NATWEST PLAYFAIR CRICKET WORLD CUP 1999

EDITED BY BILL FRINDALL

A Guide to the Seventh World Cup Tournament

Copyright © 1999 Bill Frindall

First published in 1999
by HEADLINE BOOK PUBLISHING

The right of Bill Frindall to be identified as the
author of the Work has been asserted by him in accordance
with the Copyright, Designs and Patents Act 1988.

Cover photographs: (*Front, left*) Arjuna Ranatunga (Sri Lanka) and
(*right*) Glenn McGrath (Australia); (*back*) Sanath Jayasuriya (Sri Lanka)
© Graham Morris

10 9 8 7 6 5 4 3 2 1

ISBN 0 7472 6245 4

Typeset by
Letterpart Limited, Reigate, Surrey

Printed and bound in Great Britain by
Clays Ltd. St Ives plc.

HEADLINE BOOK PUBLISHING
A division of Hodder Headline PLC
338 Euston Road
London NW1 3BH

CONTENTS

SPONSOR'S MESSAGE FROM

♻ NatWest

NatWest's long-term commitment to cricket takes on exciting new dimensions this year as we become Global Partners to the ICC 1999 Cricket World Cup. The biggest event in this summer's sporting calendar will see teams competing for the coveted World Cup trophy throughout the months of May and June. The competition will reach its climax at Lord's, the home of cricket, on Sunday 20 June.

In 1998, NatWest were pleased to be sponsors of the NatWest England Under-19 team who were crowned as the new Under-19 Cricket World Cup champions, proving that our grass roots Development of Excellence Programme is reaping rewards, holding out great hope for the future of English cricket. As sponsors of the Cricket World Cup this year we hope to be cheering on some of the world's finest players as they battle through to the final at Lord's and look forward to hailing the new world champions at close of play on 20 June.

Our support for the game remains strong both on and off the field, with the opening of the new NatWest Media Centre at Lord's, in partnership with the MCC. We look forward to welcoming the world's media to this new facility, from which they will broadcast the World Cup and cricket coverage all over the globe for many years to come. We are also sponsoring not only the *NatWest Playfair Cricket Annual* in 1999, providing the latest facts and figures for domestic and international competitions, but also this definitive guide to the ICC 1999 Cricket World Cup.

We hope 1999 will provide exhilarating cricket as we look forward to the sport going from strength to strength both domestically and internationally.

Derek Wanless
Group Chief Executive
NatWest

EDITORIAL PREFACE

The 1999 Cricket World Cup will undoubtedly live up to its billing as one of the great events of the international sporting calendar. Returning to Britain for the first time since 1983 it is bound to engender colossal interest throughout its 38 days and record tally of 42 matches. How different it will be from the inaugural event staged here 24 years ago which lasted just 15 days. Hopefully this, cricket's seventh World Cup, will be blessed with the uninterrupted sunshine of that inaugural event which, incidentally, was coyly billed as 'International Championship Cricket' by the ICC.

Twelve teams, the nine Full ICC Members plus the top three countries from last year's ICC Trophy played in Malaysia, will convene in the UK on 4 May. For ten days they will each be hosted by a first-class county (the 12 without a Test match ground) and play three warm-up 50-over games against their hosts and neighbouring counties. Seeded into two groups of six, they will play each of the others in their group in a 30-match Round Robin lasting 18 days. The top three teams from each group will then progress into the Super Six phase, taking with them points scored in their group games. The nine Super Six games will be played on Test match grounds with those surviving from Group A playing each of those from Group B. The top four teams will qualify for the semi-finals. It is an exciting format and a marked improvement on its immediate predecessor.

Lord's will stage the opening match, preceded by a short ceremony, between England and the holders, Sri Lanka, as well as the Final, when the winners will receive the ICC Cricket World Cup Trophy and US$300,000. In all a record prize kitty of US$1million will be at stake, a far cry from the inaugural pot of £4,000.

For the first time the Scottish, Irish and Dutch Cricket Unions will stage full internationals, with the Scotland team due to play its inaugural limited-overs 'Test' when it takes on Australia at Worcester.

I am delighted that NatWest, one of the major players supporting this tournament, have agreed to sponsor this publication. It is good to see the NatWest/ *Playfair* partnership, masterminded by Barbara Quinn, extended to include this second World Cup guide.

In preparing this material I have been assisted by a worldwide band of support. Thanks are due to Allan Miller (Australia), Andrew Samson (South Africa), Tony Cozier (West Indies), Cheryl Styles (New Zealand), Rajesh Kumar and Mohandas Menon (India), John Ward (Zimbabwe), Alex Ritchie (Scottish Cricket Union), Ahmed Sajjadul Alam (Bangladesh), Harilal Shah and Fatuma Dafala (Kenya), and Shilpa Patel (BBC Radio). Clive Hitchcock and Issy Wood (ICC), Peta Dee and Warren Deutrom (ECB), and Philip Bailey (ACS) have each been generous with their provision of vital data. Production of this sister work could not have been accomplished without the expertise and dedication of the well established *Playfair* alliance between Ian Marshall and his colleagues at Headline and Chris Leggett and his tireless flock at Letterpart. I am also indebted to my wife Debbie for contributing in many ways and for seldom complaining about my neglect of the garden.

BILL FRINDALL
Urchfont, 29 March 1998

WORLD CUP MATCH RESULTS

GROUP A MATCHES

May	Venue		Score		Score	Winners	Award
14	Lord's	ENGLAND	......	SRI LANKA	....	......	......
15	Hove	SOUTH AFRICA	......	INDIA	....	......	......
15	Taunton	ZIMBABWE	......	KENYA	....	......	......
18	Canterbury	ENGLAND	......	KENYA	....	......	......
19	Northampton	SOUTH AFRICA	......	SRI LANKA	....	......	......
19	Leicester	INDIA	......	ZIMBABWE	....	......	......
22	The Oval	ENGLAND	......	SOUTH AFRICA	....	......	......
22	Worcester	SRI LANKA	......	ZIMBABWE	....	......	......
23	Bristol	INDIA	......	KENYA	....	......	......
25	Nottingham	ENGLAND	......	ZIMBABWE	....	......	......
26	Taunton	INDIA	......	SRI LANKA	....	......	......
26	Amsterdam	SOUTH AFRICA	......	KENYA	....	......	......
29	Birmingham	ENGLAND	......	INDIA	....	......	......
29	Chelmsford	SOUTH AFRICA	......	ZIMBABWE	....	......	......
30	Southampton	SRI LANKA	......	KENYA	....	......	......

GROUP A RESULTS TABLE

	P	W	L	Points
ENGLAND	...	...	...	......
INDIA	...	...	...	......
KENYA	...	...	...	......
SOUTH AFRICA	...	...	...	......
SRI LANKA	...	...	...	......
KENYA	...	...	...	......

Hundreds		Four or More Wickets	
Batsman	Score	Bowler	Analysis
....	......	....	......
....	......	....	......
....	......	....	......
....	......	....	......
....	......	....	......
....	......	....	......
....	......	....	......
....	......	....	......

WORLD CUP MATCH RESULTS

GROUP B MATCHES

May	Venue		Score		Score	Winners	Award
16	Worcester	AUSTRALIA	......	SCOTLAND	....		
16	Bristol	WEST INDIES	......	PAKISTAN	....		
17	Chelmsford	NEW ZEALAND	......	BANGLADESH	....		
20	Cardiff	AUSTRALIA	......	NEW ZEALAND	....		
20	Chester-le-St	PAKISTAN	......	SCOTLAND	....		
21	Dublin	WEST INDIES	.....	BANGLADESH	....		
23	Leeds	AUSTRALIA	......	PAKISTAN	....		
24	Southampton	WEST INDIES	......	NEW ZEALAND	....		
24	Edinburgh	SCOTLAND	......	BANGLADESH	....		
27	Leicester	WEST INDIES	......	SCOTLAND	....		
27	Chester-le-St	AUSTRALIA	......	BANGLADESH	....		
28	Derby	NEW ZEALAND	......	PAKISTAN	....		
30	Manchester	AUSTRALIA	......	WEST INDIES	....		
31	Edinburgh	SCOTLAND	......	NEW ZEALAND	....		
31	Northampton	PAKISTAN	......	BANGLADESH	....		

GROUP B RESULTS TABLE

	P	W	L	Points
AUSTRALIA	...	...	...	......
BANGLADESH	...	...	...	......
NEW ZEALAND	...	...	...	......
PAKISTAN	...	...	...	......
SCOTLAND	...	...	...	......
WEST INDIES	...	...	...	......

Hundreds

Batsman	Score
....	......
....	......
....	......
....	......
....	......
....	......
....	......
....	......

Four or More Wickets

Bowler	Analysis
....	......
....	......
....	......
....	......
....	......
....	......
....	......
....	......

SUPER SIX ROUND

Jun	Venue	Score		Score	Winners	Award
4	The Oval	Group A – 2nd	...... Group B – 2nd	....	......	......
5	Nottingham	Group A – 1st	...... Group B – 1st	....	......	......
6	Leeds	Group A – 3rd	...... Group B – 3rd	....	......	......
8	Manchester	Group A – 2nd	...... Group B – 1st	....	......	......
9	Lord's	Group A – 3rd	...... Group B – 2nd	....	......	......
10	Birmingham	Group A – 1st	...... Group B – 3rd	....	......	......
11	The Oval	Group A – 3rd	...... Group B – 1st	....	......	......
12	Nottingham	Group A – 2nd	...... Group B – 3rd	....	......	......
13	Leeds	Group A – 1st	...... Group B – 2nd	....	......	......

SUPER SIX RESULTS TABLE

	P	W	L	Points
....	...	...	...	......
....	...	...	...	......
....	...	...	...	......
....	...	...	...	......
....	...	...	...	......
....	...	...	...	......

Hundreds

Four or More Wickets

Batsman	Score	Bowler	Analysis
....	......	....	......
....	......	....	......
....	......	....	......
....	......	....	......
....	......	....	......

SEMI-FINALS

Jun	Venue	Score		Score	Winners	Award
16	Manchester	....	....	......	......	......
17	Birmingham	....	....	......	......	......

FINAL

Jun	Venue	Score		Score	Winners	Award
20	Lord's	....	....	......	......	......

Hundreds

Four or More Wickets

Batsman	Score	Bowler	Analysis
....	......	....	......
....	......	....	......
....	......	....	......

Player of the Tournament: ....

1999 CRICKET WORLD CUP PLAYING CONDITIONS

FORMAT OF THE COMPETITION

The 1999 Cricket World Cup will be contested by 12 teams which have been 'seeded' and divided into two groups:

Group A	Group B
Sri Lanka	Australia
India	West Indies
South Africa	Pakistan
England	New Zealand
Zimbabwe	Bangladesh
Kenya	Scotland

The first phase of the competition will be the Group Matches.

Each team will play every other team in its group. Points will be allocated for each match Win, Tie or No Result in accordance with the system described in Section 11 of these Playing Conditions, which will apply throughout the Tournament.

Following the Group Matches the top three teams from each group will progress to the next phase, the Super Six. The teams will be placed in order of merit based on the points gained in the Group Matches and will take forward into the Super Six phase the points scored against the other teams which have qualified from their group.

In the Super Six phase of competition, each of the three qualifying teams from Group A will play each of the three qualifying teams from Group B.

The top four teams at the end of the Super Six phase of the competition will progress to the Semi-finals where the team placed first will play the team placed fourth and the team placed second will play the team placed third.

The winners of the Semi-finals will contest the Final which will be held at Lord's.

PLAYING CONDITIONS

The Playing Conditions for Test Matches as printed in the ICC Code of Conduct Standard Playing Conditions and Other Regulations Booklet, September 1998 will apply, except where specified.

1. Duration

All matches will consist of one innings per side, and each innings will be limited to 50 six-ball overs. A minimum of 25 overs per team will constitute a match (subject to the provisions of Clause 10.1 below). Matches will be of one day's scheduled duration with one reserve day allocated (two reserve days in the case of the Final). The reserve day(s) will be used if necessary to continue a match which has not been completed on the first scheduled day.

2. Hours of Play, Intervals and Minimum Overs in the Day

2.1 Scheduled Start and Cessation Times

The scheduled hours of play will be 10.45am to 6.30pm. If there is a delayed start or one or more interruptions in play, the Umpires may order extra time on the first day if they consider that a result can be obtained on that day. If the Umpires are satisfied that a result cannot be obtained on the first day, the timing for the cessation of play on that day will be 8.00pm, subject to conditions of ground, weather and light.

2.2 Sessions of Play and Interval between Innings

There will normally be two sessions of play of 3 hours 30 minutes each, separated by an interval of 45 minutes between 2.15pm and 3.00pm. The innings of the team batting second shall not commence before the scheduled time for the commencement of the second session unless the team batting first has completed its innings at least 30 minutes prior to the scheduled interval. In such circumstances, a 10-minute break will occur and the team batting second will commence its innings and the interval will occur as scheduled.

Where the innings of the side batting first is delayed or interrupted, the Umpires will reduce the length of the interval.

In the event of time being lost up to and including 60 minutes in aggregate, the length of the interval shall be reduced from 45 to 30 minutes. In the event of more than 60 minutes being lost in aggregate, the duration of the interval shall be agreed mutually by the Umpires, both Captains and the Referee subject to no interval being of more than 35 minutes' duration or less than 10 minutes' duration. In the event of disagreement, the interval shall be of 25 minutes' duration.

Note: Refer also to the provisions of Clause 4.2

2.3 Intervals for Drinks

Two drinks intervals per innings shall be permitted, each 1 hour 10 minutes apart. The provisions of Law 16.6 shall be strictly observed, except that under conditions of extreme heat the Umpires may permit extra intervals for drinks.

An individual player may be given a drink either on the boundary edge or at the fall of a wicket, on the field, provided that no playing time is wasted. No other drinks shall be taken on to the field without the permission of the Umpires. Any player taking drinks on to the field shall be dressed in proper cricket attire.

3. Appointment of Umpires and Referees

The ICC shall appoint Umpires from the World Cup Panel for On-Field and Third Umpire duties. ECB will appoint Fourth Umpires from their First Class Panel. The three participating Associate Member Countries will provide one Umpire each whom ICC will appoint for Fourth Umpire duties.

The ICC shall appoint a Referee for each World Cup Match.

4. Length of Innings

4.1 Uninterrupted Matches (i.e. Matches Which Are Neither Delayed Nor Interrupted)

(a)   Each team shall bat for 50 (six ball) overs unless all out earlier. A team shall not be permitted to declare its innings closed.

(b)   If the team fielding first fails to bowl the required number of overs by the scheduled time for the cessation of the first session, play shall continue until the required number of overs has been bowled.

Unless otherwise determined by the Referee, the innings of the team batting second shall be limited to the same number of overs that it bowled by the scheduled time for the cessation of the first session. The over in progress at the scheduled cessation time shall count as a complete over. The interval shall not be extended and the second session shall commence at the scheduled time (3.00 pm).

The Referee may increase the number of overs to be bowled by the team bowling second if, after consultation with the Umpires, he is of the opinion that events beyond the control of the team bowling first prevented that team from bowling the required number of overs by the scheduled time for the cessation of the first innings.

(c)   If the team batting first is all out and the last wicket falls at or after the scheduled time for the interval, the innings of the team batting second shall be limited to the same number of overs bowled to the team batting first at the scheduled time for the interval.

(d)   If the team batting first is dismissed in less than 50 overs, the team batting second shall be entitled to bat for 50 overs except as provided for in (c) above.

(e)   If the team fielding second fails to bowl 50 overs or the number of overs as provided for in (b), (c), or (d) above by the scheduled cessation time, the hours of play shall be extended until the required number of overs has been bowled or a result achieved.

(f)   Penalties shall apply for slow over-rates (refer ICC Code of Conduct).

4.2 Delayed or Interrupted Matches

4.2.1 General

Any rearrangement of the number of overs that may be necessary due to a delayed start or one or more interruptions in play as a result of adverse ground, weather or light conditions or any other reason, shall only be made on the second day (third day in the case of the Final). The timing and duration of all suspensions of play (including all intervals) or delays on any day will be taken into account when calculating the length of time available for either innings.

(a)   The object shall always be to rearrange the number of overs so that, if possible, both teams have the opportunity of batting for the same number of overs. A team shall not be permitted to declare its innings closed.

A minimum of 25 overs must be bowled to the team batting second in order to constitute a match (subject to the provisions of Clause 10.1.below).

Except as provided for in Clause 4.2.3 below, the calculation of the number of overs to be bowled shall be based on a rate of 14.28 overs per hour in the total time available for play up to 6.30pm on the last scheduled day of the match. If a reduction of the number of overs is required, any recalculation must not cause the match to be rescheduled to finish earlier than the original cessation time. This time may be extended to allow for one extra over for both teams to be added if required.

(b)   If the team fielding second fails to bowl the required number of overs by the scheduled cessation time, the hours of play shall be extended until the overs have been bowled or a result achieved.

(c)   The team batting second shall not bat for a greater number of overs than the team batting first unless the latter has been all out in less than the agreed number of overs.

(d)   Fractions are to be ignored in all calculations regarding the number of overs.

11

4.2.2 Delay or Interruption to the Innings of the Team Batting First

(a) If the number of overs of the team batting first is reduced, a fixed time will be specified for the completion of the first session, as calculated by applying the provisions of Clauses 2.2 and Clause 4.2.1(a) (if appropriate).

(b) If the team fielding first fails to bowl the required number of overs by the scheduled time for the cessation of the first session, play shall continue until the required number of overs has been bowled, and Clause 4.1(b) shall apply.

(c) If the team batting first is all out and the last wicket falls at or after the scheduled time for the interval, Clause 4.1(c) shall apply.

4.2.3 Delay or Interruption to the Innings of the Team Batting Second

When the innings of the team batting second has had to be reduced to less than 50 overs under the provisions of Clause 4.2.1(a), any subsequent interruption to the innings of the team batting second will result in the overs being reduced at a rate of 14.28 overs per hour for time lost. Overs will always be reduced on the basis of time lost, as above, when the innings of the team batting second has commenced at or after 3.00pm on the last scheduled day of the match.

5. Restrictions on the Placement of Fieldsmen

Two semi-circles shall be drawn on the field of play. The semi-circles shall have as their centre the middle stump at either end of the pitch. The radius of each of the semi-circles shall be 30 yards (27.5m). The ends of each semi-circle shall be joined to the other by a straight line drawn on the field on the same side of the pitch. The field restriction area should be marked by continuous painted white lines or 'dots' at five-yard (4.5m) intervals, each 'dot' to be covered by a white plastic or rubber (but not metal) disc measuring seven inches (18cm) in diameter.

At the instant of delivery, there may not be more than five fieldsmen on the leg side.

For the first 15 overs only two fieldsmen are permitted to be outside the field restriction marking at the instant of delivery.

For the remaining overs only five fieldsmen are permitted to be outside the field restriction marking at the instant of delivery.

Two inner circles shall be drawn on the field of play. The circles have as their centres the centre point of the popping crease at either end of the pitch. The radius of each of the circles is 15 yards (13.72 metres). The field restriction area should be marked by 'dots'. The segment of the circles reserved for the slip positions shall not be demarcated. (Refer attached Appendix 1).

In the first 15 overs there must be a minimum of two stationary fieldsmen within the 15-yard field restriction of the striker at the instant of delivery. The two stationary fieldsmen may be permitted to stand deeper than 15 yards (in the un-demarcated area) provided only that they are standing in slip, leg slip and gully positions.

In circumstances where the number of overs for the team batting first is reduced, the number of overs in regard to the above fielding restrictions shall be reduced proportionately in a ratio of 15:50 (30%) in accordance with the table below. Fractions are to be ignored in all calculations re. the number of overs.

12

Total overs in Innings	Number of overs for which restrictions above will apply
25-26	7
27-29	8
30-33	9
34-36	10
37-39	11
40-43	12
44-46	13
47-49	14
50	15

Where the number of overs for the team batting second is reduced (including under the provisions of Clauses 4.1(b) and/or 4.1(c) above), the aim will be to maintain the above fielding restrictions for the same proportion of the second innings that they were maintained for the first innings (fractions to be ignored).

In the event of an infringement of any of the above fielding restrictions, the square leg Umpire shall call and signal 'No Ball'.

6. Number of Overs per Bowler

No bowler shall bowl more than 10 overs in an innings.

In a delayed or interrupted match where the overs are reduced for both teams or for the team bowling second, no bowler may bowl more than one-fifth of the total overs allowed. This restriction shall not apply to the team fielding second where the provisions of Clause 4.1(b) have been applied.

Where the total overs are not divisible by five, one additional over shall be allowed to the maximum number per bowler necessary to make up the balance.

In the event of a bowler breaking down and being unable to complete an over, the remaining balls will be bowled by another bowler. Such part of an over will count as a full over only in so far as each bowler's limit is concerned.

The scoreboard shall show the total number of overs bowled and the number of overs bowled by each bowler.

7. No Ball

Short Pitched Bowling – if the ball passes or would have passed above the shoulder height of the striker standing upright at the crease, either Umpire shall call and signal 'No Ball'. The penalty shall be one run for the no ball, plus any runs scored from that delivery.

8. Wide Bowling – Judging a Wide

Umpires are instructed to apply a very strict and consistent interpretation in regard to this Law in order to prevent negative bowling wide of the wicket.

Any offside or legside delivery which, in the opinion of the Umpire, does not give the batsman a reasonable opportunity to score shall be called a wide. As a guide, on the leg side a ball landing clearly outside the leg stump going further away shall be called wide.

A penalty of one run for a wide shall be scored if no runs are made otherwise.

9. The Ball

The ECB shall provide Grade 1 BSI-approved cricket balls manufactured by Dukes.

Coloured clothing, black sightscreens and white balls shall be used.

Each fielding team shall have one new ball for its innings.

In the event of a ball becoming wet and soggy as a result of play continuing in inclement weather or it being affected by dew, or a white ball becoming significantly discoloured and in the opinion of the Umpires being unfit for play, the ball may be replaced for a ball that has had a similar amount of wear, even though it has not gone out of shape.

Either bowler or batsman may raise the matter with the Umpires and the Umpires' decision, as to a replacement or otherwise, will be final.

10. The Result

10.1 A result can be achieved only if both teams have had the opportunity of batting for at least 25 overs (subject to the provisions of Clauses 4.1(b) and 4.2.2(b) above), unless one team has been all out in less than 25 overs or unless the team batting second scores enough runs to win in less than 25 overs.

All matches in which both teams have not had the opportunity of batting for a minimum of 25 overs (subject to the provisions of this clause) shall be declared 'No Result'.

10.2 Where the maximum number of overs available to both sides remains unaltered once play has commenced (other than through the application of 4.1(b)), the team scoring the higher number of runs shall be the winner. If the scores are equal, the result shall be a Tie and no account shall be taken of the number of wickets which have fallen.

10.3 If, due to suspension of play after the start of the match, the number of overs in the innings of either team has to be revised to a lesser number than originally allotted (minimum 25 overs unless the provisions of 4.1(b) or 4.2.2 (b) apply), then a revised target score (to win) should be set for the number of overs which the team batting second will have the opportunity of facing – this revised target being calculated by the Duckworth/Lewis method. The target set will always be a whole number and one run less will constitute a Tie.

10.4 At the interval between innings or whenever a revised target has been set, a print-out of 'par' scores (the score for which if the match was abandoned the match would be tied) for the end of each over will be supplied to both teams' dressing rooms and to the Match Umpires, Referee and Ground Authority.

10.5 If a match is abandoned before it has been played to a conclusion and before the team batting second has received its allotted number of overs (minimum 25 overs required to constitute a match unless the provisions of Clause 10.1 apply), then the result shall be decided by the Duckworth/Lewis method. If the second innings score is equal to the 'par' score for the given number of overs remaining and wickets lost, the result shall be a Tie.

11. Points

11.1 The following points system will apply:

Win	2
Tie or No Result	1
Loss	0

11.2 Group Matches

In the event of teams finishing on equal points in either Group, the right to play in the Super Six stage will be decided in the following order of priority:

(a)   The most wins in the Group Matches.

14

(b)   When two teams have both equal points and equal wins, the team which was the winner of the Group Match played between them will be placed in the higher position.

When more than two teams have equal points and equal wins, the team which was the winner of the most number of matches played between those teams will be placed in the higher position.

(c)   If still equal, the team with the higher net run rate in the Group Matches will be placed in the higher position (refer to 11.6 below for the calculation of net run rate).

(d)   If still equal, the team with the higher number of wickets taken per balls bowled in the Group Matches in which results were achieved, will be placed in the higher position.

(e)   In the highly unlikely event that teams cannot be separated by (a) to (d) above this will be done by drawing lots.

11.3 Super Six Matches

The six teams that qualify for the Super Six stage carry forward the points that they have gained against the other teams that have qualified from their respective groups. The points carried forward by each team are added to those they gain in the Super Six Matches, to form the Super Six league table.

In the event of teams finishing on equal points at the end of the Super Six stage, the right to play in the Semi-final will be decided in the following order of priority:

(a)   The most wins in all of the matches throughout the competition against the other Super Six qualifiers.

(b)   When two teams have both equal points and equal wins, the team which was the winner of the match played between them (in either the Group or Super Six Matches) will be placed in the higher position.

When more than two teams have equal points and equal wins, the team which was the winner of the most number of matches played between those teams (in both the Group and Super Six Matches) will be placed in the higher position.

(c)   If still equal, the team with the higher net run rate in all matches played against the other Super Six qualifiers (in both the Group and Super Six Matches) will be placed in the higher position (refer to 11.6 below for the calculation of net run rate).

(d)   If still equal, the team with the higher number of wickets taken per balls bowled in all of the matches throughout the competition against the other Super Six qualifiers in which results were achieved, will be placed in the higher position.

(e)   In the highly unlikely event that teams cannot be separated by (a) to (d) above this will be done by drawing lots.

11.4 Semi-final

If a Semi-final is tied or there is no result, the team that finished higher at the end of the Super Six stage as decided by clause 11.3 shall proceed to the Final.

11.5 Final

In the event of a tied Final or if there is no result in the three days allocated, the World Cup will be shared by the finalists.

11.6 Net Run Rate

A team's net run rate is calculated by deducting from the average runs per over scored by that team, the average runs per over scored against that team – see 11.2(c) for the Group Matches and 11.3(c) for the Super Six matches. Only those matches where results were achieved and where the D/L method for recalculating the target score was not utilised will count for the purpose of net run rate calculations.

In the event of a team being all out in less than its full quota of overs, the calculation of its net run rate shall be based on the full quota of overs to which it would have been entitled and not on the number of overs in which the team was dismissed.

12. Code of Conduct

All Players, Team Officials and Umpires shall be bound by the terms of the ICC Code of Conduct.

13. Prize Money

Prize Money for the 1999 Cricket World Cup totals US$1,000,000 and will be distributed as follows:

Winner	US$300,000
Runner-up	US$150,000
Losing Semi-finalists	US$100,000 each
Fifth Place Super Six	US $52,500
Sixth Place Super Six	US $27,500
Group Match Winners	US $6,000 each
Group Match Losers	US $3,000 each

14. Technical Committee

A three-man Technical Committee appointed by ICC will adjudicate on:

- Any match-related dispute regarding the interpretation of Playing Conditions (other than that which is the responsibility of the Umpires and Referee).

- Any application by a Competing Team for a replacement player.

  Decisions of the Technical Committee will be final.

  The Technical Committee is not responsible for the application of the Code of Conduct or any non-match related dispute.

1999 CRICKET WORLD CUP

RESTRICTIONS ON THE PLACEMENT OF FIELDSMEN

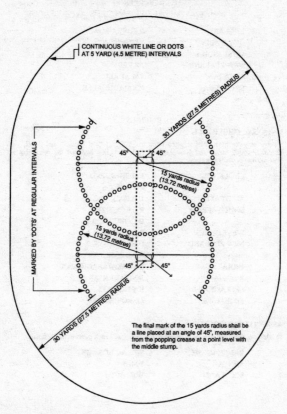

CONTINUOUS WHITE LINE OR DOTS AT 5 YARD (4.5 METRE) INTERVALS

MARKED BY 'DOTS' AT REGULAR INTERVALS

30 YARDS (27.5 METRES) RADIUS

45°   45°

15 yards radius (13.72 metres)

15 yards radius (13.72 metres)

45°   45°

30 YARDS (27.5 METRES) RADIUS

The final mark of the 15 yards radius shall be a line placed at an angle of 45°, measured from the popping crease at a point level with the middle stump.

1999 WORLD CUP OFFICIALS

REFEREES

Six referees have been selected to officiate in the 42-match World Cup tournament.

ENGLAND	R.SUBBA ROW
AUSTRALIA	P.J.P.BURGE
WEST INDIES	C.W.SMITH
NEW ZEALAND	J.R.REID
PAKISTAN	TALAT ALI
SRI LANKA	R.S.MADUGALLE

UMPIRES

NATIONAL GRID PANEL

Twelve umpires have been selected from the National Grid International Panel, with England, South Africa and New Zealand each providing two and the remaining six Test-playing countries one apiece:

ENGLAND	D.R.SHEPHERD
	P.WILLEY
AUSTRALIA	D.B.HAIR
SOUTH AFRICA	R.E.KOERTZEN
	D.L.ORCHARD
WEST INDIES	S.A.BUCKNOR
NEW ZEALAND	D.B.COWIE
	R.S.DUNNE
INDIA	S.VENKATARAGHAVAN
PAKISTAN	JAVED AKHTAR
SRI LANKA	K.T.FRANCIS
ZIMBABWE	I.D.ROBINSON

ASSOCIATE UMPIRES

In addition, the three Associate Member Countries will each provide one official:

BANGLADESH	SAILAB HOSSAIN
KENYA	S.MODI
SCOTLAND	W.B.SMITH

WORLD CUP REGISTER

With the exception of England's register, which includes performances on their 1998-99 tours, all first-class career statistics are updated to the end of the 1998 season (20 September).

Our production schedule has allowed later dates for international career statistics. Test records include all matches completed before 28 January 1999, while records for Limited-Overs Internationals include all games played prior to 14 February 1999.

Each of the twelve competing nations was required to submit to the ICC's organising committee a preliminary list of 19 players by the end of February 1999. Final lists of 15 players were due to be submitted by the end of March, after this publication had gone to press. Thus, apart from the sections covering England, Australia, Bangladesh, Kenya and Scotland, all of whom had nominated their final teams well ahead of the deadline, this register includes all players on the preliminary lists. In exceptional circumstances the final selections may include players not nominated on those earlier lists, as occurred with Australia's selection of Tom Moody.

Registers for England, Australia, Bangladesh, Kenya and Scotland include as 'Reserves' those omitted from their preliminary lists of 19 players. In the case of injuries, competing countries may substitute ANY qualified players for subsequent matches, subject to the Organising Committee's approval. Replaced players can take no further part in the competition.

ABBREVIATIONS

General

*	not out/unbroken partnership
BB	best innings bowling analysis
Cap	awarded 1st XI County Cap
ct	catches
f-c	first-class
HS	highest score
st	stumpings
Tests	official Test matches

County Limited-Overs Competitions

BHC	Benson and Hedges Cup
NWT	NatWest Trophy
ASL	AXA Sunday League

Countries

A	Australia
B	Bangladesh
E	England
H	Holland
I	India
K	Kenya
NZ	New Zealand
P	Pakistan
SA	South Africa
SL	Sri Lanka
UAE	United Arab Emirates
WI	West Indies
Z	Zimbabwe

WORLD CUP REGISTER

ENGLAND

All England players' Test match, LOI and first-class statistics are updated to 13 February 1999 inclusive and therefore include their 1998-99 tours. Key to abbreviations on page 19. England's selected 15 players are:

ATHERTON, Michael Andrew (Lancashire)
Born Failsworth, Manchester 23 Mar 1968. 5'11". Educated at Manchester Grammar School; Downing College, Cambridge U – BA (Hons). Right-hand batsman, occasional leg-break bowler. First captained England YC (U19) when aged 16 and led their tours to Sri Lanka 1986-87 and to Australia 1987-88. Cambridge U 1987-89 (blue 1987-88-89; captain 1988-89). Lancashire debut 1987; cap 1989; benefit 1997. Cricket Writer's Club Young Cricketer of 1990. One of *Wisden*'s Five Cricketers of 1990. Captained England 1993 to 1997-98. Awarded OBE 1997. **TESTS:** 88 (1989 to 1998-99, 52 as captain – England record – 13 won, 19 lost, 20 drawn); 6045 runs (av 38.50), 12 hundreds; 2 wkts (av 151.00); 58 ct. HS 185* v SA (Johannesburg) 1995-96. Youngest Lancastrian to score a Test hundred. BB 1-20. **L-O INTERNATIONALS:** 54 (1990 to 1998, 43 as captain – won 20, lost 21, tied 1, no result 1); 1791 runs (av 35.11), 2 hundreds; 15 ct. HS 127 v WI (Lord's) 1995. **TOURS** (f-c matches only; C = captain): A 1990-91, 1994-95C, 1998-99; SA 1995-96C; WI 1993-94C, 1995-96 (Lancs), 1997-98C; NZ 1996-97C; I/SL 1992-93; Z 1989-90 (Eng A), 1996-97C. **F-C CAREER:** 279 matches; 18,349 runs (av 41.32), 47 hundreds (inc 1 double), 1000 runs/season (6); 108 wkts (av 43.82), 5 wkts/inns (3); 218 ct. Scored 1193 in season of f-c debut. HS 210* Eng XI v Aus XI (Hobart) 1998-99. Lancs HS 199 v Durham (Gateshead) 1992. BB 6-78 v Notts (Nottingham) 1990. **1998 SEASON (f-c):** 874 runs (av 39.72); 2 hundreds; did not bowl. **COUNTY L-O:** HS 121* v Durham (Manchester) 1996 (BHC). BB 4-42 Combined U v Somerset (Taunton) 1989 (BHC).

AUSTIN, Ian David (Lancashire)
Born Haslingden, Lancs 30 May 1966. 5'10". Educated at Haslingden High School. Left-hand batsman, right-arm medium-fast bowler. Lancashire debut 1987; cap 1990. **TESTS:** 0. **L-O INTERNATIONALS:** 4 (1998 to 1998-99); 29 runs (av 14.50); 3 wkts (av 59.66); 0 ct. HS 11* v SL (Lord's) 1998; BB 2-37 v SL (Lord's) 1998 – on debut. **TOURS** (f-c matches only): WI 1995-96 (Lancs); Z 1988-89 (Lancs). **F-C CAREER:** 118 matches; 3653 runs (av 28.53), 2 hundreds; 251 wkts (av 29.79); 33 ct. HS 115* v Derbys (Blackpool) 1992. BB 5-23 (10-60 match) v Middx (Manchester) 1994. **1998 SEASON (f-c):** 304 runs (av 23.38); 36 wkts (av 27.16). **COUNTY L-O:** HS 97 v Sussex (Hove) 1997 (NWT). BB 5-56 v Derbys (Derby) 1991 (ASL).

CROFT, Robert Damien Bale (Glamorgan)
Born Morriston, Glam 25 May 1970. 5'10½". Educated at St John Lloyd Catholic Comprehensive School; West Glamorgan Institute of Higher Education (Business Studies). Right-hand batsman (who has opened in county limited-overs matches, scoring four successive fifties in 1998 BHC), off-break bowler. Glamorgan debut 1989; cap 1992. **TESTS:** 15 (1996 to 1998-99); 295 runs (av 16.38); 16 wkts (av 38.33); 8 ct. HS 37* v SA (Manchester) 1998; BB 5-95 v NZ (Christchurch) 1996-97. **L-O INTERNATIONALS:** 40 (1996 to 1998-99); 274 runs (av 16.11); 40 wkts (av 36.60); 9 ct. HS 32 v SL (Perth) 1998-99; BB 3-51 v SA (Oval) 1998. **TOURS** (f-c matches only): A 1998-99; SA 1993-94 (Eng A), 1995-96 (Glam); WI 1991-92 (Eng A), 1997-98; NZ 1996-97; Z 1990-91 (Glam), 1994-95 (Glam), 1996-97. **F-C CAREER:** 205 matches; 6100 runs (av 25.20), 2 hundreds; 550 wkts (av 36.65), 5 wkts/inns (22), 10 wkts/match (3), 50 wkts/season (5); 107 ct. HS 143 v Somerset (Taunton) 1995. BB 8-66 (14-169 match) v Warwks (Swansea) 1992. **1998 SEASON (f-c):** 343 runs (av 22.86); 20 wkts (av 57.20). **COUNTY L-O:** HS 77 v Essex (Cardiff) 1998 (BHC). BB 6-20 v Worcs (Cardiff) 1994 (ASL).

EALHAM, Mark Alan (Kent)
Born Willesborough, Ashford, Kent 27 Aug 1969. Son of A.G.E.Ealham (Kent 1966-82). 5'9". Educated at Stour Valley Secondary School, Chartham. Right-hand batsman, right-arm medium-fast bowler. Kent debut 1989; cap 1992. **TESTS:** 8 (1996 to 1998); 210 runs (av 21.00); 17 wkts (av 28.70); 4 ct. HS 53* v A (Birmingham) 1997; BB 4-21 v I (Nottingham) 1996. **L-O INTERNATIONALS:** 30 (1996 to 1998-99); 380 runs (av 18.09); 30 wkts (av 34.90); 3 ct. HS 45; BB 5-32. **TOURS** (f-c matches only): A 1996-97 (Eng A); SL 1997-98; Z 1992-93 (Kent); K 1997-98. **F-C CAREER:** 124 matches; 5432 runs (av 32.14), 5 hundreds, 1000 runs/season (1); 266 wkts (av 29.52), 5 wkts/inns (11), 10 wkts/match (1); 50 ct. HS 139 v Leics (Canterbury) 1997. BB 8-36 (10-74 match) v Warwks (Birmingham) 1996. **1998 SEASON (f-c):** 461 runs (av 24.26), 1 hundred; 23 wkts (av 25.78). **COUNTY L-O:** HS 112 v Derbys (Maidstone) 1995 (off 44 balls – Sunday League record) (ASL). BB 6-53 v Hants (Basingstoke) 1993 (ASL).

FAIRBROTHER, Neil Harvey (Lancashire)
Born Warrington, Lancashire 9 Sep 1963. 5'8". Educated at Lymm Grammar School. Left-hand batsman, occasional left-arm medium bowler. Lancashire debut 1982; cap 1985; captain 1992-93; benefit 1995. Transvaal 1994-95. **TESTS:** 10 (1987 to 1992-93). 219 runs (av 15.64); 0 wkts; 4 ct. HS 83 v I (Madras) 1992-93. **L-O INTERNATIONALS:** 66 (1986-87 to 1998-99); 1019 runs (av 40.80), 4 wickets; 32 ct. HS 113 v WI (Lord's) 1991. **TOURS** (f-c matches only): NZ 1987-88, 1991-92; I/SL 1992-93; P 1987-88, 1990-91 (Eng A); SL 1990-91 (Eng A). **F-C CAREER:** 315 matches; 17,941 runs (av 41.72), 40 hundreds (inc 3 doubles plus 1 treble), 1000 runs/season (10); 5 wkts (av 88.00); 231 ct. HS 366 v Surrey (Oval) 1990 (ground record), including 311 in a day and 100 or more in each session. BB 2-91 v Notts (Manchester) 1987. **1998 SEASON (f-c):** 759 runs (av 50.60), 3 hundreds; did not bowl. **COUNTY L-O:** HS 116* v Scot (Manchester) 1988 (BHC) and 116* v Notts (Nottingham) 1988 (ASL). BB 1-17 (BHC).

FLINTOFF, Andrew (Lancashire)
Born Preston, Lancs 6 Dec 1977. 6'4". Educated at Ribbleton Hall High School. Right-hand batsman, right-arm medium-fast bowler. Lancashire debut 1995; cap 1998. **TESTS:** 2 (1998); 17 runs (av 5.66); 1 wkt (av 112.00); 1 ct. HS 17 and BB 1-52 v SA (Nottingham) 1998. **L-O INTERNATIONALS:** 0. **TOURS** (f-c matches only) (Eng A): SA 1998-99; SL 1997-98; Z 1998-99; K 1997-98. **F-C CAREER:** 32 matches; 1501 runs (av 33.35), 3 hundreds; 10 wkts (av 68.20); 49 ct. HS 145 Eng A v Gauteng (Johannesburg) 1998-99. Lancs HS 124 v Northants (Northampton) 1998. BB 3-51 v Worcs (Lytham) 1998. **1998 SEASON (f-c):** 608 runs (av 24.32), 1 hundred; 7 wkts (av 61.28); 23 ct. **COUNTY L-O:** HS 93* v Notts (Nottingham) 1998 (ASL). BB 1-4 (NWT).

FRASER, Angus Robert Charles (Middlesex)
Born Billinge, Lancashire 8 Aug 1965. Brother of A.G.J.Fraser (Middlesex and Essex 1986-92). 6'5". Educated at Gayton High School, Harrow; Orange Senior High School, Edgware. Right-hand batsman, right-arm fast-medium bowler. Middlesex debut 1984; cap 1988; benefit 1997. MBE 1999. One of *Wisden's* Five Cricketers of 1995. **TESTS:** 46 (1989 to 1998-99); 388 runs (av 7.46); 177 wkts (av 27.32), 5 wkts/inns (13), 10 wkts/match (2); 9 ct. HS 32 v SL (Oval) 1998; BB 8-53 (11-110 match) v WI (Port-of-Spain) 1997-98 – record England analysis v WI. **L-O INTERNATIONALS:** 37 (1989-90 to 1998); 122 runs (av 13.55); 42 wkts (av 29.64), 4 wkts (1); 2 ct. HS 38* v A (Melbourne) 1990-91; BB 4-22 v A (Melbourne) 1994-95. **TOURS** (f-c matches only): A 1990-91, 1994-95 (*part*), 1998-99; SA 1995-96; WI 1989-90, 1993-94, 1997-98. **F-C CAREER:** 248 matches; 2380 runs (av 10.76); 761 wkts (av 27.17), 5 wkts/inns (33), 10 wkts/match (5), 50 wkts/season (7); 46 ct. HS 92 v Surrey (Oval) 1990. BB 8-53 (*see TESTS*). Middx BB 7-40 v Leics (Lord's) 1993. **1998 SEASON (f-c):** 134 runs (av 9.57); 61 wkts (av 20.06), 5 wkts/inns (4), 10 wkts/match (2). **COUNTY L-O:** HS 33 v Essex (Chelmsford) 1997 (ASL). BB 5-32 v Derbys (Lord's) 1995 (ASL).

GOUGH, Darren (Yorkshire)
Born Barnsley, Yorkshire 18 Sep 1970. 5'11". Educated at Priory Comprehensive School, Lundwood. Right-hand batsman, right-arm fast bowler. Yorkshire debut 1989; cap 1993. **TESTS:** 31 (1994 to 1998-99); 468 runs (av 11.41); 125 wkts (av 28.62), 5wkts/inns (5); 9 ct. HS 65 v NZ (Manchester) 1994 – on debut; BB 6-42 v SA (Leeds) 1998; hat-trick v A (Sydney) 1998-99 – first for E v A since 1899. Took wicket with his sixth ball in Tests. **L-O INTERNATIONALS:** 56 (1994 to 1998-99); 269 runs (av 11.20); 89 wkts (av 24.75), 4 wkts (6); 7 ct. HS 45 v A (Melbourne) 1994-95; BB 5-44 v Z (Sydney) 1994-95 and 5-44 v A (Lord's) 1997. Took wicket with his sixth ball in LOIs. **TOURS** (f-c matches only): A 1994-95, 1998-99; SA 1991-92 (Y), 1992-93 (Y), 1993-94 (Eng A), 1995-96; NZ 1996-97; Z 1996-97. **F-C CAREER:** matches: 2805 runs (av 16.02), 1 hundred; 536 wkts (av 27.17), 5 wkts/inns (22), 10 wkts/match (3), 50 wkts/season (4); 37 ct. HS 121 v Warwks (Leeds) 1996. BB 7-28 (10-80 match) v Lancs (Leeds) 1995 (friendly). Championship BB 7-42 (10-96 match) v Somerset (Taunton) 1993. 2 hat-tricks (1995, 1998-99); took 4 wkts in 5 balls v Kent (Leeds) 1995. **1998 SEASON (f-c):** 269 runs (av 19.21); 42 wkts (av 25.40), 5 wkts/inns (2). **COUNTY L-O:** BB 7-27 v Ire (Leeds) 1997 (NWT). HS 72* v Leics (Leicester) 1991 (ASL).

HICK, Graeme Ashley (Worcestershire)
Born Salisbury, Rhodesia (now Harare, Zimbabwe) 23 May 1966. 6'3". Educated at Prince Edward Boys' High School, Salisbury. Right-hand batsman, off-break bowler. Outstanding slip fielder. Zimbabwe 1983-84 to 1985-86. Worcestershire debut 1984; cap 1986; benefit 1999. N Districts 1987-88 to 1988-89. Queensland 1990-91. One of *Wisden*'s Five Cricketers of 1986. Scored his first hundred when aged six (for Banket Primary School). At 17 was youngest player to appear in 1983 World Cup and youngest to represent Zimbabwe. **TESTS:** 53 (1991 to 1998-99); 2993 runs (av 34.40), 5 hundreds; 22 wkts (av 56.72); 76 ct. HS 178 v I (Bombay) 1992-93; BB 4-126 v NZ (Wellington) 1991-92. **L-O INTERNATIONALS:** 87 (1991 to 1998-99); 2990 runs (av 38.83), 5 hundreds; 19 wkts (av 39.00); 40 ct. HS 126* v SL (Adelaide) 1998-99; BB 3-41 v A (Melbourne) 1994-95. **TOURS** (f-c matches only): E 1985 (Z); A 1994-95, 1998-99 (*part*); SA 1995-96; WI 1993-94; NZ 1991-92; I 1992-93; SL 1983-84 (Z), 1992-93; Z 1990-91 (Worcs), 1996-97 (Worcs). **F-C CAREER:** 369 matches; 30,189 runs (av 55.29), 104 hundreds (inc 9 doubles plus a treble and a quadruple), 1000 runs/season (15) inc 2000 (3); youngest to score 2000 (1986); scored 1019 runs before June 1988, including a record 410 runs in April; fewest innings for 10,000 runs in county cricket (179); youngest (24) to score 50 first-class hundreds; second-youngest (32) to score 100 f-c hundreds; scored 645 runs without being dismissed (UK record) in 1990; 217 wkts (av 43.71), 5 wkts/inns (5), 10 wkts/match (1); 456 ct. HS 405* (Worcs record and then the second highest in UK f-c matches) v Somerset (Taunton) 1988. BB 5-18 v Leics (Worcester) 1995. **1998 SEASON (f-c):** 1304 runs (av 43.46), 7 hundreds; 7 wkts (av 34.57); 24 ct. **COUNTY L-O:** HS 172* v Devon (Worcester) 1987 (NWT). HS 130 v Durham (Darlington) 1995. BB 4-21 v Somerset (Worcester) 1995 (ASL).

HOLLIOAKE, Adam John (Surrey)
Born Melbourne, Australia 5 Sep 1971. Brother of B.C.Hollioake (Surrey 1996-). 5'11". Educated in Australia at St Joseph's College, Sydney, and at St Patrick's College, Ballarat; in England at St George's College, Weybridge, and at Surrey Tutorial College, Guildford. Right-hand batsman, right-arm medium-fast bowler. Surrey debut 1993, scoring 13 and 123 v Derbys (Ilkeston); cap 1995; captain 1997 to date. Qualified for England 1992. **TESTS:** 4 (1997 to 1997-98); 65 runs (av 10.83); 2 wkts (av 33.50); 4 ct. HS 45 and BB 2-31 v A (Nottingham) 1997 – on debut. **L-O INTERNATIONALS:** 31 (1996 to 1998-99, 14 as captain – 6 won, 8 lost); 582 runs (av 26.45); 31 wkts (av 29.00); 12 ct. HS 83* v SA (Dhaka) 1998-99; BB 4-23 v P (Birmingham) 1996 – on debut. **TOURS** (f-c matches only): A 1996-97 (Eng A – captain); WI 1997-98. **F-C CAREER:** 97 matches; 5557 runs (av 40.56), 12 hundreds, 1000 runs/season (2); 91 wkts (av 40.16), 5 wkts/inns (1); 80 ct. HS 182 v Middx (Lord's) 1997. BB 5-62 v Glam (Swansea) 1998. **1998 SEASON (f-c):** 684 runs (av 34.20), 1 hundred; 8 wkts (av 30.87). **COUNTY L-O:** HS 93 v Kent (Canterbury) 1995 (ASL). BB 5-38 v Kent (Canterbury) 1997 (ASL).

22

KNIGHT, Nicholas Verity (Warwickshire)
Born Watford, Herts 28 Nov 1969. 6'0". Educated at Felsted School; Loughborough U. Left-hand batsman, occasional right-arm medium bowler. Essex 1991-94; cap 1994. Warwickshire debut 1994-95 (SA tour); cap 1995. **TESTS:** 12 (1995 to 1998); 585 runs (av 27.85), 1 hundred; 21 ct. HS 113 v P (Leeds) 1996. **L-O INTERNATIONALS:** 40 (1996 to 1998-99); 1498 runs (av 40.48), 3 hundreds; 14 ct. HS 125* v P (Nottingham) 1996 – carrying bat through innings of 246. **TOURS** (f-c matches only): SA 1994-95 (Warwks); NZ 1996-97; I 1994-95 (Eng A); SL 1997-98 (Eng A – captain); P 1995-96 (Eng A); Z 1996-97; K 1997-98 (Eng A – captain). **F-C CAREER:** 128 matches; 7842 runs (av 40.63), 20 hundreds, 1000 runs/season (2); 1 wkt (av 191.00); 176 ct. HS 192 v Lancs (Birmingham) 1998. BB 1-61. **1998 SEASON (f-c):** 1069 runs (av 44.54), 4 hundreds; 0 wkts. **COUNTY L-O:** HS 151 v Somerset (Birmingham) 1995 (NWT). BB 1-14 (ASL).

MULLALLY, Alan David (Leicestershire)
Born Southend-on-Sea, Essex 12 Jul 1969. 6'5". Educated at Cannington High School, Perth, Australia; Wembley & Carlisle Technical College. Right-hand batsman, left-arm fast-medium bowler. W Australia 1987-88 to 1989-90. Victoria 1990-91. Hampshire (1 match) 1988. Leicestershire debut 1990; cap 1993. **TESTS:** 13 (1996 to 1998-99); 99 runs (av 6.60); 40 wkts (av 32.27), 5 wkts/inns (1); 3 ct. HS 24 v P (Oval) 1996; BB 5-105 v A (Brisbane) 1998-99. **L-O INTERNATIONALS:** 22 (1996 to 1998-99); 42 runs (av 6.00); 28 wkts (av 27.57), 4 wkts (1); 5 ct. HS 20 v Z (Harare) 1996-97; BB 4-18 v A (Brisbane) 1998-99. **TOURS** (f-c matches only): A 1998-99; NZ 1996-97; Z 1996-97. **F-C CAREER:** 163 matches; 1234 runs (av 9.20); 471 wkts (av 30.24), 5 wkts/inns (17), 10 wkts/match (3), 50 wkts/season (4); 33 ct. HS 75 v Middx (Leicester) 1996. BB 7-55 (11-89 match) v Notts (Worksop) 1998. **1998 SEASON (f-c):** 132 runs (av 14.66); 60 wkts (av 18.80), 5 wkts/inns (3), 10 wkts/match (1). **COUNTY L-O:** HS 38 v Kent (Leicester) 1994 (ASL). BB 5-15 v Warwks (Birmingham) 1996 (ASL).

STEWART, Alec James (Surrey) (CAPTAIN)
Born Merton, Surrey 8 Apr 1963. Son of M.J.Stewart (Surrey and England 1954-72). 5'11". Educated at Tiffin Boys' School, Kingston-upon-Thames. Right-hand batsman, wicket-keeper, occasional right-arm medium bowler. Surrey debut 1981; cap 1985; captain 1992-97; benefit 1994. MBE 1998. One of *Wisden*'s Five Cricketers of 1992. **TESTS:** 86 (1989-90 to 1998-99, 13 as captain – 3 won, 7 lost, 3 drawn); 5968 runs (av 41.15), 12 hundreds; 0 wkts; 155 ct, 7 st. HS 190 v P (Birmingham) 1992. Carried his bat through the innings v P (Lord's) 1992. Only England batsman to score hundred in each innings v WI (118 and 143 at Bridgetown 1993-94). **L-O INTERNATIONALS:** 116 (1989-90 to 1998-99, 21 as captain – 8 won, 13 lost). 3211 runs (av 31.17), 2 hundreds; 101 ct, 11 st. HS 116 v I (Sharjah) 1997-98. **TOURS** (f-c matches only; C = captain): A 1990-91, 1994-95, 1998-99C; SA 1995-96; WI 1989-90, 1993-94, 1997-98; NZ 1991-92, 1996-97; I 1992-93; SL 1992-93C; Z 1996-97. **F-C CAREER:** 364 matches; 21,996 runs (av 40.73), 44 hundreds (inc 2 doubles), 1000 runs/season (8); 3 wkts (av 139.00); 521 ct, 17 st. HS 271* v Yorks (Oval) 1997. BB 1-7. Held 11 catches (equalling world f-c match record) v Leics (Leicester) 1989. **1998 SEASON (f-c):** 963 runs (av 43.77), 1 hundred; 41 ct. **COUNTY L-O:** HS 167* v Somerset (Oval) 1994 (BHC).

THORPE, Graham Paul (Surrey)
Born Farnham, Surrey 1 Aug 1969. 5'11". Educated at Weydon Comprehensive School; Farnham Sixth Form College. Left-hand batsman, occasional right-arm medium bowler, specialist slip fielder. Surrey debut 1988; cap 1991. One of *Wisden*'s Five Cricketers of 1997. **TESTS:** 53 (1993 to 1998-99); 3452 runs (av 40.14), 6 hundreds; 0 wkts; 48 ct. HS 138 v A (Birmingham) 1997; scored 114* v A (Nottingham) 1993 on debut. **L-O INTERNATIONALS:** 44 (1993 to 1997-98); 1482 runs (av 40.05); 2 wkts (av 48.50); 23 ct. HS 89 v Z (Brisbane) 1994-95 and 89 v H (Peshawar) 1995-96; BB 2-15 v I (Manchester) 1996. **TOURS** (f-c matches only): A 1992-93 (Eng A), 1994-95, 1998-99 (*part*); SA 1995-96; WI 1991-92 (Eng A), 1993-94, 1997-98; NZ 1996-97; P 1990-91

(Eng A); SL 1990-91 (Eng A); Z 1989-90 (Eng A), 1996-97. **F-C CAREER:** 237 matches; 15,403 runs (av 45.17), 33 hundreds (inc 3 doubles), 1000 runs/season (8); 25 wkts (av 49.92); 190 ct. HS 223* Eng XI v S Aus (Adelaide) 1998-99. Surrey HS 222 v Glam (Oval) 1997. BB 4-40 v A (Oval) 1993. Championship BB 2-14 v Derbys (Oval) 1996. **1998 SEASON (f-c):** 314 runs (av 26.16), 1 hundred; did not bowl. Back surgery reduced appearances to nine matches. **COUNTY L-O:** HS 145* v Lancs (Oval) 1994 (NWT). BB 3-21 v Somerset (Oval) 1991 (ASL).

WELLS, Vincent John (Leicestershire)
Born Dartford, Kent 6 Aug 1965. 6'0". Educated at Sir William Nottidge School, Whitstable, Kent. Right-hand batsman, right arm medium-fast bowler. Kent 1988-91. Leicestershire debut 1992; cap 1994. **TESTS:** 0. **LOI:** 7 (1998-99); 131 runs (av 26.20); 8 wkts (av 19.12); 3 ct. HS 39 v A (Sydney) 1998-99; BB 3-30 v A (Sydney) 1998-99. **TOURS** (f-c matches only): SA 1996-97 (Leics). **F-C CAREER:** 132 matches; 6571 runs (av 34.40), 12 hundreds (inc 3 doubles), 1000 runs/season (2); 210 wkts (av 25.54), 5 wkts/inns (3); 85 ct. HS 224 v Middx (Lord's) 1997. BB 5-18 v Notts (Worksop) 1998. Hat-trick 1994. **1998 SEASON (f-c):** 836 runs (av 36.34), 3 hundreds; 36 wkts (av 14.27), 5 wkts/inns (1). **COUNTY L-O:** 201 v Berks (Leicester) 1996 (NWT). BB 6-25 v Minor Counties (Leicester) 1998 (BHC).

WORLD CUP CAREER RECORDS

ENGLAND – BATTING AND FIELDING

	M	I	NO	HS	Runs	Avge	100	50	Ct/St
P.J.W.Allott	7	3	1	8	8	4.00	–	–	1
D.L.Amiss	4	4	–	137	243	60.75	1	1	1
G.G.Arnold	3	1	1	18*	18	–	–	–	1
M.A.Atherton	6	6	–	66	119	19.83	–	1	–
C.W.J.Athey	6	6	2	86	211	52.75	–	2	4
I.T.Botham	22	18	2	53	297	18.56	–	1	10
G.Boycott	5	5	1	57	92	23.00	–	1	–
J.M.Brearley	5	5	–	64	161	32.20	–	2	4
B.C.Broad	3	3	–	36	67	22.33	–	–	1
D.G.Cork	5	3	–	19	36	12.00	–	–	2
N.G.Cowans	1	–	–	–	–	–	–	–	1
P.A.J.DeFreitas	22	13	3	67	184	18.40	–	1	5
M.H.Denness	4	4	2	37*	113	56.50	–	–	–
G.R.Dilley	6	4	2	31*	90	45.00	–	–	1
P.R.Downton	8	5	1	9	19	4.75	–	–	8/1
P.H.Edmonds	3	2	1	5*	7	7.00	–	–	–
J.E.Emburey	8	7	2	30*	96	19.20	–	–	3
N.H.Fairbrother	14	12	4	75*	373	46.62	–	3	8
K.W.R.Fletcher	4	3	–	131	207	69.00	1	1	1
N.A.Foster	7	4	3	20*	42	42.00	–	–	1
G.Fowler	7	7	2	81*	360	72.00	–	4	–
M.W.Gatting	15	13	2	60	437	39.72	–	3	3
G.A.Gooch	21	21	1	115	897	44.85	1	8	3
D.Gough	6	4	2	26*	66	33.00	–	–	1
I.J.Gould	7	4	1	35	66	22.00	–	–	11/1
D.I.Gower	12	11	3	130	434	54.25	1	1	2
A.W.Greig	4	4	–	9	29	7.25	–	–	–
F.C.Hayes	3	3	–	52	90	30.00	–	1	–
E.E.Hemmings	6	1	1	4*	4	–	–	–	2
M.Hendrick	5	2	1	1*	1	1.00	–	–	3
G.A.Hick	15	14	2	104*	476	39.66	1	4	6
R.K.Illingworth	10	5	3	14	31	15.50	–	–	3
J.A.Jameson	2	2	–	21	32	16.00	–	–	–
A.P.E.Knott	4	2	1	18*	18	18.00	–	–	1
A.J.Lamb	19	17	4	102	656	50.46	1	3	9
W.Larkins	2	2	–	7	7	3.50	–	–	–
P.Lever	4	1	–	5	5	5.00	–	–	1
C.C.Lewis	9	6	2	33	81	20.25	–	–	4
V.J.Marks	7	3	–	8	18	6.00	–	–	2
P.J.Martin	5	4	2	3	6	3.00	–	–	–
G.Miller	1	–	–	–	–	–	–	–	–
C.M.Old	9	7	2	51*	91	18.20	–	1	2
D.R.Pringle	11	7	2	18*	50	10.00	–	–	2
D.W.Randall	5	5	1	42*	64	16.00	–	–	1
D.A.Reeve	11	7	3	35	117	29.25	–	–	5
R.T.Robinson	7	7	–	55	142	20.28	–	1	1
R.C.Russell	6	4	–	12	27	6.75	–	–	7/1
G.C.Small	13	4	1	5	8	2.66	–	–	–
N.M.K.Smith	3	3	1	31	69	34.50	–	–	1
R.A.Smith	10	10	2	91	293	36.62	–	2	4
J.A.Snow	3	1	–	2	2	2.00	–	–	–
A.J.Stewart	15	13	1	77	345	28.75	–	2	8/1

	M	I	NO	HS	Runs	Avge	100	50	Ct/St
C.J.Tavaré	7	7	–	58	212	30.28	–	1	2
R.W.Taylor	5	3	1	20*	32	16.00	–	–	4
G.P.Thorpe	6	6	2	89	254	63.50	–	2	5
P.C.R.Tufnell	4	2	2	3*	3	–	–	–	–
D.L.Underwood	2	–	–	–	–	–	–	–	2
C.White	2	1	–	13	13	13.00	–	–	–
R.G.D.Willis	11	4	1	24	25	8.33	–	–	4
B.Wood	3	2	–	77	83	41.50	–	1	–

ENGLAND – BOWLING

	O	M	R	W	Avge	Best	4w	R/O
P.J.W.Allott	80.3	10	335	8	41.87	3-41	–	4.16
G.G.Arnold	29.4	7	70	3	23.33	1-15	–	2.35
C.W.J.Athey	1	0	10	0	–	–	–	10.00
I.T.Botham	222	33	762	30	25.40	4-31	1	3.43
G.Boycott	27	1	94	5	18.80	2-14	–	3.48
B.C.Broad	1	0	6	0	–	–	–	6.00
D.G.Cork	48	2	216	8	27.00	2-33	–	4.50
N.G.Cowans	12	3	31	2	15.50	2-31	–	2.58
P.A.J.DeFreitas	187.5	30	742	29	25.58	3-28	–	3.95
G.R.Dilley	66	4	243	7	34.71	4-45	1	3.68
P.H.Edmonds	26	3	73	3	24.33	2-40	–	2.80
J.E.Emburey	79	4	295	6	49.16	2-26	–	3.73
N.A.Foster	70	1	313	9	34.77	3-47	–	4.47
M.W.Gatting	12	3	48	1	48.00	1-35	–	4.00
G.A.Gooch	23	2	115	1	115.00	1-42	–	5.00
D.Gough	51	4	238	4	59.50	2-48	–	4.66
A.W.Greig	31	2	89	6	14.83	4-45	1	2.87
E.E.Hemmings	59.3	4	274	13	21.07	4-52	1	4.60
M.Hendrick	56	14	149	10	14.90	4-15	1	2.66
G.A.Hick	34.2	0	189	5	37.80	2-44	–	5.50
R.K.Illingworth	98.1	6	424	12	35.33	3-33	–	4.31
J.A.Jameson	2	1	3	0	–	–	–	1.50
A.J.Lamb	1	0	3	0	–	–	–	3.00
W.Larkins	2	0	21	0	–	–	–	10.50
P.Lever	36	3	92	5	18.40	3-32	–	2.55
C.C.Lewis	50.4	5	214	7	30.57	4-30	1	4.22
V.J.Marks	78	9	246	13	18.92	5-39	1	3.15
P.J.Martin	44	2	198	6	33.00	3-33	–	4.50
G.Miller	2	1	1	0	–	–	–	0.50
C.M.Old	90.3	18	243	16	15.18	4- 8	1	2.68
D.R.Pringle	90.4	15	366	8	45.75	3- 8	–	4.03
D.A.Reeve	45.2	5	177	9	19.66	3-38	–	3.90
G.C.Small	103	8	458	11	41.63	2-29	–	4.44
N.M.K.Smith	25.3	2	96	4	24.00	3-29	–	3.76
J.A.Snow	36	8	65	6	10.83	4-11	1	1.80
G.P.Thorpe	8	0	45	0	–	–	–	5.62
P.C.R.Tufnell	28	2	133	3	44.33	2-36	–	4.75
D.L.Underwood	22	7	41	2	20.50	2-30	–	1.86
C.White	6.3	1	23	0	–	–	–	3.53
R.G.D.Willis	118.1	27	315	18	17.50	4-11	2	2.66
B.Wood	12	5	14	0	–	–	–	1.16

WORLD CUP REGISTER

AUSTRALIA

Career statistics deadlines: Test Matches to 28 January 1999; Limited-Overs Internationals to 14 February 1999; first-class to end of 1998 English season (20 September). Key to abbreviations on page 19. Australia's selected 15 players, plus reserves, are:

BEVAN, Michael Gwyl (New South Wales)
Born Belconnen, ACT 8 May 1970. 5'11½". Educated at Western Creek High School, Canberra. Left-hand batsman, left-arm slow bowler (Chinamen/googlies). South Australia 1989-90. NSW 1990-91 to date. Yorkshire 1995-96; cap 1995. Sussex 1998; cap 1998. Club: Manly. **TESTS:** (A): 18 (1994-95 to 1997-98); 785 runs (av 29.07); 29 wkts (av 24.24), 5 wkts/inns (1), 10 wkts/match (1); 8 ct. HS 91 v P (Lahore) 1994-95; BB 6-82 (10-113 match) v WI (Adelaide) 1996-97. **L-O INTERNATIONALS:** (A): 97 (1993-94 to 1998-99); 3244 runs (av 61.20), 3 hundreds; 30 wkts (av 42.20); 37 ct. HS 108* v E (Oval) 1997; BB 3-36 v P (Melbourne) 1996-97. **F-C CAREER:** 155 matches; 11,423 runs (av 53.13), 37 hundreds (inc 1 double), 1000 runs/season (2); 95 wkts (av 42.97), 5 wkts/inns (1), 10 wkts/match (1); 91 ct. HS 203* NSW v WA (Sydney) 1993-94. BB 6-82 (*see TESTS*). **1998 SEASON (f-c – Sussex):** 935 runs (av 55.00), 3 hundreds; 19 wkts (av 34.36). **COUNTY L-O:** HS 103* Yorks v Glos (Middlesbrough) 1995 (ASL). BB 5-29 Yorks v Sussex (Eastbourne) 1996 (ASL).

DALE, Adam Craig (Queensland)
Born Ivanhoe, Victoria 30 Dec 1968. Left-hand batsman, right-arm medium-fast swing bowler. Queensland 1996-97 to date. **TESTS:** 1 (1997-98); 5 runs (av 5.00); 0 ct; 3 wkts (av 30.66). HS 5 and BB 3-71 v I (Bangalore) 1997-98 – on debut. **L-O INTERNATIONALS:** 24 (1996-97 to 1998-99); 56 runs (av 18.66); 27 wkts (av 30.40); 9 ct. HS 15* v SA (East London) 1996-97 – on debut; BB 3-18 v SA (Port Elizabeth) 1996-97. **F-C CAREER:** 24 matches; 325 runs (av 13.00); 87 wkts (av 21.95), 5 wkts/inns (4); 6 ct. HS 55 Queensland v NZ XI (Cairns) 1997-98. BB 6-38 Queensland v WA (Perth) 1996-97. **1998 SEASON (f-c – Australia A):** 12 runs (av –); 18 wkts (av 10.16), 5 wkts/inns (1).

FLEMING, Damien William (Victoria)
Born Perth, WA 24 Apr 1970. 6'0". Educated at Heatherhill High School, Deakin U). Right-hand batsman, right-arm fast-medium bowler. Victoria 1989-90 to date. Club: South Melbourne. **TESTS:** 10 (1994-95 to 1998-99). 143 runs (av 15.88); 37 wkts (av 27.21), 1 hat-trick, 5 wkts/inns (1); 7 ct. HS 71* v E (Brisbane) 1998-99; BB 5-46 v E (Perth) 1998-99. **L-O INTERNATIONALS:** 44 (1993-94 to 1998-99); 32 runs (av 6.40); 70 wkts (av 24.34), 4 wkts (4); 3 ct. HS 5* (Bombay) 1995-96. **F-C CAREER:** 72 matches; 902 runs (av 14.54); 250 wkts (av 29.08), 5 wkts/inns (8), 10 wkts/match (1); 38 ct. HS 71 (*see TESTS*). BB 7-90 v S Aus (Adelaide) 1992-93.

GILCHRIST, Adam Craig (Western Australia)
Born Bellingen, NSW 14 Nov 1971. 6'0". Educated at Kadina High School, Lismore. Left-handed batsman, wicket-keeper. NSW 1992-93 to 1993-94. Western Australia 1994-95 to date. Club: Perth (scored 252 from 157 balls in 50-over match v Gosnells, 1997-98). **TESTS:** 0. **L-O INTERNATIONALS:** 51 (1996-97 to 1998-99); 1660 runs (av 36.88), 5 hundreds; 63 ct, 10 st. HS 154 (off 129 balls) v SL (Melbourne) 1998-99 – Australian LOI record. **F-C CAREER:** 64 matches; 3098 runs (av 39.71), 7 hundreds (inc 1 double); 269 ct, 11 st. HS 203* A v S Aus (Perth) 1997-98.

JULIAN, Brendon Paul (Western Australia)
Born Hamilton, New Zealand 10 Aug 1970. 6'5". Educated at Guildford Grammar School, WA. Right-hand batsman, left-arm fast-medium bowler. Western Australia 1989-90 to date. Surrey debut/cap 1996. Club: Midland-Guildford. **TESTS:** 7 (1993 to 1995-96); 128 runs (av 16.00); 15 wkts (av 39.93), 4 ct. HS 56* v E (Nottingham) 1993; BB 4-36 v WI

27

(Bridgetown) 1994-95. **L-O INTERNATIONALS:** 18 (1993 to 1998-99); 129 runs (av 10.75); 21 wkts (av 34.90); 3 ct. HS 25 v E (Sydney) 1998-99; BB 3-40 v P (Peshawar) 1998-99. **F-C CAREER:** 117 matches; 3290 runs (av 25.30), 4 hundreds; 378 wkts (av 29.88), 5 wkts/inns (21), 10 wkts/match (2), 50 wkts/season (1); 74 ct. HS 124 WA v Tasmania (Perth) 1997-98. BB 7-39 WA v NSW (Sydney) 1997-98. **1998 SEASON (f-c – Australia A):** 104 runs (av 34.66); 9 wkts (av 25.55). **COUNTY L-O:** BB 4-46 v Somerset (Oval) 1996 (NWT). HS 41 v Derbys (Oval) 1996 (ASL).

LEE, Shane (New South Wales)
Born Wollongong, NSW, Australia 8 Aug 1973. 6'2". Educated at Oak Flats High School; Wollongong U. Right-hand batsman, right-arm fast-medium bowler. NSW 1992-93 to date. Somerset 1996; cap 1996. Club: Mosman. **TESTS:** 0. **L-O INTERNATIONALS:** 16 (1995-96 to 1998-99); 207 runs (av 18.81); 12 wkts (av 33.75), 4 wkts (1); 9ct. HS 41 v E (Adelaide) 1998-99; BB 5-33 v SL (Melbourne) 1998-99. **F-C CAREER:** 62 matches; 3542 runs (av 44.27), 10 hundreds, 1000 runs/season (1); 105 wkts (av 42.40); 50 ct. HS 183* NSW v S Aus (Adelaide) 1997-98. BB 4-20 NSW v Tasmania (Sydney) 1995-96. **COUNTY L-O:** HS 104 v Suffolk (Taunton) 1996 (NWT). BB 4-40 v Sussex (Hove) 1996 (ASL).

LEHMANN, Darren Scott (South Australia)
Born Gawler 5 Feb 1970. 5'10. Educated at Gawler High School. Left-hand batsman, othodox left-arm slow bowler. South Australia 1987-88 to 1989-90, 1993-94 to date; captain 1998-99. Victoria 1990-91 to 1992-93. Yorkshire 1997-98; cap 1997. Club: Northern Districts. **TESTS:** 5 (1997-98 to 1998-99); 228 runs (av 28.50); 2 wkts (av 22.50); 3 ct. HS 98 v P (Rawalpindi) 1998-99; BB 1-6. **L-O INTERNATIONALS:** 38 (1996-97 to 1998-99); 1102 runs (av 35.54), 1 hundred; 7 wkts (av 46.14); 7 ct. HS 103 v P (Karachi) 1998-99; BB 2-11 v SA (Melbourne) 1997-98. **F-C CAREER:** 133 matches; 11,288 runs (av 52.01), 33 hundreds, 1000 runs/season (5); 19 wkts (av 55.10); 78 ct. HS 255 S Aus v Queensland (Adelaide) 1996-97. BB 4-42 Yorks v Kent (Maidstone) 1998. **1998 SEASON (f-c – Yorkshire):** 969 runs (av 60.56), 3 hundreds; 6 wkts (av 20.66). **COUNTY L-O:** HS 119 v Durham (Leeds) 1998 (BHC). BB 3-43 v Northants (Leeds) 1997 (ASL).

McGRATH, Glenn Donald (New South Wales)
Born Dubbo, NSW 9 Feb 1970. 6'6". Educated at Narromine High School. Right-hand batsman, right-arm fast bowler. NSW 1992-93 to date. One of *Wisden's* Five Cricketers of 1997. Club: Sutherland. **TESTS:** 45 (1993-94 to 1998-99); 172 runs (av 4.52); 202 wkts (av 23.44), 5 wkts/inns (11); 13 ct. HS 24 v WI (Sydney) 1996-97; BB 8-38 v E (Lord's) 1997. **L-O INTERNATIONALS:** 85 (1993-94 to 1998-99); 49 runs (av 4.08); 122 wkts (av 25.27), 4 wkts (7); 11 ct. HS 10 v E (Melbourne) 1994-95; BB 5-40 v SL (Adelaide) 1998-99. **F-C CAREER:** 70 matches; 221 runs (av 4.91); 286 wkts (av 23.84), 5 wkts/inns (14), 10 wkts/match (1); 13 ct. HS 24 (*see TESTS*). BB 8-38 (*see TESTS*).

MARTYN, Damian Richard (Western Australia)
Born Darwin 21 Oct 1971. 5'10". Educated at Girrawheen High School. Right-hand batsman, right-arm medium bowler, occasional wicket-keeper. Western Australia 1990-91 to date. Club: South Perth. **TESTS:** 7 (1992-93 to 1993-94); 317 runs (av 28.81); 0 wkts; 1 ct. HS 74 v NZ (Auckland) 1992-93. **L-O INTERNATIONALS:** 31 (1992-93 to 1998-99); 572 runs (av 26.00); 1 wkt (av 107.00); 7 ct. HS 59* v E (Adelaide) 1998-99; BB 1-30. **F-C CAREER:** 104 matches; 6928 runs (av 44.69), 19 hundreds (inc 1 double); 22 wkts (av 42.31); 77 ct, 2 st. HS 203* WA v Tasmania (Perth) 1995-96. BB 4-46 WA v Queensland (Brisbane) 1997-98. **1998 SEASON (f-c – Australia A):** 156 runs (av 78.00); did not bowl.

MOODY, Thomas Masson (Western Australia)
Born Adelaide, Australia 2 Oct 1965. 6'6½". Educated at Guildford Grammar School, WA. Right-handed batsman, right-arm medium bowler. W Australia 1985-86 to date; captain 1995-96 to date. Warwickshire 1990; cap 1990. Worcestershire debut/cap 1991; captain 1995 (*part*) to date. **TESTS:** 8 (1989-90 to 1992-93); 456 runs (av 32.57), 2 hundreds; 2 wkts (av 73.50); 9 ct. HS 106 v SL (Brisbane) 1989-90; BB 1-17. **L-O INTERNATIONALS:** 58 (1987-88 to 1997-98); 1013 runs (av 21.55); 37 wkts (av

28

39.70); 16 ct. HS 89 v P (Brisbane) 1989-90; BB 3-39 v Z (Ahmedabad) 1997-98. **F-C CAREER:** 279 matches; 20,143 runs (av 47.50), 63 hundreds (inc 4 doubles), 1000 runs (6); 318 wkts (av 31.06), 5 wkts/inns (9), 10 wkts/match (2); 276 ct. HS 272 WA v Tasmania (Hobart) 1994-95. BB 7-38 WA v Tasmania (Hobart) 1995-96. **1998 SEASON (f-c):** 886 runs (av 42.19), 4 hundreds; 27 wkts (av 29.25), 5 wkts/inns (1). **COUNTY L-O:** HS 180* v Surrey (Oval) 1994 (NWT). BB 4-24 v Scot (Worcester) 1998 (BHC).

PONTING, Ricky Thomas (Tasmania)
Born Launceston 19 Dec 1974. 5'10". Educated at Brooks High School. Right-hand batsman, right-arm medium pace/off-break bowler, outstanding fielder. Tasmania 1992-93 to date. Club: Mowbray. **TESTS:** 22 (1995-96 to 1998-99); 1209 runs (av 36.63), 2 hundreds; 3 wkts (av 10.33); 21 ct. HS 127 v E (Leeds) 1997; BB 1-0. **L-O INTERNA-TIONALS:** 68 (1994-95 to 1998-99); 2492 runs (av 41.53), 5 hundreds; 1 wkt (av 62.00); 16 ct. HS 145 v Z (Delhi) 1997-98; BB 1-41. **F-C CAREER:** 82 matches; 6427 runs (av 53.55), 22 hundreds (inc 1 double); 5 wkts (av 72.00); 70 ct. HS 211 Tasmania v WA (Hobart) 1994-95. BB 1-0.

REIFFEL, Paul Ronald (Victoria)
Born Box Hill, Victoria 19 Apr 1966. 6'2". Educated at Jordanville Technical School. Right-hand batsman, right-arm fast-medium bowler. Victoria 1987-88 to date. Club: Richmond. **TESTS:** 35 (1991-92 to 1997-98); 955 runs (av 26.52); 104 wkts (av 26.96), 5 wkts/inns (5); 15 ct. HS 79* v SA (Melbourne) 1997-98; BB 6-71 v E (Birmingham) 1993. **L-O INTERNATIONALS:** 83 (1991-92 to 1997-98); 496 runs (av 14.58); 97 wkts (av 28.42), 4 wkts (5); 23 ct. HS 58 v SA (Port Elizabeth) 1993-94; BB 4-13 v SA (Sydney) 1993-94. **F-C CAREER:** 126 matches; 2613 runs (av 24.19); 393 wkts (av 28.20), 5 wkts/inns (14), 10 wkts/match (2), 50 wkts/season (1); 59 ct. HS 86 and BB 6-57 v Tasmania (St Kilda, Melbourne) 1990-91.

WARNE, Shane Keith (Victoria)
Born Upper Ferntree Gully, Melbourne 13 Sep 1969. 6'0". Educated at Hampton High School; Mentone Grammar School. Right-hand batsman, right-arm leg-break/googly bowler. Victoria 1990-91 to date. One of *Wisden*'s Five Cricketers of 1993. Club: St Kilda. **TESTS:** 68 (1991-92 to 1998-99); 1240 runs (av 14.76); 315 wkts (av 24.97), 5 wkts/inns (14), 10 wkts/match (4), 1 hat-trick; 48 ct. HS 74* v NZ (Brisbane) 1993-94; BB 8-71 v E (Brisbane) 1994-95. **L-O INTERNATIONALS:** 108 (1992-93 to 1998-99, 11 as captain – 10 won, 1 lost); 512 runs (av 11.37); 169 wkts (av 25.05), 4 wkts (10); 40 ct. HS 55 v SA (Port Elizabeth) 1993-94; BB 5-33 v WI (Sydney) 1996-97. **F-C CAREER:** 123 matches; 2141 runs (av 15.62); 530 wkts (av 25.72), 5 wkts/inns (24), 10 wkts/match (4), 1 hat-trick; 77 ct. HS 74* *(see Tests)*. BB 8-71 *(see Tests)*.

WAUGH, Mark Edward (New South Wales)
Born Canterbury, Sydney 2 Jun 1965. Younger twin of S.R.Waugh. 6'1". Educated at East Hills High School. Right-hand batsman, right-arm off-break bowler. NSW 1985-86 to date. Essex 1988-90 (cap 1989), 1992 and 1995. One of *Wisden*'s Five Cricketers of 1990. Club: Bankstown-Canterbury. **TESTS:** 86 (1990-91 to 1998-99); 5840 runs (av 43.91), 16 hundreds; 48 wkts (av 40.16), 5 wkts/inns (1); 100 ct. HS 153* v I (Bangalore) 1997-98; BB 5-40 v E (Adelaide) 1994-95. **L-O INTERNATIONALS:** 174 (1988-89 to 1998-99); 6044 runs (av 38.74), 11 hundreds; 80 wkts (av 31.23), 4 wkts (2); 68 ct. HS 130 v K (Vishakapatnam) 1995-96; BB 5-24 v WI (Melbourne) 1992-93. **F-C CAREER:** 277 matches; 20,925 runs (av 54.06), 67 hundreds (inc 5 doubles); 190 wkts (av 39.21), 5 wkts/inns (3); 311 ct. HS 229* NSW v WA (Perth) 1990-91, sharing world record 5th wkt stand of 464* with S.R.Waugh. BB 6-68 Aus XI v Board President's XI (Patiala) 1996-97. **COUNTY L-O:** HS 112* Essex v Glam (Neath) 1989 (ASL). BB 3-20 Essex v Durham (Chelmsford) 1995.

WAUGH, Stephen Rodger (New South Wales) (CAPTAIN)
Born Canterbury, Sydney 2 Jun 1965. Elder twin of M.E.Waugh. 5'11". Educated at East Hills High School. Right-hand batsman, right-arm medium-fast bowler. NSW 1984-85 to date. Somerset 1987-88. Ireland 1998. One of *Wisden*'s Five Cricketers of 1988. Club: Bankstown-Canterbury. **TESTS:** 111 (1985-86 to 1998-99); 7213 runs (av 50.44), 17

hundreds; 89 wkts (av 34.88), 5 wkts/inns (3); 78 ct. HS 200 v WI (Kingston) 1994-95; BB 5-28 v SA (Cape Town) 1993-94. Holds world record for most nineties in Tests (9). **L-O INTERNATIONALS:** 251 (1985-86 to 1998-99, 32 as captain – 16 won, 16 lost); 5707 runs (av 31.01), 1 hundred; 185 wkts (av 34.45), 4 wkts (3); 87 ct. HS 102* v SL (Melbourne) 1995-96; BB 4-33 v SL (Sydney) 1987-88. **F-C CAREER:** 252 matches; 16,623 runs (av 51.94), 47 hundreds (inc 4 doubles), 1000 runs/season (2); 240 wkts (av 31.77), 5 wkts/inns (5); 213 ct. HS 216* NSW v WA (Perth) 1990-91, sharing world record 5th wkt stand of 464* with M.E.Waugh. BB 6-51 NSW v Queensland (Sydney) 1988-89. **1998 SEASON (f-c – Ireland):** 76 runs (av 38.00); 0 wkts. **COUNTY L-O:** HS 140* v Middx (Lord's) 1988 (ASL). BB 2-16 v Comb Us (Oxford) 1988 (BHC).

RESERVES

GILLESPIE, Jason Neil (South Australia)
Born Darlinghurst, NSW 19 Apr 1975. 6'5". Educated at Cabra College. Right-hand batsman, right-arm fast bowler. South Australia 1994-95 to date. Club: Adelaide. **TESTS:** 10 (1996-97 to 1998-99); 97 runs (av 12.12); 39 wkts (av 21.12), 5 wkts/inns (3); 3 ct. HS 28* v E (Manchester) 1997; BB 7-37 v E (Leeds) 1997. Took 4 wickets in 6 balls v E (Perth) 1998-99. **L-O INTERNATIONALS:** 14 (1996-97 to 1997); 65 runs (av 10.83); 13 wkts (av 46.69); 0 ct. HS 26 v SA (Johannesburg) 1996-97; BB 2-39 v WI (Melbourne) 1996-97 and 2-39 v SA (Cape Town) 1996-97. **F-C CAREER:** 37 matches; 455 runs (av 11.66); 135 wkts (av 23.54), 5 wkts/inns (6); 15 ct. HS 58 S Aus v WA (Perth) 1996-97. BB 7-34 Aus XI v Border (East London) 1996-97. **1998 SEASON (f-c – Australia A):** did not bat; 6 wkts (av 18.16).

HARVEY, Ian Joseph (Victoria)
Born Wonthaggi 10 Apr 1972. Right-hand batsman, right arm medium-fast bowler. Victoria 1993-94 to date. Club: Dandenong. **TESTS:** 0. **L-O INTERNATIONALS:** 11 (1997-98); 101 runs (av 14.42); 7 wkts (av 46.42); 6 ct. HS 43 v SA (Perth) 1997-98; BB 3-17 v NZ (Sydney) 1997-98. Yorked J.N.Rhodes with his second ball in internationals. **F-C CAREER:** 34 matches; 1469 runs (av 25.32), 2 hundreds; 73 wkts (av 35.78), 5 wkts/inns (3); 27 ct. HS 136 Victoria v S Aus (Melbourne) 1995-96. BB 7-44 Victoria v S Aus (Melbourne) 1996-97.

LAW, Stuart Grant (Queensland)
Born Herston, Brisbane 18 Oct 1968. 6'2". Educated at Craigslea State High School. Right-hand batsman, right-arm medium/leg-break bowler. Queensland 1988-89 to date; captain 1994-95 to date. Essex debut/cap 1996. One of *Wisden's* Five Cricketers of 1997. Club: Wynnum-Manly. **TESTS:** 1 (1995-96); 54 runs (av –); 1 ct. HS 54* v SL (Perth) 1995-96. **L-O INTERNATIONALS:** 54 (1994-95 to 1998-99); 1237 runs (av 26.89), 1 hundred; 12 wkts (av 52.91); 12 ct. HS 110 v Z (Hobart) 1994-95; BB 2-22 v P (Sydney) 1996-97. **F-C CAREER:** 153 matches; 10753 runs (av 46.34), 30 hundreds, 1000 runs/season (3); 67 wkts (av 47.01), 5 wkts/inns (1); 161 ct. HS 179 Queensland v Tasmania (Brisbane) 1988-89. BB 5-39 Queensland v Tasmania (Brisbane) 1995-96. **1998 SEASON (f-c):** 982 runs (av 40.91), 2 hundreds; did not bowl. **COUNTY L-O:** HS 126 Essex v Kent (Southend) 1998 (ASL). BB 4-37 Essex v Worcs (Chelmsford) 1997 (ASL).

MacGILL, Stuart Charles Glyndwr (New South Wales)
Born Mount Lawley 25 Feb 1971. Grandson of C.W.T.MacGill (WA 1938-39), son of T.M.D.MacGill (WA 1968-69). 6'0". Educated at Christ Church Grammar School, Perth. Right-hand batsman, right-arm legbreak bowler. Western Australia 1993-94. NSW 1996-97. Somerset 1997 (unregistered). Devon 1997 to 1998 (NWT only). Club: North Sydney. **TESTS:** 8 (1997-98 to 1998-99); 133 runs (av 14.77); 47 wkts (av 21.78), 5 wkts/inns (3), 10 wkts/match (1); 7 ct. HS 43 v E (Melbourne) 1998-99; BB 7-50 (12-107 match) v E (Sydney) 1998-99. **L-O INTERNATIONALS:** 0. **F-C CAREER:** 19 matches; 132 runs (av 7.76); 76 wkts (av 31.48), 5 wkts/inns (4); ct 8. HS 43 (*see TESTS*). BB 7-50 (*see TESTS*).

YOUNG, Bradley Evan (South Australia)
Born Semaphore 23 Feb 1973. Right-hand batsman, orthodox slow left-arm bowler. South Australia 1995-96 to date. Club: Port Adelaide. **TESTS:** 0. **L-O INTERNATIONALS:** 6

(1997-98 to 1998-99); 31 runs (av 15.50); 1 wkt (av 251.00); 2 ct. HS 18 v I (Dhaka) 1998-99; BB 1-26. **F-C CAREER:** 21 matches; 896 runs (av 34.46); 62 wkts (av 37.77), 5 wkts/inns (2); 18 ct. HS 91* S Aus v NSW (Adelaide) 1996-97. BB 5-64 S Aus v Queensland (Brisbane) 1997-98. **1998 SEASON (f-c – Australia A):** 63 runs (av 31.50); 5 wkts (av 22.00).

WORLD CUP CAREER RECORDS

AUSTRALIA – BATTING AND FIELDING

	M	I	NO	HS	Runs	Avge	100	50	Ct/St
M.G.Bevan	7	5	1	69	125	31.25	–	1	3
D.C.Boon	16	16	1	100	815	54.33	2	5	2
A.R.Border	25	24	–	67	452	18.83	–	1	10
G.S.Chappell	5	5	–	50	129	25.80	–	1	3
I.M.Chappell	5	5	–	62	121	24.20	–	1	–
T.M.Chappell	4	4	–	110	139	34.75	1	–	1
G.J.Cosier	3	2	–	6	6	3.00	–	–	1
W.M.Darling	3	3	–	25	51	17.00	–	–	–
G.C.Dyer	8	4	–	27	50	12.50	–	–	9/2
G.Dymock	3	2	1	10	14	14.00	–	–	–
R.Edwards	5	4	1	80*	166	55.33	–	2	–
D.W.Fleming	6	1	–	0	0	0.00	–	–	2
G.J.Gilmour	2	2	1	28*	42	42.00	–	–	1
I.A.Healy	14	11	2	31	110	12.22	–	–	18/3
A.M.J.Hilditch	3	3	–	72	143	47.66	–	1	1
T.G.Hogan	4	4	2	11	24	12.00	–	–	2
R.M.Hogg	8	5	4	19*	29	29.00	–	–	1
D.W.Hookes	6	6	–	56	133	22.16	–	1	3
K.J.Hughes	8	8	1	69	218	31.14	–	2	3
M.G.Hughes	1	1	1	0*	0	–	–	–	–
A.G.Hurst	3	2	2	3*	6	–	–	–	–
D.M.Jones	16	16	2	90	590	42.14	–	5	6
T.J.Laughlin	1	1	–	8	8	8.00	–	–	–
S.G.Law	7	6	2	72	204	51.00	–	1	–
G.F.Lawson	4	4	–	16	24	6.00	–	–	–
S.Lee	2	1	–	9	9	9.00	–	–	1
D.K.Lillee	9	3	1	16*	19	9.50	–	–	–
R.B.McCosker	5	5	–	73	120	24.00	–	1	–
C.J.McDermott	17	11	–	14	43	3.90	–	–	4
G.D.McGrath	7	1	1	0*	0	–	–	–	1
K.H.Macleay	4	4	–	9	19	4.75	–	–	1
A.A.Mallett	3	1	–	0	0	0.00	–	–	1
G.R.Marsh	13	13	1	126*	579	48.25	2	2	2
R.W.Marsh	11	11	4	52*	220	31.42	–	2	17/1
T.B.A.May	6	3	1	15	16	8.00	–	–	1
T.M.Moody	11	11	1	57	212	21.20	–	2	3
J.K.Moss	1	1	–	7	7	7.00	–	–	2
S.P.O'Donnell	7	4	–	7	15	3.75	–	–	4
R.T.Ponting	7	7	–	102	229	32.71	1	1	1
G.D.Porter	2	1	–	3	3	3.00	–	–	1
B.A.Reid	14	5	2	5*	10	3.33	–	–	4
P.R.Reiffel	5	4	3	13*	27	27.00	–	–	3
M.A.Taylor	9	9	–	74	206	22.88	–	2	1
P.L.Taylor	9	7	3	17*	34	8.50	–	–	1
J.R.Thomson	8	5	2	21	51	17.00	–	–	1
A.Turner	5	5	–	101	201	40.20	1	–	3
M.R.J.Veletta	4	4	–	48	136	45.33	–	–	–

	M	I	NO	HS	Runs	Avge	100	50	Ct/St
M.H.N.Walker	5	3	–	18	33	11.00	–	–	1
K.D.Walters	5	5	1	59	123	30.75	–	1	–
S.K.Warne	7	5	2	24	32	10.66	–	–	1
M.E.Waugh	12	12	2	130	629	62.90	3	2	5
S.R.Waugh	23	22	7	82	580	38.66	–	4	8
K.C.Wessels	3	3	–	76	92	30.66	–	1	1
M.R.Whitney	7	3	2	9*	22	22.00	–	–	1
G.M.Wood	5	5	1	73	144	36.00	–	1	1
K.J.Wright	3	2	–	23	29	14.50	–	–	5
G.N.Yallop	9	9	3	66*	247	41.16	–	2	–
A.K.Zesers	2	2	2	8*	10	–	–	–	1

Record in all World Cup matches:

	M	I	NO	HS	Runs	Avge	100	50	Ct/St
K.C.Wessels (A/SA)	12	12	2	85	405	40.50	–	4	8

AUSTRALIA – BOWLING

	O	M	R	W	Avge	Best	4w	R/O
M.G.Bevan	32	1	156	3	52.00	2-35	–	4.87
D.C.Boon	1	0	17	0	–	–	–	17.00
A.R.Border	73	1	342	9	38.00	2-27	–	4.68
G.S.Chappell	18	0	88	0	–	–	–	4.88
I.M.Chappell	7	1	23	2	11.50	2-14	–	3.28
T.M.Chappell	19.4	0	98	4	24.50	3-47	–	4.98
G.J.Cosier	27.2	4	95	5	19.00	3-54	–	3.47
G.Dymock	31	7	64	2	32.00	1-17	–	2.06
D.W.Fleming	45.2	3	221	12	18.41	5-36	1	4.87
G.J.Gilmour	24	8	62	11	5.63	6-14	2	2.58
T.G.Hogan	47	2	172	6	28.66	2-33	–	3.65
R.M.Hogg	78	9	271	10	27.10	3-40	–	3.47
M.G.Hughes	9	1	49	1	49.00	1-49	–	5.44
A.G.Hurst	32	6	119	7	17.00	5-21	1	3.71
D.M.Jones	1	0	5	0	–	–	–	5.00
T.J.Laughlin	9.1	0	38	2	19.00	2-38	–	4.14
S.G.Law	5	0	23	0	–	–	–	4.60
G.F.Lawson	38	7	127	5	25.40	3-29	–	3.34
S.Lee	7	2	31	0	–	–	–	4.42
D.K.Lillee	98	8	400	12	33.33	5-34	1	4.08
C.J.McDermott	149	8	599	27	22.18	5-44	2	4.02
G.D.McGrath	62.2	10	258	6	43.00	2-30	–	4.13
K.H.Macleay	44.5	6	163	8	20.37	6-39	1	3.63
A.A.Mallett	35	3	156	3	52.00	1-35	–	4.45
T.B.A.May	44	1	213	4	53.25	2-29	–	4.84
T.M.Moody	51	2	240	7	34.28	3-56	–	4.70
S.P.O'Donnell	60.4	6	261	9	29.00	4-39	1	4.30
G.D.Porter	18	5	33	2	11.00	2-13	–	1.83
B.A.Reid	122.4	10	512	9	56.88	2-38	–	4.17
P.R.Reiffel	36	3	163	5	32.60	2-18	–	4.52
P.L.Taylor	47.4	1	218	6	36.33	2-14	–	4.57
J.R.Thomson	76.5	10	290	7	41.42	3-51	–	3.77
M.H.N.Walker	57.2	10	210	6	35.00	3-22	–	3.66
K.D.Walters	17	1	85	1	85.00	1-29	–	5.00
S.K.Warne	68.3	3	263	12	21.91	4-34	2	3.83
M.E.Waugh	53	1	269	5	53.80	3-38	–	5.07
S.R.Waugh	155.1	7	722	24	30.08	3-36	–	4.65
M.R.Whitney	66	12	215	9	23.88	4-34	1	3.25
G.N.Yallop	22	0	110	3	36.66	2-28	–	5.00
A.K.Zesers	15	1	74	1	74.00	1-37	–	4.93

WORLD CUP REGISTER

SOUTH AFRICA

Career statistics deadlines: Test Matches to 28 January 1999; Limited-Overs Internationals to 14 February 1999; first-class to end of 1998 English season (20 September). Key to abbreviations on page 19. South Africa's provisionally selected 19 players (to be reduced to 15 by 1 April) are:

ADAMS, Paul Regan (Western Province)
Born Cape Town 20 Jan 1977. 5'8". Educated at Plumstead High School. Right-hand batsman, left-arm unorthodox slow bowler. W Province 1995-96 to date. **TESTS:** 21 (1995-96 to 1998-99); 107 runs (av 5.09); 66 wkts (av 30.89), 5 wkts/inns (1), 16 ct. HS 29 v E (Cape Town) 1995-96; BB 6-55 v I (Kanpur) 1996-97. **L-O INTERNATIONALS:** 11 (1995-96 to 1997-98); 25 runs (av 8.33); 14 wkts (av 26.92); 1 ct. HS 15* v A (Sydney) 1997-98; BB 3-26 v E (East London) 1995-96. **F-C CAREER:** 42 matches; 300 runs (av 12.00); 153 wkts (av 29.72), 5 wkts/inns (7); 21 ct. HS 38* W Province v E Province (Cape Town) 1997-98. BB 7-69 W Province v Griqualand West (Cape Town) 1997-98. **1998 SEASON (f-c – SA tour):** 60 runs (av 15.00); 17 wkts (av 39.17).

BENKENSTEIN, Dale Martin (Natal)
Born Salisbury, Rhodesia 9 Jun 1974. Son of M.M.Benkenstein (Rhodesia and Natal 1970-71 to 1980-81), younger brother of twins B.R. (Natal B 1993-94) and B.N. (Natal B and Griqualand West 1994-95 to date). Educated at Michaelhouse School. Natal 1993-94 to date. Right-hand batsman, right-arm medium/off-break bowler. Natal B 1994-95. Griqualand West 1995-96 to date. **TESTS:** 0. **L-O INTERNATIONALS:** 7 (1998-99); 188 runs (av 47.00); 1 ct. HS 69 v WI (Cape Town) 1998-99. **F-C CAREER:** 52 matches; 2829 runs (av 43.52), 7 hundreds (inc 1 double); 17 wkts (av 35.29); 30 ct. HS 203* and BB 2-26 Natal B v N Transvaal B (Durban) 1994-95.

BOJE, Nico (Free State)
Born Bloemfontein 20 Mar 1973. Younger brother of E.H.L.Boje (OFS B 1989-90). 5'10". Educated at Grey College. Left-hand batsman, left-arm orthodox slow bowler. OFS/Free State 1990-91 to date. **TESTS:** 0. **L-O INTERNATIONALS:** 13 (1995-96 to 1998-99); 62 runs (av 12.40); 16 wkts (av 28.81); 5 ct. HS 28 v SL (1998-99); BB 3-33 v WI Port Elizabeth 1998-99. **F-C CAREER:** 67 matches; 2368 runs (av 31.57), 3 hundreds; 181 wkts (av 34.20), 5 wkts/inns (7), 10 wkts/match (1); 40 ct. HS 105* SA Academy v NZ Academy (Pretoria) 1997-98. BB 6-34 Free State v Northerns (Bloemfontein) 1997-98.

BOUCHER, Mark Verdon (Border)
Born East London 3 Dec 1976. 5'9". Educated at Selborne College; Port Elizabeth U. Right-hand batsman, wicket-keeper. Border 1995-96 to date. **TESTS:** 16 (1997-98 to 1998-99); 502 runs (av 23.90), 1 hundred; 69 ct, 2 st. HS 100 v WI (Pretoria) 1998-99. Conceded no byes in five-match series v SA 1998-99. **L-O INTERNATIONALS:** 23 (1997-98 to 1998-99); 179 runs (av 13.76); 30 ct, 2 st. HS 51 v WI (East London) 1998-99. **F-C CAREER:** 35 matches; 1354 runs (av 32.23); 0 wkts; 124 ct, 9 st. HS 100 (*see Tests*). **1998 SEASON (f-c – SA tour):** 211 runs (av 23.44); 43 ct 1 st.

CRONJE Wessel Johannes (**'Hansie'**) (Free State) (CAPTAIN)
Born Bloemfontein 25 Sep 1969. Son of N.E.Cronje (OFS 1960-61 to 1971-72), younger brother of F.J.C. (OFS, Griqualand West and Boland 1986-87 to date). 6'4". Educated at Grey College, Bloemfontein; OFS U. Right-hand batsman, right-arm medium bowler. OFS/Free State 1987-88 to date; captain 1990-91 to date. Leicestershire 1995 (cap 1995). **TESTS:** 56 (1991-92 to 1998-99), 41 as captain – 20 won, 10 lost, 11 drawn); 3363 runs (av 38.21), 6 hundreds; 29 wkts (av 35.55); 28 ct. HS 135 v I (Port Elizabeth) 1992-93; BB 3-19 v WI (Durban) 1998-99. **L-O INTERNATIONALS:** 152 (1991-92 to 1998-99,

102 as captain – 77 on, 24 lost, 1 no result); 4695 runs (av 39.78), 2 hundreds; 98 wkts (av 34.15), 4 wkts (2); 60 ct. HS 112 v A (Johannesburg) 1993-94; BB 5-32 v I (Cape Town) 1992-93. **F-C CAREER:** 156 matches; 10,468 runs (av 44.16), 27 hundreds (inc 2 doubles), 1000 runs/season (1); 84 wkts (av 38.35); 97 ct. HS 251 OFS v A (Bloemfontein) 1993-94. **BB** 4-47 SA v Kent (Canterbury) 1994. **1998 SEASON (f-c – SA tour):** 704 runs (av 70.40), 2 hundreds; 1 wkt (av 97.00). **COUNTY L-O:** HS 158 Leics v Lancs (Manchester) 1995 (BHC). BB 3-37 Leics v Hants (Basingstoke) 1995 (ASL).

CROOKES, Derek Norman (Natal)
Born Durban 5 Mar 1969. Son of N.S.Crookes (Natal 1962-63 to 1969-70). 6'1". Educated at Hilton College; Durban Technical College. Right-hand batsman, off-break bowler. Natal B 1989-90. Natal 1990-91 to date. **TESTS:** 0. **L-O INTERNATIONALS:** 24 (1994-95 to 1998-99); 243 runs (av 18.69); 15 wkts (av 45.86); 16 ct. HS 54 v I (Sharjah) 1995-96; BB 3-30 v P (Nairobi) 1996-97. **F-C CAREER:** 63 matches; 3385 runs (av 40.30), 8 hundreds; 139 wkts (av 31.82), 5 wkts/inns (7); 54 ct. HS 155* SA A v Somerset (Taunton) 1996. BB 7-114 Natal v Free State (Durban) 1996-97.

CULLINAN, Daryll John (Gauteng)
Born Kimberley 4 Mar 1967. Younger brother of R.E.Cullinan (Border and OFS B 1984-85 to 1990-91). 5'10". Educated at Queens College, Queenstown; Stellenbosch U. Right-hand batsman, off-break bowler. Border 1983-84 to 1984-85 and 1994-95 to 1995-96. W Province 1985-86 to 1990-91. Transvaal/Gauteng 1991-92 to 1993-94 and 1996-97 to date. Derbyshire 1995. **TESTS:** 45 (1992-93 to 1998-99); 2680 runs (av 37.74), 6 hundreds; 1 wkts (av 46.00); 38 ct. HS 168 v WI (Cape Town) 1998-99; BB 1-32. **L-O INTERNATIONALS:** 107 (1992-93 to 1998-99); 3198 runs (av 34.76), 3 hundreds; 5 wkts (av 24.00); 45 ct. HS 124 v P (Nairobi) 1996-97; BB 2-30 v E (Manchester) 1998. **F-C CAREER:** 172 matches; 10,818 runs (av 42.25), 25 hundreds (inc 1 double and 1 triple), youngest player (16 years 304 days) to score f-c hundred in SA; 3 wkts (av 66.66); 152 ct. HS 337* v N Transvaal (Johannesburg) 1993-94 (SA f-c record). BB 2-27 Border v Natal B (East London) 1983-84. **1998 SEASON (f-c – SA tour):** 900 runs (av 69.23), 2 hundreds; 0 wkts. **COUNTY L-O:** HS 119* Derbys v Cambs (March) 1995 (NWT).

DAWSON, Alan Charles (Western Province)
Born Cape Town 27 Nov 1969. Right-hand batsman, right-arm medium-fast bowler. W Province 1992-93 to date. **TESTS:** 0. **L-O INTERNATIONALS:** 1 (1998-99); did not bat; 1 wkt (av 51.00); 0 ct. BB 1-51 v E (Dhaka) 1998-99. **F-C CAREER:** 44 matches; 1006 runs (av 19.35); 118 wkts (av 27.05), 5 wkts/inns (5); 30 ct. HS 64 W Province v Boland (Cape Town) 1996-97. BB 6-18 W Province B v Free State B 1995-96.

DONALD, Allan Anthony (Free State)
Born Bloemfontein 20 Oct 1966. 6'2". Grey College High School. Right-hand batsman, right-arm fast bowler. OFS/Free State 1985-86 to date. Warwickshire 1987-93, 1995, 1997; cap 1989; benefit 1999. One of *Wisden*'s Five Cricketers of 1991. **TESTS:** 52 (1991-92 to 1998-99); 504 runs (av 11.45); 260 wkts (av 21.64), 5 wkts/inns (17), 10 wkts/match (2); 13 ct. HS 34 v WI (Port Elizabeth) 1998-99; BB 8-71 (11-113 match) v Z (Harare) 1995-96. **L-O INTERNATIONALS:** 108 (1991-92 to 1998-99); 73 runs (av 4.86); 182 wkts (av 21.40), 4 wkts (9); 14 ct. HS 12 v SL (Nottingham) 1998; BB 6-23 v K (Nairobi) 1996-97. **F-C CAREER:** 260 matches; 2281 runs (av 12.26); 1043 wkts (av 22.18), 5 wkts/inns (59), 10 wkts/match (8); 50 wkts/season (5); 98 ct. HS 55* SA v Tasmania (Devonport) 1997-98. BB 8-37 OFS v Transvaal (Johannesburg) 1986-87. **1998 SEASON (f-c – SA tour):** 29 runs (av 9.66); 39 wkts (av 20.12), 5 wkts/inns (5). **COUNTY L-O:** HS 23* Warwks v Leics (Leicester) 1989 (BHC). BB 6-15 Warwks v Yorks (Birmingham) 1995 (ASL).

ELWORTHY, Steven (Northerns)
Born Bulawayo, Rhodesia 23 Feb 1965. 6'4". Educated at Chaplin HS, Gwelo; Sandown HS, Johannesburg; Witwatersrand U. Right-hand batsman, right-arm fast-medium bowler. Transvaal B 1987-88. N Transvaal/Northerns 1988-89 to date. Lancashire 1995-96 to 1996. **TESTS:** 1 (1997); 58 runs (av 29.00); 1 wkt (av 79.00); 0 ct. HS 48 and BB1-41 v E (Nottingham) 1997. **L-O INTERNATIONALS:** 11 (1997-98 to 1998-99); 14 runs (av 14.00); 16 wkts (av 24.81); 4 ct. HS 14* v SL (Johannesburg) 1997-98; BB 3-21 v SL (Dhaka) 1998-99. **F-C CAREER:** 92 matches; 2528 runs (av 20.55); 298 wkts (av 30.49), 5 wkts/inns (10), 10 wkts/match (2); 34 ct. HS 89 Northerns v Boland (Pretoria) 1997-98; BB 7-65 N Transvaal v Natal (Durban) 1994-95. **1998 SEASON (f-c − SA tour):** 58 runs (av 29.00); 16 wkts (av 25.93). **COUNTY L-O:** BB 4-14 Lancs v Glos (Manchester) 1996 (BHC). HS 15 Lancs v Glos and 15 Lancs v Surrey (Manchester) 1996 (ASL).

GIBBS, Herschelle Herman (Western Province)
Born Green Point, Cape Town 23 Feb 1974. 5'10". Educated at Diocesan College. Right-hand batsman, occasional right-arm medium/off break bowler, outstanding fielder. W Province 1990-91 to date. **TESTS:** 11 (1996-97 to 1998-99); 433 runs (av 20.61); 8 ct. HS 54 v A (Sydney) 1997-98. **L-O INTERNATIONALS:** 22 (1996-97 to 1998-99); 485 runs (av 22.04), 1 hundred; 11 ct. HS 125 v WI (Port Elizabeth) 1998-99. **F-C CAREER:** 64 matches; 4497 runs (av 42.03), 11 hundreds (inc 1 double); 3 wkts (av 24.66); 37 ct. HS 200* SA v India A (Nagpur) 1996-97. BB 2-14 SA A v Somerset (Taunton) 1996.

KALLIS, Jacques Henry (Western Province)
Born Pinelands 16 Oct 1975. 6'0". Educated at Wynberg High School. Right-hand batsman, right-arm fast-medium bowler. W Province B 1993-94. W Province 1994-95 to date. Middlesex 1997; cap 1997. **TESTS:** 24 (1995-96 to 1998-99); 1327 runs (av 36.86); 3 hundreds; 41 wkts (av 26.90), 5 wkts/inns (1); 23 ct. HS 132 v E (Manchester) 1998; BB 5-90 v WI (Cape Town) 1998-99. **L-O INTERNATIONALS:** 58 (1995-96 to 1998-99); 1804 runs (av 38.38), 3 hundreds; 37 wkts (av 30.40), 4 wkts (1); 23 ct. HS 113* v SL (Dhaka) 1998-99; BB 5-30 v WI (Dhaka) 1998-99. **F-C CAREER:** 80 matches; 4847 runs (av 44.46), 13 hundreds, 1000 runs/season (1); 108 wkts (av 30.40), 5 wkts/inns (2); 56 ct. HS 186* W Province v Queensland (Brisbane) 1995-96. BB 5-54 Middx v Kent (Lord's) 1997. **1998 SEASON (f-c − SA tour):** 612 runs (av 55.63), 2 hundreds; 16 wkts (av 33.06). **COUNTY L-O:** HS 100 and BB 4-47 Middx v Glos (Uxbridge) 1997 (NWT).

KIRSTEN, Gary (Western Province)
Born Cape Town 23 Nov 1967. Son of N.Kirsten (Border 1946-47 to 1960-61), younger brother of P.N. (W Province, Border, Sussex, Derbyshire and SA 1973-74 to 1996-97). A.M (W Province B 1986-87 to 1989-90) and P. (Griqualand West and W Province 1992-93 to 1996-97). 5'9". Educated at Rondebosch High School; Cape Town U. Left-hand batsman, off-break bowler, occasional wicket-keeper. W Province B 1987-88. W Province 1988-89 to date. **TESTS:** 50 (1993-94 to 1998-99, 1 as captain − 1 drawn); 3231 runs (av 38.92), 8 hundreds; 2 wkts (av 67.50); 41 ct. HS 210 v E (Manchester) 1998. BB 1-0. **L-O INTERNATIONALS:** 96 (1993-94 to 1998-99); 3600 runs (av 41.37), 8 hundreds; 0 wkts; 32 ct, 1 st. HS 188* v UAE (Rawalpindi) 1995-96 − World Cup record. **F-C CAREER:** 137 matches; 9793 runs (av 45.12), 27 hundreds (inc 5 doubles); 20 wkts (av 40.20), 5 wkts/inns (1); 102 ct. HS 244 W Province v Border (East London) 1995-96. BB 6-68 W Province v N Transvaal (Pretoria) 1993-94. **1998 SEASON (f-c − SA tour):** 892 runs (av 63.71), 4 hundreds; did not bowl.

KLUSENER, Lance (Natal)
Born Durban 4 Sep 1971. 5'10". Educated at Durban High School. Left-hand batsman, right-arm fast-medium bowler. Natal 1993-94 to date. **TESTS:** 17 (1996-97 to 1998-99); 585 runs (av 27.85), 1 hundred; 45 wkts (av 32.75), 5 wkts/inns (1); 10 ct. HS 102* v I (Cape Town) 1996-97; BB 8-64 v I (Calcutta) 1996-97 − on debut. **L-O INTERNATIONALS:** 46 (1995-96 to 1998-99); 1093 runs (av 35.25); 65 wkts (av 28.23), 4 wkts

(4); 10 ct. HS 99 v SL (Lahore) 1997-98; BB 6-49 v SL (Lahore) 1997-98. **F-C CAREER:** 59 matches; 2036 runs (av 34.50), 3 hundreds; 199 wkts (av 25.37), 5 wkts/inns (7), 10 wkts/match (1); 34 ct. HS 105 Natal B v W Province B (Durban) 1994-95. BB 8-34 Natal v W Province (Durban) 1995-96. **1998 SEASON (f-c – SA tour):** 207 runs (av 69.00); 14 wkts (av 30.28).

NTINI, Makhaya (Border)
Born King William's Town 6 Jul 1977. 6'0". Educated at Dale College; E London Technical College. Right-hand batsman, right-arm fast bowler. Border 1995-96 to date. **TESTS:** 4 (1997-98 to 1998); 9 runs (av 9.00); 10 wkts (av 35.80); 1 ct. HS 4* and BB 4-72 v E (Leeds) 1998. **L-O INTERNATIONALS:** 1 (1997-98); did not bat; 2 wkts (av 15.50); 1 ct. BB 2-31 v NZ (Perth) 1997-98. **F-C CAREER:** 31 matches; 135 runs (av 6.42); 79 wkts (av 34.06), 5 wkts/inns (1); 2 ct. HS 22 Border v Boland (Paarl) 1997-98. BB 6-49 Border v W Province (Cape Town) 1996-97. **1998 SEASON (f-c – SA tour):** 4 runs (av 4.00); 19 wkts (av 30.42).

POLLOCK, Shaun Maclean (Natal)
Born Port Elizabeth 16 Jul 1973. Son of P.M.Pollock (E Province and SA 1958-59 to 1971-72); nephew of R.G. (E Province, Transvaal and SA 1960-61 to 1986-87). 6'3". Educated at Northwood High School; Durban U. Right-hand batsman, right-arm fast bowler. Natal B 1991-92. Natal 1992-93 to date. Warwickshire 1996; cap 1996. **TESTS:** 30 (1995-96 to 1998-99); 1143 runs (av 29.30); 120 wkts (av 22.14), 5 wkts/inns (8); 13 ct. HS 92 v SL (Cape Town) 1997-98; BB 7-87 v A (Adelaide) 1997-98. **L-O INTERNATION-ALS:** 63 (1995-96 to 1998-99); 960 runs (av 30.96); 92 wkts (av 23.73), 4 wkts (4); 14 ct. HS 75 v Z (Johannesburg) 1996-97; BB v WI (East London) 1998-99. **F-C CAREER:** 72 matches; 2882 runs (av 33.90), 3 hundreds; 261 wkts (av 22.45), 5 wkts/inns (11), 10 wkts/match (1); 32 ct. HS 150* Warwks v Glam (Birmingham) 1996. BB 7-33 Natal v Border (E London) 1995-96. **1998 SEASON (f-c – SA tour):** 187 runs (av 31.16); 24 wkts (av 24.75), 5 wkts/inns (1). **COUNTY L-O:** HS 59* v Lancs (Manchester) 1996)BHC). BB 6-21 v Leics (Birmingham) 1996 – inc 4 wkts in 4 balls on Warwks debut (BHC).

POTHAS, Nic (Gauteng)
Born Johannesburg 18 Nov 1973. Educated at King Edward VII School. Right-hand batsman, wicket-keeper. Transvaal/Gauteng 1993-94 to date. **TESTS:** 0. **L-O INTER-NATIONALS:** 0. **F-C CAREER:** 54 matches; 2377 runs (av 32.56), 4 hundreds; 0 wkts; 157 ct, 17 st. HS 147 SA Students v Eng XI (Pietermaritzburg) 1995-96.

RHODES, Jonathan Neil (**'Jonty'**) (Natal)
Born Pietermaritzburg 27 Jul 1969. Elder brother of C.B.Rhodes (E Province B aand natal B 1990-91 to 1993-94). 5'8". Educated at Maritzburg College; Natal U. Right-hand batsman, right-arm medium bowler, outstanding fielder. Natal 1988-89 to date. **TESTS:** 41 (1992-93 to 1998-99); 2048 runs (av 34.71), 3 hundreds; 0 wkts; 21 ct. HS 117 v E (Lord's) 1998. **L-O INTERNATIONALS:** 146 (1991-92 to 1998-99); 3532 runs (av 33.00), 1 hundred; 70 ct – including 5 v WI (Bombay) 1993-94 (world record). HS 121 v P (Nairobi) 1996-97. **F-C CAREER:** 114 matches; 5708 runs (av 35.67), 10 hundreds; 1 wkt (av 56.00); 79 ct. HS 156* Natal v Free State (Durban) 1996-97. BB 1-13. Scored 108 v W Province (Durban) 1988-89 on f-c debut. **1998 SEASON (f-c – SA tour):** 562 runs (av 43.23), 2 hundreds; did not bowl.

SYMCOX, Patrick Leonard (Natal)
Born Kimberley 14 Apr 1960. Son of R.L.Symcox (Griqualand West 1957-58 to 1962-63). 6'3". Educated at Kimberley High School; Damelin College. Right-hand batsman, off-break bowler. Griqualand West 1977-78 to 1982-83, 1988-89 to 1989-90. N Transvaal B 1983-84 to 1987-88. Natal 1990-91 to date. **TESTS:** 20 (1993-94 to 1998-99); 741 runs (av 28.50), 1 hundred; 37 wkts (av 43.32); 5 ct. HS 108 v P (Johannesburg) 1997-98 – third hundred by a No. 10 in Tests; BB 4-69 v A (Melbourne) 1997-98. **L-O INTERNATIONALS:** 77 (1993-94 to 1998-99); 694 runs (av 17.35); 72

wkts (av 36.41), 4 wkts (1); 22 ct. HS 61 v I (Sharjah) 1995-96; BB 4-28 v A (Sydney) 1997-98. **F-C CAREER:** 109 matches; 3751 runs (av 27.18), 2 hundreds; 229 wkts (av 32.30), 5 wkts/inns (5); 65 ct. HS 108 (*see Tests*). BB 7-93 N Transvaal B v Transvaal B (Pretoria) 1987-88. **1998 SEASON (f-c – SA tour):** 21 runs (av –); 12 wkts (av 17.25), 5 wkts/inns (1).

WORLD CUP CAREER RECORDS

SOUTH AFRICA – BATTING AND FIELDING

	M	I	NO	HS	Runs	Avge	100	50	Ct/St
P.R.Adams	2	1	–	10	10	10.00	–	–	–
T.Bosch	1	–	–	–	–	–	–	–	–
W.J.Cronje	14	12	4	78	378	47.25	–	2	6
D.J.Cullinan	6	6	2	69	255	63.75	–	2	3
P.S.de Villiers	1	1	–	12	12	12.00	–	–	–
A.A.Donald	13	1	–	3	3	3.00	–	–	1
O.Henry	1	1	–	11	11	11.00	–	–	–
A.C.Hudson	12	12	–	161	571	47.58	1	4	2
J.H.Kallis	5	4	2	26	63	31.50	–	–	1
G.Kirsten	6	6	1	188*	391	78.20	1	1	2
P.N.Kirsten	8	8	2	90	410	68.33	–	4	2
A.P.Kuiper	9	8	1	36	113	16.14	–	–	3
B.M.McMillan	15	9	4	33*	145	29.00	–	–	8
C.R.Matthews	6	2	2	9*	17	–	–	–	1
S.J.Palframan	6	3	–	28	45	15.00	–	–	8
S.M.Pollock	6	3	1	20*	38	19.00	–	–	2
M.W.Pringle	7	1	1	5*	5	–	–	–	1
J.N.Rhodes	13	11	1	43	191	19.10	–	–	5
D.J.Richardson	9	5	2	28	66	22.00	–	–	14/1
M.W.Rushmere	3	3	–	35	49	16.33	–	–	1
R.P.Snell	9	4	2	11*	24	12.00	–	–	1
P.L.Symcox	4	2	–	24	25	12.50	–	–	–
K.C.Wessels	9	9	2	85	313	44.71	–	3	7

Record in all World Cup matches:

	M	I	NO	HS	Runs	Avge	100	50	Ct/St
K.C.Wessels (A/SA)	12	12	2	85	405	40.50	–	4	8

SOUTH AFRICA – BOWLING

	O	M	R	W	Avge	Best	4w	R/O
P.R.Adams	18	0	87	3	29.00	2-45	–	4.83
T.Bosch	2.3	0	19	0	–	–	–	7.60
W.J.Cronje	42	2	172	4	43.00	2-17	–	4.09
D.J.Cullinan	2	0	7	0	–	–	–	3.50
P.S.de Villiers	7	1	27	2	13.50	2-27	–	3.85
A.A.Donald	112	5	455	21	21.66	3-21	–	4.06
O.Henry	10	0	31	1	31.00	1-31	–	3.10
J.H.Kallis	13	1	57	0	–	–	–	4.38
G.Kirsten	3	1	9	0	–	–	–	3.00
P.N.Kirsten	18	1	87	5	17.40	3-31	–	4.83
A.P.Kuiper	41	0	235	9	26.11	3-40	–	5.73
B.M.McMillan	116	12	433	17	25.47	3-11	–	3.73
C.R.Matthews	59.3	2	226	7	32.28	2-30	–	3.79
S.M.Pollock	53	4	219	6	36.50	2-16	–	4.13
M.W.Pringle	57	6	236	8	29.50	4-11	1	4.14
R.P.Snell	72.5	10	310	8	38.75	3-42	–	4.25
P.L.Symcox	40	2	149	6	24.83	2-22	–	3.72

WORLD CUP REGISTER

WEST INDIES

Career statistics deadlines: Test Matches to 28 January 1999; Limited-Overs Internationals to 14 February 1999; first-class to end of 1998 English season (20 September). Key to abbreviations on page 19. West Indies' provisionally selected 19 players (to be reduced to 15 by 1 April) are:

ADAMS, James Clive (Jamaica)
Born Port Maria, Jamaica 9 Jan 1968. 5'11". Educated at Jamaica College, Kingston. Left-hand batsman, left-arm orthodox slow bowler, occasional wicket-keeper. Jamaica 1984-85 to date. Nottinghamshire 1994. **TESTS:** 33 (1991-92 to 1997-98); 2104 runs (av 51.31), 5 hundreds; 16 wkts (av 42.06), 5 wkts/inns (1). 32 ct. HS 208* v NZ (St John's) 1995-96; BB 5-17 v NZ (Bridgetown) 1995-96. **L-O INTERNATIONALS:** 74 (1992-93 to 1996-97); 1038 runs (av 28.05); 22 wkts (av 30.40), 4 wkts (1); 48 ct, 5 st. HS 81* v P (Sharjah) 1993-94; BB 5-37 v P (Adelaide) 1996-97. **F-C CAREER:** 142 matches; 8581 runs (av 43.78), 21 hundreds (inc 2 doubles); 73 wkts (av 37.08), 5 wkts/inns (1); 127 ct. HS 208* (see Tests). BB 5-17 (see Tests). **COUNTY L-O:** 93* Notts v Surrey (Nottingham) 1994 (ASL). BB 2-26 Notts v Glam (Nottingham) 1994 (ASL).

AMBROSE, Curtly Elconn Lynwall (Leeward Islands)
Born Swetes Village, Antigua 21 Sep 1963. Cousin of R.M.Otto (Leeward Is 1979-80 to 1990-91). 6'7". Educated at All Saints Village Secondary School. Left-hand batsman, right-arm fast bowler. Leeward Islands 1985-86 to date. Northamptonshire 1989-96; cap 1990. One of Wisden's Five Cricketers of 1991. **TESTS:** 84 (1987-88 to 1998-99); 1244 runs (av 12.95); 350 wkts (av 21.26), 5 wkts/inns (21), 10 wkts/match (3); 16 ct. HS 53 v A (P-of-S) 1990-91; BB 8-45 v E (Bridgetown) 1989-90. **L-O INTERNATIONALS:** 157 (1987-88 to 1998-99); 588 runs (av 11.30); 210 wkts (av 23.51), 4 wkts (10); 41 ct. HS 31* v P (Melbourne) 1996-97; BB 5-17 v A (Melbourne) 1988-89. **F-C CAREER:** 212 matches; 3063 runs (av 14.72); 839 wkts (av 20.45), 5 wkts/inns (46), 10 wkts/match (8), 50 wkts/season (6), 83 ct. HS 78 Northants v Somerset (Taunton) 1994. BB 8-45 (see Tests). **COUNTY L-O:** HS 48 Northants v Lancs (Lord's) 1990 (NWT). BB 4-7 Northants v Yorks (Northampton) 1992 (NWT).

ARTHURTON, Keith Lloyd Thomas (Leeward Islands)
Born Charlestown, Nevis 21 Feb 1965. 5'8". Educated at Charlestown Secondary School. Left-hand batsman, left-arm orthodox slow bowler. Leeward Islands 1985-86 to date. **TESTS:** 33 (1988 to 1995); 1382 runs (av 30.71), 2 hundreds; 1 wkt (av 183.00); 22 ct. HS 157* v A (Brisbane) 1992-93; BB 1-17. **L-O INTERNATIONALS:** 98 (1988-89 to 1998-99); 1871 runs (av 27.11); 40 wkts (av 24.75), 4 wkts (3); 27 ct. HS 84 v P (Sharjah) 1993-94; BB 4-31 v P (Dhaka) 1998-99. **F-C CAREER:** 120 matches; 7504 runs (av 46.60), 19 hundreds (inc 1 double), 1000 runs/season (1); 28 wkts (av 35.53), 65 ct. HS 200* MCC v Pakistan A (Shenley) 1997. BB 3-14 WI U-23 v P (Castries) 1987-88.

BRYAN, Henderson Ricardo (Barbados)
Born Barbados 21 Mar 1970. Right-hand batsman, right-arm fast-medium bowler. Barbados 1994-95 to date. Griqualand West 1997-98. **TESTS:** 0. **L-O INTERNATIONALS:** 0. **F-C CAREER:** 24 matches; 575 runs (av 17.96); 74 wkts (av 27.00), 5 wkts/inns (3), 10 wkts/match (1); 11 ct. HS 71 Griqualand West v Natal (Kimberley) 1997-98. BB 6-71 Griqualand West v Free State (Bloemfontein) 1997-98.

CHANDERPAUL, Shivnarine (Guyana)
Born Unity Village, Guyana 18 Aug 1974. 5'6". Left-hand batsman, right-arm leg-break bowler. Guyana 1991-92 to date. **TESTS:** 35 (1993-94 to 1998-99); 2145 runs (av 42.05), 2 hundreds; 5 wkts (av 130.80); 15 ct. HS 137* v I (Bridgetown) 1996-97; BB 1-2. **L-O**

INTERNATIONALS: 61 (1994-95 to 1998-99); 1909 runs (av 35.35), 2 hundreds; 12 wkts (av 39.08), 19 ct. HS 150 v SA (East London) 1998-99. **F-C CAREER:** 81 matches; 5413 runs (av 51.06), 14 hundreds (inc 1 triple), 1000 runs/season (1); 42 wkts (av 41.66); 58 ct. HS 303* Guyana v Jamaica (Kingston) 1995-96. BB 4-48 Guyana v Leeward Is (Basseterre) 1992-93.

DILLON, Mervyn (Trinidad & Tobago)
Born Toco, Trinidad 5 Jun 1974. Right-hand batsman, right-arm fast-medium bowler. Trinidad 1996-97 to date. **TESTS:** 6 (1996-97 to 1998-99); 84 runs (av 8.40); 18 wkts (av 34.22), 5 wkts/inns (1); 1 ct. HS 36 v SA (Cape Town) 1998-99; BB 5-111 v P (Karachi) 1997-98. **L-O INTERNATIONALS:** 11 (1997-98 to 1998-99); 5 runs (av –); 12 wkts (av 38.66); 1 ct. HS 5*; BB 3-32 v E (Kingstown) 1997-98. **F-C CAREER:** 18 matches; 144 runs (av 8.00); 56 wkts (av 30.28), 5 wkts/inns (1); 4 ct. HS 23 Trinidad v Jamaica (St Catherine, Jamaica) 1997-98. BB 5-111 (see Tests).

HOOPER, Carl Llewellyn (Guyana)
Born Georgetown, Guyana 15 Dec 1966. 6'1". Educated at Christchurch Secondary School, Georgetown. Right-hand batsman, off-break bowler. Demerara 1983-84. Guyana 1984-85 to date (captain 1996-97 to date). Kent 1992-94, 1996, 1998; cap 1992. **TESTS:** 78 (1987-88 to 1998-99); 4063 runs (av 34.14), 9 hundreds; 88 wkts (av 47.94), 5 wkts/inns (4); 89 ct. HS 178* v P (St John's) 1992-93; BB 5-26 v SL (Kingstown) 1996-97. **L-O INTERNATIONALS:** 177 (1986-87 to 1998-99, 4 as captain – 4 lost); 4500 runs (av 36.00), 6 hundreds; 160 wkts (av 33.25), 4 wkts (3); 85 ct. HS 113* v I (Gwalior) 1987-88; BB 4-34 v P (Karachi) 1991-92. **F-C CAREER:** 258 matches; 16,898 runs (av 45.54), 47 hundreds (inc 2 doubles), 1000 runs/season (7); 423 wkts (av 35.19), 5 wkts/inns (14); 288 ct. HS 236* Kent v Glam (Canterbury) 1993. BB 7-93 Kent v Surrey (Oval) 1998. **1998 SEASON (f-c – Kent):** 1215 runs (av 45.00), 6 hundreds; 31 wkts (av 30.87), 5 wkts/inns (1). **COUNTY L-O:** HS 145 Kent v Leics (Leicester) 1996 (ASL). BB 5-41 Kent v Essex (Maidstone) 1993 (ASL).

JACOBS, Ridley Detamore (Leeward Islands)
Born Antigua 26 Nov 1967. Left-hand batsman, wicket-keeper. Leeward Is 1991-92 to date. **TESTS:** 5 (1998-99); 317 runs (av 45.28); 20 ct. HS 78 v SA (Pretoria) 1998-99. **L-O INTERNATIONALS:** 18 (1995-96 to 1998-99); 103 runs (av 9.36); 18 ct, 6 st. HS 28* v E (Bridgetown) 1997-98. **F-C CAREER:** 46 matches; 2355 runs (av 42.81), 5 hundreds; 138 ct, 14 st. HS 119* Leeward Is v Trinidad (Port-of-Spain) 1992-93.

JOSEPH, David Rolston Emmanuel (Leeward Islands)
Born Antigua 15 Nov 1969. Right-hand batsman. Leeward Is 1990-91 to date. **TESTS:** 0. **L-O INTERNATIONALS:** 0. **F-C CAREER:** 37 matches; 1697 runs (av 33.27), 4 hundreds; 43 ct. HS 131 Leeward Is v Trinidad (Pointe-à-Pierre) 1994-95.

KING, Reon Dane (Guyana)
Born Guyana 6 Oct 1975. Right-hand batsman, right-arm fast-medium bowler. Guyana 1995-96 to date. **TESTS:** 1 (1998-99); 2 runs (av 2.00); 0 wkts; 1 ct. HS 2* v SA (Pretoria) 1998-99. **L-O INTERNATIONALS:** 9 (1998-99); 26 runs (av 26.00); 9 wkts (av 35.55); 2 ct. HS 7*; BB 3-40 v SA (East London) 1998-99. **F-C CAREER:** 17 matches; 113 runs (av 5.65); 58 wkts (av 25.58), 5 wkts/inns (4); 3 ct. HS 30 Guyana v Leeward Is (Charlestown) 1996-97. BB 7-82 Guyana v I (Georgetown) 1996-97.

LAMBERT, Clayton Benjamin (Guyana)
Born New Amsterdam, Guyana 10 Feb 1962. Left-hand batsman, off-break bowler. Guyana 1983-84 to date. **TESTS:** 5 (1991 to 1998-99); 284 runs (av 31.55), 1 hundred; 1 wkt (av 5.00); 8 ct. HS 104 v E (St John's) 1997-98; BB 1-4. **L-O INTERNATIONALS:** 11 (1989-90 to 1998-99); 368 runs (av 33.45), 1 hundred; 0 wkts; 0 ct. HS 119 v E (Port-of-Spain) 1997-98. **F-C CAREER:** 106 matches; 7757 runs (av 45.36), 21 hundreds (inc 3 doubles); 4 wkts (av 30.00); 143 ct. HS 236* Guyana v Windward Is (Skeldon, Berbice) 1992-93. BB 2-33 WI XI v World XI (Scarborough) 1991.

LARA, Brian Charles (Trinidad) (CAPTAIN – tbc)
Born Santa Cruz, Trinidad 2 May 1969. 5'8". Left-hand batsman, right-arm leg-break bowler. Trinidad 1987-88 to date; captain 1995-96 to date. Warwickshire 1994, 1998; cap 1994; captain 1998. One of *Wisden*'s Five Cricketers of 1994. **TESTS:** 59 (1990-91 to 1998-99, 12 as captain – 4 won, 6 lost, 2 drawn); 4860 runs (av 49.59), 10 hundreds; 0 wkts; 80 ct. HS 375 (world Test record) v E (St John's) 1993-94. **L-O INTERNATIONALS:** 137 (1990-91 to 1998-99, 14 as captain – 8 won, 6 lost); 5579 runs (av 45.72), 12 hundreds; 2 wkts (av 17.00); 63 ct. HS 169 v SL (Sharjah) 1995-96; BB 2-5 v E (Kingstown) 1993-94. **F-C CAREER:** 155 matches; 12,676 runs (av 51.11), 34 hundreds (inc 3 doubles plus a quintruple and a treble), 1000 runs/season (4 inc 2000 (1): 2066 off 2262 balls in 1994; 2 wkts (av 179.50); 197 ct. HS 501* (world f-c record) Warwks v Durham (Birmingham) 1994; scored 6 hundreds in his first 7 innings for Warwks (147, 106, 120*, 136, 26, 140, 501*). BB 1-14. **1998 SEASON (f-c):** 1033 runs (av 39.73), 3 hundreds; 0 wkts. **COUNTY L-O:** HS 133 Warwks v Kent (Birmingham) 1998 (NWT).

LEWIS, Rawl Nicholas (Windward Islands)
Born Grenada 5 Sep 1974. Right-hand batsman, right-arm leg-break and googly bowler. Windward Is 1991-92 to date. **TESTS:** 3 (1997-98 to 1998-99); 26 runs (av 4.33); 1 wkt (av 318.00); 0 ct. HS 12 and BB 1-67 v SA (Johannesburg) 1998-99. **L-O INTERNATIONALS:** 16 (1997-98 to 1998-99); 157 runs (av 17.44); 12 wkts (av 51.16); 5 ct. HS 49 v SA (Bloemfontein) 1998-99; BB 2-40 v E (Bridgetown) 1997-98. **F-C CAREER:** 41 matches; 991 runs (av 18.01); 112 wkts (av 32.66), 5 wkts/inns (5); 25 ct. HS 59 WI v Dr Khan's XI (Rawalpindi) 1997-98. BB 7-66 Windward Is v Guyana (Roseau) 1995-96.

McGARRELL, Neil Christopher (Guyana)
Born Guyana 12 Jul 1972. Right-hand batsman, slow left-arm orthodox bowler. Guyana 1995-96 to date. **TESTS:** 0. **L-O INTERNATIONALS:** 5 (1997-98 to 1998-99); 25 runs (av 12.50); 3 wkts (av 70.33); 4 ct. HS 19 v SA (Durban) 1998-99; BB 2-43 v SA (Johannesburg) 1998-99. **F-C CAREER:** 18 matches; 408 runs (av 18.54); 65 wkts (av 24.80), 5 wkts/inns (5), 10 wkts/match (2); 23 ct. HS 73 Guyana v Windward Is (St George's) 1996-97. BB 7-71 Guyana v Eng XI (Georgetown) 1997-98.

MURRAY, Junior Randalph (Windward Islands)
Born St George's, Grenada 20 Jan 1968. 6'0". Educated at Grenada Secondary School. Right-hand batsman, wicket-keeper. Windward Islands 1986-87 to date. **TESTS:** 31 (1992-93 to 1998-99); 917 runs (av 24.13), 1 hundred; 96 ct, 3 st. HS 101* v NZ (Wellington) 1994-95. **L-O INTERNATIONALS:** 55 (1992-93 to 1998-99); 678 runs (av 22.60); 46 ct, 7 st. HS 86 v E (Oval) 1995. **F-C CAREER:** 99 matches; 4074 runs (av 29.30), 6 hundreds (inc 1 double); 218 ct, 20 st. HS 218 Windward Is v Guyana ((St George's) 1996-97.

RAGOONATH, Suruj (Trinidad & Tobago)
Born Trinidad 4 Jun 1975. Right-hand batsman. Trinidad 1988-89 to date. **TESTS:** 0. **L-O INTERNATIONALS:** 0. **F-C CAREER:** 51 matches; 2754 runs (av 32.02), 2 hundreds; 23 ct. HS 128 Trinidad v Barbados (Port-of-Spain) 1996-97.

SIMMONS, Philip Verant (Trinidad & Tobago)
Born Arima, Trinidad 18 Apr 1963. 6'3½". Educated at Holy Cross College, Arima. Right-hand batsman, right-arm medium bowler. Debut (N Trinidad) 1982-83. Debut for N Trinidad 1982-83. Trinidad 1982-83 to date; captain 1988-89. Durham 1989-90 (NWT only). Leicestershire 1994-96, 1998; cap 1994. Eastern (SA) 1996-97. One of *Wisden*'s Five Cricketers of 1996. **TESTS:** 26 (1987-88 to 1997-98); 1002 runs (av 22.26), 1 hundred; 4 wkts (av 64.25); 26 ct. HS 110 and BB 2-34 v A (Melbourne) 1992-93. **L-O INTERNATIONALS:** 133 (1987-88 to 1998-99); 3532 runs (av 28.92), 5 hundreds; 74 wkts (av 35.21), 4 wkts (2); 53 ct. HS 122 v SA (Kingston) 1992-92; BB 4-3 v P (Sydney) 1992-93. **F-C CAREER:** 193 matches; 11,095 runs (av 36.14), 23 hundreds (inc 2 doubles), 1000 runs/season (2), 193 wkts (av 28.82), 5 wkts/inns (5), 50 wkts/season (1);

226 ct. HS 261 v Northants (Leicester) 1994 – on Leics debut *(county record)*. BB 7-49 v Durham (Darlington) 1998. **1998 SEASON (f-c):** 464 runs (av 24.42), 1 hundred; 23 wkts (av 21.34), 5 wkts/inns (1). **COUNTY L-O:** BB 5-33 Leics v Kent (Leicester) 1998 (BHC). HS 140 Leics v Middx (Leicester) 1994 (ASL).

WALSH, Courtney Andrew (Jamaica)
Born Kingston, Jamaica 30 Oct 1962. 6'5½". Educated at Excelsior High School. Right-hand batsman, right-arm fast bowler. Jamaica 1981-82 to date (captain 1990-91 to date). Gloucestershire 1984-96, 1998; cap 1985; captain 1993-94 and 1996; benefit 1992; testimonial 1998. One of *Wisden*'s Five Cricketers of 1986. **TESTS:** 106 (1984-85 to 1998-99, 22 as captain – 6 won, 7 lost, 9 drawn); 812 runs (av 8.54); 397 wkts (av 25.40), 5 wkts/inns (16), 10wkts/match (2), 1 hat-trick; 24 ct. HS 30* v A (Melbourne) 1988-89; BB 7-37 (13-55 match) v NZ (Wellington) 1994-95. **L-O INTERNATIONALS:** 185 (1984-85 to 1997-98, 43 as captain – 22 won, 20 lost, 1 no result); 292 runs (av 7.48); 204 wkts (av 30.94), 4 wkts (6); 27 ct. HS 30 v I (Calcutta) 1994-95; BB 5-1 v SL (Sharjah) 1986-87. **F-C CAREER:** 386 matches; 4299 runs (av 12.04); 1621 wkts (av 21.93), 5 wkts/inns (96), 10 wkts/match (19), 50 wkts/season (11) inc 100 (2): 118 (1986) and 106 (1998), 1 hat-trick 1988-89 (WI); 111 ct. HS 66 v Kent (Cheltenham) 1994. BB 9-72 v Somerset (Bristol) 1986. **1998 SEASON (f-c):** 111 runs (av 8.53), 106 wkts (av 17.31), 5 wkts/inns (7), 10 wkts/match (2). **COUNTY L-O:** HS 38 Glos v Derbys (Derby) 1996 (ASL). BB 6-21 Glos v Kent (Bristol) 1990 and 6-21 Glos v Cheshire (Bristol) 1992 (NWT).

WILLIAMS, Stuart Clayton (Leeward Islands)
Born Charlestown, Nevis 12 Aug 1969. 5'7". Right-hand batsman. Leeward Islands 1988-89 to date. **TESTS:** 28 (1993-94 to 1998-99); 1092 runs (av 24.26), 1 hundred; 0 wkts; 26 ct. HS 128 v I (Kingston) 1996-97. **L-O INTERNATIONALS:** 46 (1994-95 to 1998-99); 1501 runs (av 35.73) 1 hundred; 1 wkts (av 30.00); 11 ct. HS 105* v I (Sharjah) 1997-98; BB 1-30. **F-C CAREER:** 95 matches; 5274 runs (av 35.39), 14 hundreds; 1 wkt (av 85.00); 77 ct. HS 170 WI A v SL A (Matara) 1996-97. BB 1-25.

WORLD CUP CAREER RECORDS

WEST INDIES – BATTING AND FIELDING

	M	I	NO	HS	Runs	Avge	100	50	Ct/St
J.C.Adams	4	4	2	17*	41	20.50	–	–	6/1
C.E.L.Ambrose	13	8	2	15*	46	7.66	–	–	1
K.L.T.Arthurton	13	12	1	58*	235	21.36	–	2	2
S.F.A.F.Bacchus	8	5	1	80*	157	39.25	–	1	–
E.A.E.Baptiste	1	1	–	14	14	14.00	–	–	1
W.K.M.Benjamin	13	10	5	24*	69	13.80	–	–	4
C.A.Best	2	2	–	18	23	11.50	–	–	1
I.R.Bishop	6	4	1	17	35	11.66	–	–	1
K.D.Boyce	5	2	–	34	41	20.50	–	–	–
C.O.Browne	5	4	–	26	64	16.00	–	–	3/2
S.L.Campbell	4	4	–	47	57	14.25	–	–	1
S.Chanderpaul	6	6	–	80	211	35.16	–	2	1
C.E.H.Croft	4	1	1	0*	0	–	–	–	–
C.E.Cuffy	1	1	–	1	1	1.00	–	–	1
A.C.Cummins	6	2	1	6	11	11.00	–	–	–
W.W.Daniel	3	1	1	16*	16	–	–	–	–
W.W.Davis	5	1	1	0*	0	–	–	–	–
P.J.L.Dujon	14	9	1	46	112	14.00	–	–	19/1
R.C.Fredericks	5	5	–	58	116	23.20	–	1	2
J.Garner	8	5	3	37	52	26.00	–	–	4
L.R.Gibbs	1	–	–	–	–	–	–	–	–
O.D.Gibson	3	2	–	6	7	3.50	–	–	1
H.A.Gomes	8	7	3	78	258	64.50	–	3	3

	M	I	NO	HS	Runs	Avge	100	50	Ct/St
C.G.Greenidge	15	15	2	106*	591	45.46	2	4	1
R.A.Harper	14	13	2	24	118	10.72	–	–	6
D.L.Haynes	25	25	2	105	854	37.13	1	3	12
R.I.C.Holder	2	2	–	5	5	2.50	–	–	–
V.A.Holder	5	2	1	16	22	22.00	–	–	2
M.A.Holding	11	5	–	20	36	7.20	–	–	5
C.L.Hooper	14	12	3	63	162	18.00	–	1	8
B.D.Julien	5	3	2	26*	48	48.00	–	–	–
A.I.Kallicharran	9	8	1	78	251	35.85	–	2	6
R.B.Kanhai	5	4	2	55	109	54.50	–	1	3
C.L.King	4	3	–	86	132	44.00	–	1	2
B.C.Lara	14	14	2	111	602	50.16	1	5	4
C.H.Lloyd	17	11	2	102	393	43.66	1	2	12
A.L.Logie	15	13	2	65*	282	25.63	–	2	4
M.D.Marshall	11	7	–	18	40	5.71	–	–	–
D.L.Murray	9	5	2	61*	122	40.66	–	1	16
B.P.Patterson	7	2	–	4*	4	–	–	–	2
I.V.A.Richards	23	21	5	181	1013	63.31	3	5	9
R.B.Richardson	20	20	3	110	639	37.58	1	4	6
A.M.E.Roberts	16	8	3	37*	85	17.00	–	–	1
P.V.Simmons	8	8	–	110	323	40.37	1	2	1
C.A.Walsh	12	6	2	9*	31	7.75	–	–	3
D.Williams	8	6	2	32*	52	13.00	–	–	11/3

WEST INDIES – BOWLING

	O	M	R	W	Avge	Best	4w	R/O
J.C.Adams	22	0	110	3	36.66	3-53	–	5.00
C.E.L.Ambrose	125	15	405	17	23.82	3-28	–	3.24
K.L.T.Arthurton	35	0	178	3	59.33	2-40	–	5.08
E.A.E.Baptiste	8	1	33	0	–	–	–	4.12
W.K.M.Benjamin	123	10	515	14	36.78	3-27	–	4.18
I.R.Bishop	49	6	194	3	64.66	2-35	–	3.95
K.D.Boyce	52	3	185	10	18.50	4-50	1	3.55
C.E.H.Croft	43	3	140	8	17.50	3-29	–	3.25
C.E.Cuffy	8	0	31	1	31.00	1-31	–	3.87
A.C.Cummins	59	1	246	12	20.50	4-33	1	4.16
W.W.Daniel	24	6	84	3	28.00	3-28	–	3.50
W.W.Davis	54.3	6	206	8	25.75	7-51	1	3.77
J.Garner	90	12	289	13	22.23	5-38	1	3.21
L.R.Gibbs	4	0	17	0	–	–	–	4.25
O.D.Gibson	19.4	1	90	1	90.00	1-27	–	4.57
H.A.Gomes	74	4	304	9	33.77	2-46	–	4.10
R.A.Harper	132	10	488	18	27.11	4-47	1	3.69
V.A.Holder	43.2	4	184	5	36.80	3-30	–	4.24
M.A.Holding	115.5	16	341	20	17.05	4-33	1	2.94
C.L.Hooper	121	2	493	15	32.86	3-42	–	4.07
B.D.Julien	60	11	177	10	17.70	4-20	2	2.95
C.L.King	32	2	128	2	64.00	1-36	–	4.00
C.H.Lloyd	36	4	125	3	41.66	1-31	–	3.47
M.D.Marshall	113	13	349	14	24.92	3-28	–	3.08
B.P.Patterson	66	2	278	15	18.53	3-31	–	4.21
I.V.A.Richards	83	2	345	10	34.50	3-41	–	4.15
R.B.Richardson	4	0	24	0	–	–	–	6.00
A.M.E.Roberts	170.1	29	552	26	21.23	3-32	–	3.24
P.V.Simmons	20	1	91	3	30.33	2-40	–	4.55
C.A.Walsh	111	15	439	16	27.43	4-40	1	3.95

WORLD CUP REGISTER

NEW ZEALAND

Career statistics deadlines: Test Matches to 28 January 1999; Limited-Overs Internationals to 14 February 1999; first-class to end of 1998 English season (20 September). Key to abbreviations on page 19. New Zealand's provisionally selected 19 players (to be reduced to 15 by 1 April) are:

ALLOTT, Geoffrey Ian (Canterbury)
Born Christchurch 24 Dec 1971. Right-hand batsman, left-arm fast-medium bowler. Canterbury 1994-95 to date. **TESTS:** 6 (1995-96 to 1997-98); 18 runs (av 2.57); 11 wkts (av 60.63); 1 ct. HS 8* and BB 4-74 v E (Christchurch) 1996-97. **L-O INTERNATIONALS:** 6 (1996-97 to 1998-99); 24 runs (av 7.00); 9 wkts (av 24.66); 3 ct. HS 7*; BB 3-54 v Z (Dhaka) 1998-99. **F-C CAREER:** 20 matches; 80 runs (av 4.70); 75 wkts (av 26.21), 5 wkts/inns (4), 10 wkts/match (1); 4 ct. HS 11* Canterbury v Wellington (Wellington) 1995-96. BB 6-60 Canterbury v Otago (Oamaru) 1997-98.

ASTLE, Nathan John (Canterbury)
Born Christchurch 15 Sep 1971. 5'10". Right-hand batsman, right-arm medium bowler. Educated at Shirley High School. Canterbury 1991-92 to date. **TESTS:** 22 (1995-96 to 1998-99); 1251 runs (av 32.92), 4 hundreds; 13 wkts (av 43.15); 19 ct. HS 125 v WI (Bridgetown) 1995-96; BB 2-26 v E (Christchurch) 1996-97. **L-O INTERNATIONALS:** 75 (1994-95 to 1998-99); 2512 runs (av 34.41), 5 hundreds; 50 wkts (av 33.32), 4 wkts (1); 27 ct. HS 120 v Z (Auckland) 1995-96; BB 4-43 v P (Chandigarh) 1996-97. **F-C CAREER:** 66 matches; 3461 runs (av 36.43), 9 hundreds; 72 wkts (av 32.02), 5 wkts/inns (2); 47 ct. HS 191 Canterbury v Wellington (Christchurch) 1994-95. BB 6-22 Canterbury v Otago (Christchurch) 1996-97. **COUNTY L-O:** HS 75 v Northants (Milton Keynes) 1997 (ASL). BB 3-20 v Staffs (Nottingham) 1997 (NWT).

BELL, Mark David (Northern Districts)
Born Hamilton 26 Nov 1970. Right-hand batsman, right-arm medium bowler. N Districts 1989-90 to date. **TESTS:** 2 (1998-99); 29 runs (av 7.25); 2 ct. HS 25 v I (Hamilton) 1998-99. **L-O INTERNATIONALS:** 2 (1998-99); 18 runs (av 9.00); 0 ct. HS 16 v SL (Dhaka) 1998-99. **F-C CAREER:** 34 matches; 1993 runs (av 38.32), 2 hundreds (inc 1 double); 31 ct. HS 216 Wellington v Auckland (Auckland) 1997-98.

BULFIN, Carl Edwin (Central Districts)
Born Blenheim 19 Aug 1973. Right-hand batsman, right-arm fast-medium bowler. **TESTS:** 0. **L-O INTERNATIONALS:** 0. **F-C CAREER:** 13 matches; 142 runs (av 9.46); 38 wkts (av 23.44), 5 wkts/inns (3), 10 wkts/match (1); 4 ct. HS 37 C Districts v Canterbury (Palmerston North) 1997-98. BB 5-53 (10-164 match) C Districts v Canterbury (Blenheim) 1996-97.

CAIRNS, Christopher Lance (Canterbury)
Born Picton 13 Jun 1970. Son of B.L.Cairns (C Districts, Otago, N Districts and NZ 1971-72 to 1985-86). 6'2". Educated at Christchurch High School. Right-hand batsman, right-arm fast-medium bowler. Nottinghamshire 1988-89, 1992-93 and 1995-96; cap 1993. N Districts 1988-89. Canterbury 1990-91 to date. **TESTS:** 35 (1989-90 to 1998-99); 1634 runs (av 27.69), 2 hundreds; 109 wkts (av 32.73), 5 wkts/inns (5); 12 ct. HS 126 v I (Hamilton) 1998-99; BB 6-52 v E (Auckland) 1991-92. **L-O INTERNATIONALS:** 100 (1990-91 to 1998-99); 2335 runs (av 27.15), 2 hundreds; 93 wkts (av 33.03); 31 ct. HS 115 v I (Christchurch) 1998-99; BB 5-42 v A (Napier) 1997-98. **F-C CAREER:** 157 matches; 7337 runs (av 33.65), 7 hundreds, 1000 runs/ season (1); 472 wkts (av 28.22), 5 wkts/inns (19), 10 wkts/match (4), 50 wkts/season (3), 67 ct. HS 120 (see Tests). BB 8-47 (15-83 match) Notts v Sussex (Arundel) 1995. **COUNTY L-O:** HS 126* Notts v Surrey (Oval) 1993 (ASL). BB 6-52 Notts v Kent (Nottingham) 1993 (ASL).

DOULL, Simon Blair (Northern Districts)
Born Pukekohe 6 Aug 1969. Right-hand batsman, right-arm medium-fast bowler. N Districts 1989-90 to date. **TESTS:** 26 (1992-93 to 1998-99); 389 runs (av 12.54); 95 wkts (av 25.78), 5 wkts/inns (6); 16 ct. HS 31* v SA (Johannesburg) 1994-95; BB 7-65 v I (Wellington) 1998-99. **L-O INTERNATIONALS:** 38 (1992-93 to 1998-99); 166 runs (av 12.76); 34 wkts (av 39.29), 4 wkts; 9 ct. HS 22 v E (Napier) 1996-97; BB 4-25 v A (Auckland) 1997-98. **F-C CAREER:** 72 matches; 1151 runs (av 16.68), 1 hundred; 209 wkts (av 26.63), 5 wkts/inns (11), 10 wkts/match (1); 28 ct. HS 108 N Districts v Canterbury (Christchurch) 1991-92. BB 7-65 (see Tests).

DRUM, Christopher John (Auckland)
Born Auckland 10 Jul 1974. Right-hand batsman, right-arm fast-medium bowler. Auckland 1996-97 to date. **TESTS:** 0. **L-O INTERNATIONALS:** 1 (1998-99); did not bat; 0 wkts; 1 ct. **F-C CAREER:** 16 matches; 96 runs (av 5.64); 57 wkts (av 18.84), 5 wkts/inns (2); 6 ct. HS 20 Auckland v Canterbury (Auckland) 1997-98. BB 6-47 Auckland v Canterbury (Christchurch) 1996-97.

FLEMING, Stephen Paul (Canterbury) (CAPTAIN)
Born Christchurch 1 Apr 1973. 6'3". Educated at Cashmere High School; Christchurch College of Education. Left-hand batsman, occasional right-arm slow-medium bowler. (Canterbury) 1991-92 to date. **TESTS:** 39 (1993-94 to 1998-99, 15 as captain – 6 won, 5 lost, 4 drawn); 2426 runs (av 36.75), 2 hundreds; 65 ct. HS 176* v SL (Colombo) 1997-98. **L-O INTERNATIONALS:** 96 (1993-94 to 1998-99, 36 as captain – 14 won, 19 lost, 1 tied, 2 no result); 2799 runs (av 32.92), 3 hundreds; 1 wkt (av 28.00); 43 ct. HS 116* v A (Melbourne) 1997-98; BB 1-8. **F-C CAREER:** 83 matches; 5080 runs (av 40.31), 9 hundreds; 0 wkts; 99 ct. HS 176* (see Tests).

HARRIS, Chris Zinzan (Canterbury)
Born Christchurch 20 Nov 1969. Son of P.G.Z.Harris (Canterbury and NZ 1949-50 to 1964-65), younger brother of B.Z. (Canterbury 1988-89 to 1994-95). Left-hand batsman, right-arm medium bowler. Canterbury 1989-90 to date. **TESTS:** 14 (1992-93 to 1998-99); 390 runs (av 15.60); 9 wkts (av 68.11); 12 ct. HS 71 v Z (Bulawayo) 1997-98; BB 2-57 v P (Rawalpindi) 1996-97. **L-O INTERNATIONALS:** 120 (1990-91 to 1998-99); 2198 runs (av 30.52), 1 hundred; 117 wkts (av 34.23), 4 wkts (2); 45 ct. HS 130 v A (Madras) 1995-96; BB 5-42 v P (Sialkot) 1996-97. **F-C CAREER:** 68 matches; 3739 runs (av 43.98), 7 hundreds (inc 2 doubles); 73 wkts (av 40.65); 54 ct. HS 251* Canterbury v C Districts (Rangiora) 1996-97. BB 4-22 Canterbury v Wellington (Christchurch) 1996-97.

HART, Matthew Norman (Northern Districts)
Born Hamilton 16 May 1972. 6'0". Te Puke High School; Waikato Polytechnic. Left-hand batsman, left-arm orthodox slow bowler. N Districts 1990-91 to date. **TESTS:** 14 (1993-94 to 1995-96); 353 runs (av 17.65); 29 wkts (av 49.58), 5 wkts/inns (1); 9 ct. HS 45 v WI (Christchurch) 1994-95; BB 5-77 v SA (Johannesburg) 1994-95. **L-O INTERNATIONALS:** 11 (1993-94 to 1996-97); 49 runs (av 8.16); 13 wkts (av 26.69), 4 wkts (1); 7 ct. HS 16 v I (Delhi) 1994-95. BB 5-22 v WI (Margao) 1994-95. **F-C CAREER:** 87 matches; 2300 runs (av 21.69); 187 wkts (av 33.68), 5 wkts/inns (6); 79 ct. HS 87* N Districts v Wellington (Wellington) 1995-96. BB 6-73 NZ v Indian Colts (Hyderabad) 1995-96.

HORNE, Matthew Jeffrey (Otago)
Born Auckland 5 Dec 1970. Younger brother of P.A. (Auckland 1979-80 to 1990-91). Right-hand batsman, right-arm medium bowler. Auckland 1992-93 to 1995-96. Otago 1996-97 to date. **TESTS:** 13 (1996-97 to 1998-99); 849 runs (av 36.91), 2 hundreds; 0 wkts; 11 ct. HS 157 v Z (Auckland) 1997-98. **L-O INTERNATIONALS:** 29 (1996-97 to 1998-99); 542 runs (av 19.35); 8 ct. HS 61 v I (Napier) 1998-99. **F-C CAREER:** 34 matches; 2609 runs (av 44.22), 9 hundreds (inc 1 double); 0 wkts; 34 ct. HS 241 Otago v Auckland (Auckland) 1997-98.

LARSEN, Gavin Rolf (Wellington)
Born Wellington 27 Sep 1962. 5'11". Educated at Onslow College. Right-hand batsman, right-arm medium bowler. Wellington 1984-85 to date. **TESTS**: 8 (1994 to 1995-96); 127 runs (av 14.11); 24 wkts (av 28.70); 5 ct. HS 26* and BB 3-57 v SA (Auckland) 1994-95. **L-O INTERNATIONALS**: 106 (1989-90 to 1998-99, 3 as captain – 1 won, 2 lost); 572 runs (av 14.66); 103 wkts (av 34.22), 4 wkts (1); 21 ct. HS 37 v P (Christchurch) 1991-92; BB 4-24 v P (Auckland) 1993-94. Appeared in 55 LOIs before making his Test debut. **F-C CAREER**: 100 matches; 3326 runs (av 27.94), 1 hundred; 156 wkts (av 29.36), 5 wkts/inns (5); 67 ct. HS 161 Wellington v C Districts (Levin) 1987-88. BB 6-37 Wellington v N Districts (Wellington) 1994-95.

McMILLAN, Craig Douglas (Canterbury)
Born Christchurch 13 Sep 1976. Right-hand batsman, right-arm medium bowler. Canterbury 1994-95 to date. **TESTS**: 10 (1997-98 to 1998-99); 834 runs (av 49.05), 2 hundreds; 8 wkts (av 39.75); 5 ct. HS 142 v SL (Colombo) 1997-98; BB 2-27 v SL (Colombo) 1997-98. **L-O INTERNATIONALS**: 36 (1996-97 to 1998-99); 884 runs (av 26.78); 16 wkts (av 28.87);11 ct. HS 86 v SA (Adelaide) 1997-98; BB 2-17 v Z (Harare) 1997-98. **F-C CAREER**: 39 matches; 2606 runs (av 42.03), 6 hundreds; 19 wkts (av 43.15); 21 ct. HS 159 Canterbury v N Districts (Christchurch) 1996-97. BB 3-9 Canterbury v Central Districts (Palmerston North) 1997-98.

NASH, Dion Joseph (Northern Districts)
Born Auckland 20 Nov 1971. 6'1". Educated at Dargaville High School; Auckland Grammar School; Otago U. Right-hand batsman, right-arm fast-medium bowler. N Districts 1990-91 to 1991-92, 1995-96 to date. Otago 1992-93 to 1993-94. Middlesex 1995-96; cap 1995. **TESTS**: 18 (1992-93 to 1998-99); 452 runs (av 25.11); 57 wkts (av 27.14), 5 wkts/inns (2), 10 wkts/match (1); 9 ct. HS 89* v I (Wellington) 1998-99; BB 6-76 (11-169 match) v E (Lord's) 1994. **L-O INTERNATIONALS**: 51 (1992-93 to 1998-99, 4 as captain – 1 won, 2 lost, 1 no result); 382 runs (av 15.28); 44 wkts (av 39.40), 4 wkts (1); 17 ct. HS 40* v SL (PSS, Colombo) 1992-93; BB 4-38 v I (Sharjah) 1997-98. **F-C CAREER**: 82 matches; 2006 runs (av 21.56), 2 hundreds; 180 wkts (av 28.86), 5 wkts/inns (7), 10 wkts/match (1), 50 wkts/season (1); 36 ct. HS 125 N Districts v C Districts (Masterton) 1997-98. BB 6-30 NZ Academy v N Districts (Rotorua) 1993-94. **COUNTY L-O**: HS 54 Middx v Comb Us (Lord's) 1995 (BHC). BB 3-34 Middx v Glos (Bristol) 1995 (ASL).

O'CONNOR, Shayne Barry (Otago)
Born Hastings 15 Nov 1973. Left-hand batsman, left-arm fast-medium bowler. Otago 1994-95 to date. **TESTS**: 6 (1997-98); 26 runs (av 5.20); 18 wkts (av 35.38); 4 ct. HS 7; BB 4-52 v Z (Wellington) 1997-98. **L-O INTERNATIONALS**: 23 (1996-97 to 1997-98); 21 runs (av 5.25); 29 wkts (av 27.37), 4 wkts (2); 7 ct. HS 8. BB 5-39 v Z (Wellington) 1997-98. **F-C CAREER**: 29 matches; 445 runs (av 15.34); 101 wkts (av 26.43), 5 wkts/inns (4), 10 wkts/match (1); 13 ct. HS 47 Otago v Auckland (Dunedin) 1996-97. BB 6-31 Otago v Wellington (Wellington) 1997-98.

PARORE, Adam Craig (Auckland)
Born Auckland 23 Jan 1971. 5'9". Educated at Auckland U. Right-hand batsman, wicket-keeper. Auckland 1988-89 to date. **TESTS**: 46 (1990 to 1998-99); 1979 runs (av 27.48), 1 hundred; 96 ct, 3 st. HS 100* v WI (Christchurch) 1994-95. **L-O INTERNA-TIONALS**: 107 (1992-93 to 1998-99); 2500 runs (av 29.76), 1 hundred; 61 ct, 15 st. HS 108 v SA (Pretoria) 1994-95. **F-C CAREER**: 113 matches; 5193 runs (av 34.16), 7 hundreds; 0 wkts; 218 ct, 16 st. HS 155* Auckland v Otago (Dunedin) 1991-92.

TWOSE, Roger Graham (Wellington)
Born Torquay, England 17 Apr 1968. Nephew of R.W.Tolchard (Leics and England 1965-83). 6'0". Educated at King's College, Taunton. Left-hand batsman, right-arm medium bowler. Warwickshire 1989-95 (cap 1992). N Districts 1989-90. C Districts 1991-92 to 1993-94 (captain 1993-94). Wellington 1994-95 to date. Devon 1988-89.

MCC YC. **TESTS:** 9 (1995-96 to 1998-99); 436 runs (av 31.14); 3 wkts (av 43.33); 2 ct. HS 94 v Z (Auckland) 1995-96; BB 2-36 v Z (Hamilton) 1995-96. **L-O INTERNATIONALS:** 30 (1995-96 to 1998-99); 745 runs (av 26.60); 4 wkts (av 59.25); 7 ct. HS 92 v UAE (Faisalabad) 1995-96; BB 2-31 v P (Wellington) 1995-96. **F-C CAREER:** 155 matches; 8649 runs (av 37.76), 17 hundreds (inc 2 doubles), 1000 runs/season (3); 132 wkts (av 31 25), 5 wkts/inns (2); 81 ct. HS 277* Warwks v Glam (Birmingham) 1994. BB 6-28 Warwks v Surrey (Guildford) 1994. **COUNTY L-O:** HS 110 Warwks v Beds (Birmingham) 1994 (NWT). BB 3-31 Warwks v Durham (Darlington) 1993 (ASL).

VETTORI, Daniel Luca (Northern Districts)
Born Auckland 27 Jan 1979. Right-hand batsman, left-arm orthodox slow bowler. N Districts 1996-97 to date. **TESTS:** 16 (1996-97 to 1998-99); 377 runs (av 17.95); 54 wkts (av 32.55), 5 wkts/inns (2); 9 ct. HS 90 v Z (Bulawayo) 1997-98; BB 6-64 v SL (Colombo) 1997-98. Youngest cricketer (18y 10d) to represent NZ. **L-O INTERNATIONALS:** 31 (1996-97 to 1998-99); 159 runs (av 14.45); 25 wkts (av 39.72); 4 wkts (1); 10 ct. HS 25* v SA (Hobart) 1997-98; BB 4-49 v Z (Hamilton) 1997-98. **F-C CAREER:** 28 matches; 535 runs (av 14.45); 110 wkts (av 27.10), 5 wkts/inns (7); 17 ct. HS 90 (see Tests). BB 6-64 (see Tests).

YOUNG, Bryan Alexander (Northern Districts)
Born Whangerei 3 Nov 1964. 5'10". Right-hand batsman, former wicket-keeper. N Districts 1983-84 to date. **TESTS:** 33 (1993-94 to 1997-98); 1954 runs (av 32.03), 2 hundreds; 53 ct. HS 267* v SL (Dunedin) 1996-97. **L-O INTERNATIONALS:** 73 (1990-91 to 1998-99); 1644 runs (av 24.53); 28 ct. HS 74 v SA (Hobart) 1993-94. **F-C CAREER:** 154 matches; 7155 runs (av 32.67), 9 hundreds; 1 wkt (av 76.00); 289 ct, 11 st. HS 267* (see Tests). BB 1-76.

WORLD CUP CAREER RECORDS

NEW ZEALAND – BATTING AND FIELDING

	M	I	NO	HS	Runs	Avge	100	50	Ct/St
N.J.Astle	6	6	–	101	111	18.50	1	–	2
S.L.Boock	4	3	2	12	19	19.00	–	–	4
J.G.Bracewell	7	7	2	34	80	16.00	–	–	1
M.G.Burgess	4	2	–	35	45	22.50	–	–	2
B.L.Cairns	11	9	–	14	43	4.77	–	–	4
C.L.Cairns	11	9	3	52	160	26.66	–	1	10
E.J.Chatfield	13	8	7	19*	45	45.00	–	–	2
R.O.Collinge	4	2	–	6	6	3.00	–	–	1
J.V.Coney	10	8	2	66*	244	40.66	–	2	4
J.J.Crowe	8	8	1	88*	220	31.42	–	1	4
M.D.Crowe	21	21	5	100*	880	55.00	1	8	8
B.A.Edgar	8	8	1	84*	194	27.71	–	1	5
S.P.Fleming	6	6	–	66	193	32.16	–	1	3
L.K.Germon	6	6	3	89	191	63.66	–	1	2/1
M.J.Greatbatch	7	7	–	73	313	44.71	–	3	4
B.G.Hadlee	1	1	–	19	19	19.00	–	–	–
D.R.Hadlee	4	3	1	20	28	14.00	–	–	–
R.J.Hadlee	13	10	1	42	149	16.55	–	–	3
C.Z.Harris	13	10	1	130	200	22.22	1	–	5
B.F.Hastings	4	4	1	34	76	25.33	–	–	3
P.A.Horne	1	1	–	18	18	18.00	–	–	–
G.P.Howarth	11	11	1	76	374	37.40	–	4	2
H.J.Howarth	4	2	1	1*	1	1.00	–	–	2
A.H.Jones	13	13	2	78	416	37.81	–	4	3
R.J.Kennedy	3	1	–	2	2	2.00	–	–	1

	M	I	NO	HS	Runs	Avge	100	50	Ct/St
G.R.Larsen	11	3	1	37	46	23.00	–	–	6
R.T.Latham	7	7	–	60	136	19.42	–	1	3
W.K.Lees	8	6	1	26	88	17.60	–	–	10
B.J.McKechnie	8	4	2	27	45	22.50	–	–	2
D.K.Morrison	11	4	3	12	27	27.00	–	–	2
J.F.M.Morrison	6	5	–	55	102	20.40	–	1	3
D.J.Nash	4	2	1	8	13	13.00	–	–	–
J.M.Parker	4	4	–	66	71	17.75	–	–	1
A.C.Parore	5	5	–	55	144	28.80	–	1	1
D.N.Patel	17	11	2	40	97	10.77	–	–	3
K.R.Rutherford	14	12	2	75	416	41.60	–	4	5
I.D.S.Smith	17	13	3	29	138	13.80	–	–	9
M.C.Snedden	9	8	–	64	218	27.25	–	1	2
C.M.Spearman	6	6	–	78	191	31.83	–	2	1
L.W.Stott	1	–	–	–	–	–	–	–	1
S.A.Thomson	5	5	2	31*	101	33.66	–	–	3
G.B.Troup	3	1	1	3*	3	–	–	–	1
G.M.Turner	14	14	4	171*	612	61.20	2	2	2
R.G.Twose	6	6	–	92	175	29.16	–	1	1
K.J.Wadsworth	4	4	–	25	68	17.00	–	–	3/1
W.Watson	14	5	4	12*	29	29.00	–	–	2
J.G.Wright	18	18	–	69	493	27.38	–	3	4

NEW ZEALAND – BOWLING

	O	M	R	W	Avge	Best	4w	R/O
N.J.Astle	27	1	129	3	43.00	2-10	–	4.77
S.L.Boock	32.4	2	156	4	39.00	2-42	–	4.77
J.G.Bracewell	59	0	310	1	310.00	1-66	–	5.25
B.L.Cairns	115.2	16	436	14	31.14	3-36	–	3.78
C.L.Cairns	68.5	5	368	4	92.00	2-43	–	5.34
E.J.Chatfield	131.3	16	524	14	37.42	2-24	–	3.98
R.O.Collinge	48	13	137	6	22.83	3-28	–	2.85
J.V.Coney	89	7	303	12	25.25	3-28	–	3.40
M.D.Crowe	18	2	116	1	116.00	1-15	–	6.44
S.P.Fleming	2	0	8	1	8.00	1- 8	–	4.00
M.J.Greatbatch	1	0	5	0	–	–	–	5.00
D.R.Hadlee	46	5	162	8	20.25	3-21	–	3.52
R.J.Hadlee	146.1	38	421	22	19.13	5-25	1	2.88
C.Z.Harris	105.1	5	477	21	22.71	3-15	–	4.53
H.J.Howarth	40	5	148	5	29.60	3-29	–	3.70
A.H.Jones	12	0	52	2	26.00	2-42	–	4.33
R.J.Kennedy	21	2	88	4	22.00	2-36	–	4.19
G.R.Larsen	94	9	336	12	28.00	3-16	–	3.57
R.T.Latham	23	0	136	1	136.00	1-35	–	5.91
B.J.McKechnie	89.5	9	304	13	23.38	3-24	–	3.38
D.K.Morrison	79	2	396	8	49.50	3-42	–	5.01
J.F.M.Morrison	8	0	31	0	–	–	–	3.87
D.J.Nash	35	4	153	6	25.50	3-27	–	4.37
D.N.Patel	140	9	554	13	42.61	3-36	–	3.95
K.R.Rutherford	1.4	0	11	0	–	–	–	6.62
M.C.Snedden	81.5	6	455	10	45.50	2-36	–	5.56
L.W.Stott	12	1	48	3	16.00	3-48	–	4.00
S.A.Thomson	42.3	2	197	5	39.40	3-20	–	4.63
G.B.Troup	32	3	104	4	26.00	2-36	–	3.25
R.G.Twose	13	0	79	0	–	–	–	6.07
W.Watson	132	14	571	19	30.05	3-37	–	4.32

WORLD CUP REGISTER

INDIA

Career statistics deadlines: Test Matches to 28 January 1999; Limited-Overs Internationals to 14 February 1999; first-class to end of 1998 English season (20 September). Key to abbreviations on page 19. India's provisionally selected 19 players (to be reduced to 15 by 1 April) are:

AGARKAR, Ajit Bhalchandra (Bombay)
Born Bombay 4 Dec 1977. Right-hand batsman, right-arm fast-medium bowler. Bombay 1996-97 to date. **TESTS:** 1 (1998-99); 9 runs (av 4.50); 2 wkts (av 50.00); 0 ct. HS 5 and BB 1-40 v Z (Harare) 1998-99. **L-O INTERNATIONALS:** 30 (1997-98 to 1998-99); 177 runs (av 16.09); 58 wkts (23.75), 4 wkts (3); 13 ct. HS 30 v SL (Colombo) 1997-98; BB 4-35 v NZ (Sharjah) 1997-98. **F-C CAREER:** 13 matches; 441 runs (av 44.10), 1 hundred; 40 wkts (av 22.60), 5 wkts/inns (3); 8 ct.

AZHARUDDIN, Mohammed (Hyderabad) (CAPTAIN)
Born Hyderabad 8 Feb 1963. 5'11". Educated at Nizam College; Osmania U. Right-hand batsman, right-arm medium/leg-break bowler. Hyderabad 1981-82 to date. Derbyshire 1991 and 1994 (cap 1991). One of *Wisden's* Five Cricketers of 1990. **TESTS:** 94 (1984-85 to 1998-99, 43 as captain – 13 won, 12 lost, 18 drawn); 5860 runs (av 45.78), 21 hundreds; 0 wkts; 103 ct. HS 199 v SL (Kanpur) 1986-87. **L-O INTERNATIONALS:** 310 (*record*) (1984-85 to 1998-99, 160 as captain – 85 won, 68 lost, 2 tied, 5 no result); 8868 runs (av 37.89), 7 hundreds; 12 wkts (av 39.91); 147 ct. HS 153* v Z (Cuttack) 1997-98; BB 3-19 v A (Delhi) 1987-88. **F-C CAREER:** 211 matches; 14,504 runs (av 51.98), 50 hundreds (inc 3 doubles); 12 wkts (av 56.83); 207 ct. HS 226 S Zone v C Zone (Jamadoba) 1983-84. BB 2-22. **COUNTY L-O:** HS 111* v Northants (Northampton) 1994 (ASL). BB 1-17 (BHC).

CHOPRA, Nikhil (Delhi)
Born Allahabad 26 Dec 1973. Delhi 1993-94 to date. Right-hand batsman, right-arm off-break bowler. **TESTS:** 0. **L-O INTERNATIONALS:** 11 (1997-98 to 1998-99); 77 runs (av 15.40); 7 wkts (av 46.00); 2 ct. HS 39 v Z (Sharjah) 1998-99. BB 2-21 v Z (Sharjah) 1998-99. **F-C CAREER:** 24 matches; 679 runs (av 29.52); 60 wkts (av 38.46), 5 wkts/inns (3); 10 ct. HS 84. BB 7-66.

DRAVID, Rahul (Karnataka)
Born Indore 11 Jan 1973. 5'11½". Educated at St Joseph's High School; Bangalore U. Right-hand batsman, right-arm off-break bowler. Karnataka 1990-91 to date. **TESTS:** 25 (1996 to 1998-99); 2126 runs (av 57.45), 4 hundreds; 0 wkts; 30 ct. HS 190 v NZ (Hamilton) 1998-99 – scored 103* in second innings. **L-O INTERNATIONALS:** 70 (1995-96 to 1998-99); 2017 runs (av 34.77), 2 hundreds; 0 wkts; 33 ct. HS 123* v NZ (Taupo) 1998-99. **F-C CAREER:** 96 matches; 7218 runs (av 56.83), 18 hundreds (inc 2 doubles); 0 wkts; 94 ct, 1 st. HS 215 Karnataka v Uttar Pradesh (Bangalore) 1997-98.

GANGULY, Sourav Chandidas (Bengal)
Born Calcutta 8 Jul 1973. Younger brother of Snehasish C. Ganguly (Bengal 1986-87 to 1996-97). 5'11". Educated at St Xavier's College. Left-hand batsman, right-arm medium bowler. Bengal 1989-90 to date. **TESTS:** 23 (1996 to 1998-99); 1731 runs (av 50.91), 6 hundreds; 17 wkts (av 31.47); 6 ct. HS 173 v SL (Bombay) 1997-98; BB 3-28 v A (Calcutta) 1997-98. **L-O INTERNATIONALS:** 90 (1991-92 to 1998-99); 3146 runs (av 40.33), 5 hundreds; 26 wkts (av 38.96), 4 wkts (1); 26 ct. HS 124 v P (Dhaka) 1997-98; BB 5-16 v P (Toronto) 1997. **F-C CAREER:** 86 matches; 5609 runs (av 50.08), 13 hundreds (inc 2 doubles); 73 wkts (av 36.67), 5 wkts/inns (1); 59 ct. HS 200* for Bengal (Calcutta) v Tripura 1993-94 and v Bihar 1994-95. BB 6-87.

JADEJA, Ajaysinhji (Haryana)
Born Jamnagar 1 Feb 1971. 5'10". Educated at Sardar Patel Vidhyalay, New Delhi. Right-hand batsman, right-arm medium bowler. Haryana 1988-89 to date. **TESTS:** 13 (1992-93 to 1998-99); 538 runs (av 28.31); 4 ct. HS 96 v WI (St John's) 1996-97. **L-O INTERNATIONALS:** 154 (1991-92 to 1998-99, 3 as captain – 2 won, 1 lost); 4020 runs (av 35.89), 4 hundreds; 14 wkts (av 74.57); 45 ct. HS 119 v sl (Colombo) 1997-98; BB 2-16 v SA (Chandigarh) 1993-94. **F-C CAREER:** 74 matches; 5576 runs (av 54.13), 13 hundreds (inc 5 doubles); 38 wkts (av 41.52); 51 ct. HS 264 N Zone v C Zone (Baroda) 1993-94. BB 4-37.

KAMBLI, Vinod Ganpat (Bombay)
Born Bombay 18 Jan 1972. Left-hand batsman, right-arm off-break bowler. Bombay 1989-90 to date. **TESTS:** 17 (1992-93 to 1995-96); 1084 runs (av 54.20), 4 hundreds; 7 ct. HS 227 v Z (Delhi) 1992-93. **L-O INTERNATIONALS:** 86 (1991-92 to 1997-98); 2225 runs (av 37.08), 2 hundreds; 1 wkt (av 7.00); 12 ct. HS 106 v Z (Kanpur) 1995-96; BB 1-7. **F-C CAREER:** 81 matches; 6883 runs (av 70.23), 25 hundreds (inc 7 doubles); 4 wkts (av 72.75); 39 ct. HS 262 Bombay v Saurashtra (Bombay) 1991-92. BB 1-4.

KANITKAR, Hrishikesh Hemant (Maharashtra)
Born Poona 14 Nov 1974. Left-hand batsman, right-arm off-break bowler. Maharashtra 1994-95 to date. **TESTS:** 0. **L-O INTERNATIONALS:** 27 (1997-98 to 1998-99); 290 runs (av 22.30); 17 wkts (av 44.11); 11 ct. HS 57 v A (Cochin) 1997-98; 2-22 v P (Toronto) 1998. **F-C CAREER:** 28 matches; 2113 runs (av 68.16), 11 hundreds (inc 1 double); 38 wkts (av 44.07); 19 ct. HS 205 Maharashtra v Gujarat (Poona) 1996-97. BB 3-26.

KHURASIYA, Amay Ramsevak (Madhya Pradesh)
Born Jabalpur 18 May 1972. Left-hand batsman, left-arm orthodox slow bowler. Madhya Pradesh 1989-90 to date. **TESTS:** 0. **L-O INTERNATIONALS:** 0. **F-C CAREER:** 62 matches; 4130 runs (av 46.40), 15 hundreds (inc 2 doubles); 0 wkts; 45 ct. HS 238 Madhya Pradesh v Vidarbha (Korba) 1992-93.

KUMBLE, Anil (Karnataka)
Born Bangalore 17 Oct 1970. 6'1½". Educated at National High School; R.V. Engineering C, Bangalore. Right-hand batsman, right-arm leg-break and googly bowler. Karnataka 1989-90 to date. Northamptonshire 1995 (cap 1995) – taking 105 f-c wickets. One of *Wisden*'s Five Cricketers of 1995. **TESTS:** 49 (1990 to 1998-99); 905 runs (av 18.10); 213 wkts (av 28.50), 5 wkts/inns (13), 10 wkts/match (1); 23 ct. HS 88 v SA (Calcutta) 1996-97; BB 7-59 (11-128 match) v SL (Lucknow) 1993-94. **L-O INTERNATIONALS:** 158 (1989-90 to 1998-99); 518 runs (av 10.15); 212 wkts (av 27.55), 4 wkts (7); 58 ct. HS 24 v E (Bangalore) 1992-93; BB 6-12 v WI (Calcutta) 1993-94. **F-C CAREER:** 121 matches; 3295 runs (av 27.92), 5 hundreds; 557 wkts (av 23.40), 5 wkts/inns (39), 10 wkts/match (9), 50 wkts/season (1); no 100 (1); 61 ct. HS 154*. BB 8-41 Karnataka v Kerala (Bijapur) 1991-92. **COUNTY L-O:** BB 4-50 v Holland (Northampton) 1995 (NWT). HS 8 (ASL).

MONGIA, Nayan Ramlal (Baroda)
Born Baroda 19 Dec 1969. 5'6". Educated at M.S. University, Baroda. Right-hand batsman, wicket-keeper. Baroda 1989-90 to date. **TESTS:** 36 (1993-94 to 1998-99); 1245 runs (av 25.93), 1 hundred; 81 ct, 6 st. HS 152 v A (Delhi) 1996-97. **L-O INTERNATIONALS:** 123 (1993-94 to 1998-99); 1125 runs (av 19.73); 97 ct, 38 st. HS 69 v P (Sharjah) 1995-96. **F-C CAREER:** 93 matches; 4871 runs (av 40.93), 9 hundreds; 0 wkts; 195 ct, 24 st. HS 165.

PANDEY, Gyanendrakumar Kedarnath (Uttar Pradesh)
Born Lucknow 12 Aug 1972. Left-hand batsman, left-arm orthodox slow bowler. Uttar Pradesh 1988-89 to date. **TESTS:** 0. **L-O INTERNATIONALS:** 0. **F-C CAREER:** 65 matches; 3055 runs (av 40.19), 6 hundreds; 88 wkts (av 42.04), 5 wkts/inns (1); 36 ct. HS 178. BB 7-167.

PRASAD, Bapu Krishnarao Venkatesh (Karnataka)
Born Bangalore 5 Aug 1969. 6'3½". Right-hand batsman, right-arm medium-fast bowler. Karnataka 1990-91 to date. **TESTS:** 20 (1996 to 1998-99); 117 runs (av 6.88); 63 wkts (av 33.68), 5 wkts/inns (5), 10 wkts/match (1); 5 ct. HS 30* v NZ (Hamilton) 1998-99; BB 6-104 v SA (Calcutta) 1996-97. **L-O INTERNATIONALS:** 104 (1993-94 to 1998-99); 121 runs (av 5.50); 119 wkts (av 34.48), 4 wkts (3); 28 ct. HS 19 v K (Gwalior) 1997-98; BB 4-17 v P (Colombo) 1997-98. **F-C CAREER:** 72 matches; 344 runs (av 8.19); 199 wkts (av 28.24), 5 wkts/inns (10), 10 wkts/match (2); 38 ct. HS 28. BB 7-37.

RAMESH, Sadagoppan (Tamil Nadu)
Born Madras 16 Oct 1975. Younger brother of S.Mahesh (Tamil Nadu 1993-94 to date). Left-hand batsman, right-arm off-break bowler. Tamil Nadu 1995-96 to date. **TESTS:** 0. **L-O INTERNATIONALS:** 0. **F-C CAREER:** 25 matches; 1979 runs (av 52.07), 7 hundreds; 0 wkts; 21 ct. HS 187.

SHEWAG, Virender (Delhi)
Born Delhi 20 Oct 1978. Right-hand batsman, right-arm off-break bowler. Delhi 1997-98 to date. **TESTS:** 0. **L-O INTERNATIONALS:** 0. **F-C CAREER:** 1 match; did not bat; 1 wkt (av 31.00); 1 ct. BB 1-31.

SHUKLA, Laxmi Ratan (Bengal)
Born Howrah 6 May 1981. Right-hand batsman, right-arm medium bowler. Bengal 1997-98 to date. **TESTS:** 0. **L-O INTERNATIONALS:** 0. **F-C CAREER:** 2 matches; 26 runs (av 26.00); 2 wkts (av 49.50); 5 ct. HS 26. BB 1-29.

SINGH, Rabindra Ramanarayan (**'Robin'**) (Tamil Nadu)
Born Princes Town, Trinidad 14 Sep 1963. Left-hand batsman, right-arm medium-fast bowler. South-Central Trinidad 1982-83 (1 match). Tamil Nadu 1985-86 to date. **TESTS:** 1 (1998-99); 27 runs (av 13.50); 0 wkts; 5 ct. HS 15 v Z (Harare) 1998-99. **L-O INTERNATIONALS:** 72 (1988-89 to 1998-99); 1215 runs (av 28.92), 1 hundred; 44 wkts (av 40.40), 4 wkts (1); 15 ct. HS 100 v SL (Colombo) 1997-98; BB 5-22 v SL (Gauhati) 1997-98. Appeared in 60 LOIs before making his Test debut. **F-C CAREER:** 108 matches; 5906 runs (av 49.21), 20 hundreds; 134 wkts (av 37.09), 5 wkts/inns (4), 10 wkts/match (1); 85 ct. BB 155. BB 7-54.

SRINATH, Javagal (Karnataka)
Born Mysore 31 Aug 1969. 6'3". Right-hand batsman, right-arm fast-medium bowler. Karnataka 1989-90 to date. Gloucestershire 1995 (cap 1995). **TESTS:** 35 (1991-92 to 1998-99); 609 runs (av 17.91); 124 wkts (av 31.19), 5 wkts/inns (3); 15 ct. HS 76 v NZ (Hamilton) 1998-99; BB 6-21 v SA (Ahmedabad) 1996-97. **L-O INTERNATIONALS:** 153 (1991-92 to 1998-99); 643 runs (av 11.69); 212 wkts (av 27.14), 4 wkts (5); 24 ct. HS 53 v SA (Rajkot) 1996-97; BB 5-23 v B (Dhaka) 1997-98. **F-C CAREER:** 92 matches; 1468 runs (av 15.45); 331 wkts (av 26.06), 5 wkts/inns (11), 10 wkts/match (2); 47 ct. HS 76 (*see Tests*). BB 9-76 Glos v Glam (Abergavenny) 1995. **COUNTY L-O:** HS 11* Glos v Durham (Chester-le-St) 1995 (NWT). BB 4-33 Glos v Comb Us (Bristol) 1995 (BHC).

TENDULKAR, Sachin Ramesh (Bombay)
Born Bombay 24 Apr 1973. 5'5". Educated at Kirti College. Right-hand batsman, right-arm medium bowler. Bombay 1988-89 (scoring 100* v Gujarat when record 15yr 232d) to date. Yorkshire 1992 (cap 1992). One of *Wisden's* Five Cricketers of 1996. **TESTS:** 64 (1989-90 to 1998-99, 17 as captain – 3 won, 4 lost, 10 drawn); 4820 runs (av 54.77), 17 hundreds; 9 wkts (av 40.55); 48 ct. HS 179 v WI (Nagpur) 1994-95; BB 2-7 v NZ (Wellington) 1998-99. **L-O INTERNATIONALS:** 211 (1989-90 to 1998-99, 54 as captain – 17 won, 31 lost, 1 tied, 5 no result); 7800 runs (av 42.39), 21 hundreds; 78 wkts (av 46.74), 4 wkts (3); 71 ct. HS 142 v A (Sharjah) 1997-98; BB 5-32 v A (Cochin) 1997-98. **F-C CAREER:** 139 matches; 11,181 runs (av 60.11), 34 hundreds (inc 1 double); 27 wkts (av 69.44); 96 ct. HS 204* Bombay v A (Bombay) 1997-98. BB 3-60. **COUNTY L-O:** BB 2-21 v Kent (Leeds) 1992 (BHC). HS 107 v Lancs (Leeds) 1992 (ASL).

WORLD CUP CAREER RECORDS

INDIA – BATTING AND FIELDING

	M	I	NO	HS	Runs	Avge	100	50	Ct/St
S.Abid Ali	3	1	–	70	70	70.00	–	1	–
M.Amarnath	14	12	–	80	254	21.16	–	1	2
P.K.Amre	4	3	1	22	27	13.50	–	–	–
S.A.Ankola	1	–	–	–	–	–	–	–	–
K.Azad	3	2	–	15	15	7.50	–	–	–
M.Azharuddin	22	18	3	93	665	44.33	–	7	6
S.T.Banerjee	2	1	1	25*	36	36.00	–	–	2
B.S.Bedi	5	4	1	13	25	8.33	–	–	–
R.M.H.Binny	9	7	–	27	73	10.42	–	–	2
F.M.Engineer	3	2	1	54*	78	78.00	–	1	2
A.D.Gaekwad	6	5	–	37	113	22.60	–	–	2
S.M.Gavaskar	19	19	3	103*	561	35.06	1	4	4
K.D.Ghavri	4	3	–	20	35	11.66	–	–	–
A.Jadeja	13	11	2	53	237	26.33	–	1	4
V.G.Kambli	12	11	3	106	205	25.62	1	–	1
Kapil Dev	26	24	6	175*	669	37.16	1	1	12
A.R.Kapoor	2	1	–	0	0	0.00	–	–	–
S.C.Khanna	3	3	–	10	17	5.66	–	–	1
S.M.H.Kirmani	8	6	1	24*	61	12.20	–	–	12/2
A.Kumble	7	3	1	17	27	13.50	–	–	8
Madan Lal	11	7	3	27	122	30.50	–	–	1
Maninder Singh	7	2	1	4	4	4.00	–	–	1
S.V.Manjrekar	11	11	–	62	295	26.81	–	1	5
N.R.Mongia	7	6	3	27	69	23.00	–	–	4/3
K.S.More	14	10	5	42*	100	20.00	–	–	12/6
C.S.Pandit	2	1	–	24	24	24.00	–	–	1
B.P.Patel	6	5	1	38	88	22.00	–	–	–
S.M.Patil	8	8	1	51*	216	30.85	–	2	2
M.Prabhakar	19	11	2	11*	45	5.00	–	–	4
B.K.V.Prasad	7	2	1	0*	0	0.00	–	–	1
S.L.V.Raju	11	3	1	3*	4	2.00	–	–	2
B.S.Sandhu	8	4	2	11*	28	14.00	–	–	2
C.Sharma	4	1	–	0	0	0.00	–	–	–
R.J.Shastri	14	11	1	57	185	18.50	–	1	6
N.S.Sidhu	12	10	–	93	454	45.40	–	6	3
L.Sivaramakrishnan	2	–	–	–	–	–	–	–	1

	M	I	NO	HS	Runs	Avge	100	50	Ct/St
E.D.Solkar	3	2	–	13	21	10.50	–	–	1
K.Srikkanth	23	23	1	75	521	23.68	–	2	9
J.Srinath	15	9	6	12*	59	19.66	–	–	3
S.R.Tendulkar	15	14	2	137	806	67.16	2	6	4
D.B.Vengsarkar	11	10	3	63	252	36.00	–	1	3
S.Venkataraghavan	6	4	3	26*	49	49.00	–	–	1
G.R.Viswanath	6	5	–	75	145	29.00	–	1	–
Yashpal Sharma	8	8	1	89	240	34.28	–	2	2

INDIA – BOWLING

	O	M	R	W	Avge	Best	4w	R/O
S.Abid Ali	36	7	115	6	19.16	2-22	–	3.19
M.Amarnath	110.3	9	431	16	26.93	3-12	–	3.90
S.A.Ankola	5	0	28	0	–	–	–	5.60
K.Azad	17	1	42	1	42.00	1-28	–	2.47
M.Azharuddin	23.5	0	109	5	21.80	3-19	–	4.57
S.T.Banerjee	13	1	85	1	85.00	1-45	–	6.53
B.S.Bedi	60	17	148	2	74.00	1- 6	–	2.46
R.M.H.Binny	95	9	382	19	20.10	4-29	1	4.02
K.D.Ghavri	43	4	195	0	–	–	–	4.53
A.Jadeja	24.2	0	120	2	60.00	2-31	–	4.93
Kapil Dev	237	27	892	28	31.85	5-43	1	3.76
A.R.Kapoor	20	2	81	1	81.00	1-41	–	4.05
A.Kumble	69.4	3	281	15	18.73	3-28	–	4.03
Madan Lal	116.2	12	426	22	19.36	4-20	1	3.66
Maninder Singh	70	1	280	14	20.00	3-21	–	4.00
S.M.Patil	9	0	61	0	–	–	–	6.77
M.Prabhakar	145.1	10	640	24	26.66	4-19	1	4.40
B.K.V.Prasad	65	1	312	8	39.00	3-45	–	4.80
S.L.V.Raju	88.1	7	366	13	28.15	3-30	–	4.15
B.S.Sandhu	83	10	297	8	37.12	2-26	–	3.57
C.Sharma	36.1	2	170	6	28.33	3-51	–	4.70
R.J.Shastri	92.3	2	389	12	32.41	3-26	–	4.20
L.Sivaramakrishnan	17	0	70	1	70.00	1-36	–	4.11
E.D.Solkar	4	0	28	0	–	–	–	7.00
K.Srikkanth	2.1	0	15	0	–	–	–	6.94
J.Srinath	118.5	6	542	16	33.87	3-34	–	4.56
S.R.Tendulkar	77	1	329	4	82.25	2-34	–	4.27
S.Venkataraghavan	72	7	217	0	–	–	–	3.01

WORLD CUP REGISTER

PAKISTAN

Career statistics deadlines: Test Matches to 28 January 1999; Limited-Overs Internationals to 14 February 1999; first-class to end of 1998 English season (20 September). Key to abbreviations on page 19. Pakistan's provisionally selected 19 players (to be reduced to 15 by 1 April) are:

ABDUL RAZZAK (Lahore)
Born Lahore 2 Dec 1979. 5'11". Educated at Furqan Model Secondary School, Lahore. Right-hand batsman, right-arm fast-medium bowler. First-class debut 1996-97. **TESTS:** 0. **L-O INTERNATIONALS:** 13 (1996-97 to 1998); 101 runs (av 12.62); 12 wkts (36.25); 1 ct. HS 46* v SA (Durban) 1997-98; BB 3-48 v I (Toronto) 1998. **F-C CAREER:** 16 matches; 626 runs (av 32.94), 2 hundreds; 70 wkts (av 29.80), 5 wkts/inns (3); 5 ct. HS 117. BB 7-51.

ARSHAD KHAN (Peshawar and Allied Bank)
Born Peshawar 22 Mar 1971. Right-hand batsman, right-arm off-break bowler. First-class debut 1988-89. **TESTS:** 2 (1997-98 to 1998-99); 11 runs (av 5.50); 5 wkts (av 49.00); 0 ct. HS 7 and BB 3-72 v A (Karachi) 1998-99. **L-O INTERNATIONALS:** 12 (1994-95 to 1998-99); 42 runs (av 21.00); 10 wkts (av 43.70); 3 ct. HS 13* v WI (Dhaka) 1998-99; BB 3-70 v A (Karachi) 1998-99. **F-C CAREER:** 90 matches; 1045 runs (av 9.95); 286 wkts (av 24.01), 5 wkts/inns (14), 10 wkts/match (2); 46 ct. HS 50*. BB 8-115.

AZHAR MAHMOOD (Islamabad and United Bank)
Born Multan 28 Feb 1975. 5'11". Educated at F.G. High School, Islamabad. Right-hand batsman, right-arm fast-medium bowler. First-class debut 1993-94. **TESTS:** 14 (1997-98 to 1998-99); 687 runs (av 40.41), 3 hundreds; 25 wkts (av 37.64); 10 ct. HS 136 v SA (Johannesburg) 1997-98; BB 4-53 v WI (Rawalpindi) 1997-98. Scored 128* v SA (Rawalpindi) 1997-98 on debut. **L-O INTERNATIONALS:** 49 (1996-97 to 1998-99); 452 runs (av 16.74); 34 wkts (av 49.47); 16 ct. HS 65* v A (Karachi) 1998-99; BB 3-34 v I (Lahore) 1997-98. **F-C CAREER:** 59 matches; 2279 runs (av 29.59), 4 hundreds; 220 wkts (av 22.37), 5 wkts/inns (9), 10 wkts/match (2); 40 ct. HS 136. BB 7-55.

IJAZ AHMED (Habib Bank)
Born Sialkot 20 Sep 1968. 5'9". Educated at Islamia College. Right-hand batsman, left-arm medium bowler. First-class debut 1983-84. **TESTS:** 50 (1986-87 to 1998-99); 2799 runs (av 39.98), 10 hundreds; 2 wkts (av 34.50); 35 ct. HS 155 v A (Peshawar) 1998-99; BB 1-9. **L-O INTERNATIONALS:** 215 (1986-87 to 1998-99); 5577 runs (av 32.42), 9 hundreds; 3 wkts (av 90.66); 4 wkts (av 116.00); 79 ct. HS 139* v I (Lahore) 1997-98; BB 2-31 v NZ (Sialkot) 1990-91. **F-C CAREER:** 143 matches; 8536 runs (av 39.33), 21 hundreds (inc 1 double); 33 wkts (av 31.84), 5 wkts/inns (1); 98 ct. HS 201* PACO v Karachi (Krachi) 1984-85. BB 5-95.

IMRAN NAZIR (WPDA and Lahore)
Born Gujranwala 16 Dec 1981. Right-hand batsman, right-arm leg-break bowler. First-class debut 1998-99. **TESTS:** 0. **L-O INTERNATIONALS:** 0. **F-C CAREER:** 0 matches.

INZAMAM-UL-HAQ (Faisalabad and United Bank)
Born Multan 3 Mar 1970. Brother of Intizar-ul-Haq (Multan). 6'2". Educated at Government College, Multan. Right-hand batsman, occasional left-arm orthodox slow bowler. First-class debut 1985-86. **TESTS:** 51 (1992 to 1998-99); 3160 runs (av 42.70), 6 hundreds; 0 wkts; 46 ct. HS 177 v WI (Rawalpindi) 1997-98. **L-O INTERNATIONALS:** 171 (1991-92 to 1998-99); 5369 runs (av 38.35), 5 hundreds; 2 wkts (av 26.00); 46 ct. HS 137* v NZ (Sharjah) 1993-94; BB 1-4. **F-C CAREER:** 150 matches; 9902 runs (av

50.26), 26 hundreds (inc 2 doubles); 37 wkts (av 34.97), 5 wkts/inns (2); 121 ct. HS 201*
United Bank v PNSC (Karachi) 1988-89. BB 5-80.

MOHAMMAD WASIM (Rawalpindi)
Born Rawalpindi 8 Aug 1977. 6'0". Educated in Rawalpindi at F.G. High School and
Government College. Right-hand batsman, occasional right-arm leg-break bowler,
wicket-keeper. First-class debut 1994-95. **TESTS:** 11 (1996-97 to 1998-99); 463 runs (av
33.07), 2 hundreds; 15 ct, 2 st. HS 192 v Z (Harare) 1997-98. Scored 109* v NZ (Lahore)
1996-97 on debut. **L-O INTERNATIONALS:** 20 (1996-97 to 1997-98); 479 runs (av
26.61); 6 ct. HS 76 v Z (Harare) 1997-98. **F-C CAREER:** 44 matches; 2135 runs (av
33.35), 7 hundreds; 3 wkts (av 36.66); 49 ct, 2 st. HS 192.

MOIN KHAN (Karachi and PIA)
Born Rawalpindi 23 Sep 1971. Younger brother of Nadeem Khan (Karachi and PIA 1986-87
to date). 5'8". Educated at Government College of Commerce, Rawalpindi. Right-hand
batsman, wicket-keeper. First-class debut 1986-87. **TESTS:** 42 (1990-91 to 1998-99); 1 as
captain – 1 drawn); 1683 runs (av 30.05), 3 hundreds; 74 ct, 11 st. HS 117* v SL (Sialkot)
1995-96. **L-O INTERNATIONALS:** 118 (1990-91 to 1998-99, 2 as captain, 2 won); 1684
runs (av 23.71); 104 ct, 41 st. HS 69* v I (Toronto) 1998. **F-C CAREER:** 129 matches; 4756
runs (av 29.35), 8 hundreds; 2 wkts (av 40.50); 303 ct, 37 st. HS 129. BB 2-78.

MUSHTAQ AHMED (United Bank)
Born Sahiwal 28 Jun 1970. 5'5". Right-hand batsman, right-arm leg-break and googly
bowler. Multan 1986-87 to 1990-91. United Bank 1986-87 to date. Somerset 1993-95,
1997-98; cap 1993. One of *Wisden*'s Five Cricketers of 1996. **TESTS:** 41 (1989-90 to
1998-99); 592 runs (av 12.59); 165 wkts (av 29.01), 5 wkts/inns (10), 10 wkts/match (3);
17 ct. HS 59 v SA (Rawalpindi) 1997-98; BB 7-56 (10-171 match) v NZ (Christchurch)
1995-96. **L-O INTERNATIONALS:** 130 (1988-89 to 1997-98); 343 runs (av 9.02); 144
wkts (av 33.62), 4 wkts (3); 28 ct. HS 26 v SL (Sharjah) 1995-96; BB 5-36 v I (Toronto)
1996. **F-C CAREER:** 168 matches; 2648 runs (av 14.23); 741 wkts (av 25.33), 5
wkts/inns (52), 10 wkts/match (15), 50 wkts/season (5); 82 ct. HS 90 v Sussex (Taunton)
1993. BB 9-93 Multan v Peshawar (Sahiwal) 1990-91. **1998 SEASON (f-c – Somerset):**
121 runs (av 15.12); 14 wkts (av 29.35). **COUNTY L-O:** BB 7-24 Somerset v Ire
(Taunton) 1997 (BHC). HS 41 Somerset v Durham (Taunton) 1998 (ASL).

SAEED ANWAR (ADBP)
Born Karachi 6 Sep 1968. 5'8½". Left-hand batsman, left-arm orthodox slow bowler.
Karachi 1986-87 to 1989-90. United Bank 1987-88 to 1989-90. ADBP 1990-91 to date.
One of *Wisden*'s Five Cricketers of 1996. **TESTS:** 36 (1990-91 to 1998-99, 5 as captain –
1 won, 2 lost, 2 drawn); 2693 runs (av 44.64), 7 hundreds; 0 wkts; 15 ct. HS 176 v E
(Oval) 1996. **L-O INTERNATIONALS:** 161 (1988-89 to 1998-99, 8 as captain – 5 won,
3 lost); 5688 runs (av 40.33), 15 hundreds; 3 wkts (av 55.66); 30 ct. HS 194 (*record*) v I
(Madras) 1996-97; BB 1-9. **F-C CAREER:** 111 matches; 7629 runs (av 44.61), 23
hundreds (inc 2 doubles); 9 wkts (av 45.77); 57 ct. HS 221 Karachi Whites v Multan
(Karachi) 1989-90. BB 3-83.

SAJID SHAH (Peshawar and PNSC)
Born Mardan 19 Oct 1974. Right-hand batsman, right-arm fast-medium bowler. First-
class debut 1993-94. **TESTS:** 0. **L-O INTERNATIONALS:** 0. **F-C CAREER:** 50
matches; 630 runs (av 11.05); 188 wkts (av 23.22), 5 wkts/inns (13), 10 wkts/match (2);
15 ct. HS 50. BB 7-63.

SAQLAIN MUSHTAQ (PIA)
Born Lahore 29 Dec 1976. Younger brother of Sibtain Mushtaq (Lahore 1988-89). 5'11".
Right-hand batsman, off-break bowler. Educated in Lahore at Government Muslim
League High School and M.A.O. College. Islamabad 1994-95. PIA 1994-95 to date.
Surrey debut 1997; cap 1998. **TESTS:** 17 (1995-96 to 1998-99); 315 runs (av 16.57); 65

wkts (av 32.41), 5 wkts/inns (4); 5 ct. HS 79 v Z (Sheikhupura) 1996-97; BB 5-32 v Z (Lahore) 1998-99. **L-O INTERNATIONALS:** 88 (1995-96 to 1998-99); 415 runs (av 11.85); 176 wkts (av 18.72), 4 wkts (13); 27 ct. HS 30* v A (Melbourne) 1996-97; BB 5-29 v A (Adelaide) 1996-97. **F-C CAREER:** 63 matches; 1032 runs (av 15.87); 264 wkts (av 22.62), 5 wkts/inns (18), 10 wkts/match (6), 50 wkts/season (2); hat-trick 1997; 29 ct. Took 52 wickets in debut season. HS 79 (*see Tests*). BB 8-65 (11-107 match) v Derbys (Oval) 1988. **1998 SEASON (f-c):** 176 runs (av 17.60); 63 wkts (av 17.76), 5 wkts/inns (3), 10 wkts/match (3). **COUNTY L-O:** BB 4-46 Surrey v Lancs (Oval) 1998 (BHC). HS 29* Surrey v Warwks (Birmingham) 1997 (ASL).

SHAHID AFRIDI (Karachi)

Born Kohat 1 Mar 1980. Right-hand batsman, right-arm leg-break and googly bowler. First-class debut 1995-96. **TESTS:** 1 (1998-99); 16 runs (av 8.00); 5 wkts (av 20.20), 5 wkts/inns (1); 2 ct. HS 10 and BB 5-52 v A (Karachi) 1998-99 – on debut. **L-O INTERNATIONALS:** 71 (1997-98 to 1998-99); 1604 runs (av 24.30), 2 hundreds; 45 wkts (av 54.24); 24 ct. HS 109 v I (Toronto) 1998; BB 3-33 v WI (Sydney) 1996-97. Scored a 37-ball hundred (*record*) which included 11 sixes (*equalled record*) v SL (Nairobi) 1996-97 in his first LOI innings. **F-C CAREER:** 18 matches; 906 runs (av 34.84), 2 hundreds; 43 wkts (av 29.27), 5 wkts/inns (3); 8 ct. HS 123. BB 6-101.

SHAHID NAZIR (Habib Bank)

Born Faisalabad 4 Dec 1977. 5'11". M.M. High School, Faisalabad; M.A.O. College, Lahore). Right-hand batsman, right-arm fast-medium bowler. First-class debut 1995-96. **TESTS:** 7 (1996-97 to 1997-98); 45 runs (av 7.50); 16 wkts (av 30.87), 5 wkts/inns (1); 2 ct. HS 18 v WI (Peshawar) 1997-98; BB 5-53 v Z (Sheikhupura) 1996-97. **L-O INTERNATIONALS:** 14 (1996 to 1997-98); 25 runs (av 25.00); 15 wkts (av 33.20); 2 ct. HS 8; BB 3-14 v WI (Melbourne) 1996-97. **F-C CAREER:** 21 matches; 295 runs (av 15.52); 78 wkts (av 20.92), 5 wkts/inns (5); 7 ct. HS 60*. BB 6-64.

SHOAIB AKHTAR (Rawalpindi and ADBP)

Born Rawalpindi 13 Jun 1975. 6'0". Educated in Rawalpindi at Elliot High School and Asgar Mal Government College. Right-hand batsman, right-arm fast bowler. First-class debut 1994-95. **TESTS:** 8 (1997-98 to 1998-99); 38 runs (av 7.60); 18 wkts (av 43.83), 5 wkts/inns (1); 4 ct. HS 11 v Z (Lahore) 1998-99; BB 5-43 v SA (Durban) 1997-98. **L-O INTERNATIONALS:** 5 (1997-98 to 1998-99); 44 runs (av 44.00); 5 wkts (av 41.40); 1 ct. HS 36 and BB 3-44 v A (Karachi) 1998-99. **F-C CAREER:** 54 matches; 342 runs (av 8.34); 187 wkts (av 28.42), 5 wkts/inns (15); 19 ct. HS 23. BB 6-69.

WAJAHATULLAH WASTI (Peshawar and Allied Bank)

Born Peshaar 11 Nov 1974. Right-hand batsman, right-arm fast-medium bowler. First-class debut 1994-95. **TESTS:** 0. **L-O INTERNATIONALS:** 0. **F-C CAREER:** 40 matches; 1739 runs (av 28.98), 1 hundred; 3 wkts (av 51.33); 38 ct. HS 103. BB 2-32.

WAQAR YOUNIS (United Bank)

Born Vehari 16 Nov 1971. 6'0". Educated at Government College, Vehari. Right-hand batsman, right-arm fast bowler. First-class debut 1987-88. Multan 1987-88 to 1990-91. United Bank 1988-89 to date. Surrey 1990-91 and 1993; cap 1990. Glamorgan 1997-98; cap 1997. One of *Wisden*'s Five Cricketers of 1991. **TESTS:** 55 (1989-90 to 1998-99, 1 as captain – 1 won); 587 runs (av 10.12); 275 wkts (av 21.56), 5 wkts/inns (21), 10 wkts/match (5); 7 ct. HS 45 v SA (Rawalpindi) 1997-98; BB 7-76 v NZ (Faisalabad) 1990-91. **L-O INTERNATIONALS:** 172 (1989-90 to 1998-99, 1 as captain, 1 lost); 537 runs (av 9.94); 283 wkts (av 23.12), 4 wkts (20); 19 ct. HS 37 v WI (Johannesburg) 1992-93; BB 6-26 v SL (Sharjah) 1989-90. **F-C CAREER:** 167 matches; 1875 runs (av 12.50); 752 wkts (av 21.19), 5 wkts/inns (57), 10 wkts/match (14), 50 wkts/season (8) inc 100 (1): 113 (1991), hat-trick 1997; 39 ct. HS 55 P v Natal (Durban) 1994-95. BB 8-17 Glam v Sussex (Swansea) 1997. **1998 SEASON (f-c):** 39 runs (av 6.50); 12 wkts (av 33.08). **COUNTY L-O:** HS 45 Glam v Sussex (Hove) 1998 (BHC). BB 5-26 Surrey v Kent (Oval) 1990 (SL)

WASIM AKRAM (PIA) (CAPTAIN)
Born Lahore 3 Jun 1966. 6'3". Educated at Islamia College. Left-hand batsman, left-arm fast bowler. PACO 1984-85 to 1985-86. Lahore 1985-86 to 1986-87. PIA 1987-88 to date. Lancashire 1988-98; cap 1989; captain 1998; benefit 1998. One of *Wisden*'s Five Cricketers of 1992. **TESTS:** 83 (1984-85 to 1998-99, 17 as captain – 9 won, 4 lost, 4 drawn); 2111 runs (av 21.11), 2 hundreds; 354 wkts (av 22.85), 5 wkts/inns (22), 10 wkts/match (4); 31 ct. HS 257* v Z (Sheikhupura) 1996-97; BB 7-119 v NZ (Wellington) 1993-94. **L-O INTERNATIONALS:** 254 (1984-85 to 1998-99, 72 as captain – 43 won, 28 lost, 1 tied); 2508 runs (av 15.29); 363 wkts (*record*) (av 23.10), 4 wkts (20); 62 ct. HS 86 v A (Melbourne) 1989-90; BB 5-15 v Z (Karachi) 1993-94. **F-C CAREER:** 219 matches; 6044 runs (av 22.80), 6 hundreds (inc 1 double); 912 wkts (av 21.34), 5 wkts/inns (64), 10 wkts/match (15), 50 wkts/season (5), hat-trick 1988; 78 ct. HS 257* (*see Tests*). BB 8-30 (13-147 match) Lancs v Somerset (Southport) 1994. **1998 SEASON (f-c):** 531 runs (av 31.23), 1 hundred; 48 wkts (av 21.35), 5 wkts/inns (1). **COUNTY L-O:** HS 89* Lancs v Notts (Nottingham) 1998 (BHC). BB 5-10 Lancs v Leics (Leicester) 1993 (BHC)

YOUSUF YOUHANA (Bahawalpur)
Born Lahore 27 Aug 1974. Right-hand batsman. First-class debut 1996-97. **TESTS:** 7 (1997-98 to 1998-99); 448 runs (av 40.72), 1 hundred; 8 ct. HS 120* v Z (Lahore) 1998-99. **L-O INTERNATIONALS:** 13 (1997-98 to 1998-99); 479 runs (av 53.22), 1 hundred; 3ct. HS 100 v A (Lahore) 1998-99. **F-C CAREER:** 16 matches; 1171 runs (av 48.79), 2 hundreds; 0 wkts: 12 ct. HS 163*.

WORLD CUP CAREER RECORDS

PAKISTAN – BATTING AND FIELDING

	M	I	NO	HS	Runs	Avge	100	50	Ct/St
Aamir Sohail	16	16	–	114	598	37.37	2	4	4
Abdul Qadir	13	9	7	41*	118	59.00	–	–	3
Aqib Javed	15	3	3	6*	8	–	–	–	2
Asif Iqbal	5	4	–	61	182	45.50	–	3	5
Asif Masood	3	1	–	6	6	6.00	–	–	–
Ata-ur-Rehman	1	1	–	0	0	0.00	–	–	–
Haroon Rashid	4	4	1	37*	69	23.00	–	–	–
Ijaz Ahmed	20	17	3	70	340	24.28	–	3	7
Ijaz Faqih	6	5	1	42*	61	15.25	–	–	1
Imran Khan	28	24	5	102*	666	35.05	1	4	6
Inzamam-ul-Haq	16	15	2	60	370	28.46	–	2	4
Iqbal Sikander	4	1	1	1*	1	–	–	–	–
Javed Miandad	33	30	5	103	1083	43.32	1	8	10/1
Majid Khan	7	7	–	84	359	51.28	–	5	1
Mansoor Akhtar	8	8	–	33	108	13.50	–	–	2
Manzoor Elahi	1	1	1	4*	4	–	–	–	1
Mohsin Khan	7	7	–	82	223	31.85	–	2	3
Moin Khan	10	5	2	20*	44	14.66	–	–	11/3
Mudassar Nazar	12	10	1	40	149	16.55	–	–	6
Mushtaq Ahmed	15	5	1	17	27	6.75	–	–	5
Mushtaq Mohammed	3	3	–	55	89	29.66	–	1	1
Naseer Malik	3	1	1	0*	0	–	–	–	–
Parvez Mir	2	2	1	4*	8	8.00	–	–	1
Ramiz Raja	16	16	3	119*	700	53.84	3	2	4
Rashid Khan	7	1	–	9	9	9.00	–	–	1
Rashid Latif	6	2	–	26	26	13.00	–	–	7/2
Sadiq Mohammed	7	7	1	74	189	31.50	–	2	3

	M	I	NO	HS	Runs	Avge	100	50	Ct/St
Saeed Anwar	6	6	2	83*	329	82.25	–	3	–
Salim Jaffer	5	3	2	8*	9	9.00	–	–	–
Salim Malik	23	19	5	100	572	40.85	1	4	5
Salim Yousuf	7	6	3	56	112	37.33	–	1	9
Saqlain Mushtaq	1	–	–	–	–	–	–	–	1
Sarfraz Nawaz	11	8	1	17	65	9.28	–	–	2
Shahid Mahboob	5	3	–	77	100	33.33	–	1	1
Shoaib Mohammed	1	1	–	0	0	0.00	–	–	1
Sikander Bakht	4	2	1	2	3	3.00	–	–	1
Tahir Naqqash	1	1	1	0*	0	–	–	–	1
Tausif Ahmed	6	2	–	1	1	0.50	–	–	1
Waqar Younis	6	1	1	4*	4	–	–	–	2
Wasim Akram	22	16	4	39	207	17.25	–	–	3
Wasim Bari	14	8	4	34	87	21.75	–	–	18/4
Wasim Haider	3	2	–	13	26	13.00	–	–	1
Wasim Raja	8	8	–	58	154	19.25	–	1	4
Zaheer Abbas	14	14	2	103*	597	49.75	1	4	7
Zahid Fazal	2	2	–	11	13	6.50	–	–	1

PAKISTAN – BOWLING

	O	M	R	W	Avge	Best	4w	R/O
Aamir Sohail	86	3	384	8	48.00	2-26	–	4.46
Abdul Qadir	135.4	8	506	24	21.08	5-44	3	3.72
Aqib Javed	124.2	1	517	18	28.72	3-21	–	4.15
Asif Iqbal	59	5	215	10	21.50	4-56	1	3.64
Asif Masood	30	3	128	2	64.00	1-50	–	4.26
Ata-ur-Rehman	10	0	40	1	40.00	1-40	–	4.00
Ijaz Ahmed	40	1	170	1	170.00	1-28	–	4.25
Ijaz Faqih	37	2	125	0	–	–	–	3.37
Imran Khan	169.3	18	655	34	19.26	4-37	2	3.86
Iqbal Sikander	35	2	147	3	49.00	1-30	–	4.20
Javed Miandad	22	2	73	4	18.25	2-22	–	3.31
Majid Khan	47	8	117	7	16.71	3-27	–	2.48
Mansoor Akhtar	17	2	75	2	37.50	1- 7	–	4.41
Manzoor Elahi	9.4	0	32	1	32.00	1-32	–	3.31
Mohsin Khan	1	0	3	0	–	–	–	3.00
Mudassar Nazar	105	8	397	8	49.62	3-43	–	3.78
Mushtaq Ahmed	135	5	549	26	21.11	3-16	–	4.06
Mushtaq Mohammed	7	0	23	0	–	–	–	3.28
Naseer Malik	30	5	98	5	19.60	2-37	–	3.26
Parvez Mir	15	2	59	2	29.50	1-17	–	3.93
Rashid Khan	71	11	266	8	33.25	3-47	–	3.74
Sadiq Mohammed	6	1	20	2	10.00	2-20	–	3.33
Salim Jaffer	39.4	2	210	5	42.00	3-30	–	5.29
Salim Malik	56	2	282	4	70.50	2-41	–	5.03
Saqlain Mushtaq	10	1	38	2	19.00	2-38	–	3.80
Sarfraz Nawaz	119	15	435	16	27.18	4-44	1	3.65
Shahid Mahboob	52	4	228	4	57.00	1-37	–	4.38
Sikander Bakht	41	10	108	7	15.42	3-32	–	2.63
Tahir Naqqash	8	0	49	1	49.00	1-49	–	6.12
Tausif Ahmed	60	4	230	5	46.00	1-35	–	3.83
Waqar Younis	54	5	253	13	19.46	4-26	1	4.68
Wasim Akram	186.2	7	768	28	27.42	4-32	1	4.12
Wasim Haider	19	1	79	1	79.00	1-36	–	4.15
Wasim Raja	13.4	4	46	1	46.00	1- 7	–	3.36
Zaheer Abbas	19.4	2	74	2	37.00	1- 8	–	3.76

WORLD CUP REGISTER

SRI LANKA

Career statistics deadlines: Test Matches to 28 January 1999; Limited-Overs Internationals to 14 February 1999; first-class to end of 1998 English season (20 September). Key to abbreviations on page 19. Sri Lanka's provisionally selected 19 players (to be reduced to 15 by 1 April) are:

ATAPATTU, Marvin Samson (Sinhalese)
Born Kalutara 22 Nov 1970. 5'9". Educated at Ananda College. Right hand batsman, right-arm leg-break bowler. First-class debut 1988-89. **TESTS:** 20 (1990-91 to 1998); 1005 runs (av 29.55), 2 hundreds; 1 wkt (av 24.00); 12 ct. HS 223 v Z (Kandy) 1997-98; BB 1-9. **L-O INTERNATIONALS:** 66 (1990-91 to 1998-99); 1972 runs (av 34.59), 2 hundreds; 0 wkts; 26 ct. HS 132* v E (Lord's) 1998. **F-C CAREER:** 126 matches; 8012 runs (av 56.42), 27 hundreds (inc 4 doubles), 1000 runs/season (3); 19 wkts (av 36.42); 91 ct. HS 253* Sinhalese v Galle (Colombo) 1995-96. BB 3-19. **1998 SEASON (f-c – Sri Lanka):** 316 runs (av 52.66), 1 hundred; 0 wkts.

BOTEJU, Hemantha (Bloomfield)
Born Colombo 3 Nov 1977. Right hand batsman, right-arm medium bowler. First-class debut 1995-96. **TESTS:** 0. **L-O INTERNATIONALS:** 0. **F-C CAREER:** 14 matches; 317 runs (av 21.13); 29 wkts (av 27.37); 9 ct. HS 74. BB 4-32.

CHANDANA, Umagiliya Durage Upul (Tamil Union)
Born Galle 5 Jul 1972. 5'5". Right hand batsman, left-arm leg-break and googly bowler. First-class debut 1991-92. **TESTS:** 0. **L-O INTERNATIONALS:** 47 (1993-94 to 1998-99); 466 runs (av 16.06); 44 wkts (av 31.93), 4 wkts (2); 23 ct. HS 50 v E (Melbourne) 1998-99; BB 4-31 v Z (Colombo) 1997-98. **F-C CAREER:** 76 matches; 3064 runs (av 34.81), 7 hundreds; 148 wkts (av 24.62), 5 wkts/inns (4); 62 ct. HS 163. BB 6-25. **1998 SEASON (f-c – Sri Lanka):** 78 runs (av 26.00); 4 wkts (av 32.25).

De SILVA, Pinnaduwage Aravinda (Nondescripts)
Born Colombo 17 Oct 1965. 5'3½". Right-hand batsman, off-break bowler. Debut (for SL) 1983-84. Nondescripts 1988-89 to date. Kent 1995 (cap 1995). One of *Wisden*'s Five Cricketers of 1995. **TESTS:** 74 (1984 to 1998, 5 as captain – 3 lost, 2 drawn); 5129 runs (av 43.10), 17 hundreds; 24 wkts (av 37.66), 36 ct. HS 267 v NZ (Wellington) 1990-91; BB 3-30 v NZ (Colombo) 1997-98. **L-O INTERNATIONALS:** 250 (1983-84 to 1998-99, 18 as captain – 5 won, 12 lost, 1 no result); 7863 runs (av 36.06), 11 hundreds; 81 wkts (av 39.90), 4wkts (1); 77 ct. HS 145 v K (Kandy) 1995-96; BB 4-45 v P (Paarl) 1997-98. **F-C CAREER:** 178 matches; 12,286 runs (av 48.75), 37 hundreds (inc 7 doubles), 1000 runs/season (1); 80 wkts (av 34.53), 5 wkts/inns (4); 94 ct. HS 267 (*see Tests*). BB 7-24 Nondescripts v Panadura (Panadura) 1994-95. **1998 SEASON (f-c – Sri Lanka):** 153 runs (av 76.50), 1 hundred; 1 wkt (av 30.00). **COUNTY L-O:** HS 124 Kent v Surrey (Canterbury) 1995 (ASL). BB 4-28 Kent v Middx (Lord's) 1995 (ASL).

DHARMASENA, Handunettige Deepthi Priyantha Kumar (Bloomfield)
Born Colombo 24 Apr 1971. 5'11". Right-hand batsman, off-break bowler. First-class debut 1988-89. **TESTS:** 20 (1993-94 to 1998); 660 runs (av 22.00); 50 wkts (av 37.86), 5 wkts/inns (3); 11 ct. HS 62* v P (Sialkot) 1995-96; BB 6-72 v NZ (Galle) 1997-98. **L-O INTERNATIONALS:** 94 (1994-95 to 1998-99); 849 runs (av 26.53); 92 wkts (av 38.02), 4 wkts (1); 26 ct. HS 69* v SA (Lahore) 1997-98; BB 4-37 v SA (Port Elizabeth) 1994-95. **F-C CAREER:** 73 matches; 2626 runs (av 31.26), 3 hundreds; 222 wkts (av 23.15), 5 wkts/inns (15), 10 wkts/match (3); 50 wkts/season (1); 43 ct. HS 155*. BB 7-111. **1998 SEASON (f-c – Sri Lanka):** 68 runs (av 22.66); 3 wkts (av 86.00).

GUNAWARDENA, Dihan Avishka (Nondescripts)
Born Colombo 26 May 1977. Left-hand batsman. First-class debut 1996-97. **TESTS:** 0. **L-O INTERNATIONALS:** 7 (1997-98 to 1998-99); 164 runs (av 23.42); 1 ct. HS 75 v A (Melbourne) 1998-99. **F-C CAREER:** 16 matches; 681 runs (av 37.83), 2 hundreds; 11 ct. HS 120*.

HATHURUSINGHE, Upul Chandika (Tamil Union)
Born Colombo 13 Sep 1968. 5'7". Educated at Ananda College. Right-hand batsman, right-arm medium bowler. First-class debut 1988-89. **TESTS:** 24 (1990-91 to 1995-96); 1260 runs (av 30.73); 16 wkts (av 41.75); 6 ct. HS 83 v P (Faisalabad) 1995-96; BB 4-66 v A (Colombo) 1992-93. **L-O INTERNATIONALS:** 34 (1991-92 to 1998); 669 runs (av 21.58); 14 wkts (av 47.85), 4 wkts (1); 6 ct. HS 66 v Z (Sharjah) 1992-93; BB 4-57 v WI (Berri, S Australia) 1991-92. **F-C CAREER:** 135 matches; 7206 runs (av 37.33), 12 hundreds; 237 wkts (av 24.46), 5 wkts/inns (9), 10 wkts/match (2); 101 ct. HS 143. BB 8-29 Tamil Union v Burgher (Colombo) 1996-97. **1998 SEASON (f-c – Sri Lanka):** 255 runs (av 51.00), 1 hundred; 6wkts (av 59.66).

JAYASURIYA, Sanath Teran (Bloomfield)
Born Matara 30 Jun 1969. 5'6". Educated at St Servatius College. Left-hand batsman, left-arm orthodox slow bowler. First-class debut 1988-89. One of *Wisden*'s Five Cricketers of 1996. **TESTS:** 38 (1990-91 to 1998); 2612 runs (av 45.82), 5 hundreds; 25 wkts (av 45.80); 35 ct. HS 340 v I (Colombo) 1997-98; BB 4-53 v SA (Cape Town) 1997-98. **L-O INTERNATIONALS:** 178 (1989-90 to 1998-99); 4672 runs (av 28.66), 7 hundreds; 152 wkts (av 35.18), 4 wkts (6); 59 ct. HS 151* v I (Bombay) 1996-97; BB 6-29 v E (Moratuwa) 1992-93. Scored fastest LOI fifty (17 balls) v P (Singapore) 1995-96. **F-C CAREER:** 138 matches; 7586 runs (av 41.22), 16 hundreds (inc 3 doubles and a treble); 83 wkts (av 34.92); 95 ct. HS 340 (*see Tests*). BB 4-44. **1998 SEASON (f-c – Sri Lanka):** 382 runs (av 47.75), 1 hundred; 3 wkts (av 48.00).

JAYAWARDENA, Denagamage Proboth Mahela DeSilva (Sinhalese)
Born Colombo 27 May 1977. 5'9". Nalanda College. Right-hand batsman, right-arm medium bowler. First-class debut 1995-96. **TESTS:** 6 (1997-98 to 1998); 398 runs (av 44.22), 1 hundred; 0 wkts; 11 ct. HS 167 v NZ (Galle) 1997-98. **L-O INTERNATIONALS:** 16 (1997-98 to 1998-99); 319 runs (av 22.78), 1 hundred; 1 wkt (av 187.00); 7 ct. HS 120 v E (Adelaide) 1998-99; BB 1-24. **F-C CAREER:** 36 matches; 2076 runs (av 41.52), 6 hundreds (inc 1 double); 23 wkts (av 32.60), 5 wkts/inns (1); 42 ct. HS 200* Sinhalese v Kurunegala Youth (Colombo) 1997-98. BB 5-72. **1998 SEASON (f-c – Sri Lanka):** 266 runs (av 29.55); 0 wkts.

KALPAGE, Ruwan Senani (Bloomfield)
Born Kandy 19 Feb 1970. Left-hand batsman, off-break bowler. First-class debut 1988-89. **TESTS:** 10 (1993-94 to 1997-98); 292 runs (av 18.25); 8 wkts (av 75.87); 9 ct. HS 63 v I (Bangalore) 1993-94; BB 2-27 v WI (Moratuwa) 1993-94. **L-O INTERNATIONALS:** 82 (1991-92 to 1997-98); 810 runs (av 21.31); 71 wkts (av 39.15), 4 wkts (1); 31 ct. HS 51 v I (Hyderabad) 1993-94; BB 4-36 v P (Colombo) 1994-95. **F-C CAREER:** 107 matches; 4318 runs (av 36.28), 11 hundreds; 276 wkts (av 25.15), 5 wkts/inns (9), 10 wkts/match (4); 70 ct. HS 189. BB 7-37.

KALUWITHARANA, Romesh Shantha (Colts)
Born Colombo 24 Nov 1969. 5'4½". Educated at St Sebastian's College. Right-hand batsman, wicket-keeper. First-class debut 1988-89. **TESTS:** 24 (1992-93 to 1998); 1191 runs (av 32.18), 2 hundreds; 47 ct, 11 st. HS 132* v A (SSC, Colombo) 1992-93 – on debut. **L-O INTERNATIONALS:** 112 (1990-91 to 1998-99); 1930 runs (av 18.92), 1 hundred; 74 ct, 49 st. HS 100* v K (Nairobi) 1996-97. **F-C CAREER:** 83 matches; 5184 runs (av 43.93), 12 hundreds, 1000 runs/season (2); 171 ct, 29 st. HS 179. **1998 SEASON (f-c – Sri Lanka):** 152 runs (av 38.00); 11 ct, 2 st.

MURALITHARAN, Muthiah (Tamil Union)
Born Kandy 17 Apr 1972. 5'5". Educated at St Anthony's College, Kandy. Right-hand batsman, off-break bowler. Central Province 1989-90 to date. Tamil Union 1991-92 to date. **TESTS:** 42 (1992-93 to 1998); 458 runs (av 13.87); 203 wkts (av 26.91), 5 wkts/inns (16), 10 wkts/match (2); 23 ct. HS 39 v I (Colombo) 1997-98; BB 9-65 (16-220 match) v E (Oval) 1998. **L-O INTERNATIONALS:** 110 (1993-94 to 1998-99); 151 runs (av 5.80); 151 wkts (av 27.97), 4 wkts (5); 53 ct. HS 18 v E (Lord's) 1998; BB 5-23 v P (Benoni) 1997-98. **F-C CAREER:** 94 matches; 882 runs (av 11.91); 448 wkts (av 21.10), 5 wkts/inns (36), 10 wkts/match (6), 50 wkts/season (2); 57 ct. HS 39 *(see Tests)*. BB 9-65 *(see Tests)*. **1998 SEASON (f-c – Sri Lanka):** 47 runs (av 23.50); 34 wkts (av 13.61), 5 wkts/inns (5), 10 wkts/match (2).

PERERA, Anhettige Suresh Asanka (Sinhalese)
Born Colombo 16 Feb 1978. 5'11". Right-hand batsman, right-arm fast-medium bowler. First-class debut 1997-98. **TESTS:** 1 (1998); 43 runs (av –); 1 wkt (av 126.00); 0 ct. HS 43* and B 1-104 v E (Oval) 1998. **L-O INTERNATIONALS:** 6 (1997-98 to 1998); 17 runs (av 17.00); 8 wkts (av 28.87); 0 ct. HS 17 v E (Lord's) 1998; BB 2-25 v I (Colombo) 1997-98. **F-C CAREER:** 15 matches; 211 runs (av 26.37); 43 wkts (av 24.18); 2 ct. HS 45*. BB 4-15. **1998 SEASON (f-c – Sri Lanka):** 79 runs (av 39.50); 7 wkts (av 49.00).

RANATUNGA, Arjuna (Sinhalese) (CAPTAIN)
Born Colombo 1 Dec 1963. 5'8". Educated at Ananda College. Left-hand batsman, right-arm medium bowler. First-class debut 1981-82. **TESTS:** 82 (1981-82 to 1998, 55 as captain – 12 won, 19 lost, 24 drawn); 4595 runs (av 35.34), 4 hundreds; 16 wkts (av 64.18); 35 ct. HS 135* v P (Colombo) 1985-86; BB 2-17 v NZ (Kandy) 1983-84. **L-O INTERNATIONALS:** 260 (1981-82 to 1998-99, 184 as captain – 86 won, 89 lost, 1 tied, 8 no result); 7248 runs (av 36.42), 4 hundreds; 79 wkts (av 47.55), 4 wkts (1); 61 ct. HS 131* v I (Colombo) 1997-98; BB 4-14 v I (Kanpur) 1986-87. **F-C CAREER:** 180 matches; 10,053 runs (av 42.87), 22 hundreds, inc 4 doubles; 92 wkts (av 33.09), 5 wkts/inns (2); 95 ct. HS 238* Sinhalese v Sebastianites (Colombo) 1992-93. BB 5-45. **1998 SEASON (f-c – Sri Lanka):** 181 runs (av 45.25), 1 hundred; did not bowl.

TILLEKERATNE, Hashan Prasantha (Nondescripts)
Born Colombo 14 Jul 1967. 5'6". Educated at D.S.Senanayake College. Left-hand batsman, right-arm off-break bowler, occasional wicket-keeper. First-class debut 1984-85. **TESTS:** 53 (1989-90 to 1998); 2879 runs (av 38.90), 6 hundreds; 0 wkts; 85 ct. HS 126* v Z (Colombo) 1996-97. **L-O INTERNATIONALS:** 176 (1986-87 to 1998-99); 3303 runs (av 29.23), 2 hundreds; 6 wkts (av 23.50); 76 ct, 5 st. HS 104 v WI (Bombay) 1993-94; BB 1-3. **F-C CAREER:** 154 matches; 7893 runs (av 45.88), 23 hundreds; 21 wkts (av 36.04); 193 ct, 5 st. HS 176*. BB 4-37. **1998 SEASON (f-c – Sri Lanka):** 317 runs (av 39.62), 1 hundred; 0 wkts.

UPASHANTHA, Kalutarage Eric Amila (Colts)
Born Kurunegala 10 Jun 1972. Right-hand batsman, right-arm fast-medium bowler. First-class debut 1990-91. **TESTS:** 0. **L-O INTERNATIONALS:** 3 (1995-96); 11 runs (av 11.00); 3 wkts (av 30.33); 1 ct. HS 8*; BB 2-24 v WI (Sharjah) 1995-96. **F-C CAREER:** 56 matches; 1299 runs (av 21.29); 123 wkts (av 28.04), 5 wkts/inns (1); 44 ct. HS 77. BB 5-108.

VAAS, Warnakulasooriya Patabendige Ushantha Chaminda Joseph (Colts)
Born Colombo 27 Jan 1974. Left-hand batsman, left-arm medium-fast bowler. First-class debut 1990-91. **TESTS:** 26 (1994-95 to 1997-98); 580 runs (av 17.05); 83 wkts (av 29.02), 5 wkts/inns (4), 10 wkts/match (1); 10 ct. HS 57 v NZ (Dunedin) 1996-97; BB 6-87 v NZ (Dunedin) 1994-95. **L-O INTERNATIONALS:** 105 (1993-94 to 1998-99); 506 runs (av 12.97); 132 wkts (av 26.60), 4 wkts (3); 16 ct. HS 33 v P (Colombo) 1994-95; BB 4-20 v Z (Harare) 1994-95. **F-C CAREER:** 56 matches; 829 runs (av 15.94); 207 wkts (av 22.97), 5 wkts/inns (12), 10 wkts/match (1);`18 ct. HS 58*. BB 6-12.

WICKREMASINGHE, Gallage **Pramodya** (Sinhalese)
Born Matara 14 Aug 1971. Right-hand batsman, right-arm fast-medium bowler. First-class debut 1988-89. **TESTS:** 31 (1991-92 to 1998); 481 runs (av 10.68); 60 wkts (av 46.43), 5 wkts/inns (1); 11 ct. HS 51 v SA (Cape Town) 1997-98; BB 5-73 v P (Faisalabad) 1991-92. **L-O INTERNATIONALS:** 107 (1990-91 to 1998-99); 235 runs (av 7.83); 79 wkts (av 42.94); 16 ct. HS 21* v WI (Berri, S Australia) 1991-92; BB 3-20 v SA (Nottingham) 1998. **F-C CAREER:** 93 matches; 1177 runs (av 13.22); 260 wkts (av 28.70), 5 wkts/inns (7), 10 wkts/match (2), 50 wkts/season (1); 40 ct. HS 76*. BB 10-41 Sinhalese v Kalutara (Colombo) 1991-92. **1998 SEASON (f-c – Sri Lanka):** 24 runs (av 8.00); 13 wkts (av 30.53).

ZOYSA, Demuni **Nuwan** Tharanga (Sinhalese)
Born Colombo 13 May 1978. Left-hand batsman, left-arm fast-medium bowler. First-class debut 1996-97. **TESTS:** 4 (1996-97 to 1997-98); 57 runs (av 9.50); 8 wkts (av 38.37); 1 ct HS 16* v NZ (Dunedin) 1996-97 – on debut; BB 3-47 v NZ (Hamilton) 1996-97. **L-O INTERNATIONALS:** 9 (1996-97 to 1998-99); 9 runs (av 4.50); 12 wkts (av 25.91); 0 ct. HS 4; BB 2-22 v E (Melbourne) 1998-99. **F-C CAREER:** 13 matches; 139 runs (av 13.90); 50 wkts (av 21.26), 5 wkts/inns (2); 3 ct. HS 32*. BB 7-58.

WORLD CUP CAREER RECORDS

SRI LANKA – BATTING AND FIELDING

	M	I	NO	HS	Runs	Avge	100	50	Ct/St
S.D.Anurasiri	11	5	2	11	21	7.00	–	–	3
R.G.de Alwis	6	6	3	59*	167	55.66	–	2	5
A.L.F.de Mel	9	7	–	27	66	9.42	–	–	–
D.L.S.de Silva	2	1	–	10	10	10.00	–	–	1
D.S.de Silva	11	10	1	35	148	16.44	–	–	2
G.R.A.de Silva	2	2	1	2*	2	2.00	–	–	–
P.A.de Silva	20	19	3	145	724	45.25	2	3	7
H.D.P.K.Dharmasena	6	1	–	9	9	9.00	–	–	1
R.L.Dias	10	10	1	80	310	34.44	–	3	5
E.R.Fernando	3	3	–	22	47	15.66	–	–	1
F.R.M.D.Goonatilleke	1	–	–	–	–	–	–	–	–
A.P.Gurusinha	18	17	–	87	488	28.70	–	3	6
U.C.Hathurusinghe	4	3	–	16	26	8.66	–	–	1
P.D.Heyn	2	2	–	2	3	1.50	–	–	1
S.A.Jayasinghe	2	1	–	1	1	1.00	–	–	1
S.T.Jayasuriya	12	11	–	82	295	26.81	–	2	9
S.Jeganathan	3	3	1	20*	24	12.00	–	–	1
V.B.John	11	9	7	15	46	23.00	–	–	1
R.S.Kalpage	7	6	2	14	67	16.75	–	–	3
L.W.S.Kaluperuma	3	2	2	13*	19	–	–	–	–
R.S.Kaluwitharana	6	6	–	33	73	12.16	–	–	2/3
D.S.B.P.Kuruppu	11	11	–	72	251	22.81	–	2	4/1
G.F.Labrooy	1	1	–	19	19	19.00	–	–	–
R.S.Madugalle	11	10	–	60	193	19.30	–	1	4
R.S.Mahanama	20	16	3	89	460	35.38	–	5	5
L.R.D.Mendis	16	16	2	64	412	29.42	–	3	2
M.Muralitharan	6	1	1	5*	5	–	–	–	2
A.R.M.Opatha	5	3	–	18	29	9.66	–	–	3
S.P.Pasqual	2	2	1	23*	24	24.00	–	–	–
H.S.M.Pieris	3	3	1	16	19	9.50	–	–	–
K.R.Pushpakumara	2	–	–	–	–	–	–	–	–

	M	I	NO	HS	Runs	Avge	100	50	Ct/St
C.P.H.Ramanayake	8	6	2	12	25	6.25	–	–	4
A.N.Ranasinghe	3	3	1	14*	23	11.50	–	–	–
A.Ranatunga	25	24	8	88*	835	52.18	–	6	6
R.J.Ratnayake	9	8	2	20*	81	13.50	–	–	3
J.R.Ratnayeke	6	5	–	22	52	10.40	–	–	–
M.A.R.Samarasekera	8	8	–	75	224	28.00	–	1	1
A.P.B.Tennekoon	4	4	–	59	137	34.25	–	1	3
H.P.Tillekeratne	14	12	4	70*	208	26.00	–	1	6/1
M.H.Tissera	3	3	–	52	78	26.00	–	1	–
W.P.U.C.J.Vaas	6	1	–	23	23	23.00	–	–	–
B.Warnapura	5	5	–	31	79	15.80	–	–	3
S.Wettimuny	6	6	–	50	128	21.33	–	1	–
S.R.D.Wettimuny	3	3	1	67	136	68.00	–	2	–
G.P.Wickremasinghe	12	4	4	21*	34	–	–	–	2
K.I.W.Wijegunawardene	3	–	–	–	–	–	–	–	–

SRI LANKA – BOWLING

	O	M	R	W	Avge	Best	4w	R/O
S.D.Anurasiri	105	4	455	9	50.55	3-41	–	4.33
A.L.F.de Mel	90.2	13	449	18	24.94	5-32	2	4.97
D.L.S.de Silva	20	2	54	2	27.00	2-36	–	2.70
D.S.de Silva	110	12	463	10	46.30	3-29	–	4.20
G.R.A.de Silva	19	2	85	1	85.00	1-39	–	4.47
P.A.de Silva	60	0	310	7	44.28	3-42	–	5.16
H.D.P.K.Dharmasena	56	1	249	6	41.50	2-30	–	4.44
F.R.M.D.Goonatilleke	9	1	34	0	–	–	–	3.77
A.P.Gurusinha	53	0	307	7	43.85	2-67	–	5.79
U.C.Hathurusinghe	17	0	97	5	19.40	4-57	1	5.70
S.T.Jayasuriya	57	1	275	7	39.28	3-12	–	4.82
S.Jeganathan	29	2	123	4	30.75	2-45	–	4.24
V.B.John	99.2	10	477	4	119.25	1-49	–	4.80
R.S.Kalpage	50	0	241	4	60.25	2-33	–	4.82
L.W.S.Kaluperuma	27.4	2	102	1	102.00	1-50	–	3.68
G.F.Labrooy	10	1	68	1	68.00	1-68	–	6.80
M.Muralitharan	57.1	3	216	7	30.85	2-37	–	3.77
A.R.M.Opatha	42.1	1	180	5	36.00	3-31	–	4.26
S.P.Pasqual	4.4	0	20	0	–	–	–	4.29
H.S.M.Pieris	22	0	135	2	67.50	2-68	–	6.13
K.R.Pushpakumara	15	0	99	1	99.00	1-53	–	6.60
C.P.H.Ramanayake	64.4	6	265	5	53.00	2-37	–	4.09
A.N.Ranasinghe	10	0	65	0	–	–	–	6.50
A.Ranatunga	81.1	2	460	6	76.66	2-26	–	5.66
R.J.Ratnayake	89	6	437	12	36.41	2-18	–	4.91
J.R.Ratnayeke	54	2	313	10	31.30	3-41	–	5.79
M.A.R.Samarasekera	16.2	2	71	0	–	–	–	4.34
H.P.Tillekeratne	1	0	4	0	–	–	–	4.00
W.P.U.C.J.Vaas	49	6	193	6	32.16	2-30	–	3.93
B.Warnapura	36	0	159	4	39.75	3-42	–	4.41
S.Wettimuny	3	0	15	0	–	–	–	5.00
G.P.Wickremasinghe	87.1	5	417	7	59.57	2-29	–	4.78
K.I.W.Wijegunawardene	17	1	88	0	–	–	–	5.17

WORLD CUP REGISTER

ZIMBABWE

Career statistics deadlines: Test Matches to 28 January 1999; Limited-Overs Internationals to 14 February 1999; first-class to end of 1998 English season (20 September). Key to abbreviations are page 19. Zimbabwe's provisionally selected 19 players (to be reduced to 15 by 1 April) are:

BRANDES, Eddo Andre (Mashonaland)
Born Port Shepstone, Natal, South Africa 5 Mar 1963. Right-hand batsman, right-arm fast-medium bowler. First-class debut 1985 (Zimbabwe v Minor Counties at Cleethorpes). **TESTS:** 9 (1992-93 to 1996-97); 111 runs (av 10.09); 22 wkts (av 40.57); 4 ct. HS 39 v NZ (Auckland) 1995-96; BB 3-45 v P (Lahore) 1993-94. **L-O INTERNATIONALS:** 54 (1987-88 to 1998-99); 330 runs (av 11.37); 67 wkts (av 31.19), 4 wkts (3); 10 ct. HS 55 v SL (Sharjah) 1992-93; BB 5-28 (inc hat-trick) v E (Harare) 1996-97. **F-C CAREER:** 53 matches; 1058 runs (av 16.79), 1 hundred; 152 wkts (av 31.15), 5 wkts/inns (7), 10 wkts/match (1); 25 ct. HS 165*. BB 7-38.

BRENT, Gary Benzil (Mashonaland)
Born Sinoia 13 Jan 1976. Right-hand batsman, right-arm medium-fast bowler. First-class debut 1994-95. **TESTS:** 0. **L-O INTERNATIONALS:** 3 (1996-97 to 1998-99); 25 runs (av 8.33); 1 wkt (av 108.00); 0 ct. HS 24 v I (Cuttack) 1997-98; BB 1-53. **F-C CAREER:** 12 matches; 202 runs (av 20.20); 21 wkts (av 37.00); 6 ct. HS 40. BB 4-22.

CAMPBELL, Alistair Douglas Ross (CAPTAIN)
Born Salisbury 23 Sep 1972. Elder brother of D.J.R.Campbell (Mashonaland 1992-93 to date). 6'1". Educated at Eaglesvale High School. Left-hand batsman, right-arm leg-break bowler. First-class debut 1990-91. **TESTS:** 33 (1992-93 to 1998-99); 1589 runs (av 27.87); 0 wkts; 33 ct. HS 99 v SL (Harare) 1994-95. **L-O INTERNATIONALS:** 92 (1991-92 to 1998-99, 55 as captain – 19 won, 34 lost, 2 tied); 2293 runs (av 28.66), 3 hundreds; 4 wkts (av 44.75); 35 ct. HS 131* v SL (Harare) 1994-95; BB 2-22 v SA (Harare) 1995-96. **F-C CAREER:** 75 matches; 3850 runs (av 32.62), 4 hundreds; 19 wkts (av 41.73); 76 ct. HS 196. BB 4-82.

CARLISLE, Stuart Vance (Mashonaland)
Born Salisbury 10 May 1972. Son of A.M.Carlisle (Transvaal B 1966-67). Right-hand batsman, right-arm medium bowler. First-class debut 1993-94. **TESTS:** 6 (1994-95 to 1996-97); 175 runs (av 19.44); 10 ct. HS 58 v NZ (Auckland) 1995-96. **L-O INTERNATIONALS:** 8 (1994-95 to 1996-97); 79 runs (av 11.28); 4 ct. HS 28 v NZ (Wellington) 1995-96. **F-C CAREER:** 25 matches; 1459 runs (av 36.47), 3 hundreds; 0 wkts; 23 ct. HS 147.

FLOWER, Andrew (Mashonaland)
Born Cape Town, South Africa 28 Apr 1968. Elder brother of G.W.Flower. 5'10". Educated at Jainona High School. Left-hand batsman, occasional right-arm medium/off-break bowler, wicket-keeper. First-class debut 1986-87. **TESTS:** 33 (1992-93 to 1998-99, 11 as captain – 1 won, 5 lost, 6 drawn); 2090 runs (av 43.54), 5 hundreds; 0 wkts; 80 ct, 5 st. HS 156 v P (Harare) 1994-95 sharing with Grant Flower a fourth-wicket partnership of 269, the highest stand between brothers in Test cricket. **L-O INTERNATIONALS:** 100 (1991-92 to 1998-99, 28 as captain – 5 won, 19 lost, 2 tied, 2 no result); 2942 runs (av 31.97), 1 hundred; 0 wkts; 72 ct, 20 st. HS 115* v SL (New Plymouth) 1991-92 – on debut. **F-C CAREER:** 76 matches; 4959 runs (av 48.14), 15 hundreds (inc 1 double); 4 wkts (av 40.75); 144 ct, 14 st. HS 201 Mashonaland v Mashonaland A (Harare) 1997-98. BB 1-1.

FLOWER, Grant William (Mashonaland)
Born Salisbury 20 Dec 1970. Younger brother of A.Flower. 5'10". Educated at St George's College. Right-hand batsman, left-arm orthodox slow bowler. First-class debut 1989-90. **TESTS:** 32 (1992-93 to 1998-99); 2061 runs (av 37.47), 5 hundreds; 3 wkts (av 118.00); 15 ct. HS 201* v P (Harare) 1994-95 sharing with Andrew Flower a fourth-wicket partnership of 269, the highest stand between brothers in Test cricket. BB 1-4. **L-O INTERNATIONALS:** 87 (1992-93 to 1998-99); 2867 runs (av 35.39), 2 hundreds; 34 wkts (av 35.91); 35 ct. HS 84* v 112 v SL (Colombo) 1997-98; BB 3-15 v A (Perth) 1994-95. **F-C CAREER:** 79 matches; 5616 runs (av 45.53), 11 hundreds (inc 2 doubles); 55 wkts (av 38.20), 5 wkts/inns (1); 70 ct. HS 243* Mashonaland v Matebeleland (Harare) 1996-97. BB 5-37.

GOODWIN, Murray William (Mashonaland)
Born Salisbury 11 Dec 1972. Right-hand batsman, right-arm leg-break bowler. Western Australia 1994-95 to 1996-97 scoring 926 runs (av 44.09 with 1 hundred) in 14 f-c matches. Emigrated to Australia when 13. Gained Zimbabwean citizenship in Sep 1997. Mashonaland debut 1997-98. **TESTS:** 9 (1997-98 to 1998-99); 404 runs (av 53.60), 1 hundred; 0 wkts; 6 ct. HS 166* v P (Bulawayo) 1997-98. **L-O INTERNATIONALS:** 26 (1997-98 to 1998-99); 722 runs (av 27.76), 1 hundred; 3 wkts (av 57.66); 7 ct. HS 111 v SL (Colombo) 1997-98; BB 1-12. **F-C CAREER:** 24 matches; 1844 runs (av 48.52), 2 hundreds; 4 wkts (av 41.50); 23 ct. HS 166* (*see Tests*). BB 2-34.

HUCKLE, Adam George (Matabeleland)
Born Bulawayo 21 Sep 1971. Son of M.R.Huckle (Rhodesia 1966-67). Right-hand batsman, right-arm leg-break bowler. Zimbabwe debut 1990-91. Eastern Province 1992-93 to 1995-96. **TESTS:** 8 (1997-98 to 1998-99); 74 runs (av 6.72); 25 wkts (av 34.88), 5 wkts/inns (2), 10 wkts/match (1); ct. HS 28* v I (Harare) 1998-99; BB 6-109 (11-255 match) v NZ (Bulawayo) 1997-98. **L-O INTERNATIONALS:** 13 (1997-98 to 1998-99); 9 runs (av 4.50); 3 wkts (av 158.66); 3 ct. HS 5*; BB 2-27 v B (Nairobi) 1997-98. **F-C CAREER:** 41 matches; 187 runs (av 5.50); 104 wkts (av 40.02), 5 wkts/inns (4), 10 wkts/match (2); 12 ct. HS 28* (*see Tests*). BB 6-59.

JOHNSON, Neil Clarkson (Matabeleland)
Born Salisbury 24 Jan 1970. 6'2". Educated in South Africa at Howick High School, Natal and Port Elizabeth U. Left-hand batsman, right-arm fast-medium bowler. Eastern Province B 1989-90 to 1991-92. Natal 1992-93 to 1997-98. Leicestershire 1997; cap 1997. Zimbabwe debut 1998-99. **TESTS:** 3 (1998-99); 126 runs (av 31.50), 1 hundred; 7 wkts (av 37.85); 4 ct. HS 107 v P (Peshawar) 1998-99; BB 3-41 v I (Harare) 1998-99 – on debut. **L-O INTERNATIONALS:** 9 (1998-99); 351 runs (av 39.00), 1 hundred; 5 wkts (av 74.40); 5 ct. HS 103 and BB 2-51 v P (Sheikhupura) 1998-99. **F-C CAREER:** 74 matches; 3198 runs (av 33.66), 5 hundreds; 126 wkts (av 29.97), 5 wkts/inns (2); 85 ct. HS 150 Leics v Lancs (Leicester) 1997. BB 5-79 Natal v Boland (Stellenbosch) 1993-94. **COUNTY L-O:** HS 79* Leics v Middx (Lord's) 1997 (ASL). BB 3-37 Leics v Notts (Leicester) 1997 (ASL).

MATAMBANADZO, Everton Zvikomborero (Mashonaland)
Born Salisbury 13 Apr 1976. Right-hand batsman, right-arm fast-medium bowler. First-class debut 1993-94. **TESTS:** 2 (1996-97 to 1997-98); 11 runs (av 5.50); 2 wkts (av 77.50); 0 ct. HS 7 and BB 2-62 v P (Faisalabad) 1996-97 – on debut. **L-O INTERNATIONALS:** 7 (1996-97 to 1997-98); 8 runs (av 4.00); 11 wkts (av 19.72), 4 wkts (1); 1 ct. HS 5*; BB 4-32 v P (Lahore) 1996-97 – on debut. **F-C CAREER:** 15 matches; 79 runs (av 8.11); 32 wkts (av 34.40); 7 ct. HS 32*. BB 3-20.

MBANGWA, Mpumelelo (Matebeleland)
Born Plumtree 26 Jun 1976. Right-hand batsman, right-arm fast-medium bowler. First-class debut 1995-96. **TESTS:** 9 (1996-97 to 1998-99); 16 runs (av 1.33); 24 wkts (av 24.58); 2 ct. HS 4; BB 3-23 v P (Peshawar) 1998-99. **L-O INTERNATIONALS:** 13

(1996-97 to 1998-99); 24 runs (av 4.80); 7 wkts (av 78.00); 2ct. HS 11 v P (Lahore) 1996-97; BB 2-24 v K (Nairobi) 1997-98. **F-C CAREER:** 25 matches; 81 runs (av 3.52); 46 wkts (av 33.63); 8 ct. HS 14*. BB 4-49.

OLONGA, Henry Khaaba (Matebeleland)
Born Lusaka, Zambia 3 Jul 1976. Right-hand batsman, right-arm fast-medium bowler. First-class debut 1993-94. **TESTS:** 10 (1994-95 to 1998-99); 30 runs (av 2.50); 25 wkts (av 29.96), 5 wkts/inns (1); 7 ct. HS 7; BB 5-70 v I (Harare) 1998-99. **L-O INTERNA-TIONALS:** 6 (1995-96 to 1998-99); 8 runs (av 8.00); 7 wkts (av 41.00), 4 wkts (1); 1 ct. HS 6; BB 4-46 v I (Sharjah) 1998-99. **F-C CAREER:** 27 matches; 273 runs (av 9.10); 66 wkts (av 33.07), 5 wkts/inns (1); 18 ct. HS 41. BB 5-80.

RENNIE, Gavin James (Mashonaland)
Born Fort Victoria 12 Jan 1976. Younger brother of J.A.Rennie (Mashonaland, Matabeleland and Zimbabwe 1992-93 to date). Left-hand batsman, left-arm orthodox slow bowler. First-class debut 1993-94. **TESTS:** 10 (1997-98 to 1998-99); 499 runs (av 26.26); 8 ct. HS 84 v I (Harare) 1998-99. **L-O INTERNATIONALS:** 16 (1996-97 to 1998-99); 332 runs (av 25.53); 9 ct. HS 76 v K (Nairobi) 1997-98. **F-C CAREER:** 36 matches; 1335 runs (av 21.88), 1 hundred; 21 wkts (av 40.14); 21 ct. HS 101. BB 3-15.

STRANG, Paul Andrew (Mashonaland)
Born Bulawayo 28 Jul 1970. Elder brother of B.C.Strang (Mashonaland and Zimbabwe 1994-95 to date). Educated at Falcon College; Cape Town U. Right-hand batsman, right-arm leg-break bowler. Debut (Zimbabwe B) 1992-93. Mashonaland Country Dists 1993-94 to 1995-96. Mashonaland 1996-97. Kent 1997; cap 1997. Nottinghamshire 1998. **TESTS:** 20 (1994-95 to 1997-98); 747 runs (av 27.66), 1 hundred; 57 wkts (av 37.78), 5 wkts/inns (3); 12 ct. HS 106* v P (Sheikhupura) 1996-97; BB 5-106 v SL (Colombo) 1996-97. **L-O INTERNATIONALS:** 69 (1994-95 to 1998-99); 955 runs (av 25.13); 72 wkts (av 31.16), 4 wkts (3); 20 ct. HS 47 v I (Paarl) 1996-97; BB 5-21 v K (Patna) 1995-96. **F-C CAREER:** 82 matches; 2685 runs (av 27.12), 2 hundreds; 262 wkts (av 31.83), 5 wkts/inns (16), 10 wkts/match (2), 50 wkts (1); 75 ct. HS 106* (*see Tests*). BB 7-75 Mashonaland CD v Mashonaland U-24 (Harare South) 1994-95. **1998 SEASON (f-c):** 300 runs (av 20.00); 30 wkts (av 32.76), 5 wkts/inns (1). **COUNTY L-O:** HS 40 Kent v Warwks (Tunbridge Wells) 1997 (ASL) and 40 v Somerset (Nottingham) 1998 (NWT). BB 6-32 v Warwks (Birmingham) 1998 (ASL).

STREAK, Heath Hilton (Matebeleland)
Born Bulawayo 16 Mar 1974. Son of D.H.Streak (Rhodesia 1976-77 to 1978-79). 6'1". Educated at Falcon College. Right-hand batsman, right-arm fast-medium bowler. Debut for Zimbabwe B v Kent (Harare) 1992-93. Matabeleland 1993-94 to date. Hampshire 1995. **TESTS:** 26 (1993-94 to 1998-99); 533 runs (av 15.67); 106 wkts (av 24.83), 5 wkts/inns (3); 7 ct. HS 53 v SA (Harare) 1995-96 and 53 v P (Bulawayo) 1997-98; BB 6-90 v P (Harare) 1994-95. **L-O INTERNATIONALS:** 69 (1993-94 to 1998-99); 755 runs (av 19.86); 85 wkts (av 31.36), 4 wkts (4); 15 ct. HS 59 v I (Sharjah) 1998-99; BB 5-32 v I (Bulawayo) 1996-97. **F-C CAREER:** 71 matches; 2058 runs (av 23.93), 2 hundreds; 208 wkts (av 27.85), 5 wkts/inns (4), 50 wkts/season (1); 28 ct. HS 131. BB 7-69. **COUNTY L-O:** HS 32* Hants v Yorks (Southampton) 1995 (ASL). BB 4-56 Hants v Worcs (Southampton) 1995 (ASL).

VILJOEN, Dirk Peter (Mashonaland)
Born Salisbury 11 Mar 1977. Left-hand batsman, left-arm orthodox slow bowler. First-class debut 1994-95. **TESTS:** 1 (1997-98); 0 runs (av 0.00); 1 wkt (av 14.00); 1 ct. HS 0 ('pair') and BB 1-14 v P (Bulawayo) 1997-98. **L-O INTERNATIONALS:** 9 (1996-97 to 1997-98); 125 runs (av 15.62); 4 wkts (av 33.50); 1 ct. HS 36 v NZ (Wellington) 1997-98; BB 2-31 v NZ (Christchurch) 1997-98. **F-C CAREER:** 12 matches; 290 runs (av 14.50); 4 wkts (av 35.50); 6 ct. HS 47. BB 3-93.

WHITTALL, Andrew Richard (Matebeleland)
Born Mutare 28 Mar 1973. Cousin of G.J.Whittall. 6'3". Educated at Falcon College; Trinity College, Cambridge U. Right-hand batsman, right-arm off-break bowler. Cambridge U 1993-96; blue 1993-94-95-96; captain 1994-95. **TESTS:** 9 (1996-97 to 1998-99); 106 runs (av 7.57); 6 wkts (av 105.16); 8 ct. HS 17 v P (Bulawayo) 1997-98; BB 3-73 v SL (Kandy) 1997-98. **L-O INTERNATIONALS:** 40 (1996-97 to 1998-99); 135 runs (av 10.38); 32 wkts (av 44.68); 12 ct. HS 31 v I (Sharjah) 1998-99; BB 3-23 v K (Nairobi) 1997-98. **F-C CAREER:** 52 matches; 825 runs (av 14.47); 99 wkts (av 56.31), 5 wkts/inns (3), 10 wkts/match (1); 30 ct. HS 91* Cambridge U v Oxford U (Lord's) 1994. BB 6-46 (11-113 match) v Essex (Cambridge) 1995. **COUNTY L-O:** HS 21 and BB 2-49 Combined U v Glos (Bristol) 1995 (BHC).

WHITTALL, Guy James (Matebeleland)
Born Chipinga 5 Sep 1972. Cousin of A.R.Whittall. 5'8". Educated at Falcon College. Right-hand batsman, right-arm medium bowler. First-class debut 1990-91. **TESTS:** 25 (1993-94 to 1997-98); 1072 runs (av 26.80), 2 hundreds; 36 wkts (av 36.50); 12 ct. HS 203* v NZ (Bulawayo) 1996-97; BB 4-18 v E (Harare) 1996-97. **L-O INTERNATIONALS:** 68 (1993-94 to 1997-98); 1360 runs (av 22.66); 49 wkts (av 37.93); 18 ct. HS 83 v K (Nairobi) 1997-98; BB 3-43 v K (Nairobi) 1997-98. **F-C CAREER:** 64 matches; 2940 runs (av 28.00), 7 hundreds (inc 1 double); 101 wkts (av 34.15), 5 wkts/inns (2); 41 ct. HS 203* (*see Tests*). BB 6-34.

WISHART, Craig Brian (Mashonaland)
Born Salisbury 9 Jan 1974. Right-hand batsman, right-arm medium bowler. First-class debut 1992-93. **TESTS:** 11 (1995-96 to 1998-99); 292 runs (av 15.36); 5 ct. HS 63 v I (Harare) 1998-99. **L-O INTERNATIONALS:** 39 (1996-97 to 1998-99); 644 runs (av 20.12), 1 hundred; 0 wkts; 13 ct. HS 102 v I (Harare) 1998-99. **F-C CAREER:** 51 matches; 2057 runs (av 25.08), 2 hundreds; 24 wkts (av 30.58), 5 wkts/inns (1); 37 ct. HS 144. BB 5-24.

WORLD CUP CAREER RECORDS

ZIMBABWE – BATTING AND FIELDING

	M	I	NO	HS	Runs	Avge	100	50	Ct/St
K.J.Arnott	9	8	1	60	206	29.42	–	3	2
E.A.Brandes	14	10	3	23	99	14.14	–	–	4
R.D.Brown	7	7	–	38	110	15.71	–	–	5
M.G.Burmester	4	3	1	12	17	8.50	–	–	1
I.P.Butchart	17	14	2	54	240	20.00	–	1	4
A.D.R.Campbell	10	9	–	75	127	14.11	–	1	6
K.M.Curran	11	11	–	73	287	26.09	–	2	1
S.G.Davies	1	1	–	9	9	9.00	–	–	–
K.G.Duers	6	2	1	5	7	7.00	–	–	2
C.N.Evans	6	5	2	39*	92	30.66	–	–	–
D.A.G.Fletcher	6	6	2	71*	191	47.75	–	2	–
A.Flower	14	14	3	115*	295	26.81	1	–	6/2
G.W.Flower	6	6	1	45	150	30.00	–	3	3
J.G.Heron	6	6	–	18	50	8.33	–	–	1
V.R.Hogg	2	1	1	7*	7	–	–	–	–
D.L.Houghton	20	19	–	142	567	29.84	1	4	14/2
W.R.James	4	3	–	17	35	11.66	–	–	1
M.P.Jarvis	10	5	3	17	37	18.50	–	–	1
A.C.I.Lock	6	3	2	5	8	8.00	–	–	–
M.A.Meman	1	1	–	19	19	19.00	–	–	–

	M	I	NO	HS	Runs	Avge	100	50	Ct/St
G.A.Paterson	10	10	–	27	123	12.30	–	–	2
S.G.Peall	5	2	–	9	9	4.50	–	–	1
G.E.Peckover	3	3	1	16*	33	16.50	–	–	–
A.J.Pycroft	20	19	2	61	295	17.35	–	2	6
P.W.E.Rawson	10	8	3	24*	80	16.00	–	–	4
A.H.Shah	16	16	1	60*	266	17.73	–	1	3
B.C.Strang	4	2	–	3	3	1.50	–	–	2
P.A.Strang	6	4	3	22*	52	52.00	–	–	1
H.H.Streak	6	5	1	30	80	20.00	–	–	1
A.J.Traicos	20	12	5	19	70	10.00	–	–	2
A.C.Waller	20	20	3	83*	479	28.17	–	2	3
G.J.Whittall	6	6	–	35	83	13.83	–	–	–

ZIMBABWE – BOWLING

	O	M	R	W	Avge	Best	4w	R/O
E.A.Brandes	118.1	11	586	16	36.62	4-21	1	4.95
M.G.Burmester	21.5	0	138	4	34.50	3-36	–	6.32
I.P.Butchart	117	6	640	12	53.33	3-57	–	5.47
A.D.R.Campbell	3	0	13	0	–	–	–	4.33
K.M.Curran	84.2	3	398	9	44.22	3-65	–	4.71
K.G.Duers	50	2	256	5	85.33	1-17	–	5.12
D.A.G.Fletcher	50.1	5	221	7	31.57	4-42	1	4.40
G.W.Flower	11	2	54	0	–	–	–	4.90
V.R.Hogg	15	4	49	0	–	–	–	3.26
D.L.Houghton	2	0	19	1	19.00	1-19	–	9.50
M.P.Jarvis	83.1	5	384	7	54.85	1-21	–	4.61
A.C.I.Lock	32	3	141	3	47.00	2-57	–	4.40
M.A.Meman	6.5	0	34	0	–	–	–	4.97
S.G.Peall	23	1	101	1	101.00	1-23	–	4.39
P.W.E.Rawson	95.1	10	427	12	35.58	3-47	–	4.48
A.H.Shah	104.3	9	456	11	41.45	2-17	–	4.36
B.C.Strang	18	1	66	3	22.00	2-24	–	3.66
P.A.Strang	42.1	4	192	12	16.00	5-21	2	4.55
H.H.Streak	44	9	175	4	43.75	3-60	–	3.97
A.J.Traicos	188	13	673	16	42.06	3-35	–	3.57
G.J.Whittall	14	0	79	0	–	–	–	5.64

WORLD CUP REGISTER

BANGLADESH

Career statistics in Limited-Overs Internationals are up to 14 February 1999. Key to abbreviations on page 19. Bangladesh's selected 15 players, plus reserves, are:

AKRAM KHAN (Abahani)
(Mohammad Akram Khan)
Born Chittagong 1 Feb 1967. Right-hand batsman, occasional right-arm medium bowler.
L-O INTERNATIONALS: 21 (1988-89 to 1997-98, 15 as captain – 1 won, 14 lost); 453 runs (av 22.65); 0 wkts; 6 ct. HS 59 v Z (Nairobi) 1997-98.

AMINUL ISLAM (Biman) (CAPTAIN)
(Mohammad Aminul Islam Bulbul)
Born Dhaka 2 Feb 1968. Right-hand batsman, right-arm off-break bowler. **L-O INTERNATIONALS:** 21 (1988-89 to 1997-98, 1 as captain – 1 lost); 497 runs (av 31.06); 3 wkts (av 73.00); 7 ct. HS 70 v I (Chandigarh) 1997-98; BB 3-57 v Z (Nairobi) 1997-98.

ENAMUL HUQ (Surjotorun)
(Enamul Huq Moni)
Born Comilla 27 Feb 1966. Left-hand batsman, left-arm orthodox slow bowler. **L-O INTERNATIONALS:** 12 (1989-90 to 1997-98); 71 (av 7.88); 5 wkts (av 73.00); 3 ct. HS 18 v A (Sharjah) 1989-90; BB 2-46 v K (Hyderabad) 1997-98.

FARUQUE AHMED (Biman)
Born Dhaka 3 Mar 1966. Right-hand batsman, occasional right-arm off-break bowler.
L-O INTERNATIONALS: 5 (1988-89 to 1990-91); 89 runs (av 17.80); 1 ct. HS 57 v I (Chandigarh) 1990-91.

HASIBUL HUSSAIN (Abahani)
(Mohammad Hasibul Hussain Shanto)
Born Dhaka 3 Jun 1977. Right-hand batsman, right-arm medium-fast bowler. **L-O INTERNATIONALS:** 15 (1994-95 to 1997-98); 96 runs (av 8.72); 13 wkts (av 48.92); 3 ct. HS 21* v K (Nairobi) 1997-98; BB 2-44 v K (Madras) 1997-98.

JAHANGIR ALAM (Brothers Union)
Born Narayangonj 5 Mar 1974. Right-hand batsman, wicket-keeper. **L-O INTERNATIONALS:** 2 (1997-98); 4 runs (av 2.00); 0 ct. HS 3.

KHALED MAHMUD (Brothers Union)
(Khaled Mahmud Sujan)
Born Dhaka 21 Jul 1971. Right-hand batsman, right-arm medium bowler. **L-O INTERNATIONALS:** 6 (1997-98); 132 runs (av 26.40); 7 wkts (av 23.14); 0 ct. HS 47 v I (Dhaka) 1997-98 – on debut; BB 2-12 v I (Bombay) 1997-98.

KHALED MASUD (Surjotorun)
(Mohammad Khaled Masud Pilot)
Born Rajshahi 8 Feb 1976. Right-hand batsman, wicket-keeper. **L-O INTERNATIONALS:** 16 (1994-95 to 1997-98); 117 runs (av 10.63); 13 ct, 2 st. HS 27* v P (Sharjah) 1994-95.

MEHRAB HOSSAIN (Abahani)
(Mehrab Hossain Opee)
Born Dhaka 22 Sep 1979. Right-hand batsman. **L-O INTERNATIONALS:** 1 (1997-98); 6 runs (av 6.00); 0 ct. HS 6 v I (Chandigarh) 1997-98.

MOHAMMED RAFIQUE (Mohammedan)
Born Dhaka 5 Oct 1971. Right-hand batsman, left-arm orthodox slow bowler. **L-O INTERNATIONALS:** 12 (1994-95 to 1997-98); 194 runs (av 16.16); 15 wkts (av 32.00); 1 ct. HS 77 and BB 3-55 v K (Hyderabad) 1997-98.

MONJURUL ISLAM (Mohammedan)
Born Khulna 7 Nov 1979. Left-hand batsman, left-arm medium-fast bowler. **L-O INTERNATIONALS:** 0.

NAIMUR RAHMAN (Abahani)
(Naimur Rahman Durjoy)
Born Dhaka 19 Sep 1974. Right-hand batsman, right-arm off-break bowler. **L-O INTERNATIONALS:** 8 (1994-95 to 1997-98); 135 runs (av 19.28); 2 wkts (av 104.50); 4 ct. HS 47 v SL (Colombo) 1997-98; BB 1-29.

NEEYAMUR RASHID (Abahani)
Born Pabna 1 Jan 1975. Right-hand batsman, right-arm medium-fast bowler. **L-O INTERNATIONALS:** 0.

SHAFIUDDIN AHMED (Brothers Union)
(Shafiuddin Ahmed Babu)
Born Dhaka 1 Jun 1973. Right-hand batsman, right-arm medium-fast bowler. **L-O INTERNATIONALS:** 5 (1997-98); 27 runs (av 13.50); 6 wkts (av 32.00); 0 ct. HS 11 and BB 3-42 v Z (Nairobi) 1997-98

SHAHRIAR HOSSAIN (Brothers Union)
(Mohammad Shariar Hossain Bidyut)
Born Narayangonj 1 Jun 1976. Right-hand batsman. **L-O INTERNATIONALS:** 5 (1997-98); 41 runs (av 8.20); 2 ct. HS 16 v K (Nairobi) 1997-98.

RESERVES

AL SHARIAR (Surjotorun)
(Al Shariar Rokon)
Born Dhaka 23 Apr 1978. Right-hand batsman, right-arm leg-break bowler. **L-O INTERNATIONALS:** 0.

AMINUL ISLAM BHOLA (Ajax)
(Also known as Aminul Islam jr)
Born Rajshahi 1 Apr 1975. Right-hand batsman, right-arm medium-fast bowler. **L-O INTERNATIONALS:** 0.

JAVED OMER (Biman)
(Mohammad Javed Omer Belim Golla)
Born Dhaka 25 Nov 1976. Right-hand batsman. **L-O INTERNATIONALS:** 4 (1994-95 to 1997-98); 48 runs (av 12.00); 0 ct. HS 18 v I (Sharjah) 1994-95 – on debut.

MAHBUBUR RAHMAN (Kalabagan)
Born Mymensingh 1 Feb 1969. Right-hand batsman. **L-O INTERNATIONALS:** 0.

WORLD CUP REGISTER

KENYA

Career statistics in Limited-Overs Internationals are up to 14 February 1999. Key to abbreviations on page 19. Kenya's selected 15 players, plus reserves, are:

ANGARA, Joseph Oduol (Swamibapa)
Born Nairobi 8 Nov 1971. Right-hand batsman, right-arm medium-fast bowler. **L-O INTERNATIONALS:** 3 (1997-98); 6 runs (av 6.00); 2 wkts (45.00); 0 ct. HS 3*; BB 1-19.

ASIF KARIM (Jaffery) (CAPTAIN)
Born Mombasa 15 Dec 1963. Right-hand batsman, left-arm orthodox slow bowler. **L-O INTERNATIONALS:** 20 (1995-96 to 1997-98, 11 as captain – 4 won, 7 lost); 135 runs (av 11.25); 17 wkts (av 38.52), 4 wkts (1); 2 ct. HS 53 v Z (Nairobi) 1997-98; BB 5-33 v B (Nairobi) 1997-98.

CHUDASAMA, Dipak (Nairobi Gymkhana)
Born Mombasa 20 May 1963. Right-hand batsman. **L-O INTERNATIONALS:** 18 (1995-96 to 1997-98); 432 runs (av 25.41), 1 hundred; 2 ct. HS 122 v B (Nairobi) 1997-98.

GUPTA, Sandip Kumar (Nairobi Gymkhana)
Born Nairobi 7 Apr 1967. Right-hand batsman. **L-O INTERNATIONALS:** 3 (1996-97); 43 runs (av 14.33); 0 ct. HS 41 v SL (Nairobi) 1996-97 – on debut.

KAMANDE, James (Nairobi Gymkhana)
Born Muranga 12 Dec 1978. Right-hand batsman, right-arm fast-medium bowler. **L-O INTERNATIONALS:** 0.

MODI, Hitesh Subashchandra (Nairobi Gymkhana)
Born Kisumu 13 Oct 1971. Left-hand batsman, right-arm off-break bowler. **L-O INTERNATIONALS:** 20 (1995-96 to 1997-98); 453 runs (av 28.31); 0 wkts; 5 ct. HS 78* v SL (Nairobi) 1996-97.

ODOYO, Thomas (Nairobi Gymkhana)
Born Nairobi 12 May 1978. Right-hand batsman, right-arm fast-medium bowler. **L-O INTERNATIONALS:** 19 (1995-96 to 1997-98); 217 runs (av 14.46); 11 wkts (av 53.09); 5 ct. HS 41 v Z (Nairobi) 1997-98; BB 3-25 v P (Nairobi) 1996-97.

ODUMBE, Maurice Omondi (Aga Khan)
Born Nairobi 15 Jun 1969. Right-hand batsman, right-arm off-break bowler. **L-O INTERNATIONALS:** 20 (1995-96 to 1997-98, 9 as captain – 1 won, 7 lost, 1 no result); 446 runs (av 26.23); 17 wkts (av 34.64); 2 ct. HS 83 and 3-14 v I (Gwalior) 1997-98.

OTIENO, Kennedy (Aga Khan)
(Kennedy Otieno Obuya)
Born Nairobi 11 Mar 1972. Right-hand batsman, wicket-keeper. **L-O INTERNATIONALS:** 20 (1995-96 to 1997-98); 592 runs (av 32.88), 1 hundred; 7 ct, 4 st. HS 144 v B (Nairobi) 1997-98.

SHAH, Ravindu (Nairobi Gymkhana)
Born Nairobi 28 Aug 1972. Right-hand batsman, right-arm medium-fast bowler. **L-O INTERNATIONALS:** 5 (1997-98); 213 runs (av 42.60); 0 wkts; 3 ct. HS 70 v I (Gwalior) 1997-98.

SHEIKH, Mohammed (Nairobi Gymkhana)
Born Nairobi 29 Aug 1980. Left-hand batsman, left-arm orthodox slow bowler. **L-O INTERNATIONALS:** 11 (1997-98); 19 runs (av 6.33); 10 wkts (av 33.70); 5 ct. HS 6*; BB 2-41 v I (Bangalore) 1997-98.

SUJI, Anthony (Aga Khan)
(Anthony Suji Ondik)
Born Nairobi 5 Feb 1976. Right-hand batsman, right-arm medium bowler. **L-O INTERNATIONALS:** 8 (1996-97 to 1997-98); 115 runs (av 19.16); 3 wkts (av 51.33); 1 ct. HS 67 v Z (Nairobi) 1996-97; BB 1-16.

SUJI, Martin (Aga Khan)
Born Nairobi 2 Jun 1971. Right-hand batsman, right-arm fast-medium bowler. **L-O INTERNATIONALS:** 19 (1995-96 to 1997-98); 46 runs (av 11.50); 14 wkts (av 45.92), 4 wkts (1); 5 ct. HS 15 v Z (Patna) 1995-96; BB 4-24 v B (Nairobi) 1997-98.

TIKOLO, Stephen Ogonji (Swamibapa)
Born Nairobi 25 Jun 1971. Right-hand batsman, right-arm off-break bowler. Border 1995-96. **L-O INTERNATIONALS:** 20 (1995-96 to 1997-98); 501 runs (av 26.36); 13 wkts (av 34.15); 11 ct. HS 96 v SL (Kandy) 1995-96; BB 3-29 v I (Gwalior) 1997-98.
F-C CAREER: 6 matches; 240 runs (av 24.00); 2 ct. HS 64 Border v N Transvaal (East London) 1995-96.

VADHER, Alpesh (Premier)
Born Nairobi 7 Sep 1974. Right-hand batsman. **L-O INTERNATIONALS:** 8 (1997-98); 93 runs (av 31.00); 4 ct. HS 42* v B (Nairobi) 1997-98.

RESERVES

ONGONDO, Peter Jimmy (Swamibapa)
Born Nairobi 10 Feb 1997. Right-hand batsman, right-arm medium-fast bowler.

ONYANGO, Lameck (Swamibapa)
(Lameck Onyango Ngoche)
Born Nairobi 22 Sep 1973. Right-hand batsman, right-arm fast-medium bowler. **L-O INTERNATIONALS:** 3 (1995-96 to 1997-98); 29 runs (av 9.66); 1 wkt (av 96.00); 1 ct. HS 23 v SL (Kandy) 1995-96 – on debut; BB 1-45.

OTIENO, Francis (Ruaraka)
Born Nairobi 25 Aug 1979. Right-hand batsman, right-arm slow-medium bowler. **L-O INTERNATIONALS:** 0.

PATEL, Bhijal (Premier)
Born Nairobi 14 Nov 1977. Right-hand batsman, left-arm orthodox slow bowler. **L-O INTERNATIONALS:** 0.

WORLD CUP CAREER RECORDS

KENYA – BATTING AND FIELDING

	M	I	NO	HS	Runs	Avge	100	50	Ct/St
R.Ali	6	2	2	6*	6	–	–	–	1
Asif Karim	6	3	1	11	17	8.50	–	–	–
D.Chudasama	6	5	–	34	103	20.60	–	–	1
H.S.Modi	6	5	–	41	84	16.80	–	–	3
T.Odoyo	5	4	–	24	42	10.50	–	–	–
E.T.Odumbe	6	5	1	20	54	13.50	–	–	3
M.O.Odumbe	6	5	–	50	112	22.40	–	1	1
L.Onyango	1	1	–	23	23	23.00	–	–	1
K.Otieno	6	5	–	85	147	29.40	–	1	1
M.Suji	6	4	2	15	18	9.00	–	–	3
Tariq Iqbal	3	2	–	16	17	8.50	–	–	2
D.L.Tikolo	3	2	2	25*	36	–	–	–	2
S.O.Tikolo	6	5	–	96	196	39.20	–	2	3

KENYA – BOWLING

	O	M	R	W	Avge	Best	4w	R/O
R.Ali	41.2	3	190	10	19.00	3-17	–	4.59
Asif Karim	48	4	171	4	42.75	1-19	–	3.56
T.Odoyo	19	0	112	0	–	–	–	5.89
E.T.Odumbe	16.5	0	95	4	23.75	2- 8	–	5.64
M.O.Odumbe	42.5	6	187	6	31.16	3-15	–	4.36
L.Onyango	4	0	31	0	–	–	–	7.75
M.Suji	45.2	4	224	4	56.00	2-55	–	4.94
D.L.Tikolo	8	0	55	0	–	–	–	6.87
S.O.Tikolo	10	0	83	1	83.00	1-26	–	8.30

WORLD CUP REGISTER

SCOTLAND

Scotland will be playing their inaugural Limited-Overs International match when they meet Australia at Worcester on 16 May 1999. First-class and Scotland career statistics are to end of 1998 UK season (20 September). Key to abbreviations on page 19. Scotland's selected 15 players (and 4 reserves) are:

ALLINGHAM, Michael James de Grey (Heriot's FP)
Born Inverness 6 Jan 1965. 6'0". Right-hand batsman, right-arm medium bowler. First-class debut (Scotland) 1996. **F-C CAREER:** 4 matches; 187 runs (av 37.40); 4 wkts (av 37.50); 3 ct. HS 50*. BB 3-53. **Scotland (all matches):** 42 matches; 804 runs (av 29.77); 34 wkts av 35.76). HS 64*. Teacher at Fettes College, Edinburgh.

ASIM BUTT (Heriot's FP)
Born Lahore, Pakistan 24 Oct 1967. 6'2". Right-hand batsman, left-arm medium-fast bowler. First-class debut (Lahore) 1983-84. Scotland debut 1998. **F-C CAREER:** 23 matches; 362 runs (av 17.23); 38 wkts (av 26.92), 5 wkts/inns (1); 11 ct. HS 44. BB 5-53. **Scotland (all matches):** 15 matches; 72 runs (av 18.00); 21 wkts (av 29.42). HS 21. Assistant retail manager.

BLAIN, John Angus Rae
Born Edinburgh 4 Jan 1979. 6'1". Educated at Penicuik High School; Jewel & Esk Valley College. Right-hand batsman, right-arm medium-fast bowler. First-class debut (Scotland) 1996. Northamptonshire debut 1997. **F-C CAREER:** 3 matches; 0 runs (av 0.00); 2 wkts (av 104.00); 2 ct. HS 0 and BB 1-18 v Worcs (Northampton) 1997. **COUNTY L-O:** HS 10* Scot v Notts (Nottingham) 1996 (BHC). BB 5-24 Northants v Derbys (Derby) 1997 (ASL). **Scotland (all matches):** 18 matches; 36 runs (av 7.20); 22 wkts (av 30.90). HS 12. Captained Scotland in U-19 World Cup.

BRINKLEY, James Edward (Essex)
Born Helensburgh 13 Mar 1974. 6'3". Educated at Marist College, Canberra; Trinity College, Perth. Right-hand batsman, right-arm fast-medium bowler. Worcestershire 1993-94 (Z tour) to 1995. Matabeleland 1994-95. Scotland debut 1998. Essex (one SL appearance) 1998. **F-C CAREER:** 15 matches; 89 runs (av 6.84); 35 wkts (av 34.71), 5 wkts/inns (2); 5 ct. HS 29 Matabeleland v Mashonaland U-24 (Harare) 1994-95. BB 6-35 Matabeleland v Mashonaland CD (Harare South) 1994-95. **COUNTY L-O:** HS 30* Scot v Yorks (Linlithgow) 1998 (BHC). BB 2-26 Wo v Hants (Worcester) 1996 (ASL). **Scotland (all matches):** 19 matches; 189 runs (av 13.50); 24 wkts (av 28.91). HS 43.

DAVIES, Alec George (West Lothian)
Born Rawalpindi, Pakistan 14 Aug 1962. 6'1½". Educated at Monmouth School; Bullmershe College, Reading. Right-hand batsman, wicket-keeper. First-class debut (Surrey – one match, v Zimbabwe) 1985. Scotland debut 1993. **F-C CAREER:** 5 matches; 80 runs (av 20.00); 10 ct, 2 st. HS 26*. **Scotland (all matches):** 59 matches; 556 runs (av 16.84); 73 ct, 14 st. HS 45*. Sports development officer.

DYER, Nicholas Rayner (Chichester)
Born Edinburgh 10 Jun 1969. 5'5". Right-hand batsman, right-arm off-break bowler. First-class debut (Scotland) 1997. **F-C CAREER:** 2 matches; 0 runs (av –); 6 wkts (av 31.16); 1 ct. HS 0*. BB 4-48. **Scotland (all matches):** 16 matches; 10 runs (av 3.33); 17 wkts (av 38.41). HS 7. Primary school teacher.

HAMILTON, Gavin Mark
Born Broxburn, Scotland 16 Sep 1974. 6'1". Educated at Hurstmere Secondary School, Kent. Left-hand batsman. right-arm fast-medium bowler. Scotland 1993-94. Yorkshire debut 1994; cap 1998. **F-C CAREER:** 40 matches; 1054 runs (av 24.51); 118 wkts (av 27.50), 5 wkts/inns (6), 10 wkts/match (2), 50 wkts/season (1); 13 ct. HS 79 Yorks v Glam (Cardiff) 1998. BB 7-50 (11-72 match) Yorks v Surrey (Leeds) 1998. Match double (79, 70; 5-69, 5-43) v Glam (Cardiff) 1998 – first instance for Yorks since 1964 (R.Illingworth). **COUNTY L-O:** HS 39 v Lancs (Manchester) 1998 (NWT). BB 5-16 v Hants (Leeds) 1998 (ASL). **Scotland (all matches):** 10 matches; 49 runs (av 12.25); 12 wkts (av 34.41). HS 21. Playing for Scotland in the World Cup will not affect his eligibility to represent England.

PATTERSON, Bruce Mathew Winston (Ayr)
Born Ayr 29 Jan 1965. 6'0½". Right-hand batsman. First-class debut (Scotland) 1988. **F-C CAREER:** 9 matches; 776 runs (av 51.03), 3 hundreds; 10 ct. HS 114. **Scotland (all matches):** 98 matches; 3406 runs (av 33.39); 0 wkts. HS 114. Estate agent.

PHILIP, Iain Lindsay (Stenhousemuir)
Born Larbert 9 Jun 1958. 5'11". Right-hand batsman, occasional left-arm orthodox slow bowler, occasional wicket-keeper. First-class debut (Scotland) 1986. **F-C CAREER:** 12 matches; 831 runs (av 43.73), 4 hundreds; 0 wkts; 11 ct. HS 145. **Scotland (all matches):** 129 matches; 4730 runs (av 35.03), 11 hundreds; 0 wkts. HS 234 v MCC (Glasgow) 1991. Holds national records for most appearances, most runs, most hundreds and highest score.

SALMOND, George (CAPTAIN)
Born Dundee 1 Dec 1969. 5'8". Right-hand batsman. First-class debut (Scotland) 1991. **F-C CAREER:** 8 matches; 709 runs (av 59.08), 2 hundreds; 5 ct. HS 181. **Scotland (all matches):** 104 matches; 2445 runs (av 25.46). HS 181. Primary school teacher.

SHERIDAN, Keith Lamont Paton (Poloc)
Born Bellshill 26 Mar 1971. 5'7". Right-hand batsman, left-arm orthodox slow bowler. First-class debut (Scotland) 1992. **F-C CAREER:** 4 matches; 12 runs (av 12.00); 9 wkts (av 40.11); 2 ct. HS 12*. BB 4-43. **Scotland (all matches):** 63 matches; 148 runs (av 9.25); 83 wkts (av 28.45). HS 25*. Civil engineer.

SMITH, Michael Jonathon (Aberdeenshire)
Born Edinburgh 30 Mar 1966. 5'9½". Right-hand batsman, right-arm off-break bowler. First-class debut (Scotland) 1987. **F-C CAREER:** 3 matches; 145 runs (av 36.25); 2 wkts (av 25.50); 3 ct. HS 79 v Ireland () 1987 – on debut. BB 2-30. **Scotland (all matches):** 67 matches; 1397 runs (av 22.90); 13 wkts (av 40.38). HS 100* v MCC (Lord's) 1994. Salesman.

STANGER, Ian Michael (Clydesdale)
Born Glasgow 5 Oct 1971. 6'0". Educated at Hutcheson's Grammar School, Glasgow; Duncan of Jordanstone Art College, Dundee. Right-hand batsman, right-arm medium-fast bowler. First-class debut (Scotland) 1997. Leicestershire 1994 (Sunday League only). **F-C CAREER:** 3 matches; 78 runs (av 26.00); 4 wkts (av 57.00); 3 ct. HS 52*. BB 3-57. **COUNTY L-O:** HS 6 (ASL). BB 3-34 Leics v Surrey (Oval) 1994 (ASL). **Scotland (all matches):** 57 matches; 842 runs (av 26.31); 41 wkts (av 52.75). HS 74.

STEINDL, Peter David (Grange)
Born Bundaberg, Australia 14 Jun 1970. 5'9". Right-hand batsman, right-arm medium bowler. First-class debut (Scotland) 1998. **F-C CAREER:** 1 match; 14 runs (av 14.00); 0 wkts; 0 ct. HS 14. **Scotland (all matches):** 23 matches; 132 runs (av 26.40); 18 wkts (av 43.72). HS 23*. Development Officer for the Scottish Cricket Union.

WILLIAMSON, John Greig (Clydesdale)
Born Glasgow 28 Dec 1968. 6'2". Right-hand batsman, right-arm medium bowler. First-class debut (Scotland) 1994. **F-C CAREER:** 4 matches; 115 runs (av 28.75); 5 wkts (av 71.40); 1 ct. HS 55. BB 2-51. **Scotland (all matches):** 77 matches; 1184 runs (av 19.09); 87 wkts (av 29.80). HS 67. Solicitor.

RESERVES

COWAN, David (Freuchie)
Born St Andrews, Fife 30 Mar 1964. 6'1½". Left-hand batsman, right-arm medium-fast bowler. First-class debut (Scotland) 1991. **F-C CAREER:** 1 match; 2 runs (av –); 5 wkts (av 26.60); 1 ct. HS 2* and BB 3-41 v Ireland (Malahide) 1991. **Scotland (all matches):** 25 matches; 88 runs (av 9.77); 47 wkts (av 28.80). HS 22*. Employed by Fife Council

GOURLAY, Scott (Freuchie)
Born 8 Jan 1971. 5'10½". Right-hand batsman, right-arm medium bowler. **F-C CAREER:** 0 matches. **Scotland (all matches):** 19 matches; 118 runs (av 10.72); 15 wkts (av 33.60). HS 24. Storeman.

LOCKHART, Douglas Ross (Glasgow Academicals and Oxford University)
Born Glasgow 19 Jan 1976. 6'1". Educated at The Glasgow Academy; Durham U; Keble College, Oxford. Right-hand batsman, occasional wicket-keeper. First-class debut (Scotland) 1996. Oxford U 1998; blue 1998. **F-C CAREER:** 11 matches; 377 runs (av 20.94); 9 ct. HS 77*. **Scotland (all matches):** 36 matches; 1076 runs (av 26.90). HS 119*.

WRIGHT, Craig McIntyre (West of Scotland)
Born Paisley 28 Apr 1974. 5'10½". Educated at Glasgow Caledonian U. Right-hand batsman, right-arm fast-medium bowler. First-class debut (Scotland) 1997. **F-C CAREER:** 1 match; 0 runs (av 0.00); 3 wkts (av 29.66); 0 ct. HS 0. BB 3-66. **Scotland (all matches):** 19 matches; 132 runs (av 12.00); 26 wkts (av 25.53). HS 23. Current student who is also a part-time Development Officer for the Scottish Cricket Union.

THE 1975 WORLD CUP

The inaugural World Cup tournament was held within five years of the birth of limited-overs internationals, the very first of which had been a hastily arranged affair played on the final day (5 January 1971) of a rain-aborted Melbourne Test match to appease the disappointed local public. Like all of England's home one-day matches between the first in 1972 and the end of the third World Cup in 1983, the competition was sponsored by Prudential Assurance who contributed over £100,000 for the privilege.

This initial competition was a very modest affair, consisting of just 15 matches on only five playing days. That it was such a resounding success was due as much to the fact that its 15-day span coincided with the start of one of Britain's rare long, hot summers, as to the standard of cricket played. For that number of 60-overs matches to be completed without the loss of a single minute to inclement weather in Britain in June constituted a miracle of major proportions, particularly as an inch-deep covering of snow had prevented play in a county match at Buxton just five days before the tournament began. Pessimistically, the organisers had set aside three days for each contest. All 15 matches were staged at Test match venues, with Edgbaston, Headingley and The Oval each hosting three games and Lord's, Old Trafford and Trent Bridge two apiece.

The six current Test-playing countries were joined by two associate members, Sri Lanka and East Africa, the eight teams being divided into two groups of four, each playing the other once, but with England and Australia seeded. Group A comprised England, East Africa, India and New Zealand, while Pakistan, Sri Lanka and West Indies joined Australia in Group B. The leading two teams in each group qualified for the semi-finals.

A crowd of almost 20,000 (receipts £19,000) watched England amass 334 for 4, then the highest total in a 60-overs match in Britain, with Dennis Amiss (137) recording the first World Cup hundred and the left-handed Chris Old scoring an undefeated 51 off 30 balls. The game was reduced to farcical boredom when India decided that the target on a slow pitch was totally beyond them and played for a draw! The chief culprit was opening batsman Sunil Gavaskar who took it upon himself to use the 60 overs for batting practice and managed to score just 36 runs from 174 balls, a performance which incurred the public wrath of both his manager, G.S.Ramchand, and his captain, Srini Venkataraghavan. England's margin of victory, 202 runs, remains the largest by any side batting first in World Cup matches.

Australia's clash with Pakistan attracted Headingley's first full house for nine years (21,000 plus). Chasing 279, Pakistan looked set for a sensational win at 181 for 4, but their last six wickets clattered for 24 runs, Dennis Lillee returning the competition's first five-wicket haul. His partner in pace, Jeff Thomson, could find no rhythm and was no-balled 12 times, five of them in the first over.

Sri Lanka were totally outclassed by West Indies, being dismissed in 37.2 overs on a blameless pitch for just 86, the lowest total of this tournament. As the match was completed by 3.30pm, the players entertained a disappointed Old Trafford crowd with a 20-overs exhibition game.

East Africa fared little better against New Zealand, thanks to an exceptional batting display by Glenn Turner. Imperious driving featured prominently in the Worcestershire opener's unbeaten 171, the World Cup's highest score until Kapil Dev surpassed it four years later.

The Kiwis' captain was unable to reproduce this form in the second round of matches and his team was easily beaten by England. At Headingley, India's ten-wicket defeat of East Africa attracted a paying attendance of only 720. Lancashire-born Don Pringle, father of a future England and Essex all-rounder Derek, made his World Cup debut for East Africa.

West Indies and Pakistan produced an epic match at Edgbaston, the eventual champions scraping home by one wicket with two balls to spare thanks to a last-wicket partnership of 64 in 14 overs between Deryck Murray and Andy Roberts. At The Oval, Sri Lanka, facing a daunting total of 328 (Alan Turner contributing the only pre-lunch hundred in World Cup matches), batted with extraordinary bravery against a hostile Australian attack. Remember that this was before the introduction of helmets and arm guards. Despite two of their batsmen being put in hospital by Thomson, they fell only 52 runs short of their target and lost just four wickets. This outstanding performance gained Sri Lanka considerable support in their quest for Test-playing status, eventually granted six years later.

Sri Lanka and East Africa were emphatically beaten by Pakistan and England respectively in the final round of matches, while New Zealand beat India by four wickets with seven balls to spare thanks to another magnificent hundred by their captain. From the time the draw was made a year earlier, the most eagerly awaited contest was that between the favourites, West Indies and Australia. Although it produced some marvellously entertaining action, the encounter failed to provide a memorable finish, West Indies cantering home by seven wickets with 14 overs to spare. This was the first time I had scored an international match not involving England, a curious experience. The main recollection is of the diminutive and hatless Alvin Kallicharran hooking and cutting a succession of ferocious short-pitched deliveries from Lillee to the tune of 35 runs from ten balls: 4 4 4 4 4 1 4 6 0 4.

The final group placings eliminated India, Pakistan and the two associate member teams:

GROUP A	P	W	L	Pts	GROUP B	P	W	L	Pts
ENGLAND	3	3	0	12	WEST INDIES	3	3	0	12
NEW ZEALAND	3	2	1	8	AUSTRALIA	3	2	1	8
India	3	1	2	4	Pakistan	3	1	2	4
East Africa	3	0	3	0	Sri Lanka	3	0	3	0

A typical Headingley pitch produced a low-scoring semi-final and 65 overs of frenzied excitement. Put in by Ian Chappell in ideal bowling conditions, a heavy atmosphere allied to a damp, green pitch which had staged the Australia-Pakistan match eleven days previously, England were dismissed in the 37th over for 93, Gary Gilmour returning the tournament's first six-wicket analysis. Bowling left-arm fast-medium, he could full advantage of those conditions to swing the ball late and seam it either way. At one stage England were 37 for 7. Although Chris Old, John Snow and Geoff Arnold inflicted similar damage, reducing Australia to 39 for 6, Gilmour, at 24 the team's youngest member, completed an outstanding day by contributing 28, the game's highest innings, to an unbroken winning partnership of 55 with Doug Walters.

At The Oval, West Indies coasted to the final, defeating New Zealand by five wickets with almost 20 overs in hand. At lunch, New Zealand, 92 for 1 after 29 overs and with Glenn Turner and Geoff Howarth (on the ground of his adopted county) in prime form, were promisingly placed after being put in to bat. An astonishing slip catch by the 39-year-old Rohan Kanhai ended their 90-run stand in the first over after the interval and the remaining eight wickets could add only 60 runs. Gordon Greenidge and Alvin Kallicharran provided rich entertainment with their second-wicket stand of 125, New Zealand gaining some consolation from an aggressive display of left-arm fast bowling by Richard Collinge.

It was fortunate that the first World Cup final was played on the longest day of the year as this epic battle fully absorbed its vast audience, with millions viewing on television, from 11am until 8.42pm, the most protracted day's cricket at international level. Australia, having elected to bowl, made an early if freakish breakthrough when Roy Fredericks slipped while hooking a Lillee bouncer and kicked his wicket as the ball soared over the long-leg boundary. At 50 for 3 in the 19th over and with their semi-final heroes Greenidge and Kallicharran both out, West Indies were under pressure. Clive Lloyd swiftly swung the match with a breathtaking exhibition of hooking and effortless driving off the back foot. Tall, strong-wristed and armed with one of cricket's most weighty bats, its handle adorned with five rubber grips, he survived a chance at mid-wicket when he had made 26, reached fifty from 52 balls and completed his hundred just 30 balls later. His timing, and power of stroke prompted radio commentator John Arlott, for whom I was privileged to be scoring, to describe one pull as being played with 'the ease of a man knocking off a thistle-top with a walking stick' and to label a delivery which failed to produce a run as 'a maiden ball'.

Lloyd's partnership with his fellow Guyanan, Kanhai, added 149 in 26 overs, the latter playing a passive anchor role and remaining on 16 for ten overs. The West Indies captain batted 148 minutes during which he faced just 85 balls, hitting two sixes and a dozen fours. Although Richards failed (one of another five wickets for Gilmour), Keith Boyce and Bernard Julian added 50 from ten overs to take West Indies towards their highest total so far in limited-overs internationals.

Undaunted by their immense task, Australia maintained their challenge to the end and might well have achieved a remarkable win if half their wickets had not fallen to run outs, three by Richards, including direct hits from mid-wicket and cover. A defiant last-wicket partnership of 41 between Thomson and Lillee took Australia within range of their target before Thomson, sent back when attempting a bye to the keeper, was beaten by Murray's underarm lob.

Most of the crowd swarmed on to the field and the huge Caribbean element produced their own carnival of dances and song as, shortly before 9pm, HRH The Duke of Edinburgh presented the Prudential Cup to Clive Lloyd. Made in 1890, the elegant 18 inch high trophy was styled on the work of Paul de Lamerie (1688-1751), one of the most renowned silversmiths of all time.

That this tournament proved to be an outstanding success was a great relief to the organisers. The ICC had carefully avoided the title 'World Cup' and had designated the series as 'International Championship Cricket'. Unlike soccer's similar competition, this had involved only eight of the 21 member nations of the ICC. Indeed it had been referred to as the 'World without South Africa Cup'.

Overall takings (excluding the sponsor's fee of £100,000 which covered the cost of staging the matches plus fares and a month's subsistence for the teams) exceeded £200,000, the total attendance for the 15 games being 158,000. The Lord's final accounted for 26,000 and gross receipts of £66,950, then a record for a one-day match in Britain. The winners received £4,000, runners-up Australia gained £2,000 and the two losing semi-finalists, England and New Zealand won £1,000 each. As hosts, the Test and County Cricket Board received 10% of the profits, the other seven participants each receiving 7%. The ICC distributed the balance to the non-participating associate member countries, the international coaching fund and to a reserve for promoting the next World Cup in 1979.

When the ICC membership congregated for its AGM in London soon after the final, suggestions were invited for the next tournament. Although India were keen to act as hosts, it was thought that England with its longer period of daylight in midsummer was the ideal venue for 60-overs matches.

ENGLAND v INDIA

At Lord's, London, on 7 June 1975.   Toss: England.
Result: **ENGLAND** won by 202 runs.   Award: D.L.Amiss.
LOI debuts: India – M.Amarnath, A.D.Gaekwad, K.D.Ghavri.

ENGLAND		Runs	Balls	4/6
J.A.Jameson	c Venkataraghavan b Amarnath	21	42	2
D.L.Amiss	b Madan Lal	137	147	18
K.W.R.Fletcher	b Abid Ali	68	107	4/1
A.W.Greig	lbw b Abid Ali	4	8	–
*M.H.Denness	not out	37	31	2/1
C.M.Old	not out	51	30	4/2
B.Wood				
†A.P.E.Knott				
J.A.Snow				
P.Lever				
G.G.Arnold				
Extras	(lb 12, w 2, nb 2)	16		
Total	(60 overs; 4 wickets)	**334**		

INDIA		Runs	Balls	4/6
S.M.Gavaskar	not out	36	174	1
E.D.Solkar	c Lever b Arnold	8	34	–
A.D.Gaekwad	c Knott b Lever	22	46	2
G.R.Viswanath	c Fletcher b Old	37	59	5
B.P.Patel	not out	16	57	–
M.Amarnath				
†F.M.Engineer				
S.Abid Ali				
Madan Lal				
*S.Venkataraghavan				
K.D.Ghavri				
Extras	(lb 3, w 1, nb 9)	13		
Total	(60 overs; 3 wickets)	**132**		

INDIA	O	M	R	W		FALL OF WICKETS		
Madan Lal	12	1	64	1	Wkt	E	I
Amarnath	12	2	60	1	1st	54	21
Abid Ali	12	0	58	2	2nd	230	50
Ghavri	11	1	83	0	3rd	237	108
Venkataraghavan	12	0	41	0	4th	245	–
Solkar	1	0	12	0	5th	–	–
					6th	–	–
ENGLAND					7th	–	–
Snow	12	2	24	0	8th	–	–
Arnold	10	2	20	1	9th	–	–
Old	12	4	26	1	10th	–	–
Greig	9	1	26	0			
Wood	5	2	4	0			
Lever	10	0	16	1			
Jameson	2	1	3	0			

Umpires: D.J.Constant (4) and J.G.Langridge (1).

NEW ZEALAND v EAST AFRICA

At Edgbaston, Birmingham, on 7 June 1975. Toss: New Zealand.
Result: **NEW ZEALAND** won by 181 runs. Award: G.M.Turner.
LOI debuts: New Zealand – B.J.McKechnie; East Africa – all.

NEW ZEALAND		Runs	Balls	4/6
*G.M.Turner	not out	171		16/2
J.F.M.Morrison	c and b Nana	14		2
G.P.Howarth	b Mehmood	20		2
J.M.Parker	c Zulfiqar b Sethi	66		7
B.F.Hastings	c Sethi b Zulfiqar	8		1
†K.J.Wadsworth	b Nagenda	10		–/1
R.J.Hadlee	not out	6		–
B.J.McKechnie				
D.R.Hadlee				
H.J.Howarth				
R.O.Collinge				
Extras	(b 1, lb 8, w 5)	14		
Total	(60 overs; 5 wickets)	**309**		

EAST AFRICA		Runs	Balls	4/6
Frasat Ali	st Wadsworth b H.J.Howarth	45		1/1
S.Walusimba	b D.R.Hadlee	15		1
R.K.Sethi	run out	1		–
S.Sumar	b D.R.Hadlee	4		–
Jawahir Shah	c and b H.J.Howarth	5		–
*Harilal Shah	lbw b H.J.Howarth	0		–
Mehmood Quaraishy	not out	16		–
Zulfiqar Ali	b D.R.Hadlee	30		4
†H.McLeod	b Collinge	5		–
P.G.Nana	not out	1		–
J.Nagenda				
Extras	(lb 5, nb 1)	6		
Total	(60 overs; 8 wickets)	**128**		

EAST AFRICA	O	M	R	W		FALL OF WICKETS		
Nagenda	9	1	50	1		Wkt	NZ	EA
Frasat Ali	9	0	50	0		1st	51	30
Nana	12	2	34	1		2nd	103	32
Sethi	10	1	51	1		3rd	252	36
Zulfiqar Ali	12	0	71	1		4th	278	59
Mehmood Quaraishy	8	0	39	1		5th	292	59
						6th	–	84
NEW ZEALAND	O	M	R	W		7th	–	121
Collinge	12	5	23	1		8th	–	126
R.J.Hadlee	12	6	10	0		9th	–	–
McKechnie	12	2	39	0		10th	–	–
D.R.Hadlee	12	1	21	3				
H.J.Howarth	12	3	29	3				

Umpires: H.D.Bird (4) and A.E.Fagg (3).

AUSTRALIA v PAKISTAN

At Headingley, Leeds, on 7 June 1975.   Toss: Australia.
Result: **AUSTRALIA** won by 73 runs.   Award: D.K.Lillee.
LOI debuts: Australia – R.B.McCosker, A.Turner; Pakistan – Naseer Malik.

AUSTRALIA		**Runs**	**Balls**	**4/6**
A.Turner	c Mushtaq b Asif Iqbal	46	54	4
R.B.McCosker	c Wasim Bari b Naseer	25	76	2
*I.M.Chappell	c Wasim Raja b Sarfraz	28	30	5
G.S.Chappell	c Asif Iqbal b Imran	45	56	5
K.D.Walters	c Sarfraz b Naseer	2	13	–
R.Edwards	not out	80	94	6
†R.W.Marsh	c Wasim Bari b Imran	1	5	–
M.H.N.Walker	b Asif Masood	18	28	2
J.R.Thomson	not out	20	14	2/1
A.A.Mallett				
D.K.Lillee				
Extras	(lb 7, nb 6)	13		
Total	(60 overs; 7 wickets)	**278**		

PAKISTAN		**Runs**	**Balls**	**4/6**
Sadiq Mohammed	b Lillee	4	12	–
Majid Khan	c Marsh b Mallett	65	76	11
Zaheer Abbas	c Turner b Thomson	8	10	2
Mushtaq Mohammed	c G.S.Chappell b Walters	8	32	–
*Asif Iqbal	b Lillee	53	95	8
Wasim Raja	c Thomson b Walker	31	57	4
Imran Khan	c Turner b Walker	9	19	1
Sarfraz Nawaz	c Marsh b Lillee	0	2	–
†Wasim Bari	c Marsh b Lillee	2	18	–
Asif Masood	c Walker b Lillee	6	7	1
Naseer Malik	not out	0	13	–
Extras	(lb 4, w 3, nb 12)	19		
Total	(53 overs)	**205**		

PAKISTAN	O	M	R	W
Naseer Malik	12	2	37	2
Asif Masood	12	0	50	1
Sarfraz Nawaz	12	0	63	1
Asif Iqbal	12	0	58	1
Imran Khan	10	0	44	2
Wasim Raja	2	0	13	0

AUSTRALIA	O	M	R	W
Lillee	12	2	34	5
Thomson	8	2	25	1
Walker	12	3	32	2
Mallett	12	1	49	1
Walters	6	0	29	1
G.S.Chappell	3	0	17	0

FALL OF WICKETS		
Wkt	A	P
1st	63	15
2nd	99	27
3rd	110	68
4th	124	104
5th	184	181
6th	195	189
7th	243	189
8th	–	195
9th	–	203
10th	–	205

Umpires: W.E.Alley (2) and T.W.Spencer (3).

WEST INDIES v SRI LANKA

At Old Trafford, Manchester, on 7 June 1975.   Toss: West Indies.
Result: **WEST INDIES** won by 9 wickets.   Award: B.D.Julien.
LOI debuts: West Indies – I.V.A.Richards, A.M.E.Roberts; Sri Lanka – all.

SRI LANKA		Runs	Balls	4/6
†E.R.Fernando	c Murray b Julien	4		–
B.Warnapura	c Murray b Boyce	8		2
*A.P.B.Tennekoon	c Murray b Julien	0		–
P.D.Heyn	c Lloyd b Roberts	2		–
M.H.Tissera	c Kallicharran b Julien	14		1
L.R.D.Mendis	c Murray b Boyce	8		1
A.N.Ranasinghe	b Boyce	0		–
H.S.M.Pieris	c Lloyd b Julien	3		–
A.R.M.Opatha	b Roberts	11		1
D.S.de Silva	c Lloyd b Holder	21		2
L.W.S.Kaluperuma	not out	6		–
Extras	(b 3, lb 3, nb 3)	9		
Total	(37.2 overs)	**86**		

WEST INDIES		Runs	Balls	4/6
R.C.Fredericks	c Warnapura b De Silva	33		4
†D.L.Murray	not out	30		2/1
A.I.Kallicharran	not out	19		–
R.B.Kanhai				
*C.H.Lloyd				
I.V.A.Richards				
B.D.Julien				
K.D.Boyce				
V.A.Holder				
A.M.E.Roberts				
L.R.Gibbs				
Extras	(b 2, lb 1, w 1, nb 1)	5		
Total	(20.4 overs; 1 wicket)	**87**		

WEST INDIES	O	M	R	W		FALL OF WICKETS		
						Wkt	SL	WI
Roberts	12	5	16	2		1st	5	52
Boyce	8	1	22	3		2nd	5	–
Julien	12	3	20	4		3rd	16	–
Gibbs	4	0	17	0		4th	21	–
Holder	1.2	0	2	1		5th	41	–
						6th	41	–
SRI LANKA	O	M	R	W		7th	42	–
Opatha	4	0	19	0		8th	48	–
De Silva	8	1	33	1		9th	58	–
Pieris	2	0	13	0		10th	86	–
Kaluperuma	6.4	1	17	0				

Umpires: W.L.Budd (2) and A.Jepson (2).

ENGLAND v NEW ZEALAND

At Trent Bridge, Nottingham, on 11 June 1975.   Toss: New Zealand.
Result: **ENGLAND** won by 80 runs.   Award: K.W.R.Fletcher.
LOI debuts: None.

ENGLAND		Runs	Balls	4/6
J.A.Jameson	c Wadsworth b Collinge	11	31	–
D.L.Amiss	b Collinge	16	18	3
K.W.R.Fletcher	run out	131	147	13
F.C.Hayes	lbw b R.J.Hadlee	34	80	5
*M.H.Denness	c Morrison b D.R.Hadlee	37	52	1/1
A.W.Greig	b D.R.Hadlee	9	19	–
C.M.Old	not out	20	16	–/1
†A.P.E.Knott				
D.L.Underwood				
G.G.Arnold				
P.Lever				
Extras	(lb 6, w 1, nb 1)	8		
Total	(60 overs; 6 wickets)	**266**		

NEW ZEALAND		Runs	Balls	4/6
J.F.M.Morrison	c Old b Underwood	55	85	6/1
*G.M.Turner	b Lever	12	34	1
B.G.Hadlee	b Greig	19	77	1
J.M.Parker	b Greig	1	8	–
B.F.Hastings	c Underwood b Old	10	26	1
†K.J.Wadsworth	b Arnold	25	24	3
R.J.Hadlee	b Old	0	6	–
B.J.McKechnie	c Underwood b Greig	27	50	4
D.R.Hadlee	c Arnold b Greig	20	42	2
H.J.Howarth	not out	1	7	–
R.O.Collinge	b Underwood	6	6	–/1
Extras	(b 1, lb 4, w 1, nb 4)	10		
Total	(60 overs)	**186**		

NEW ZEALAND	O	M	R	W
Collinge	12	2	43	2
R.J.Hadlee	12	2	66	1
D.R.Hadlee	12	1	55	2
McKechnie	12	2	38	0
Howarth	12	2	56	0

ENGLAND	O	M	R	W
Arnold	12	3	35	1
Lever	12	0	37	1
Old	12	2	29	2
Greig	12	0	45	4
Underwood	12	2	30	2

FALL OF WICKETS		
Wkt	E	NZ
1st	27	30
2nd	28	83
3rd	111	91
4th	177	95
5th	200	129
6th	266	129
7th	–	129
8th	–	177
9th	–	180
10th	–	186

Umpires: W.E.Alley (3) and T.W.Spencer (4).

INDIA v EAST AFRICA

At Headingley, Leeds, on 11 June 1975.   Toss: East Africa.
Result: **INDIA** won by 10 wickets.   Award: F.M.Engineer.
LOI debuts: East Africa – P.S.Mehta, D.J.Pringle, Yunus Badat.

EAST AFRICA		Runs	Balls	4/6
Frasat Ali	b Abid Ali	12		1
S.Walusimba	lbw b Abid Ali	16		1
†P.S.Mehta	run out	12		–
Yunus Badat	b Bedi	1		–
Jawahir Shah	b Amarnath	37		5
*Harilal Shah	c Engineer b Amarnath	0		–
R.K.Sethi	c Gaekwad b Madan Lal	23		2
Mehmood Quaraishy	run out	6		–
Zulfiqar Ali	not out	2		–
P.G.Nana	lbw b Madan Lal	0		–
D.J.Pringle	b Madan Lal	2		–
Extras	(lb 8, nb 1)	9		
Total	(55.3 overs)	**120**		

INDIA		Runs	Balls	4/6
S.M.Gavaskar	not out	65		9
†F.M.Engineer	not out	54		7
A.D.Gaekwad				
G.R.Viswanath				
B.P.Patel				
E.D.Solkar				
S.Abid Ali				
Madan Lal				
M.Amarnath				
*S.Venkataraghavan				
B.S.Bedi				
Extras	(b 4)	4		
Total	(29.5 overs; 0 wickets)	**123**		

INDIA	O	M	R	W		FALL OF WICKETS		
Abid Ali	12	5	22	2		Wkt	EA	I
Madan Lal	9.3	2	15	3		1st	26	–
Bedi	12	8	6	1		2nd	36	–
Venkataraghavan	12	4	29	0		3rd	37	–
Amarnath	10	0	39	2		4th	56	–
						5th	56	–
EAST AFRICA	O	M	R	W		6th	98	–
Frasat Ali	6	1	17	0		7th	116	–
Pringle	3	0	14	0		8th	116	–
Zulfiqar Ali	11	3	32	0		9th	116	–
Nana	4.5	0	36	0		10th	120	–
Sethi	5	0	20	0				

Umpires: H.D.Bird (5) and A.Jepson (3).

AUSTRALIA v SRI LANKA

At Kennington Oval, London, on 11 June 1975. Toss: Sri Lanka.
Result: **AUSTRALIA** won by 52 runs. Award: A.Turner.
LOI debuts: Sri Lanka – S.R.de S.Wettimuny.

AUSTRALIA		**Runs**	**Balls**	**4/6**
R.B.McCosker	b De Silva	73	111	2
A.Turner	c Mendis b De Silva	101	113	9/1
*I.M.Chappell	b Kaluperuma	4	7	1
G.S.Chappell	c Opatha b Pieris	50	50	5/1
K.D.Walters	c Tennekoon b Pieris	59	66	5
J.R.Thomson	not out	9	7	–
†R.W.Marsh	not out	9	7	–
R.Edwards				
M.H.N.Walker				
D.K.Lillee				
A.A.Mallett				
Extras	(b 1, lb 20, w 1, nb 1)	23		
Total	(60 overs; 5 wickets)	**328**		

SRI LANKA		**Runs**	**Balls**	**4/6**
S.R.de S.Wettimuny	retired hurt	53	102	7
†E.R.Fernando	b Thomson	22	18	4
B.Warnapura	st Marsh b Mallett	31	39	5
L.R.D.Mendis	retired hurt	32	45	5
*A.P.B.Tennekoon	b I.M.Chappell	48	71	6
M.H.Tissera	c Turner b I.M.Chappell	52	72	7
A.N.Ranasinghe	not out	14	18	3
H.S.M.Pieris	not out	0	3	–
A.R.M.Opatha				
D.S.de Silva				
L.W.S.Kaluperuma				
Extras	(b 6, lb 8, w 8, nb 2)	24		
Total	(60 overs; 4 wickets)	**276**		

SRI LANKA	O	M	R	W
Opatha	9	0	32	0
Pieris	11	0	68	2
Warnapura	9	0	40	0
Ranasinghe	7	0	55	0
De Silva	12	3	60	2
Kaluperuma	12	0	50	1

AUSTRALIA	O	M	R	W
Lillee	10	0	42	0
Thomson	12	5	22	1
Mallett	12	0	72	1
Walters	6	1	33	0
Walker	12	1	44	0
G.S.Chappell	4	0	25	0
I.M.Chappell	4	0	14	2

FALL OF WICKETS		
Wkt	A	SL
1st	182	30
2nd	187	84
3rd	191	246
4th	308	268
5th	308	–
6th	–	–
7th	–	–
8th	–	–
9th	–	–
10th	–	–

Umpires: W.L.Budd (3) and A.E.Fagg (4).

WEST INDIES v PAKISTAN

At Edgbaston, Birmingham, on 11 June 1975.　Toss: Pakistan.
Result: **WEST INDIES** won by 1 wicket.　Award: Sarfraz Nawaz.
LOI debuts: Pakistan – Javed Miandad, Parvez Mir; West Indies – C.G.Greenidge.

PAKISTAN		Runs	Balls	4/6
*Majid Khan	c Murray b Lloyd	60		6
Sadiq Mohammed	c Kanhai b Julien	7		1
Zaheer Abbas	lbw b Richards	31		4
Mushtaq Mohammed	b Boyce	55		3
Wasim Raja	b Roberts	58		6
Javed Miandad	run out	24		2
Parvez Mir	run out	4		–
†Wasim Bari	not out	1		–
Sarfraz Nawaz	not out	0		–
Asif Masood				
Naseer Malik				
Extras	(b 1, lb 15, w 4, nb 6)	26		
Total	(60 overs; 7 wickets)	**266**		

WEST INDIES		Runs	Balls	4/6
R.C.Fredericks	lbw b Sarfraz	12		2
C.G.Greenidge	c Wasim Bari b Sarfraz	4		1
A.I.Kallicharran	c Wasim Bari b Sarfraz	16		1
R.B.Kanhai	b Naseer	24		3
*C.H.Lloyd	c Wasim Bari b Miandad	53		8
I.V.A.Richards	c Zaheer b Parvez	13		2
B.D.Julien	c Miandad b Asif	18		2
†D.L.Murray	not out	61		6
K.D.Boyce	b Naseer	7		
V.A.Holder	c Parvez b Sarfraz	16		1
A.M.E.Roberts	not out	24		3
Extras	(lb 10, w 1, nb 8)	19		
Total	(59.4 overs; 9 wickets)	**267**		

WEST INDIES	O	M	R	W
Roberts	12	1	47	1
Boyce	12	2	44	1
Julien	12	1	41	1
Holder	12	3	56	0
Richards	4	0	21	1
Lloyd	8	1	31	1

PAKISTAN	O	M	R	W
Asif Masood	12	1	64	1
Sarfraz Nawaz	12	1	44	4
Naseer Malik	12	2	42	2
Parvez Mir	9	1	42	1
Javed Miandad	12	0	46	1
Mushtaq Mohammed	2	0	7	0
Wasim Raja	0.4	0	3	0

FALL OF WICKETS		
Wkt	P	WI
1st	21	6
2nd	83	31
3rd	140	36
4th	202	84
5th	249	99
6th	263	145
7th	265	151
8th	–	166
9th	–	203
10th	–	–

Umpires: D.J.Constant (5) and J.G.Langridge (2).

ENGLAND v EAST AFRICA

At Edgbaston, Birmingham, on 14 June 1975.　Toss: East Africa.
Result: **ENGLAND** won by 196 runs.　Award: J.A.Snow.
LOI debuts: None.

ENGLAND		Runs	Balls	4/6
B.Wood	b Mehmood	77		6
D.L.Amiss	c Nana b Zulfiqar	88		7
F.C.Hayes	b Zulfiqar	52		6/2
A.W.Greig	lbw b Zulfiqar	9		–
†A.P.E.Knott	not out	18		–
C.M.Old	b Mehmood	18		3
*M.H.Denness	not out	12		1
K.W.R.Fletcher				
J.A.Snow				
P.Lever				
D.L.Underwood				
Extras	(b 7, lb 7, w 1, nb 1)	16		
Total	**(60 overs; 5 wickets)**	**290**		

EAST AFRICA		Runs	Balls	4/6
Frasat Ali	b Snow	0		–
S.Walusimba	lbw b Snow	7		–
Yunus Badat	b Snow	0		–
Jawahir Shah	lbw b Snow	4		–
R.K.Sethi	b Lever	30		3
*Harilal Shah	b Greig	6		–
Mehmood Quaraishy	c Amiss b Greig	19		2
Zulfiqar Ali	b Lever	7		–
†H.McLeod	b Lever	0		–
P.G.Nana	not out	8		–
D.J.Pringle	b Old	3		–
Extras	(lb 6, w 1, nb 3)	10		
Total	**(52.3 overs)**	**94**		

EAST AFRICA	O	M	R	W
Frasat Ali	9	0	40	0
Pringle	12	0	41	0
Nana	12	2	46	0
Sethi	5	0	29	0
Zulfiqar Ali	12	0	63	3
Mehmood Quaraishy	10	0	55	2

ENGLAND	O	M	R	W
Snow	12	6	11	4
Lever	12	3	32	3
Underwood	10	5	11	0
Wood	7	3	10	0
Greig	10	1	18	2
Old	1.3	0	2	1

FALL OF WICKETS		
Wkt	E	EA
1st	158	7
2nd	192	7
3rd	234	15
4th	244	21
5th	277	42
6th	–	72
7th	–	76
8th	–	79
9th	–	88
10th	–	94

Umpires: W.E.Alley (4) and J.G.Langridge (3).

NEW ZEALAND v INDIA

At Old Trafford, Manchester, on 14 June 1975.　Toss: India.
Result: **NEW ZEALAND** won by 4 wickets.　Award: G.M.Turner.
LOI debuts: None.

INDIA		Runs	Balls	4/6
S.M.Gavaskar	c R.J.Hadlee b D.R.Hadlee	12		2
†F.M.Engineer	lbw b R.J.Hadlee	24		3
A.D.Gaekwad	c Hastings b R.J.Hadlee	37		3
G.R.Viswanath	lbw b McKechnie	2		–
B.P.Patel	c Wadsworth b H.J.Howarth	9		1
E.D.Solkar	c Wadsworth b H.J.Howarth	13		2
S.Abid Ali	c H.J.Howarth b McKechnie	70		5/1
Madan Lal	c and b McKechnie	20		4
M.Amarnath	c Morrison b D.R.Hadlee	1		–
*S.Venkataraghavan	not out	26		3
B.S.Bedi	run out	6		–
Extras	(b 5, w 1, nb 4)	10		
Total	(60 overs)	**230**		

NEW ZEALAND		Runs	Balls	4/6
*G.M.Turner	not out	114		13
J.F.M.Morrison	c Engineer b Bedi	17		2
G.P.Howarth	run out	9		–
J.M.Parker	lbw b Abid Ali	1		–
B.F.Hastings	c Solkar b Amarnath	34		3
†K.J.Wadsworth	lbw b Madan Lal	22		3
R.J.Hadlee	b Abid Ali	15		2
D.R.Hadlee	not out	8		2
B.J.McKechnie				
H.J.Howarth				
R.O.Collinge				
Extras	(b 8, lb 5)	13		
Total	(58.5 overs; 6 wickets)	**233**		

NEW ZEALAND	O	M	R	W		FALL OF WICKETS		
Collinge	12	2	43	0		Wkt	I	NZ
R.J.Hadlee	12	2	48	2		1st	17	45
D.R.Hadlee	12	3	32	2		2nd	48	62
McKechnie	12	1	49	3		3rd	59	70
H.J.Howarth	12	0	48	0		4th	81	135
						5th	94	185
INDIA	O	M	R	W		6th	101	224
Madan Lal	11.5	1	62	1		7th	156	–
Amarnath	8	1	40	1		8th	157	–
Bedi	12	6	28	1		9th	217	–
Abid Ali	12	2	35	2		10th	230	–
Venkataraghavan	12	0	39	0				
Solkar	3	0	16	0				

Umpires: W.L.Budd (4) and A.E.Fagg (5).

AUSTRALIA v WEST INDIES

At Kennington Oval, London, on 14 June 1975.   Toss: West Indies.
Result: **WEST INDIES** won by 7 wickets.   Award: A.I.Kallicharran.
LOI debuts: None.

AUSTRALIA		Runs	Balls	4/6
R.B.McCosker	c Fredericks b Julien	0	3	–
A.Turner	lbw b Roberts	7	18	–
*I.M.Chappell	c Murray b Boyce	25	63	–
G.S.Chappell	c Murray b Boyce	15	33	–
K.D.Walters	run out	7	18	–
R.Edwards	b Richards	58	74	6
†R.W.Marsh	not out	52	84	4
M.H.N.Walker	lbw b Holder	8	22	1
J.R.Thomson	c Holder b Richards	1	3	–
D.K.Lillee	b Roberts	3	12	–
A.A.Mallett	c Murray b Roberts	0	1	–
Extras	(lb 9, w 1, nb 6)	16		
Total	(53.4 overs)	**192**		

WEST INDIES		Runs	Balls	4/6
R.C.Fredericks	c Marsh b Mallett	58	105	5
C.G.Greenidge	lbw b Walker	16	18	2
A.I.Kallicharran	c Mallett b Lillee	78	83	14/1
I.V.A.Richards	not out	15	38	2
R.B.Kanhai	not out	18	33	1
*C.H.Lloyd				
B.D.Julien				
†D.L.Murray				
K.D.Boyce				
V.A.Holder				
A.M.E.Roberts				
Extras	(b 4, lb 2, w 3, nb 1)	10		
Total	(46 overs; 3 wickets)	**195**		

WEST INDIES	O	M	R	W
Julien	12	2	31	1
Roberts	10.4	1	39	3
Boyce	11	0	38	2
Holder	10	0	31	1
Lloyd	4	1	19	0
Richards	6	0	18	2

AUSTRALIA	O	M	R	W
Lillee	10	0	66	1
Thomson	6	1	21	0
Walker	12	2	41	1
G.S.Chappell	4	0	13	0
Mallett	11	2	35	1
I.M.Chappell	3	1	9	0

FALL OF WICKETS		
Wkt	A	WI
1st	0	29
2nd	21	153
3rd	49	159
4th	56	–
5th	61	–
6th	160	–
7th	173	–
8th	174	–
9th	192	–
10th	192	–

Umpires: H.D.Bird (6) and D.J.Constant (6).

PAKISTAN v SRI LANKA

At Trent Bridge, Nottingham, on 14 June 1975.　Toss: Sri Lanka.
Result: **PAKISTAN** won by 192 runs.　Award: Zaheer Abbas.
LOI debuts: Sri Lanka – G.R.A.de Silva.

PAKISTAN		Runs	Balls	4/6
Sadiq Mohammed	c Opatha b Warnapura	74		12/1
*Majid Khan	c Tennekoon b D.S.de Silva	84		9/1
Zaheer Abbas	b Opatha	97		10/1
Mushtaq Mohammed	c Heyn b Warnapura	26		2
Wasim Raja	c Opatha b Warnapura	2		–
Javed Miandad	not out	28		1
Imran Khan	b Opatha	0		–
Parvez Mir	not out	4		–
†Wasim Bari				
Asif Masood				
Naseer Malik				
Extras	(b 4, lb 4, w 2, nb 5)	15		
Total	(60 overs; 6 wickets)	**330**		

SRI LANKA		Runs	Balls	4/6
†E.R.Fernando	c and b Miandad	21		3
B.Warnapura	b Imran	2		–
*A.P.B.Tennekoon	lbw b Naseer	30		4
M.H.Tissera	c Wasim Bari b Sadiq	12		2
P.D.Heyn	c Zaheer b Miandad	1		–
A.N.Ranasinghe	b Wasim Raja	9		–
H.S.M.Pieris	lbw b Parvez	16		1
A.R.M.Opatha	c Zaheer b Sadiq	0		–
D.S.de Silva	b Imran	26		4
L.W.S.Kaluperuma	not out	13		1
G.R.A.de Silva	c Wasim Raja b Imran	0		–
Extras	(lb 1, w 3, nb 4)	8		
Total	(50.1 overs)	**138**		

SRI LANKA	O	M	R	W
Opatha	12	0	67	2
Pieris	9	0	54	0
G.R.A.de Silva	7	1	46	0
D.S.de Silva	12	1	61	1
Kaluperuma	9	1	35	0
Warnapura	8	0	42	3
Ranasinghe	3	0	10	0

PAKISTAN	O	M	R	W
Asif Masood	6	2	14	0
Imran Khan	7.1	3	15	3
Javed Miandad	7	2	22	2
Naseer Malik	6	1	19	1
Sadiq Mohammed	6	1	20	2
Wasim Raja	7	4	7	1
Mushtaq Mohammed	5	0	16	0
Parvez Mir	6	1	17	1

FALL OF WICKETS		
Wkt	P	SL
1st	159	5
2nd	168	44
3rd	256	60
4th	268	61
5th	318	75
6th	318	79
7th	–	90
8th	–	113
9th	–	135
10th	–	138

Umpires: A.Jepson (4) and T.W.Spencer (5).

ENGLAND v AUSTRALIA (SEMI-FINAL)

At Headingley, Leeds, on 18 June 1975.　Toss: Australia.
Result: **AUSTRALIA** won by 4 wickets.　Award: G.J.Gilmour.
LOI debuts: None.

ENGLAND		Runs	Balls	4/6
D.L.Amiss	lbw b Gilmour	2	7	–
B.Wood	b Gilmour	6	19	1
K.W.R.Fletcher	lbw b Gilmour	8	45	–
A.W.Greig	c Marsh b Gilmour	7	25	1
F.C.Hayes	lbw b Gilmour	4	6	1
*M.H.Denness	b Walker	27	60	1
†A.P.E.Knott	lbw b Gilmour	0	5	–
C.M.Old	c G.S.Chappell b Walker	0	3	–
J.A.Snow	c Marsh b Lillee	2	14	–
G.G.Arnold	not out	18	30	2
P.Lever	lbw b Walker	5	13	–
Extras	(lb 5, w 7, nb 2)	14		
Total	(36.2 overs)	**93**		

AUSTRALIA		Runs	Balls	4/6
A.Turner	lbw b Arnold	7	20	–
R.B.McCosker	b Old	15	50	–
*I.M.Chappell	lbw b Snow	2	19	–
G.S.Chappell	lbw b Snow	4	9	1
K.D.Walters	not out	20	43	2
R.Edwards	b Old	0	3	–
†R.W.Marsh	b Old	5	8	–
G.J.Gilmour	not out	28	28	5
M.H.N.Walker				
D.K.Lillee				
J.R.Thomson				
Extras	(b 1, lb 6, nb 6)	13		
Total	(28.4 overs; 6 wickets)	**94**		

AUSTRALIA	O	M	R	W
Lillee	9	3	26	1
Gilmour	12	6	14	6
Walker	9.2	3	22	3
Thomson	6	0	17	0

ENGLAND	O	M	R	W
Arnold	7.4	2	15	1
Snow	12	0	30	2
Old	7	2	29	3
Lever	2	0	7	0

FALL OF WICKETS		
Wkt	E	A
1st	2	17
2nd	11	24
3rd	26	32
4th	33	32
5th	35	32
6th	36	39
7th	37	–
8th	52	–
9th	73	–
10th	93	–

Umpires: W.E.Alley (5) and D.J.Constant (7).

WEST INDIES v NEW ZEALAND (SEMI-FINAL)

At Kennington Oval, London, on 18 June 1975.　Toss: West Indies.
Result: **WEST INDIES** won by 5 wickets.　Award: A.I.Kallicharran.
LOI debuts: None.

NEW ZEALAND		Runs	Balls	4/6
*G.M.Turner	c Kanhai b Roberts	36	74	3
J.F.M.Morrison	lbw b Julien	5	26	–
G.P.Howarth	c Murray b Roberts	51	93	3
J.M.Parker	b Lloyd	3	12	–
B.F.Hastings	not out	24	57	4
†K.J.Wadsworth	c Lloyd b Julien	11	21	1
B.J.McKechnie	lbw b Julien	1	9	–
D.R.Hadlee	c Holder b Julien	0	10	–
B.L.Cairns	b Holder	10	14	1
H.J.Howarth	b Holder	0	1	–
R.O.Collinge	b Holder	2	4	–
Extras	(b 1, lb 5, w 2, nb 7)	15		
Total	(52.2 overs)	**158**		

WEST INDIES		Runs	Balls	4/6
R.C.Fredericks	c Hastings b Hadlee	6	14	–
C.G.Greenidge	lbw b Collinge	55	95	9/1
A.I.Kallicharran	c and b Collinge	72	92	7/1
I.V.A.Richards	lbw b Collinge	5	10	1
R.B.Kanhai	not out	12	18	2
*C.H.Lloyd	c Hastings b McKechnie	3	8	–
B.D.Julien	not out	4	5	1
†D.L.Murray				
K.D.Boyce				
V.A.Holder				
A.M.E.Roberts				
Extras	(lb 1, nb 1)	2		
Total	(40.1 overs; 5 wickets)	**159**		

WEST INDIES	O	M	R	W
Julien	12	5	27	4
Roberts	11	3	18	2
Holder	8.2	0	30	3
Boyce	9	0	31	0
Lloyd	12	1	37	1

NEW ZEALAND	O	M	R	W
Collinge	12	4	28	3
Hadlee	10	0	54	1
Cairns	6.1	2	23	0
McKechnie	8	0	37	1
H.J.Howarth	4	0	15	0

FALL OF WICKETS		
Wkt	NZ	WI
1st	8	8
2nd	98	133
3rd	106	139
4th	106	142
5th	125	151
6th	133	–
7th	139	–
8th	155	–
9th	155	–
10th	158	–

Umpires: W.L.Budd (5) and A.E.Fagg (6).

AUSTRALIA v WEST INDIES (FINAL)

At Lord's, London, on 21 June 1975.   Toss: Australia.
Result: **WEST INDIES** won by 17 runs.   Award: C.H.Lloyd.
LOI debuts: None.

WEST INDIES		Runs	Balls	4/6
R.C.Fredericks	hit wicket b Lillee	7	13	–
C.G.Greenidge	c Marsh b Thomson	13	61	1
A.I.Kallicharran	c Marsh b Gilmour	12	18	2
R.B.Kanhai	b Gilmour	55	105	8
*C.H.Lloyd	c Marsh b Gilmour	102	85	12/2
I.V.A.Richards	b Gilmour	5	11	1
K.D.Boyce	c G.S.Chappell b Thomson	34	37	3
B.D.Julien	not out	26	37	1
†D.L.Murray	c and b Gilmour	14	10	1/1
V.A.Holder	not out	6	2	1
A.M.E.Roberts				
Extras	(lb 6, nb 11)	17		
Total	(60 overs; 8 wickets)	**291**		

AUSTRALIA		Runs	Balls	4/6
A.Turner	run out	40	24	1
R.B.McCosker	c Kallicharran b Boyce	7	54	1
*I.M.Chappell	run out	62	93	6
G.S.Chappell	run out	15	23	2
K.D.Walters	b Lloyd	35	51	5
†R.W.Marsh	b Boyce	11	24	–
R.Edwards	c Fredericks b Boyce	28	37	2
G.J.Gilmour	c Kanhai b Boyce	14	11	2
M.H.N.Walker	run out	7	9	1
J.R.Thomson	run out	21	21	2
D.K.Lillee	not out	16	19	1
Extras	(b 2, lb 9, nb 7)	18		
Total	(58.4 overs)	**274**		

AUSTRALIA	O	M	R	W
Lillee	12	1	55	1
Gilmour	12	2	48	5
Thomson	12	1	44	2
Walker	12	1	71	0
G.S.Chappell	7	0	33	0
Walters	5	0	23	0

WEST INDIES	O	M	R	W
Julien	12	0	58	0
Roberts	11	1	45	0
Boyce	12	0	50	4
Holder	11.4	1	65	0
Lloyd	12	1	38	1

FALL OF WICKETS		
Wkt	WI	A
1st	12	25
2nd	27	81
3rd	50	115
4th	199	162
5th	206	170
6th	209	195
7th	261	221
8th	285	231
9th	–	233
10th	–	274

Umpires: H.D.Bird (7) and T.W.Spencer (6).

THE 1979 WORLD CUP

Without being graced with the exemplary weather of the initial venture, the second World Cup series proved another outstanding success. Once again West Indies, the favourites, won the Prudential Cup but against different finalists.

The tournament was run on similar lines to its predecessor with eight teams playing 15 matches spread over as many days and according to 60-over Gillette Cup rules. Again only Test match grounds were used but with a different distribution: Headingley, Old Trafford and Trent Bridge each hosting three games, while Edgbaston, Lord's and The Oval staged two apiece.

This time a special mini-tournament of 60-over matches for the ICC Trophy was held on Midlands club grounds to determine which two associate members would qualify to join the six Test-playing countries in the Prudential World Cup. Fifteen associates (all except West Africa and Hong Kong) entered this qualifying tournament and were divided into three groups. When Gibraltar withdrew they were replaced by Wales, who, not being an associate ICC member were ineligible for the competition. They did not compete for a place in the semi-finals but points scored against them counted. The three group winners plus the best of the runners-up qualified for the semi-finals. Denmark (16), Bermuda (14) and Canada (12) were joined by Sri Lanka (10), the latter being equal on points with East Africa and USA but having a superior run-rate. Apart from the final, which was staged two days prior to the World Cup final itself, all the matches were played during the fortnight immediately preceding the major tournament. Unfortunately those two weeks attracted an abnormal amount of rain and six matches were abandoned. The competition did not escape political interference, Israel gaining four points when the Sri Lanka team 'withdrew from the game'.

The two victorious semi-finalists were Sri Lanka (predictably) who thrashed Denmark by 208 runs and Canada who beat Bermuda by four wickets with seven balls to spare. The final, at the Worcester County Ground, produced an exhilarating match in which 588 runs were scored, Sri Lanka (324-8) triumphing over Canada (264-5) by 60 runs to become the ICC Trophy's first holders.

As in 1975, the eight teams contesting the Prudential Cup were divided into two groups of four, each playing the other once, but this time England and Australia were not seeded. The draw, made at the ICC meeting at Lord's in July 1978, put Australia, England and Pakistan in Group A, while West Indies, India and New Zealand were in Group B. The leading two teams in each group qualified for the semi-finals.

The final group placings again eliminated India and the two associate members, but this time they were joined by an Australian team still bereft of its Packer players. Sri Lanka provided the group stage's major highlight when they gained their first World Cup victory, defeating India by 47 runs at Old Trafford.

FINAL GROUP TABLES

GROUP A	P	W	L	Pts		GROUP B	P	W	L	NR	Pts
ENGLAND	3	3	0	12		WEST INDIES	3	2	0	1	10
PAKISTAN	3	2	1	8		NEW ZEALAND	3	2	1	0	8
Australia	3	1	2	4		Sri Lanka	3	1	1	1	6
Canada	3	0	3	0		India	3	0	3	0	0

Graced by brilliant weather, the semi-finals produced two vintage matches. At Old Trafford England scraped home against New Zealand by just 9 runs, at that time the narrowest margin of victory in a World Cup match. The holders' clash with Pakistan at The Oval provided a run feast, 543 runs coming from 116.2 overs. Despite a magnificent second-wicket partnership of 166 between Majid Khan (81) and Zaheer Abbas (93), Pakistan failed by 43 runs to match the record West Indies World Cup total of 293.

The final was also blessed with fine weather and an all-ticket capacity crowd of 25,000. They saw Clive Lloyd's team retain the World Cup with an emphatic 92-run victory after Viv Richards and Collis King rescued them from a tottering start. Richards contributed 136 not out but it was King's innings which stays in the memory, his 86 coming off just 66 balls and including 3 sixes and 10 fours. England had opted to go into the match with only four specialist bowlers, the remaining 12 overs being shared by Geoff Boycott, Graham Gooch and Wayne Larkins and producing 86 runs. Although Mike Brearley and Boycott scored 129 for the first wicket, they fell a long way behind the asking rate, the Yorkshireman taking 17 overs to reach double figures. Brearley's dismissal left England wanting 158 from the last 22 overs and the giant Joel Garner, with five wickets for 4 runs from 11 balls made sure that they were disappointed.

Although the total attendance for the competition was down by 28,000 (132,000 compared with 160,000 in 1975), the fall was caused by the poor weather. Increased prices meant that gate receipts increased to £359,700, almost double the £188,000 for the first Prudential Cup. Profits amounted to £350,000.

At their annual meeting following this tournament, the ICC agreed to make the competition a four-yearly event with the 1983 Cup again being staged in England.

WEST INDIES v INDIA

At Edgbaston, Birmingham, on 9 June 1979.   Toss: West Indies.
Result: **WEST INDIES** won by 9 wickets.   Award: C.G.Greenidge.
LOI debuts: India – S.C.Khanna.

INDIA		**Runs**	**Balls**	**4/6**
S.M.Gavaskar	c Holding b Roberts	8		
A.D.Gaekwad	c King b Holding	11		
D.B.Vengsarkar	c Kallicharran b Holding	7		
G.R.Viswanath	b Holding	75		
B.P.Patel	run out	15		
M.Amarnath	c Murray b Croft	8		
Kapil Dev	b King	12		
†S.C.Khanna	c Haynes b Holding	0		
K.D.Ghavri	c Murray b Garner	12		
*S.Venkataraghavan	not out	13		
B.S.Bedi	c Lloyd b Roberts	13		
Extras	(b 6, lb 3, w 3, nb 4)	16		
Total	(53.1 overs)	**190**		

WEST INDIES		**Runs**	**Balls**	**4/6**
C.G.Greenidge	not out	106		
D.L.Haynes	lbw b Kapil Dev	47		
I.V.A.Richards	not out	28		
A.I.Kallicharran				
*C.H.Lloyd				
C.L.King				
†D.L.Murray				
A.M.E.Roberts				
J.Garner				
M.A.Holding				
C.E.H.Croft				
Extras	(lb 6, nb 7)	13		
Total	(51.3 overs; 1 wicket)	**194**		

WEST INDIES	O	M	R	W
Roberts	9.1	0	32	2
Holding	12	2	33	4
Garner	12	1	42	1
Croft	10	1	31	1
King	10	1	36	1

INDIA	O	M	R	W
Kapil Dev	10	1	46	1
Ghavri	10	2	25	0
Venkataraghavan	12	3	30	0
Bedi	12	0	45	0
Amarnath	7.3	0	35	0

FALL OF WICKETS		
Wkt	I	WI
1st	10	138
2nd	24	–
3rd	29	–
4th	56	–
5th	77	
6th	112	–
7th	119	–
8th	155	–
9th	163	–
10th	190	–

Umpires: D.G.L.Evans (1) and J.G.Langridge (5).

NEW ZEALAND v SRI LANKA

At Trent Bridge, Nottingham, on 9 June 1979.   Toss: New Zealand.
Result: **NEW ZEALAND** won by 9 wickets.   Award: G.P.Howarth.
LOI debuts: New Zealand – J.V.Coney, W.K.Lees, L.W.Stott; Sri Lanka – D.L.S.de Silva,
R.L.Dias, S.A.Jayasinghe, S.P.Pasqual.

SRI LANKA		Runs	Balls	4/6
B.Warnapura	c and b McKechnie	20		
S.R.de S.Wettimuny	b Cairns	16		
*A.P.B.Tennekoon	b Stott	59		6
R.L.Dias	c and b Stott	25		
L.R.D.Mendis	c Turner b Troup	14		
D.S.de Silva	c Burgess b Stott	6		
†S.A.Jayasinghe	run out	1		
S.P.Pasqual	b Hadlee	1		
A.R.M.Opatha	b McKechnie	18		
D.L.S.de Silva	c Wright b McKechnie	10		
G.R.A.de Silva	not out	2		
Extras	(lb 13, w 2, nb 2)	17		
Total	(56.5 overs)	**189**		

NEW ZEALAND		Runs	Balls	4/6
G.M.Turner	not out	83		4
J.G.Wright	c Tennekoon b G.R.A.de Silva	34		6
G.P.Howarth	not out	63		8/1
J.V.Coney				
*M.G.Burgess				
†W.K.Lees				
B.J.McKechnie				
B.L.Cairns				
R.J.Hadlee				
L.W.Stott				
G.B.Troup				
Extras	(lb 7, w 2, nb 1)	10		
Total	(47.4 overs; 1 wicket)	**190**		

NEW ZEALAND	O	M	R	W
Hadlee	12	3	24	1
Troup	10	0	30	1
Cairns	12	1	45	1
McKechnie	10.5	2	25	3
Stott	12	1	48	3

SRI LANKA	O	M	R	W
Opatha	7	1	31	0
D.L.S.de Silva	8	2	18	0
Warnapura	7	0	30	0
D.S.de Silva	9	0	42	0
G.R.A.de Silva	12	1	39	1
Pasqual	4.4	0	20	0

FALL OF WICKETS		
Wkt	SL	NZ
1st	26	64
2nd	57	–
3rd	107	–
4th	137	–
5th	149	–
6th	150	–
7th	150	–
8th	154	–
9th	178	–
10th	189	–

Umpires: W.L.Budd (9) and K.E.Palmer (3).

ENGLAND v AUSTRALIA

At Lord's, London, on 9 June 1979.   Toss: England.
Result: **ENGLAND** won by 6 wickets.   Award: G.A.Gooch.
LOI debuts: None.

AUSTRALIA		Runs	Balls	4/6
A.M.J.Hilditch	b Boycott	47	108	2
W.M.Darling	lbw b Willis	25	61	3
A.R.Border	c Taylor b Edmonds	34	74	4
*K.J.Hughes	c Hendrick b Boycott	6	13	1
G.N.Yallop	run out	10	20	1
G.J.Cosier	run out	6	20	–
T.J.Laughlin	run out	8	22	–
†K.J.Wright	lbw b Old	6	15	–
G.Dymock	not out	4	12	–
R.M.Hogg	run out	0	5	–
A.G.Hurst	not out	3	10	–
Extras	(b 4, lb 5, w 1)	10		
Total	(60 overs; 9 wickets)	**159**		

ENGLAND		Runs	Balls	4/6
*J.M.Brearley	c Wright b Laughlin	44	147	2
G.Boycott	lbw b Hogg	1	5	–
D.W.Randall	c Wright b Hurst	1	3	–
G.A.Gooch	lbw b Laughlin	53	96	6
D.I.Gower	not out	22	30	2
I.T.Botham	not out	18	14	2
P.H.Edmonds				
†R.W.Taylor				
C.M.Old				
M.Hendrick				
R.G.D.Willis				
Extras	(lb 10, nb 11)	21		
Total	(47.1 overs; 4 wickets)	**160**		

ENGLAND	O	M	R	W		FALL OF WICKETS		
Willis	11	2	20	1		Wkt	A	E
Hendrick	12	2	24	0		1st	56	4
Old	12	2	33	1		2nd	97	5
Botham	8	0	32	0		3rd	111	113
Edmonds	11	1	25	1		4th	131	124
Boycott	6	0	15	2		5th	132	–
						6th	137	–
AUSTRALIA	O	M	R	W		7th	150	–
Hogg	9	1	25	1		8th	153	–
Hurst	10	3	33	1		9th	153	–
Dymock	11	2	19	0		10th	–	–
Cosier	8	1	24	0				
Laughlin	9.1	0	38	2				

Umpires: D.J.Constant (12) and B.J.Meyer (3).

PAKISTAN v CANADA

At Headingley, Leeds, on 9 June 1979. Toss: Canada.
Result: **PAKISTAN** won by 8 wickets. Award: Sadiq Mohammed.
LOI debuts: Canada – all.

CANADA		Runs	Balls	4/6
G.R.Sealy	c and b Asif	45		
C.J.D.Chappell	c and b Sikander	14		
F.A.Dennis	c Wasim b Sarfraz	25		
M.P.Stead	c Zaheer b Asif	10		
C.A.Marshall	b Imran	8		
J.C.B.Vaughan	c and b Asif	0		
*†B.M.Mauricette	c Zaheer b Sarfraz	15		
Tariq Javed	st Wasim b Majid	3		
J.M.Patel	b Sarfraz	0		
C.C.Henry	not out	1		
J.N.Valentine				
Extras	(lb 10, w 5, nb 3)	18		
Total	(60 overs; 9 wickets)	**139**		

PAKISTAN		Runs	Balls	4/6
Majid Khan	b Valentine	1		
Sadiq Mohammed	not out	57		
Zaheer Abbas	run out	36		
Haroon Rashid	not out	37		
Javed Miandad				
*Asif Iqbal				
Mudassar Nazar				
Imran Khan				
†Wasim Bari				
Sarfraz Nawaz				
Sikander Bakht				
Extras	(b 1, lb 3, w 1, nb 4)	9		
Total	(40.1 overs; 2 wickets)	**140**		

PAKISTAN	O	M	R	W		FALL OF WICKETS		
Imran Khan	11	1	27	1	Wkt	C	P	
Sarfraz Nawaz	10	1	26	3	1st	54	4	
Mudassar Nazar	4	1	11	0	2nd	85	61	
Sikander Bakht	12	5	18	1	3rd	103	–	
Majid Khan	11	4	11	1	4th	110	–	
Asif Iqbal	12	2	28	3	5th	110	–	
					6th	129	–	
CANADA	O	M	R	W	7th	134	–	
Valentine	9	3	18	1	8th	138	–	
Vaughan	5	1	21	0	9th	139	–	
Henry	5	0	26	0	10th	–	–	
Patel	11.1	0	27	0				
Sealy	6	0	21	0				
Stead	4	0	18	0				

Umpires: H.D.Bird (12) and A.G.T.Whitehead (1).

SECOND WORLD CUP (5th Match): WEST INDIES v SRI LANKA
At Kennington Oval, London, on 13, 14, 15 June 1979. Toss: –.
No result – match abandoned without a ball bowled (2 points each).

NEW ZEALAND v INDIA

At Headingley, Leeds, on 13 June 1979.   Toss: New Zealand.
Result: **NEW ZEALAND** won by 8 wickets.   Award: B.A.Edgar.
LOI debuts: None.

INDIA		Runs	Balls	4/6
S.M.Gavaskar	c Lees b Hadlee	55		5
A.D.Gaekwad	b Hadlee	10		
D.B.Vengsarkar	c Lees b McKechnie	1		
G.R.Viswanath	c Turner b Cairns	9		
B.P.Patel	b Troup	38		5
M.Amarnath	b Troup	1		
Kapil Dev	c and b Cairns	25		3
K.D.Ghavri	c Coney b McKechnie	20		
†S.C.Khanna	c Morrison b McKechnie	7		
*S.Venkataraghavan	c Lees b Cairns	1		
B.S.Bedi	not out	1		
Extras	(lb 8, w 5, nb 1)	14		
Total	(55.5 overs)	**182**		

NEW ZEALAND		Runs	Balls	4/6
J.G.Wright	c and b Amarnath	48		1
B.A.Edgar	not out	84		8
B.L.Cairns	run out	2		–
G.M.Turner	not out	43		6
J.V.Coney				
*M.G.Burgess				
J.F.M.Morrison				
B.J.McKechnie				
†W.K.Lees				
R.J.Hadlee				
G.B.Troup				
Extras	(lb 3, nb 3)	6		
Total	(57 overs; 2 wickets)	**183**		

NEW ZEALAND	O	M	R	W		FALL OF WICKETS		
					Wkt	I	NZ	
Hadlee	10	2	20	2	1st	27	100	
Troup	10	2	36	2	2nd	38	103	
Cairns	11.5	0	36	3	3rd	53	–	
McKechnie	12	1	24	3	4th	104	–	
Coney	7	0	33	0	5th	107	–	
Morrison	5	0	19	0	6th	147	–	
INDIA	O	M	R	W	7th	153	–	
Amarnath	12	1	39	1	8th	180	–	
Bedi	12	1	32	0	9th	180	–	
Venkataraghavan	12	0	34	0	10th	182	–	
Ghavri	10	1	34	0				
Kapil Dev	11	3	38	0				

Umpires: W.L.Budd (10) and A.G.T.Whitehead (2).

AUSTRALIA v PAKISTAN

At Trent Bridge, Nottingham, on 13, 14 June 1979.   Toss: Australia.
Result: **PAKISTAN** won by 89 runs.   Award: Asif Iqbal.
LOI debuts: Australia – J.K.Moss, G.D.Porter.

PAKISTAN		Runs	Balls	4/6
Sadiq Mohammed	c Moss b Porter	27	73	2
Majid Khan	b Dymock	61	100	7/1
Zaheer Abbas	c and b Cosier	16	32	1
Haroon Rashid	c Wright b Cosier	16	42	2
Javed Miandad	c Border b Cosier	46	46	4
*Asif Iqbal	c sub (D.F.Whatmore) b Hurst	61	57	7
Wasim Raja	c Moss b Border	18	12	2/1
Imran Khan	not out	15	9	–
Mudassar Nazar	not out	1	1	–
†Wasim Bari				
Sikander Bakht				
Extras	(b 6, lb 4, w 5, nb 10)	25		
Total	(60 overs; 7 wickets)	**286**		

AUSTRALIA		Runs	Balls	4/6
W.M.Darling	c Wasim Bari b Imran	13	25	1
A.M.J.Hilditch	c Sadiq b Mudassar	72	129	4
A.R.Border	b Sikander	0	5	–
*K.J.Hughes	lbw b Sikander	15	37	2
G.N.Yallop	b Majid	37	64	2
J.K.Moss	run out	7	16	–
G.J.Cosier	c and b Majid	0	1	–
†K.J.Wright	c Wasim Bari b Imran	23	37	–
G.D.Porter	c Sadiq b Majid	3	9	–
G.Dymock	lbw b Sikander	10	18	–
A.G.Hurst	not out	3	2	–
Extras	(b 1, lb 5, w 8)	14		
Total	(57.1 overs)	**197**		

AUSTRALIA	O	M	R	W		FALL OF WICKETS		
Porter	12	3	20	1	Wkt		P	A
Dymock	12	3	28	1	1st		99	22
Cosier	12	1	54	3	2nd		99	24
Hurst	12	0	65	1	3rd		133	46
Yallop	8	0	56	0	4th		152	117
Border	4	0	38	1	5th		239	136
					6th		268	137
PAKISTAN	O	M	R	W	7th		274	172
Asif Iqbal	12	0	36	0	8th		–	175
Majid Khan	12	0	53	3	9th		–	193
Mudassar Nazar	12	0	31	1	10th		–	197
Imran Khan	10.1	2	29	2				
Sikander Bakht	11	1	34	3				

Umpires: H.D.Bird (13) and K.E.Palmer (4).

ENGLAND v CANADA

At Old Trafford, Manchester, on 13 *(no play)*, 14 June 1979. Toss: Canada.
Result: **ENGLAND** won by 8 wickets.   Award: C.M.Old.
LOI debuts: Canada – R.G.Callender.

CANADA		Runs	Balls	4/6
G.R.Sealy	c Botham b Hendrick	3	9	–
C.J.D.Chappell	lbw b Botham	5	31	–
F.A.Dennis	hit wicket b Willis	21	99	2
Tariq Javed	lbw b Old	4	40	–
J.C.B.Vaughan	b Old	1	10	–
C.A.Marshall	b Old	2	7	–
*†B.M.Mauricette	b Willis	0	8	–
†M.P.Stead	b Old	0	12	–
J.M.Patel	b Willis	1	14	–
R.G.Callender	b Willis	0	3	–
J.N.Valentine	not out	3	11	–
Extras	(lb 4, nb 1)	5		
Total	(40.3 overs)	**45**		

ENGLAND		Runs	Balls	4/6
*J.M.Brearley	lbw b Valentine	0	10	–
G.Boycott	not out	14	36	–
D.W.Randall	b Callender	5	11	1
G.A.Gooch	not out	21	31	2/1
D.I.Gower				
I.T.Botham				
G.Miller				
†R.W.Taylor				
C.M.Old				
R.G.D.Willis				
M.Hendrick				
Extras	(w 3, nb 3)	6		
Total	(13.5 overs; 2 wickets)	**46**		

ENGLAND	O	M	R	W		FALL OF WICKETS		
Willis	10.3	3	11	4	Wkt		C	E
Hendrick	8	4	5	1	1st		5	3
Botham	9	5	12	1	2nd		13	11
Miller	2	1	1	0	3rd		25	–
Boycott	1	0	3	0	4th		29	–
Old	10	5	8	4	5th		37	–
					6th		38	–
CANADA	O	M	R	W	7th		41	–
Valentine	7	2	20	1	8th		41	–
Callender	6	1	14	1	9th		42	–
Stead	0.5	0	6	0	10th		45	–

Umpires: J.G.Langridge (6) and B.J.Meyer (4).

INDIA v SRI LANKA

At Old Trafford, Manchester, on 16, 18 June 1979.　Toss: India.
Result: **SRI LANKA** won by 47 runs.　Award: L.R.D.Mendis.
LOI debuts: Sri Lanka – F.R.M.de S.Goonatilleke, R.S.Madugalle.

SRI LANKA		Runs	Balls	4/6
*B.Warnapura	c Gaekwad b Amarnath	18		2
S.R.de S.Wettimuny	c Vengsarkar b Kapil Dev	67		8
R.L.Dias	c and b Amarnath	50		2
L.R.D.Mendis	run out	64		1/3
R.S.Madugalle	c Khanna b Amarnath	4		
S.P.Pasqual	not out	23		1
D.S.de Silva	not out	1		
†S.A.Jayasinghe				
A.R.M.Opatha				
D.L.S.de Silva				
F.R.M.de S.Goonatilleke				
Extras	(lb 8, w 2, nb 1)	11		
Total	(60 overs; 5 wickets)	**238**		

INDIA		Runs	Balls	4/6
S.M.Gavaskar	c Dias b Warnapura	26		2
A.D.Gaekwad	c sub‡ b D.L.S.de Silva	33		2
D.B.Vengsarkar	c D.L.S.de Silva b D.S.de Silva	36		3
G.R.Viswanath	run out	22		–
B.P.Patel	b D.S.de Silva	10		1
Kapil Dev	c Warnapura b D.L.S.de Silva	16		2
M.Amarnath	b D.S.de Silva	7		–
K.D.Ghavri	c Warnapura b Opatha	3		–
†S.C.Khanna	c Dias b Opatha	10		1
*S.Venkataraghavan	not out	9		–
B.S.Bedi	c Jayasinghe b Opatha	5		–
Extras	(lb 10, w 3, nb 1)	14		
Total	(54.1 overs)	**191**		

INDIA	O	M	R	W		FALL OF WICKETS		
Kapil Dev	12	2	53	1		Wkt	SL	I
Ghavri	12	0	53	0		1st	31	60
Amarnath	12	3	40	3		2nd	127	76
Bedi	12	2	37	0		3rd	147	119
Venkataraghavan	12	0	44	0		4th	175	132
						5th	227	147
SRI LANKA	O	M	R	W		6th	–	160
Opatha	10.1	0	31	3		7th	–	162
Goonatilleke	9	1	34	0		8th	–	170
Warnapura	12	0	47	1		9th	–	185
D.L.S.de Silva	12	0	36	2		10th	–	191
D.S.de Silva	11	1	29	3				

Umpires: K.E.Palmer (5) and A.G.T.Whitehead (3).　　　　‡(G.R.A.de Silva)

WEST INDIES v NEW ZEALAND

At Trent Bridge, Nottingham, on 16 June 1979.   Toss: New Zealand.
Result: **WEST INDIES** won by 32 runs.   Award: C.H.Lloyd.
LOI debuts: New Zealand – E.J.Chatfield.

WEST INDIES		Runs	Balls	4/6
C.G.Greenidge	c Edgar b Coney	65		3/1
D.L.Haynes	lbw b Hadlee	12		
I.V.A.Richards	c Burgess b Coney	9		
A.I.Kallicharran	b McKechnie	39		2
*C.H.Lloyd	not out	73		4
C.L.King	lbw b Cairns	12		
†D.L.Murray	c Coney b Chatfield	12		
A.M.E.Roberts	c Lees b Cairns	1		
J.Garner	not out	9		
M.A.Holding				
C.E.H.Croft				
Extras	(b 5, lb 7)	12		
Total	(60 overs; 7 wickets)	**244**		

NEW ZEALAND		Runs	Balls	4/6
B.A.Edgar	run out	12		
J.G.Wright	c Lloyd b Garner	15		
J.V.Coney	c Garner b King	36		3
G.M.Turner	c Lloyd b Roberts	20		
J.F.M.Morrison	c Murray b Garner	11		
*M.G.Burgess	c Richards b Roberts	35		3
†W.K.Lees	b Croft	5		
R.J.Hadlee	b Roberts	42		4
B.J.McKechnie	not out	13		
B.L.Cairns	b Holding	1		
E.J.Chatfield	not out	3		
Extras	(lb 14, w 4, nb 1)	19		
Total	(60 overs; 9 wickets)	**212**		

NEW ZEALAND	O	M	R	W
Hadlee	11	2	41	1
Chatfield	11	0	45	1
Cairns	12	1	48	2
Coney	12	0	40	2
McKechnie	11	0	46	1
Morrison	3	0	12	0

WEST INDIES	O	M	R	W
Roberts	12	2	43	3
Holding	12	1	29	1
Croft	12	1	38	1
Garner	12	0	45	2
King	12	1	38	1

FALL OF WICKETS		
Wkt	WI	NZ
1st	23	27
2nd	61	38
3rd	117	90
4th	152	91
5th	175	138
6th	202	143
7th	204	160
8th	–	199
9th	–	202
10th	–	–

Umpires: H.D.Bird (14) and B.J.Meyer (5).

AUSTRALIA v CANADA

At Edgbaston, Birmingham, on 16 June 1979.   Toss: Australia.
Result: **AUSTRALIA** won by 7 wickets.   Award: A.G.Hurst.
LOI debuts: Canada – S.Baksh.

CANADA		Runs	Balls	4/6
G.R.Sealy	c Porter b Dymock	25	30	4
C.J.D.Chappell	lbw b Hurst	19	42	2
F.A.Dennis	lbw b Hurst	1	8	–
Tariq Javed	c Wright b Porter	8	30	1
S.Baksh	b Hurst	0	6	–
J.C.B.Vaughan	b Porter	29	43	4
*†B.M.Mauricette	c Hilditch b Cosier	5	22	–
J.M.Patel	b Cosier	2	4	–
R.G.Callender	c Wright b Hurst	0	2	–
C.C.Henry	c Hughes b Hurst	5	11	1
J.N.Valentine	not out	0	6	–
Extras	(b 4, lb 5, w 1, nb 1)	11		
Total	(33.2 overs)	**105**		

AUSTRALIA		Runs	Balls	4/6
A.M.J.Hilditch	c Valentine b Henry	24	30	3
W.M.Darling	lbw b Valentine	13	16	2
A.R.Border	b Henry	25	53	4
*K.J.Hughes	not out	27	40	2
G.N.Yallop	not out	13	20	–
G.J.Cosier				
†K.J.Wright				
G.D.Porter				
R.M.Hogg				
G.Dymock				
A.G.Hurst				
Extras	(lb 1, nb 3)	4		
Total	(26 overs; 3 wickets)	**106**		

AUSTRALIA	O	M	R	W		FALL OF WICKETS		
Hogg	2	0	26	0	Wkt	C	A	
Hurst	10	3	21	5	1st	44	23	
Dymock	8	2	17	1	2nd	50	53	
Porter	6	2	13	2	3rd	51	72	
Cosier	7.2	2	17	2	4th	51	–	
					5th	78	–	
CANADA	O	M	R	W	6th	97	–	
Valentine	3	0	28	1	7th	97	–	
Callender	3	0	12	0	8th	98	–	
Henry	10	0	27	2	9th	104	–	
Vaughan	6	0	15	0	10th	105	–	
Patel	4	0	20	0				

Umpires: D.J.Constant (13) and J.G.Langridge (7).

ENGLAND v PAKISTAN

At Headingley, Leeds, on 16 June 1979.   Toss: Pakistan.
Result: **ENGLAND** won by 14 runs.   Award: M.Hendrick.
LOI debuts: None.

ENGLAND		Runs	Balls	4/6
*J.M.Brearley	c Wasim Bari b Imran	0	2	–
G.Boycott	lbw b Majid	18	54	2
D.W.Randall	c Wasim Bari b Sikander	1	5	–
G.A.Gooch	c Sadiq b Sikander	33	90	5
D.I.Gower	b Majid	27	40	3
I.T.Botham	b Majid	22	48	1/1
P.H.Edmonds	c Wasim Raja b Asif	2	23	–
†R.W.Taylor	not out	20	59	1
C.M.Old	c and b Asif	2	7	–
R.G.D.Willis	b Sikander	24	37	3
M.Hendrick	not out	1	1	–
Extras	(lb 3, w 7, nb 5)	15		
Total	(60 overs; 9 wickets)	**165**		

PAKISTAN		Runs	Balls	4/6
Majid Khan	c Botham b Hendrick	7	20	1
Sadiq Mohammed	b Hendrick	18	27	4
Mudassar Nazar	lbw b Hendrick	0	2	–
Zaheer Abbas	c Taylor b Botham	3	19	–
Haroon Rashid	c Brearley b Hendrick	1	2	–
Javed Miandad	lbw b Botham	0	4	–
*Asif Iqbal	c Brearley b Willis	51	104	5
Wasim Raja	lbw b Old	21	25	4
Imran Khan	not out	21	82	1
†Wasim Bari	c Taylor b Boycott	17	33	2
Sikander Bakht	c Hendrick b Boycott	2	19	–
Extras	(lb 8, w 1, nb 1)	10		
Total	(56 overs)	**151**		

PAKISTAN	O	M	R	W
Imran Khan	12	3	24	1
Sikander Bakht	12	3	32	3
Mudassar Nazar	12	4	30	0
Asif Iqbal	12	3	37	2
Majid Khan	12	2	27	3

ENGLAND	O	M	R	W
Willis	11	2	37	1
Hendrick	12	6	15	4
Botham	12	3	38	2
Old	12	2	28	1
Edmonds	3	0	8	0
Boycott	5	0	14	2
Gooch	1	0	1	0

FALL OF WICKETS		
Wkt	E	P
1st	0	27
2nd	4	27
3rd	51	28
4th	70	30
5th	99	31
6th	115	34
7th	115	86
8th	118	115
9th	161	145
10th	–	151

Umpires: W.L.Budd (11) and D.G.L.Evans (2).

ENGLAND v NEW ZEALAND (SEMI-FINAL)

At Old Trafford, Manchester, on 20 June 1979.   Toss: New Zealand.
Result: **ENGLAND** won by 9 runs.   Award: G.A.Gooch.
LOI debuts: England – W.Larkins.

ENGLAND		Runs	Balls	4/6
*J.M.Brearley	c Lees b Coney	53	115	3
G.Boycott	c Howarth b Hadlee	2	14	–
W.Larkins	c Coney b McKechnie	7	37	–
G.A.Gooch	b McKechnie	71	84	1/3
D.I.Gower	run out	1	1	–
I.T.Botham	lbw b Cairns	21	30	2
D.W.Randall	not out	42	50	1/1
C.M.Old	c Lees b Troup	0	2	–
†R.W.Taylor	run out	12	25	1
R.G.D.Willis	not out	1	2	–
M.Hendrick				
Extras	(lb 8, w 3)	11		
Total	(60 overs; 8 wickets)	**221**		

NEW ZEALAND		Runs	Balls	4/6
J.G.Wright	run out	69	137	9
B.A.Edgar	lbw b Old	17	38	1
G.P.Howarth	lbw b Boycott	7	12	1
J.V.Coney	lbw b Hendrick	11	39	–
G.M.Turner	lbw b Willis	30	51	2
*M.G.Burgess	run out	10	13	–
R.J.Hadlee	b Botham	15	32	1
†W.K.Lees	b Hendrick	23	20	–/1
B.L.Cairns	c Brearley b Hendrick	14	6	1/1
B.J.McKechnie	not out	4	9	–
G.B.Troup	not out	3	3	–
Extras	(b 5, w 4)	9		
Total	(60 overs; 9 wickets)	**212**		

NEW ZEALAND	O	M	R	W		FALL OF WICKETS		
Hadlee	12	4	32	1		Wkt	E	NZ
Troup	12	1	38	1		1st	13	47
Cairns	12	2	47	1		2nd	38	58
Coney	12	0	47	1		3rd	96	104
McKechnie	12	1	46	2		4th	98	112
						5th	145	132
ENGLAND	O	M	R	W		6th	177	162
Botham	12	3	42	1		7th	178	180
Hendrick	12	0	55	3		8th	219	195
Old	12	1	33	1		9th	–	208
Boycott	9	1	24	1		10th	–	–
Gooch	3	1	8	0				
Willis	12	1	41	1				

Umpires: J.G.Langridge (8) and K.E.Palmer (6).

WEST INDIES v PAKISTAN (SEMI-FINAL)

At Kennington Oval, London, on 20 June 1979.   Toss: Pakistan.
Result: **WEST INDIES** won by 43 runs.   Award: C.G.Greenidge.
LOI debuts: None.

WEST INDIES		Runs	Balls	4/6
C.G.Greenidge	c Wasim b Asif	73	107	5/1
D.L.Haynes	c and b Asif	65	115	4
I.V.A.Richards	b Asif	42	62	1
*C.H.Lloyd	c Mudassar b Asif	37	38	3
C.L.King	c sub (Wasim Raja) b Sarfraz	34	25	3
A.I.Kallicharran	b Imran	11	14	–
A.M.E.Roberts	not out	7	4	–
J.Garner	not out	1	1	–
†D.L.Murray				
M.A.Holding				
C.E.H.Croft				
Extras	(b 1, lb 17, w 1, nb 4)	23		
Total	(60 overs; 6 wickets)	**293**		

PAKISTAN		Runs	Balls	4/6
Majid Khan	c Kallicharran b Croft	81	124	7
Sadiq Mohammed	c Murray b Holding	2	7	–
Zaheer Abbas	c Murray b Croft	93	122	8/1
Haroon Rashid	run out	15	22	1
Javed Miandad	lbw b Croft	0	1	–
*Asif Iqbal	c Holding b Richards	17	20	1
Mudassar Nazar	c Kallicharran b Richards	2	9	–
Imran Khan	c and b Richards	6	4	1
Sarfraz Nawaz	c Haynes b Roberts	12	15	–
†Wasim Bari	c Murray b Roberts	9	12	–
Sikander Bakht	not out	1	4	–
Extras	(lb 9, w 2, nb 1)	12		
Total	(56.2 overs)	**250**		

PAKISTAN	O	M	R	W
Imran Khan	9	1	43	1
Sarfraz Nawaz	12	1	71	1
Sikander Bakht	6	1	24	0
Mudassar Nazar	10	0	50	0
Majid Khan	12	2	26	0
Asif Iqbal	11	0	56	4

WEST INDIES	O	M	R	W
Roberts	9.2	2	41	2
Holding	9	1	28	1
Croft	11	0	29	3
Garner	12	1	47	0
King	7	0	41	0
Richards	8	0	52	3

FALL OF WICKETS		
Wkt	WI	P
1st	132	10
2nd	165	176
3rd	233	187
4th	236	187
5th	285	208
6th	285	220
7th	–	221
8th	–	228
9th	–	246
10th	–	250

Umpires: W.L.Budd (12) and D.J.Constant (14).

ENGLAND v WEST INDIES (FINAL)

At Lord's, London, on 23 June 1979. Toss: England.
Result: **WEST INDIES** won by 92 runs. Award: I.V.A.Richards.
LOI debuts: None.

WEST INDIES		Runs	Balls	4/6
C.G.Greenidge	run out	9	31	–
D.L.Haynes	c Hendrick b Old	20	27	3
I.V.A.Richards	not out	138	157	11/3
A.I.Kallicharran	b Hendrick	4	17	–
*C.H.Lloyd	c and b Old	13	33	2
C.L.King	c Randall b Edmonds	86	66	10/3
†D.L.Murray	c Gower b Edmonds	5	9	1
A.M.E.Roberts	c Brearley b Hendrick	0	7	–
J.Garner	c Taylor b Botham	0	5	–
M.A.Holding	b Botham	0	6	–
C.E.H.Croft	not out	0	2	–
Extras	(b 1, lb 10)	11		
Total	(60 overs; 9 wickets)	286		

ENGLAND		Runs	Balls	4/6
*J.M.Brearley	c King b Holding	64	130	7
G.Boycott	c Kallicharran b Holding	57	105	3
D.W.Randall	b Croft	15	22	–
G.A.Gooch	b Garner	32	28	4
D.I.Gower	b Garner	0	4	–
I.T.Botham	c Richards b Croft	4	3	–
W.Larkins	b Garner	0	1	–
P.H.Edmonds	not out	5	8	–
C.M.Old	b Garner	0	2	–
†R.W.Taylor	c Murray b Garner	0	1	–
M.Hendrick	b Croft	0	5	–
Extras	(lb 12, w 2, nb 3)	17		
Total	(51 overs)	194		

ENGLAND	O	M	R	W		FALL OF WICKETS		
Botham	12	2	44	2		Wkt	WI	E
Hendrick	12	2	50	2		1st	22	129
Old	12	0	55	2		2nd	36	135
Boycott	6	0	38	0		3rd	55	183
Edmonds	12	2	40	2		4th	99	183
Gooch	4	0	27	0		5th	238	186
Larkins	2	0	21	0		6th	252	186
						7th	258	192
WEST INDIES	O	M	R	W		8th	260	192
Roberts	9	2	33	0		9th	272	194
Holding	8	1	16	2		10th	–	194
Croft	10	1	42	3				
Garner	11	0	38	5				
Richards	10	0	35	0				
King	3	0	13	0				

Umpires: H.D.Bird (15) and B.J.Meyer (6).

THE 1983 WORLD CUP

India caused one of the major sporting upsets of the century when they beat the holders and firm favourites, West Indies, by the emphatic margin of 43 runs in a low-scoring final. This was no cricketing fluke. A fortnight earlier they had beaten Clive Lloyd's team by 34 runs, successfully defending their record World Cup total of 262.

The third World Cup, the last to be sponsored by Prudential, began with another giant-killing feat when Zimbabwe beat Australia in the opening round. For the first time, all eight teams won a match. Compared with its two predecessors, this competition was almost double the size, involving 27 matches instead of the earlier 15. This was the result of expanding the programme at group stage, each team playing the others within that group twice in order to reduce the chances of a team being eliminated through ill-luck with the weather. Fortunately, after one of the wettest Mays on record, June was mainly dry and sunny and of the 27 matches staged over 16 days, only three required the assistance of the reserve day.

For the first time the World Cup was taken outside the Test match grounds, Swansea producing the then record World Cup match aggregate of 626 runs, Pakistan contributing the record total of 338 for 5 and Sri Lanka responding with the highest second innings tally of 288 for 9. Tunbridge Wells saw Kapil Dev savage its rhododendrons and the Zimbabwean bowlers with 6 sixes and 16 fours in his record World Cup innings of 175 not out. Taunton nearly reached Swansea's record aggregate when England's encounter with Sri Lanka produced 619 runs, while Leicester, Bristol, Worcester, Southampton, Derby and Chelmsford all enjoyed a unique occasion.

Again, matches were of 60 overs and bowlers were restricted to 12 apiece. To counteract negative bowling, the playing conditions empowered umpires to apply a stricter interpretation of wides and bouncers than in first-class cricket.

As before, the top two teams in each group qualified for the semi-finals, Pakistan getting the nod over New Zealand by virtue of their superior run-rate per over, both countries gaining 12 points.

FINAL GROUP TABLES

GROUP A	P	W	L	Pts	R/O	GROUP B	P	W	L	Pts	R/O
ENGLAND	6	5	1	20	4.67	WEST INDIES	6	5	1	20	4.31
PAKISTAN	6	3	3	12	4.01	INDIA	6	4	2	16	3.87
New Zealand	6	3	3	12	3.93	Australia	6	2	4	8	3.81
Sri Lanka	6	1	5	4	3.75	Zimbabwe	6	1	5	4	3.49

In financial terms this was the most bountiful tournament so far, the Prudential doubling their sponsorship from £500,000, gate receipts reaching £1,195,712 from an aggregate attendance of 232,081, and a resultant surplus in excess of £1 million.

This profit inspired other countries to bid for the next World Cup and when tenders were submitted at the end of the year the fourth tournament was awarded jointly to India and Pakistan.

ENGLAND v NEW ZEALAND

At Kennington Oval, London, on 9 June 1983.   Toss: England.
Result: **ENGLAND** won by 106 runs.   Award: A.J.Lamb.
LOI debuts: None.

ENGLAND		Runs	Balls	4/6
G.Fowler	c Coney b Cairns	8	19	1
C.J.Tavaré	c Edgar b Chatfield	45	91	4
D.I.Gower	c Edgar b Coney	39	62	6
A.J.Lamb	b Snedden	102	105	12/2
M.W.Gatting	b Snedden	43	47	3
I.T.Botham	c Lees b Hadlee	22	16	–/1
†I.J.Gould	not out	14	12	1
G.R.Dilley	not out	31	14	4
V.J.Marks				
P.J.W.Allott				
*R.G.D.Willis				
Extras	(lb 12, w 1, nb 5)	18		
Total	(60 overs; 6 wickets)	**322**		

NEW ZEALAND		Runs	Balls	4/6
G.M.Turner	lbw b Willis	14	28	2
B.A.Edgar	c Gould b Willis	3	6	–
J.G.Wright	c Botham b Dilley	10	17	1
*G.P.Howarth	c Lamb b Marks	18	44	1
J.V.Coney	run out	23	52	2
M.D.Crowe	run out	97	118	8
†W.K.Lees	b Botham	8	23	–
R.J.Hadlee	c Lamb b Marks	1	9	–
B.L.Cairns	lbw b Botham	1	2	–
M.C.Snedden	c Gould b Gatting	21	34	1
E.J.Chatfield	not out	9	24	1
Extras	(b 2, lb 4, w 4, nb 1)	11		
Total	(59 overs)	**216**		

NEW ZEALAND	O	M	R	W
Hadlee	12	4	26	1
Cairns	12	4	57	1
Snedden	12	1	105	2
Chatfield	12	1	45	1
Coney	6	1	20	1
Crowe	6	0	51	0

ENGLAND	O	M	R	W
Willis	7	2	9	2
Dilley	8	0	33	1
Botham	12	0	42	2
Allott	12	1	47	0
Marks	12	1	39	2
Gatting	8	1	35	1

FALL OF WICKETS		
Wkt	E	NZ
1st	13	3
2nd	79	28
3rd	117	31
4th	232	62
5th	271	85
6th	278	123
7th	–	136
8th	–	138
9th	–	190
10th	–	216

Umpires: B.J.Meyer (10) and D.O.Oslear (3).

PAKISTAN v SRI LANKA

At St Helen's, Swansea, on 9 June 1983.　Toss: Sri Lanka.
Result: **PAKISTAN** won by 50 runs.　Award: Mohsin Khan.
LOI debuts: Sri Lanka – M.A.R.Samarasekera.

PAKISTAN		Runs	Balls	4/6
Mohsin Khan	b John	82	121	5/1
Mudassar Nazar	c De Silva b Ratnayake	36	72	2
Zaheer Abbas	c Kuruppu b De Mel	82	81	10
Javed Miandad	lbw b De Mel	72	52	4/3
*Imran Khan	not out	56	33	6/2
Ijaz Faqih	run out	2	3	–
Tahir Naqqash	not out	0	–	–
†Wasim Bari				
Rashid Khan				
Shahid Mahboob				
Sarfraz Nawaz				
Extras	(b 4, lb 4)	8		
Total	**(60 overs; 5 wickets)**	**338**		

SRI LANKA		Runs	Balls	4/6
S.Wettimuny	c Rashid b Sarfraz	12	26	1
D.S.B.P.Kuruppu	run out	72	101	7/2
R.L.Dias	b Rashid	5	21	–
*L.R.D.Mendis	b Tahir	16	17	3
A.Ranatunga	c and b Mudassar	31	42	5
M.A.R.Samarasekera	run out	0	2	–
D.S.de Silva	c Wasim Bari b Sarfraz	35	51	1
A.L.F.de Mel	c Tahir b Shahid	11	22	–
†R.G.de Alwis	not out	59	56	5/1
R.J.Ratnayake	c Mudassar b Sarfraz	13	13	–/1
V.B.John	not out	12	11	2
Extras	(lb 8, w 10, nb 4)	22		
Total	**(60 overs; 9 wickets)**	**288**		

SRI LANKA	O	M	R	W
De Mel	12	2	69	2
John	12	2	58	1
Ratnayake	12	0	65	1
Ranatunga	9	0	53	0
De Silva	10	0	52	0
Samarasekera	5	0	33	0

PAKISTAN	O	M	R	W
Sarfraz Nawaz	12	1	40	3
Shahid Mahboob	11	0	48	1
Tahir Naqqash	8	0	49	1
Rashid Khan	12	1	55	1
Ijaz Faqih	12	1	52	0
Mudassar Nazar	4	0	18	1
Zaheer Abbas	1	0	4	0

FALL OF WICKETS		
Wkt	P	SL
1st	88	34
2nd	156	58
3rd	229	85
4th	325	142
5th	332	143
6th	–	157
7th	–	180
8th	–	234
9th	–	262
10th	–	–

Umpires: K.E.Palmer (9) and D.R.Shepherd (1).

AUSTRALIA v ZIMBABWE

At Trent Bridge, Nottingham, on 9 June 1983.   Toss: Australia.
Result: **ZIMBABWE** won by 13 runs.   Award: D.A.G.Fletcher.
LOI debuts: Zimbabwe – all.

ZIMBABWE		Runs	Balls	4/6
A.H.Shah	c Marsh b Lillee	16		–
G.A.Paterson	c Hookes b Lillee	27		2
J.G.Heron	c Marsh b Yallop	14		1
A.J.Pycroft	b Border	21		1
†D.L.Houghton	c Marsh b Yallop	0		–
*D.A.G.Fletcher	not out	69		5
K.M.Curran	c Hookes b Hogg	27		2
I.P.Butchart	not out	34		2
P.W.E.Rawson				
A.J.Traicos				
V.R.Hogg				
Extras	(lb 18, w 7, nb 6)	31		
Total	(60 overs; 6 wickets)	**239**		

AUSTRALIA		Runs	Balls	4/6
G.M.Wood	c Houghton b Fletcher	31		3
K.C.Wessels	run out	76		5
*K.J.Hughes	c Shah b Fletcher	0		–
D.W.Hookes	c Traicos b Fletcher	20		1
G.N.Yallop	c Pycroft b Fletcher	2		–
A.R.Border	c Pycroft b Curran	17		–
†R.W.Marsh	not out	50		3/2
G.F.Lawson	b Butchart	0		–
R.M.Hogg	not out	19		1
D.K.Lillee				
J.R.Thomson				
Extras	(b 2, lb 7, w 2)	11		
Total	(60 overs; 7 wickets)	**226**		

AUSTRALIA	O	M	R	W		FALL OF WICKETS		
Lawson	11	2	33	0		Wkt	A	Z
Hogg	12	3	43	1		1st	55	61
Lillee	12	1	47	2		2nd	55	63
Thomson	11	1	46	0		3rd	86	114
Yallop	9	0	28	2		4th	86	133
Border	5	0	11	1		5th	94	138
						6th	164	168
ZIMBABWE	O	M	R	W		7th	–	176
Hogg	6	2	15	0		8th	–	–
Rawson	12	1	54	0		9th	–	–
Butchart	10	0	39	1		10th	–	–
Fletcher	11	1	42	4				
Traicos	12	2	27	0				
Curran	9	0	38	1				

Umpires: D.J.Constant (19) and M.J.Kitchen (1).

WEST INDIES v INDIA

At Old Trafford, Manchester, on 9, 10 June 1983.   Toss: West Indies.
Result: **INDIA** won by 34 runs.   Award: Yashpal Sharma.
LOI debuts: None.

INDIA		Runs	Balls	4/6
S.M.Gavaskar	c Dujon b Marshall	19		
K.Srikkanth	c Dujon b Holding	14		
M.Amarnath	c Dujon b Garner	21		
S.M. Patil	b Gomes	36		
Yashpal Sharma	b Holding	89	127	9
*Kapil Dev	c Richards b Gomes	6		
R.M.H.Binny	lbw b Marshall	27		
Madan Lal	not out	21		
†S.M.H.Kirmani	run out	1		
R.J.Shastri	not out	5		
B.S.Sandhu				
Extras	(b 4, lb 10, w 1, nb 8)	23		
Total	**(60 overs; 8 wickets)**	**262**		

WEST INDIES		Runs	Balls	4/6
C.G.Greenidge	b Sandhu	24		
D.L.Haynes	run out	24		
I.V.A.Richards	c Kirmani b Binny	17		
S.F.A.F.Bacchus	b Madan Lal	14		
*C.H.Lloyd	b Binny	25		
†P.J.L.Dujon	c Sandhu b Binny	7		
H.A.Gomes	run out	8		
M.D.Marshall	st Kirmani b Shastri	2		
A.M.E.Roberts	not out	37		
M.A.Holding	b Shastri	8		
J.Garner	st Kirmani b Shastri	37		–/1
Extras	(b 4, lb 17, w 4)	25		
Total	**(54.1 overs)**	**228**		

WEST INDIES	O	M	R	W		FALL OF WICKETS		
Holding	12	3	32	2		Wkt	I	WI
Roberts	12	1	51	0		1st	21	49
Marshall	12	1	48	2		2nd	46	56
Garner	12	1	49	1		3rd	76	76
Richards	2	0	13	0		4th	125	96
Gomes	10	0	46	2		5th	141	107
						6th	214	124
INDIA	O	M	R	W		7th	243	126
Kapil Dev	10	0	34	0		8th	246	130
Sandhu	12	1	36	1		9th	–	157
Madan Lal	12	1	34	1		10th	–	228
Binny	12	1	48	3				
Shastri	5.1	0	26	3				
Patil	3	0	25	0				

Umpires: B.Leadbeater (1) and A.G.T.Whitehead (6).

ENGLAND v SRI LANKA

At County Ground, Taunton, on 11 June 1983.   Toss: England.
Result: **ENGLAND** won by 47 runs.   Award: D.I.Gower.
LOI debuts: None.

ENGLAND		Runs	Balls	4/6
G. Fowler	b John	22	59	1
C.J.Tavaré	c De Alwis b Ranatunga	32	61	4
D.I.Gower	b De Mel	130	120	12/5
A.J.Lamb	b Ratnayake	53	51	4/2
M.W.Gatting	run out	7	8	–
I.T.Botham	run out	0	1	–
†I.J.Gould	c Ranatunga b Ratnayake	35	40	2
G.R.Dilley	b De Mel	29	16	5
V.J.Marks	run out	5	5	–
P.J.W.Allott	not out	0		
*R.G.D.Willis				
Extras	(lb 11, w 9)	20		
Total	(60 overs; 9 wickets)	**333**		

SRI LANKA		Runs	Balls	4/6
S.Wettimuny	lbw b Marks	33	66	3/1
D.S.B.P.Kuruppu	c Gatting b Dilley	4	3	1
R.L.Dias	c Botham b Dilley	2	15	–
*L.R.D.Mendis	c Willis b Marks	56	64	5/1
R.S.Madugalle	c Tavaré b Marks	12	26	1
A.Ranatunga	c Lamb b Marks	34	45	4
D.S.de Silva	st Gould b Marks	28	37	2
†R.G.de Alwis	not out	58	51	6/1
A.L.F.de Mel	c Dilley b Allott	27	26	2
R.J.Ratnayake	c Lamb b Dilley	15	18	1
V.B.John	b Dilley	0	1	–
Extras	(lb 12, w 2, nb 3)	17		
Total	(58 overs)	**286**		

SRI LANKA	O	M	R	W		FALL OF WICKETS		
De Mel	12	3	62	2		Wkt	E	SL
John	12	0	55	1		1st	49	11
Ratnayake	12	0	66	2		2nd	78	17
Ranatunga	12	0	65	1		3rd	174	92
De Silva	12	0	65	0		4th	193	108
						5th	194	117
ENGLAND	O	M	R	W		6th	292	168
Willis	11	3	43	0		7th	298	192
Dilley	11	0	45	4		8th	333	246
Allott	12	1	82	1		9th	333	281
Botham	12	0	60	0		10th	–	286
Marks	12	3	39	5				

Umpires: M.J.Kitchen (2) and K.E.Palmer (10).

NEW ZEALAND v PAKISTAN

At Edgbaston, Birmingham, on 11, 12 June 1983.   Toss: Pakistan.
Result: **NEW ZEALAND** won by 52 runs.   Award: Abdul Qadir.
LOI debuts: New Zealand – J.G.Bracewell; Pakistan – Abdul Qadir.

NEW ZEALAND		Runs	Balls	4/6
G.M.Turner	c Wasim b Rashid	27	37	5
B.A.Edgar	c Imran b Qadir	44	107.	3
J.G.Wright	c Wasim b Qadir	9	14	2
B.L.Cairns	b Qadir	4	6	1
*G.P.Howarth	st Wasim b Qadir	16	35	1
J.V.Coney	c Ijaz b Shahid	33	65	3
M.D.Crowe	c Mohsin b Rashid	34	53	2
R.J.Hadlee	c Wasim b Sarfraz	13	11	1
J.G.Bracewell	lbw b Rashid	3	6	–
†W.K.Lees	not out	24	21	2
E.J.Chatfield	not out	6	8	–
Extras	(lb 20, w 4, nb 1)	25		
Total	**(60 overs; 9 wickets)**	**238**		

PAKISTAN		Runs	Balls	4/6
Mohsin Khan	lbw b Hadlee	0	3	–
Mudassar Nazar	c Lees b Cairns	0	2	–
Zaheer Abbas	b Hadlee	0	3	–
Javed Miandad	lbw b Chatfield	35	61	3
*Imran Khan	c Chatfield b Hadlee	9	26	1
Ijaz Faqih	c Edgar b Coney	12	37	1
Shahid Mahboob	c Wright b Coney	17	31	2
†Wasim Bari	c Edgar b Coney	34	71	2
Abdul Qadir	not out	41	68	2/1
Sarfraz Nawaz	c Crowe b Chatfield	13	14	2
Rashid Khan	c and b Cairns	9	21	–
Extras	(b 5, lb 6, w 3, nb 2)	16		
Total	**(55.2 overs)**	**186**		

PAKISTAN	O	M	R	W
Sarfraz Nawaz	11	1	49	1
Shahid Mahboob	10	2	38	1
Rashid Khan	11	0	47	3
Mudassar Nazar	12	1	40	0
Abdul Qadir	12	4	21	4
Ijaz Faqih	1	0	6	0
Zaheer Abbas	3	0	12	0

NEW ZEALAND	O	M	R	W
Hadlee	9	2	20	3
Cairns	9.2	3	21	2
Chatfield	12	0	50	2
Crowe	2	0	12	0
Coney	12	3	28	3
Bracewell	11	2	39	0

FALL OF WICKETS		
Wkt	NZ	P
1st	57	0
2nd	68	0
3rd	80	0
4th	109	22
5th	120	54
6th	166	60
7th	197	102
8th	202	131
9th	223	158
10th	–	186

Umpires: H.D.Bird (19) and B.Leadbeater (2).

AUSTRALIA v WEST INDIES

At Headingley, Leeds, on 11, 12 June 1983.   Toss: Australia.
Result: **WEST INDIES** won by 101 runs.   Award: W.W.Davis.
LOI debuts: None.

WEST INDIES		Runs	Balls	4/6
C.G.Greenidge	c Wood b Hogg	4		1
D.L.Haynes	c Marsh b Lawson	13		1
I.V.A.Richards	b Lawson	7		1
H.A.Gomes	c Marsh b Lillee	78		4
*C.H.Lloyd	lbw b MacLeay	19		1/1
S.F.A.F.Bacchus	c Wessels b Yallop	47		5
†P.J.L.Dujon	lbw b Lawson	12		–
A.M.E.Roberts	c Marsh b Lillee	5		–
M.A.Holding	run out	20		2
W.W.Daniel	not out	16		2
W.W.Davis				
Extras	(b 1, lb 9, w 10, nb 11)	31		
Total	(60 overs; 9 wickets)	**252**		

AUSTRALIA		Runs	Balls	4/6
G.M.Wood	retired hurt	2		–
K.C.Wessels	b Roberts	11		2
*K.J.Hughes	c Lloyd b Davis	18		–/2
D.W.Hookes	c Dujon b Davis	45		5
G.N.Yallop	c Holding b Davis	29		4
A.R.Border	c Lloyd b Davis	17		2
K.H.MacLeay	c Haynes b Davis	1		–
†R.W.Marsh	c Haynes b Holding	8		1
G.F.Lawson	c Dujon b Davis	2		–
R.M.Hogg	not out	0		–
D.K.Lillee	b Davis	0		–
Extras	(b 1, lb 4, w 5, nb 8)	18		
Total	(30.3 overs)	**151**		

AUSTRALIA	O	M	R	W		FALL OF WICKETS		
Lawson	12	3	29	3		Wkt	WI	A
Hogg	12	1	49	1		1st	7	18
MacLeay	12	1	31	1		2nd	25	55
Lillee	12	0	55	2		3rd	32	114
Yallop	5	0	26	1		4th	78	116
Border	7	0	31	0		5th	154	126
						6th	192	137
WEST INDIES	O	M	R	W		7th	208	141
Roberts	7	0	14	1		8th	211	150
Holding	8	2	23	1		9th	252	151
Davis	10.3	0	51	7		10th	–	–
Daniel	3	0	35	0				
Gomes	2	0	10	0				

Umpires: D.J.Constant (20) and D.G.L.Evans (7).

INDIA v ZIMBABWE

At Grace Road, Leicester, on 11 June 1983.   Toss: India.
Result: **INDIA** won by 5 wickets.   Award: Madan Lal.
LOI debuts: Zimbabwe – R.D.Brown.

ZIMBABWE		Runs	Balls	4/6
A.H.Shah	c Kirmani b Sandhu	8	32	1
G.A.Paterson	lbw b Madan Lal	22	51	2
J.G.Heron	c Kirmani b Madan Lal	18	30	2
A.J.Pycroft	c Shastri b Binny	14	21	1
†D.L.Houghton	c Kirmani b Madan Lal	21	47	1
*D.A.G.Fletcher	b Kapil Dev	13	32	–
K.M.Curran	run out	8	16	–
I.P.Butchart	not out	22	35	2
R.D.Brown	c Kirmani b Shastri	6	27	–
P.W.E.Rawson	c Kirmani b Binny	3	6	–
A.J.Traicos	run out	2	13	–
Extras	(lb 9, w 9)	18		
Total	(51.4 overs)	**155**		

INDIA		Runs	Balls	4/6
K.Srikkanth	c Butchart b Rawson	20	27	1
S.M.Gavaskar	c Heron b Rawson	4	11	–
M.Amarnath	c sub (G.E.Peckover) b Traicos	44	79	4
S.M.Patil	b Fletcher	50	54	7/1
R.J.Shastri	c Brown b Shah	17	27	1
Yashpal Sharma	not out	18	19	2
*Kapil Dev	not out	2	8	–
R.M.H.Binny				
Madan Lal				
†S.M.H.Kirmani				
B.S.Sandhu				
Extras	(w 2)	2		
Total	(37.3 overs; 5 wickets)	**157**		

INDIA	O	M	R	W		FALL OF WICKETS	
Kapil Dev	9	3	18	1	Wkt	Z	I
Sandhu	9	1	29	1	1st	13	13
Madan Lal	10.4	0	27	3	2nd	55	32
Binny	11	2	25	2	3rd	56	101
Shastri	12	1	38	1	4th	71	128
					5th	106	148
ZIMBABWE	O	M	R	W	6th	114	–
Rawson	5.1	1	11	2	7th	115	–
Curran	6.5	1	33	0	8th	139	–
Butchart	5	1	21	0	9th	148	–
Traicos	11	1	41	1	10th	155	–
Fletcher	6	1	32	1			
Shah	3.3	0	17	1			

Umpires: J.Birkenshaw (1) and R.Palmer (1).

ENGLAND v PAKISTAN

At Lord's, London, on 13 June 1983.   Toss: Pakistan.
Result: **ENGLAND** won by 8 wickets.   Award: Zaheer Abbas.
LOI debuts: None.

PAKISTAN		Runs	Balls	4/6
Mohsin Khan	c Tavaré b Willis	3	29	–
Mudassar Nazar	c Gould b Allott	26	98	2
Mansoor Akhtar	c Gould b Willis	3	15	–
Javed Miandad	c Gould b Botham	14	26	2
Zaheer Abbas	not out	83	104	7/1
*Imran Khan	run out	7	35	1
Wasim Raja	c Botham b Marks	9	19	2
Abdul Qadir	run out	0	2	–
Sarfraz Nawaz	c and b Botham	11	15	2
†Wasim Bari	not out	18	21	1
Rashid Khan				
Extras	(b 5, lb 8, w 3, nb 3)	19		
Total	(60 overs; 8 wickets)	**193**		

ENGLAND		Runs	Balls	4/6
G.Fowler	not out	78	151	5
C.J.Tavaré	lbw b Rashid	8	21	–
D.I.Gower	c Sarfraz b Mansoor	48	72	6
A.J.Lamb	not out	48	62	5/1
M.W.Gatting				
I.T.Botham				
†I.J.Gould				
V.J.Marks				
G.R.Dilley				
P.J.W.Allott				
*R.G.D.Willis				
Extras	(b 1, lb 12, w 2, nb 2)	17		
Total	(50.4 overs; 2 wickets)	**199**		

ENGLAND	O	M	R	W		FALL OF WICKETS		
Willis	12	4	24	2		Wkt	P	E
Dilley	12	1	33	0		1st	29	15
Allott	12	2	48	1		2nd	33	93
Botham	12	3	36	2		3rd	49	–
Marks	12	1	33	1		4th	67	–
						5th	96	–
PAKISTAN	O	M	R	W		6th	112	–
Rashid Khan	7	2	19	1		7th	118	–
Sarfraz Nawaz	11	5	22	0		8th	154	–
Wasim Raja	3	0	14	0		9th	–	–
Mudassar Nazar	8	0	30	0		10th	–	–
Abdul Qadir	9.4	0	53	0				
Mansoor Akhtar	12	2	44	1				

Umpires: B.J.Meyer (11) and A.G.T.Whitehead (7).

NEW ZEALAND v SRI LANKA

At County Ground, Bristol, on 13 June 1983.   Toss: New Zealand.
Result: **NEW ZEALAND** won by 5 wickets.   Award: R.J.Hadlee.
LOI debuts: None.

SRI LANKA		Runs	Balls	4/6
S.Wettimuny	lbw b Hadlee	7	19	1
D.S.B.P.Kuruppu	c Hadlee b Chatfield	26	60	5
R.L.Dias	b Chatfield	25	43	4
*L.R.D.Mendis	b Hadlee	43	70	2
R.S.Madugalle	c Snedden b Coney	60	87	3/1
A.Ranatunga	lbw b Hadlee	0	3	–
D.S.de Silva	b Coney	13	20	–
†R.G.de Alwis	c Howarth b Snedden	16	17	2
A.L.F.de Mel	c and b Hadlee	1	6	–
R.J.Ratnayake	b Hadlee	5	9	–
V.B.John	not out	2	5	–
Extras	(lb 6, w 1, nb 1)	8		
Total	(56.1 overs)	**206**		

NEW ZEALAND		Runs	Balls	4/6
G.M.Turner	c Mendis b De Silva	50	60	8
J.G.Wright	lbw b De Mel	45	52	8
*G.P.Howarth	c Madugalle b Ratnayake	76	79	14
M.D.Crowe	c De Alwis b De Mel	0	11	–
J.J.Crowe	lbw b John	23	26	4
J.V.Coney	not out	2	10	–
†I.D.S.Smith	not out	4	1	1
R.J.Hadlee				
B.L.Cairns				
M.C.Snedden				
E.J.Chatfield				
Extras	(lb 6, w 3)	9		
Total	(39.2 overs; 5 wickets)	**209**		

NEW ZEALAND	O	M	R	W
Hadlee	10.1	4	25	5
Snedden	10	1	38	1
Chatfield	12	4	24	2
Cairns	7	0	35	0
Coney	12	0	44	2
M.D.Crowe	5	0	32	0

SRI LANKA	O	M	R	W
De Mel	8	2	30	2
John	8.2	0	49	1
Ratnayake	12	0	60	1
De Silva	9	0	39	1
Ranatunga	2	0	22	0

FALL OF WICKETS		
Wkt	SL	NZ
1st	16	89
2nd	56	99
3rd	73	110
4th	144	176
5th	144	205
6th	171	–
7th	196	–
8th	199	–
9th	199	–
10th	206	–

Umpires: H.D.Bird (20) and D.R.Shepherd (2).

AUSTRALIA v INDIA

At Trent Bridge, Nottingham, on 13 June 1983.   Toss: Australia.
Result: **AUSTRALIA** won by 162 runs.   Award: T.M.Chappell.
LOI debuts: None.

AUSTRALIA		Runs	Balls	4/6
K.C.Wessels	b Kapil Dev	5	11	1
T.M.Chappell	c Srikkanth b Amarnath	110	131	11
*K.J.Hughes	b Madan Lal	52	86	3
D.W.Hookes	c Kapil Dev b Madan Lal	1	4	–
G.N.Yallop	not out	66	73	5
A.R.Border	c Yashpal b Binny	26	23	1
†R.W.Marsh	c Sandhu b Kapil Dev	12	15	1
K.H.MacLeay	c and b Kapil Dev	4	5	–
T.G.Hogan	b Kapil Dev	11	9	–/1
G.F.Lawson	c Srikkanth b Kapil Dev	6	3	1
R.M.Hogg	not out	2	2	–
Extras	(b 1, lb 14, w 8, nb 2)	25		
Total	(60 overs; 9 wickets)	**320**		

INDIA		Runs	Balls	4/6
R.J.Shastri	lbw b Lawson	11	18	1
K.Srikkanth	c Border b Hogan	39	63	6
M.Amarnath	run out	2	17	–
D.B.Vengsarkar	lbw b MacLeay	5	14	1
S.M.Patil	b MacLeay	0	7	–
Yashpal Sharma	c and b MacLeay	3	11	–
*Kapil Dev	b Hogan	40	27	2/1
Madan Lal	c Hogan b MacLeay	27	39	2
R.M.H.Binny	lbw b MacLeay	0	6	–
†S.M.H.Kirmani	b MacLeay	12	23	2
B.S.Sandhu	not out	9	12	–/1
Extras	(b 1, lb 4, w 3, nb 2)	10		
Total	(37.5 overs)	**158**		

INDIA	O	M	R	W
Kapil Dev	12	2	43	5
Sandhu	12	1	52	0
Binny	12	0	52	1
Shastri	2	0	16	0
Madan Lal	12	0	69	2
Patil	6	0	36	0
Amarnath	4	0	27	1

AUSTRALIA	O	M	R	W
Lawson	5	1	25	1
Hogg	7	2	23	0
Hogan	12	1	48	2
MacLeay	11.5	3	39	6
Border	2	0	13	0

FALL OF WICKETS		
Wkt	A	I
1st	11	38
2nd	155	43
3rd	159	57
4th	206	57
5th	254	64
6th	277	66
7th	289	124
8th	301	126
9th	307	136
10th	–	158

Umpires: D.O.Oslear (4) and R.Palmer (2).

WEST INDIES v ZIMBABWE

At New Road, Worcester, on 13 June 1983. Toss: West Indies.
Result: **WEST INDIES** won by 8 wickets. Award: C.G.Greenidge.
LOI debuts: Zimbabwe – G.E.Peckover.

ZIMBABWE		Runs	Balls	4/6
A.H.Shah	b Roberts	2		–
G.A.Paterson	c Dujon b Holding	4		–
J.G.Heron	st Dujon b Gomes	12	73	–
A.J.Pycroft	run out	13		1
†D.L.Houghton	c Dujon b Roberts	54		5/1
*D.A.G.Fletcher	not out	71		7
K.M.Curran	b Roberts	7		1
I.P.Butchart	lbw b Holding	0		–
G.E.Peckover	not out	16		3
P.W.E.Rawson				
A.J.Traicos				
Extras	(b 1, lb 23, w 7, nb 7)	38		
Total	(60 overs; 7 wickets)	**217**		

WEST INDIES		Runs	Balls	4/6
C.G.Greenidge	not out	105		5/1
D.L.Haynes	c Houghton b Rawson	2		–
I.V.A.Richards	lbw b Rawson	16		2
H.A.Gomes	not out	75		5
S.F.A.F.Bacchus				
*C.H.Lloyd				
†P.J.L.Dujon				
A.M.E.Roberts				
M.A.Holding				
W.W.Daniel				
W.W.Davis				
Extras	(b 1, lb 8, w 9, nb 2)	20		
Total	(48.3 overs; 2 wickets)	**218**		

WEST INDIES	O	M	R	W		FALL OF WICKETS		
Roberts	12	4	36	3		Wkt	Z	WI
Holding	12	2	33	2		1st	7	3
Daniel	12	4	21	0		2nd	7	23
Davis	12	2	34	0		3rd	35	–
Gomes	8	0	42	1		4th	65	–
Richards	4	1	13	0		5th	157	–
						6th	181	–
ZIMBABWE	O	M	R	W		7th	183	–
Rawson	12	1	39	2		8th	–	–
Curran	10.3	1	37	0		9th	–	–
Butchart	9	1	40	0		10th	–	–
Fletcher	4	0	22	0				
Traicos	9	0	37	0				
Shah	4	0	23	0				

Umpires: J.Birkenshaw (2) and D.G.L.Evans (8).

ENGLAND v NEW ZEALAND

At Edgbaston, Birmingham, on 15 June 1983. Toss: England.
Result: **NEW ZEALAND** won by 2 wickets. Award: J.V.Coney.
LOI debuts: None.

ENGLAND		Runs	Balls	4/6
G.Fowler	c J.J.Crowe b Chatfield	69	112	9
C.J.Tavaré	c Cairns b Coney	18	44	1
I.T.Botham	c and b Bracewell	12	9	1/1
D.I.Gower	not out	92	96	6/4
A.J.Lamb	c J.J.Crowe b Cairns	8	14	1
M.W.Gatting	b Cairns	1	5	–
†I.J.Gould	lbw b Cairns	4	14	–
V.J.Marks	b Hadlee	5	15	–
G.R.Dilley	b Hadlee	10	19	–
P.J.W.Allott	c Smith b Hadlee	0	1	–
*R.G.D.Willis	lbw b Chatfield	0	3	–
Extras	(b 4, lb 10, w 1)	15		
Total	**(55.2 overs)**	**234**		

NEW ZEALAND		Runs	Balls	4/6
G.M.Turner	lbw b Willis	2	5	–
B.A.Edgar	c Gould b Willis	1	6	–
*G.P.Howarth	run out	60	104	5/1
J.J.Crowe	b Allott	17	46	1
M.D.Crowe	b Marks	20	40	2
J.V.Coney	not out	66	97	9
†I.D.S.Smith	b Botham	4	6	1
R.J.Hadlee	b Willis	31	45	3
B.L.Cairns	lbw b Willis	5	6	–
J.G.Bracewell	not out	4	7	1
E.J.Chatfield				
Extras	(b 2, lb 22, w 1, nb 3)	28		
Total	**(59.5 overs; 8 wickets)**	**238**		

NEW ZEALAND	O	M	R	W
Hadlee	10	3	32	3
Cairns	11	0	44	3
Coney	12	2	27	1
Bracewell	12	0	66	1
Chatfield	10.2	0	50	2

ENGLAND	O	M	R	W
Willis	12	1	42	4
Dilley	12	1	43	0
Botham	12	1	47	1
Allott	11.5	2	44	1
Marks	12	1	34	1

FALL OF WICKETS		
Wkt	E	NZ
1st	63	2
2nd	77	3
3rd	117	47
4th	143	75
5th	154	146
6th	162	151
7th	203	221
8th	233	231
9th	233	–
10th	234	–

Umpires: J.Birkenshaw (3) and K.E.Palmer (11).

WEST INDIES v INDIA

At Kennington Oval, London, on 15 June 1983.   Toss: West Indies.
Result: **WEST INDIES** won by 66 runs.   Award: I.V.A.Richards.
LOI debuts: None.

WEST INDIES		Runs	Balls	4/6
C.G.Greenidge	c Vengsarkar b Kapil Dev	9		
D.L.Haynes	c Kapil Dev b Amarnath	38		
I.V.A.Richards	c Kirmani b Sandhu	119	146	6/1
*C.H.Lloyd	run out	41		
S.F.A.F.Bacchus	b Binny	8		
†P.J.L.Dujon	c Shastri b Binny	9		
H.A.Gomes	not out	27		
A.M.E.Roberts	c Patil b Binny	7		
M.D.Marshall	run out	4		
M.A.Holding	c sub (K.Azad) b Madan Lal	2		
W.W.Davis	not out	0		
Extras	(lb 13, w 5)	18		
Total	(60 overs; 9 wickets)	**282**		

INDIA		Runs	Balls	4/6
K.Srikkanth	c Dujon b Roberts	2		
R.J.Shastri	c Dujon b Roberts	6		
M.Amarnath	c Lloyd b Holding	80		
D.B.Vengsarkar	retired hurt	32		
S.M.Patil	c and b Gomes	21		
Yashpal Sharma	run out	9		
*Kapil Dev	c Haynes b Holding	36		
R.M.H.Binny	lbw b Holding	1		
Madan Lal	not out	8		
†S.M.H.Kirmani	b Marshall	0		
B.S.Sandhu	run out	0		
Extras	(b 3, lb 13, nb 5)	21		
Total	(53.1 overs)	**216**		

INDIA	O	M	R	W		FALL OF WICKETS		
Kapil Dev	12	0	46	1		Wkt	WI	I
Sandhu	12	2	42	1		1st	17	2
Binny	12	0	71	3		2nd	118	21
Amarnath	12	0	58	1		3rd	198	130
Madan Lal	12	0	47	1		4th	213	143
						5th	239	193
WEST INDIES	O	M	R	W		6th	240	195
Roberts	9	1	29	2		7th	257	212
Holding	9.1	0	40	3		8th	270	214
Marshall	11	3	20	1		9th	280	216
Davis	12	2	51	0		10th	–	–
Gomes	12	1	55	1				

Umpires: B.J.Meyer (12) and D.R.Shepherd (3).

PAKISTAN v SRI LANKA

At Headingley, Leeds, on 16 June 1983.   Toss: Sri Lanka.
Result: **PAKISTAN** won by 11 runs.   Award: Abdul Qadir.
LOI debuts: None.

PAKISTAN		Runs	Balls	4/6
Mohsin Khan	c Ranatunga b De Mel	3	14	–
Mansoor Akhtar	c De Alwis b De Mel	6	32	–
Zaheer Abbas	c Dias b De Mel	15	28	2
Javed Miandad	lbw b Ratnayake	7	14	1
*Imran Khan	not out	102	133	11
Ijaz Faqih	lbw b Ratnayake	0	1	–
Shahid Mahboob	c De Silva b De Mel	77	126	6
Sarfraz Nawaz	c Madugalle b De Mel	9	10	1
Abdul Qadir	not out	5	7	–
†Wasim Bari				
Rashid Khan				
Extras	(b 1, lb 4, w 4, nb 2)	11		
Total	(60 overs; 7 wickets)	**235**		

SRI LANKA		Runs	Balls	4/6
S.Wettimuny	c Shahid b Rashid	50	127	4
D.S.B.P.Kuruppu	b Rashid	12	36	1
R.L.Dias	st Wasim b Qadir	47	73	7
*L.R.D.Mendis	c Wasim b Qadir	33	49	5
R.J.Ratnayake	st Wasim b Qadir	1	6	–
R.S.Madugalle	c Qadir b Shahid	26	20	1/1
A.Ranatunga	c Zaheer b Qadir	0	1	–
D.S.de Silva	run out	1	3	–
†R.G.de Alwis	c Miandad b Qadir	4	5	1
A.L.F.de Mel	c Imran b Sarfraz	17	19	1
V.B.John	not out	6	15	–
Extras	(lb 8, w 17, nb 2)	27		
Total	(58.3 overs)	**224**		

SRI LANKA	O	M	R	W
De Mel	12	1	39	5
John	12	1	48	0
Ratnayake	12	2	42	2
Ranatunga	11	0	49	0
De Silva	12	1	42	0
Wettimuny	1	0	4	0

PAKISTAN	O	M	R	W
Rashid Khan	12	4	31	2
Sarfraz Nawaz	11.3	2	25	1
Shahid Mahboob	10	0	62	1
Mansoor Akhtar	1	0	8	0
Ijaz Faqih	12	0	27	0
Abdul Qadir	12	1	44	5

FALL OF WICKETS		
Wkt	P	SL
1st	6	22
2nd	25	101
3rd	30	162
4th	43	162
5th	43	166
6th	187	166
7th	204	171
8th	–	193
9th	–	199
10th	–	224

Umpires: D.O.Oslear (5) and A.G.T.Whitehead (8).

AUSTRALIA v ZIMBABWE

At County Ground, Southampton, on 16 June 1983.   Toss: Australia.
Result: **AUSTRALIA** won by 32 runs.   Award: D.L.Houghton.
LOI debuts: None.

AUSTRALIA		Runs	Balls	4/6
G.M.Wood	c Rawson b Traicos	73	123	5
T.M.Chappell	c Traicos b Rawson	22	33	4
*K.J.Hughes	b Traicos	31	58	2
D.W.Hookes	c Brown b Fletcher	10	28	–
G.N.Yallop	c Houghton b Curran	20	39	3
A.R.Border	b Butchart	43	56	2
†R.W.Marsh	not out	35	25	2/1
K.H.MacLeay	c Rawson b Butchart	9	5	–/1
T.G.Hogan	not out	5	3	–
D.K.Lillee				
R.M.Hogg				
Extras	(lb 16, w 2, nb 6)	24		
Total	(60 overs; 7 wickets)	**272**		

ZIMBABWE		Runs	Balls	4/6
R.D.Brown	c Marsh b Hogan	38	87	4
G.A.Paterson	lbw b Hogg	17	40	1
J.G.Heron	run out	3	14	–
A.J.Pycroft	run out	13	36	1
†D.L.Houghton	c Hughes b Chappell	84	91	9/1
*D.A.G.Fletcher	b Hogan	2	9	–
K.M.Curran	lbw b Chappell	35	51	2
I.P.Butchart	lbw b Hogg	0	1	–
P.W.E.Rawson	lbw b Hogg	0	1	–
A.J.Traicos	b Chappell	19	29	1
V.R.Hogg	not out	7	14	–
Extras	(b 1, lb 10, w 1, nb 10)	22		
Total	(59.5 overs)	**240**		

ZIMBABWE	O	M	R	W
Hogg	9	2	34	0
Rawson	9	0	50	1
Fletcher	9	1	27	1
Butchart	10	0	52	2
Traicos	12	1	28	2
Curran	11	0	57	1

AUSTRALIA	O	M	R	W
Hogg	12	0	40	3
Lillee	9	1	23	0
Hogan	12	0	33	2
MacLeay	9	0	45	0
Border	9	1	30	0
Chappell	8.5	0	47	3

FALL OF WICKETS

Wkt	A	Z
1st	46	48
2nd	124	53
3rd	150	79
4th	150	97
5th	219	109
6th	231	212
7th	249	213
8th	–	213
9th	–	213
10th	–	240

Umpires: D.G.L.Evans (9) and R.Palmer (3).

126

ENGLAND v PAKISTAN

At Old Trafford, Manchester, on 18 June 1983.   Toss: Pakistan.
Result: **ENGLAND** won by 7 wickets.   Award: G.Fowler.
LOI debuts: None.

PAKISTAN		Runs	Balls	4/6
Mohsin Khan	c Marks b Allott	32	98	3
Mudassar Nazar	c Gould b Dilley	18	23	2
Zaheer Abbas	c Gould b Dilley	0	8	–
Javed Miandad	run out	67	100	6
*Imran Khan	c Willis b Marks	13	28	2
Wasim Raja	c Willis b Marks	15	24	3
Ijaz Faqih	not out	42	52	5
Sarfraz Nawaz	b Willis	17	20	1/1
Abdul Qadir	run out	6	7	–
†Wasim Bari	not out	2	3	–
Rashid Khan				
Extras	(b 3, lb 14, w 2, nb 1)	20		
Total	(60 overs; 8 wickets)	**232**		

ENGLAND		Runs	Balls	4/6
G.Fowler	c Miandad b Mudassar	69	96	7
C.J.Tavaré	c Wasim Raja b Zaheer	58	116	5
D.I.Gower	c Zaheer b Mudassar	31	48	3
A.J.Lamb	not out	38	57	4
M.W.Gatting	not out	14	27	1
I.T.Botham				
†I.J.Gould				
V.J.Marks				
G.R.Dilley				
P.J.W.Allott				
*R.G.D.Willis				
Extras	(b 1, lb 15, w 7)	23		
Total	(57.2 overs; 3 wickets)	**233**		

ENGLAND	O	M	R	W		FALL OF WICKETS		
Willis	12	3	37	1		Wkt	P	E
Dilley	12	2	46	2		1st	33	115
Allott	12	1	33	1		2nd	34	165
Botham	12	1	51	0		3rd	87	181
Marks	12	0	45	2		4th	116	–
						5th	144	–
PAKISTAN	O	M	R	W		6th	169	–
Rashid Khan	11	1	58	0		7th	204	–
Sarfraz Nawaz	10.2	2	22	0		8th	221	–
Abdul Qadir	11	0	51	0		9th	–	–
Ijaz Faqih	6	0	19	0		10th	–	–
Mudassar Nazar	12	2	34	2				
Zaheer Abbas	7	0	26	1				

Umpires: H.D.Bird (21) and D.O.Oslear (6).

NEW ZEALAND v SRI LANKA

At County Ground, Derby, on 18 June 1983.   Toss: Sri Lanka.
Result: **SRI LANKA** won by 3 wickets.   Award: A.L.F.de Mel.
LOI debuts: None.

NEW ZEALAND		Runs	Balls	4/6
G.M.Turner	c Dias b De Mel	6	10	1
J.G.Wright	c De Alwis b De Mel	0	7	–
*G.P.Howarth	b Ratnayake	15	23	2
M.D.Crowe	lbw b Ratnayake	8	32	–
B.A.Edgar	c Samarasekera b De Silva	27	77	3
J.V.Coney	c sub (E.R.N.S.Fernando) b De Silva	22	50	2
R.J.Hadlee	c Madugalle b De Mel	15	39	3
†W.K.Lees	c Ranatunga b De Mel	2	16	–
B.L.Cairns	c Dias b De Mel	6	7	1
M.C.Snedden	run out	40	55	5
E.J.Chatfield	not out	19	48	2
Extras	(b 4, lb 5, w 11, nb 1)	21		
Total	(58.2 overs)	**181**		

SRI LANKA		Runs	Balls	4/6
S.Wettimuny	b Cairns	4	30	–
D.S.B.P.Kuruppu	c and b Snedden	62	120	10
A.Ranatunga	b Crowe	15	22	2
R.L.Dias	not out	64	101	9
*L.R.D.Mendis	lbw b Chatfield	0	2	–
R.S.Madugalle	c Lees b Snedden	6	18	–
M.A.R.Samarasekera	c Lees b Hadlee	5	11	–
D.S.de Silva	run out	2	10	–
†R.G.de Alwis	not out	11	10	1
A.L.F.de Mel				
R.J.Ratnayake				
Extras	(b 1, lb 4, w 10)	15		
Total	(52.5 overs; 7 wickets)	**184**		

SRI LANKA	O	M	R	W		FALL OF WICKETS		
De Mel	12	4	32	5	Wkt		NZ	SL
Ratnayake	11	4	18	2	1st		8	15
Ranatunga	10	2	50	0	2nd		8	49
De Silva	12	5	11	2	3rd		32	129
Samarasekera	11.2	2	38	0	4th		47	130
Wettimuny	2	0	11	0	5th		88	139
					6th		91	151
NEW ZEALAND	O	M	R	W	7th		105	161
Hadlee	12	3	16	1	8th		115	–
Cairns	10	2	35	1	9th		116	–
Snedden	10.5	1	58	2	10th		181	–
Chatfield	12	3	23	1				
Crowe	4	2	15	1				
Coney	4	1	22	0				

Umpires: D.J.Constant (21) and B.Leadbeater (3).

AUSTRALIA v WEST INDIES

At Lord's, London, on 18 June 1983.   Toss: Australia.
Result: **WEST INDIES** won by 7 wickets.   Award: I.V.A.Richards.
LOI debuts: None.

AUSTRALIA		Runs	Balls	4/6
G.M.Wood	b Marshall	17	24	–
T.M.Chappell	c Dujon b Marshall	5	14	1
*K.J.Hughes	b Gomes	69	124	8
D.W.Hookes	c Greenidge b Davis	56	74	4/2
G.N.Yallop	not out	52	74	3
A.R.Border	c and b Gomes	11	24	1
†R.W.Marsh	c Haynes b Holding	37	26	4/2
T.G.Hogan	not out	0	1	–
J.R.Thomson				
D.K.Lillee				
R.M.Hogg				
Extras	(b 1, lb 18, w 6, nb 1)	26		
Total	(60 overs; 6 wickets)	**273**		

WEST INDIES		Runs	Balls	4/6
C.G.Greenidge	c Hughes b Hogg	90	140	8
D.L.Haynes	b Hogan	33	46	3
I.V.A.Richards	not out	95	117	9/3
H.A.Gomes	b Chappell	15	26	1
*C.H.Lloyd	not out	19	22	3
S.F.A.F.Bacchus				
†P.J.L.Dujon				
M.D.Marshall				
A.M.E.Roberts				
M.A.Holding				
W.W.Davis				
Extras	(b 3, lb 18, w 1, nb 2)	24		
Total	(57.5 overs; 3 wickets)	**276**		

WEST INDIES	O	M	R	W
Roberts	12	0	51	0
Marshall	12	0	36	2
Davis	12	0	57	1
Holding	12	1	56	1
Gomes	12	0	47	2

AUSTRALIA	O	M	R	W
Hogg	12	0	25	1
Thomson	11	0	64	0
Hogan	12	0	60	1
Lillee	12	0	52	0
Chappell	10.5	0	51	1

FALL OF WICKETS		
Wkt	A	WI
1st	10	79
2nd	37	203
3rd	138	228
4th	176	–
5th	202	–
6th	266	–
7th	–	–
8th	–	–
9th	–	–
10th	–	–

Umpires: K.E.Palmer (12) and A.G.T.Whitehead (9).

INDIA v ZIMBABWE

At Nevill Ground, Tunbridge Wells, on 18 June 1983.   Toss: India.
Result: **INDIA** won by 31 runs.   Award: Kapil Dev.
LOI debuts: None.

INDIA		**Runs**	**Balls**	**4/6**
S.M.Gavaskar	lbw b Rawson	0	6	–
K.Srikkanth	c Butchart b Curran	0		–
M.Amarnath	c Houghton b Rawson	5		1
S.M.Patil	c Houghton b Curran	1		–
Yashpal Sharma	c Houghton b Rawson	9		1
Kapil Dev	not out	175		16/6
*R.M.H.Binny	lbw b Traicos	22		2
R.J.Shastri	c Pycroft b Fletcher	1		–
Madan Lal	c Houghton b Curran	17		1
†S.M.H.Kirmani	not out	24		2
B.S.Sandhu				
Extras	(lb 9, w 3)	12		
Total	(60 overs; 8 wickets)	**266**		

ZIMBABWE		**Runs**	**Balls**	**4/6**
R.D.Brown	run out	35		2
G.A.Paterson	lbw b Binny	23		4
J.G.Heron	run out	3		–
A.J.Pycroft	c Kirmani b Sandhu	6		1
†D.L.Houghton	lbw b Madan Lal	17		1/2
*D.A.G.Fletcher	c Kapil Dev b Amarnath	13		–
K.M.Curran	c Shastri b Madan Lal	73		8
I.P.Butchart	b Binny	18		1
G.E.Peckover	c Yashpal b Madan Lal	14		–
P.W.E.Rawson	not out	2		–
A.J.Traicos	c and b Kapil Dev	3		–
Extras	(lb 17, w 7, nb 4)	28		
Total	(57 overs)	**235**		

ZIMBABWE	O	M	R	W		FALL OF WICKETS		
Rawson	12	4	47	3		Wkt	I	Z
Curran	12	1	65	3		1st	0	44
Butchart	12	2	38	0		2nd	6	48
Fletcher	12	2	59	1		3rd	6	61
Traicos	12	0	45	1		4th	9	86
						5th	17	103
INDIA	O	M	R	W		6th	77	113
Kapil Dev	11	1	32	1		7th	78	168
Sandhu	11	2	44	1		8th	140	189
Binny	11	2	45	2		9th	–	230
Madan Lal	11	2	42	3		10th	–	235
Amarnath	12	1	37	1				
Shastri	1	0	7	0				

Umpires: M.J.Kitchen (3) and B.J.Meyer (13).

ENGLAND v SRI LANKA

At Headingley, Leeds, on 20 June 1983.   Toss: England.
Result: **ENGLAND** won by 9 wickets.   Award: R.G.D.Willis.
LOI debuts: None.

SRI LANKA		Runs	Balls	4/6
S.Wettimuny	lbw b Botham	22	49	3
D.S.B.P.Kuruppu	c Gatting b Willis	6	36	1
A.Ranatunga	c Lamb b Botham	0	16	–
R.L.Dias	c Gould b Cowans	7	24	1
*L.R.D.Mendis	b Allott	10	38	–
R.S.Madugalle	c Gould b Allott	0	6	–
D.S.de Silva	c Gower b Marks	15	36	1
†R.G.de Alwis	c Marks b Cowans	19	20	2/1
A.L.F.de Mel	c Lamb b Marks	10	23	2
R.J.Ratnayake	not out	20	32	1/1
V.B.John	c Cowans b Allott	15	27	1
Extras	(b 5, lb 2, w 3, nb 2)	12		
Total	(50.4 overs)	**136**		

ENGLAND		Runs	Balls	4/6
G.Fowler	not out	81	77	11
C.J.Tavaré	c De Alwis b De Mel	19	48	1/1
D.I.Gower	not out	27	24	3
A.J.Lamb				
M.W.Gatting				
I.T.Botham				
†I.J.Gould				
V.J.Marks				
P.J.W.Allott				
*R.G.D.Willis				
N.G.Cowans				
Extras	(b 1, lb 3, w 3, nb 3)	10		
Total	(24.1 overs; 1 wicket)	**137**		

ENGLAND	O	M	R	W		FALL OF WICKETS		
Willis	9	4	9	1		Wkt	SL	E
Cowans	12	3	31	2		1st	25	68
Botham	9	4	12	2		2nd	30	–
Allott	10.4	0	41	3		3rd	32	–
Gatting	4	2	13	0		4th	40	–
Marks	6	2	18	2		5th	43	–
						6th	54	–
SRI LANKA	O	M	R	W		7th	81	–
De Mel	10	1	33	1		8th	97	–
Ratnayake	5	0	23	0		9th	103	–
John	6	0	41	0		10th	136	–
De Silva	3	0	29	0				
Ranatunga	0.1	0	1	0				

Umpires: B.Leadbeater (4) and R.Palmer (4).

NEW ZEALAND v PAKISTAN

At Trent Bridge, Nottingham, on 20 June 1983. Toss: Pakistan.
Result: **PAKISTAN** won by 11 runs. Award: Imran Khan.
LOI debuts: None.

PAKISTAN		Runs	Balls	4/6
Mohsin Khan	c Cairns b Coney	33	64	3
Mudassar Nazar	b Coney	15	60	–
Javed Miandad	b Hadlee	25	45	1
Zaheer Abbas	not out	103	121	6
*Imran Khan	not out	79	74	7/1
Ijaz Faqih				
Shahid Mahboob				
Sarfraz Nawaz				
Abdul Qadir				
†Wasim Bari				
Rashid Khan				
Extras	(b 1, lb 2, w 2, nb 1)	6		
Total	(60 overs; 3 wickets)	**261**		

NEW ZEALAND		Runs	Balls	4/6
G.M.Turner	c Wasim b Sarfraz	4	16	–
J.G.Wright	c Imran b Qadir	19	57	1
*G.P.Howarth	c Miandad b Zaheer	39	51	3
M.D.Crowe	b Mudassar	43	62	4
B.A.Edgar	lbw b Shahid	6	22	–
J.V.Coney	run out	51	78	3
R.J.Hadlee	c Mohsin b Mudassar	11	20	1
B.L.Cairns	c Imran b Qadir	0	3	–
†W.K.Lees	c sub (Mansoor Akhtar) b Mudassar	26	25	4
J.G.Bracewell	c Mohsin b Sarfraz	34	24	7
E.J.Chatfield	not out	3	6	–
Extras	(lb 8, w 5, nb 1)	14		
Total	(59.1 overs)	**250**		

NEW ZEALAND	O	M	R	W
Hadlee	12	1	61	1
Cairns	12	1	45	0
Chatfield	12	0	57	0
Coney	12	0	42	2
Bracewell	12	0	50	0

PAKISTAN	O	M	R	W
Rashid Khan	6	1	24	0
Sarfraz Nawaz	9.1	1	50	2
Abdul Qadir	12	0	53	2
Ijaz Faqih	6	1	21	0
Shahid Mahboob	10	0	37	1
Mudassar Nazar	12	0	43	3
Zaheer Abbas	4	1	8	1

FALL OF WICKETS		
Wkt	P	NZ
1st	48	13
2nd	54	44
3rd	114	85
4th	–	102
5th	–	130
6th	–	150
7th	–	152
8th	–	187
9th	–	246
10th	–	250

Umpires: D.G.L.Evans (10) and M.J.Kitchen (4).

AUSTRALIA v INDIA

At County Ground, Chelmsford, on 20 June 1983.   Toss: India.
Result: **INDIA** won by 118 runs.   Award: R.M.H.Binny.
LOI debuts: None.

INDIA		Runs	Balls	4/6
S.M.Gavaskar	c Chappell b Hogg	9	10	1
K.Srikkanth	c Border b Thomson	24	22	3
M.Amarnath	c Marsh b Thomson	13	20	2
Yashpal Sharma	c Hogg b Hogan	40	40	1
S.M.Patil	c Hogan b MacLeay	30	25	4
*Kapil Dev	c Hookes b Hogg	28	32	3
K.Azad	c Border b Lawson	15	18	1
R.M.H.Binny	run out	21	32	2
Madan Lal	not out	12	15	–
†S.M.H.Kirmani	lbw b Hogg	10	20	1
B.S.Sandhu	b Thomson	8	18	1
Extras	(lb 13, w 9, nb 15)	37		
Total	(55.5 overs)	**247**		

AUSTRALIA		Runs	Balls	4/6
T.M.Chappell	c Madan Lal b Sandhu	2	5	–
G.M.Wood	c Kirmani b Binny	21	32	2
G.N.Yallop	c and b Binny	18	30	2
*D.W.Hookes	b Binny	1	2	–
A.R.Border	b Madan Lal	36	49	5
†R.W.Marsh	lbw b Madan Lal	0	2	–
K.H.MacLeay	c Gavaskar b Madan Lal	5	6	1
T.G.Hogan	c Srikkanth b Binny	8	10	2
G.F.Lawson	b Sandhu	16	20	1
R.M.Hogg	not out	8	12	1
J.R.Thomson	b Madan Lal	0	5	–
Extras	(lb 5, w 5, nb 4)	14		
Total	(38.2 overs)	**129**		

AUSTRALIA	O	M	R	W
Lawson	10	1	40	1
Hogg	12	2	40	3
Hogan	11	1	31	1
Thomson	10.5	0	51	3
MacLeay	12	2	48	1

INDIA	O	M	R	W
Kapil Dev	8	2	16	0
Sandhu	10	1	26	2
Madan Lal	8.2	3	20	4
Binny	8	2	29	4
Amarnath	2	0	17	0
Azad	2	0	7	0

FALL OF WICKETS		
Wkt	I	A
1st	27	3
2nd	54	46
3rd	65	48
4th	118	52
5th	157	52
6th	174	69
7th	207	78
8th	215	115
9th	232	129
10th	247	129

Umpires: J.Birkenshaw (4) and D.R.Shepherd (4).

WEST INDIES v ZIMBABWE

At Edgbaston, Birmingham, on 20 June 1983. Toss: Zimbabwe.
Result: **WEST INDIES** won by 10 wickets. Award: S.F.A.F.Bacchus.
LOI debuts: None.

ZIMBABWE		Runs	Balls	4/6
R.D.Brown	c Lloyd b Marshall	14		–
G.A.Paterson	c Richards b Garner	6		1
J.G.Heron	c Dujon b Garner	0		–
A.J.Pycroft	c Dujon b Marshall	4		–
†D.L.Houghton	c Lloyd b Daniel	0		–
*D.A.G.Fletcher	b Richards	23		2
K.M.Curran	b Daniel	62		4/1
I.P.Butchart	c Haynes b Richards	8		–
G.E.Peckover	c and b Richards	3		–
P.W.E.Rawson	b Daniel	19		1
A.J.Traicos	not out	1		–
Extras	(b 4, lb 13, w 7, nb 7)	31		
Total	(60 overs)	**171**		

WEST INDIES		Runs	Balls	4/6
D.L.Haynes	not out	88		9
S.F.A.F.Bacchus	not out	80		8
A.L.Logie				
I.V.A.Richards				
H.A.Gomes				
*C.H.Lloyd				
†P.J.L.Dujon				
M.D.Marshall				
J.Garner				
W.W.Daniel				
W.W.Davis				
Extras	(lb 1, w 3)	4		
Total	(45.1 overs; 0 wickets)	**172**		

WEST INDIES	O	M	R	W		FALL OF WICKETS	
Marshall	12	3	19	2	Wkt	Z	WI
Garner	7	4	13	2	1st	17	–
Davis	8	2	13	0	2nd	17	–
Daniel	9	2	28	3	3rd	41	–
Gomes	12	2	26	0	4th	42	–
Richards	12	1	41	3	5th	42	–
					6th	79	–
ZIMBABWE	O	M	R	W	7th	104	–
Rawson	12	3	38	0	8th	115	–
Butchart	4	0	23	0	9th	170	–
Traicos	12	2	24	0	10th	171	–
Curran	9	0	44	0			
Fletcher	8.1	0	39	0			

Umpires: H.D.Bird (22) and D.J.Constant (22).

ENGLAND v INDIA (SEMI-FINAL)

At Old Trafford, Manchester, on 22 June 1983.   Toss: England.
Result: **INDIA** won by 6 wickets.   Award: M.Amarnath.
LOI debuts: None.

ENGLAND		Runs	Balls	4/6
G.Fowler	b Binny	33	59	3
C.J.Tavaré	c Kirmani b Binny	32	51	4
D.I.Gower	c Kirmani b Amarnath	17	30	1
A.J.Lamb	run out	29	58	1
M.W.Gatting	b Amarnath	18	46	1
I.T.Botham	b Azad	6	26	–
†I.J.Gould	run out	13	36	–
V.J.Marks	b Kapil Dev	8	18	–
G.R.Dilley	not out	20	26	2
P.J.W.Allott	c Patil b Kapil Dev	8	14	–
*R.G.D.Willis	b Kapil Dev	0	2	–
Extras	(b 1, lb 17, w 7, nb 4)	29		
Total	(60 overs)	**213**		

INDIA		Runs	Balls	4/6
S.M.Gavaskar	c Gould b Allott	25	41	3
K.Srikkanth	c Willis b Botham	19	44	3
M.Amarnath	run out	46	92	4/1
Yashpal Sharma	c Allott b Willis	61	115	3/2
S.M.Patil	not out	51	32	8
*Kapil Dev	not out	1	6	–
K.Azad				
R.M.H.Binny				
Madan Lal				
†S.M.H.Kirmani				
B.S.Sandhu				
Extras	(b 5, lb 6, w 1, nb 2)	14		
Total	(54.4 overs; 4 wickets)	**217**		

INDIA	O	M	R	W		FALL OF WICKETS		
Kapil Dev	11	1	35	3		Wkt	E	I
Sandhu	8	1	36	0		1st	69	46
Binny	12	1	43	2		2nd	84	50
Madan Lal	5	0	15	0		3rd	107	142
Azad	12	1	28	1		4th	141	205
Amarnath	12	1	27	2		5th	150	–
						6th	160	–
ENGLAND	O	M	R	W		7th	175	–
Willis	10.4	2	42	1		8th	177	–
Dilley	11	0	43	0		9th	202	–
Allott	10	3	40	1		10th	213	–
Botham	11	4	40	1				
Marks	12	1	38	0				

Umpires: D.G.L.Evans (11) and D.O.Oslear (7).

PAKISTAN v WEST INDIES (SEMI-FINAL)

At Kennington Oval, London, on 22 June 1983.　Toss: West Indies.
Result: **WEST INDIES** won by 8 wickets.　Award: I.V.A.Richards.
LOI debuts: None.

PAKISTAN		Runs	Balls	4/6
Mohsin Khan	b Roberts	70	176	1
Mudassar Nazar	c and b Garner	11	39	–
Ijaz Faqih	c Dujon b Holding	5	19	–
Zaheer Abbas	b Gomes	30	38	1
*Imran Khan	c Dujon b Marshall	17	41	–
Wasim Raja	lbw b Marshall	0	3	–
Shahid Mahboob	c Richards b Marshall	6	10	–
Sarfraz Nawaz	c Holding b Roberts	3	12	–
Abdul Qadir	not out	10	21	–
†Wasim Bari	not out	4	7	–
Rashid Khan				
Extras	(b 6, lb 13, w 4, nb 5)	28		
Total	**(60 overs; 8 wickets)**	**184**		

WEST INDIES		Runs	Balls	4/6
C.G.Greenidge	lbw b Rashid	17		
D.L.Haynes	b Qadir	29		
I.V.A.Richards	not out	80		11/1
H.A.Gomes	not out	50		3
*C.H.Lloyd				
S.F.A.F.Bacchus				
†P.J.L.Dujon				
M.D.Marshall				
A.M.E.Roberts				
J.Garner				
M.A.Holding				
Extras	(b 2, lb 6, w 4)	12		
Total	**(48.4 overs; 2 wickets)**	**188**		

WEST INDIES	O	M	R	W
Roberts	12	3	25	2
Garner	12	1	31	1
Marshall	12	2	28	3
Holding	12	1	25	1
Gomes	7	0	29	1
Richards	5	0	18	0

PAKISTAN	O	M	R	W
Rashid Khan	12	2	32	1
Sarfraz Nawaz	8	0	23	0
Abdul Qadir	11	1	42	1
Shahid Mahboob	11	1	43	0
Wasim Raja	1	0	9	0
Zaheer Abbas	4.4	1	24	0
Mohsin Khan	1	0	3	0

FALL OF WICKETS		
Wkt	P	WI
1st	23	34
2nd	34	56
3rd	88	–
4th	139	–
5th	139	–
6th	159	–
7th	164	–
8th	171	–
9th	–	–
10th	–	–

Umpires: D.J.Constant (23) and A.G.T.Whitehead (10).

WEST INDIES v INDIA (FINAL)

At Lord's, London, on 25 June 1983.   Toss: West Indies.
Result: **INDIA** won by 43 runs.   Award: M.Amarnath.
LOI debuts: None.

INDIA		Runs	Balls	4/6
S.M.Gavaskar	c Dujon b Roberts	2	12	–
K.Srikkanth	lbw b Marshall	38	57	7/1
M.Amarnath	b Holding	26	80	3
Yashpal Sharma	c sub (A.L.Logie) b Gomes	11	32	1
S.M.Patil	c Gomes b Garner	27	29	–/1
*Kapil Dev	c Holding b Gomes	15	8	3
K.Azad	c Garner b Roberts	0	3	–
R.M.H.Binny	c Garner b Roberts	2	8	–
Madan Lal	b Marshall	17	27	–/1
†S.M.H.Kirmani	b Holding	14	43	–
B.S.Sandhu	not out	11	30	1
Extras	(b 5, lb 5, w 9, nb 1)	20		
Total	(54.4 overs)	**183**		

WEST INDIES		Runs	Balls	4/6
C.G.Greenidge	b Sandhu	1	12	–
D.L.Haynes	c Binny b Madan Lal	13	33	2
I.V.A.Richards	c Kapil Dev b Madan Lal	33	28	7
*C.H.Lloyd	c Kapil Dev b Binny	8	17	1
H.A.Gomes	c Gavaskar b Madan Lal	5	16	–
S.F.A.F.Bacchus	c Kirmani b Sandhu	8	25	–
†P.J.L.Dujon	b Amarnath	25	73	–/1
M.D.Marshall	c Gavaskar b Amarnath	18	51	–
A.M.E.Roberts	lbw b Kapil Dev	4	14	–
J.Garner	not out	5	19	–
M.A.Holding	lbw b Amarnath	6	24	–
Extras	(lb 4, w 10)	14		
Total	(52 overs)	**140**		

WEST INDIES	O	M	R	W		FALL OF WICKETS		
Roberts	10	3	32	3		Wkt	I	WI
Garner	12	4	24	1		1st	2	5
Marshall	11	1	24	2		2nd	59	50
Holding	9.4	2	26	2		3rd	90	57
Gomes	11	1	49	2		4th	92	66
Richards	1	0	8	0		5th	110	66
						6th	111	76
INDIA	O	M	R	W		7th	130	119
Kapil Dev	11	4	21	1		8th	153	124
Sandhu	9	1	32	2		9th	161	126
Madan Lal	12	2	31	3		10th	183	140
Binny	10	1	23	1				
Amarnath	7	0	12	3				
Azad	3	0	7	0				

Umpires: H.D.Bird (23) and B.J.Meyer (14).

THE 1987 WORLD CUP

Cricket's first oriental World Cup was a resounding success, the Indo-Pakistan Joint Management Committee overcoming the enormous logistical problems created by spreading the 27 matches around 21 venues scattered throughout an area roughly the size of the present European Community. Officially known as the Reliance Cup, this fourth world tournament began with its closest finishes to date, Australia defeating India in Madras by a single run, New Zealand scraping home by three runs against Zimbabwe despite Dave Houghton's record innings of 142, and England storming home against West Indies with two wickets and three balls to spare despite chasing 35 runs off the last three overs.

This tournament was also the longest, taking six weeks, much of the time spent travelling, many of them in airport transit lounges awaiting delayed flights. Sri Lanka had the worst deal, four of their successive journeys each involving two days of travel: from Peshawar in Pakistan's North-West Frontier Province, they went to Kanpur in central India, before crossing back to Faisalabad and finally returning to Poona.

Because of the fewer daylight hours, matches were of 50 overs per innings. Despite the early starts (9am), morning dew appeared to pose few batting problems and 19 of the 27 games were won by the team batting first. So batting friendly were the pitches that many totals reached the norm for the 60-over contests of the England-based World Cups. Indeed, West Indies against Sri Lanka in Karachi broke the team (360 for 4) and individual (Viv Richards 181) World Cup records. Rain interrupted only one match, Australia and New Zealand being reduced to 30 overs apiece in Indore. The new ruling that matches could not be carried over into a second day was never brought to trial.

FINAL GROUP TABLES

GROUP A	P	W	L	Pts	R/O	GROUP B	P	W	L	Pts	R/O
INDIA	6	5	1	20	5.39	PAKISTAN	6	5	1	20	5.01
AUSTRALIA	6	5	1	20	5.19	ENGLAND	6	4	2	16	5.12
New Zealand	6	2	4	8	4.88	West Indies	6	3	3	12	5.16
Zimbabwe	6	0	6	0	3.76	Sri Lanka	6	0	6	0	4.04

Co-hosts India and Pakistan had been expected to meet in the final but neither survived the previous stage, England trouncing India by 35 runs in Bombay thanks to a masterly innings by Graham Gooch who swept the spinners to distraction during his 136-ball innings of 115. Australia had a closer encounter in Lahore before a decisive burst of fast bowling by Craig McDermott condemned Pakistan to their third successive semi-final defeat. Attempts to arrange a third-place play-off between India and Pakistan were aborted as a result of excessive financial demands by key players.

Calcutta's vast Eden Gardens Stadium staged the most colourful and noisy final so far, crammed with a crowd three times the capacity of Lord's. Australia took full advantage of winning the toss, compiling a total of 253 for 5 thereby setting England a target in excess of any so far achieved in the second innings of a final. Despite a late assault from Phillip DeFreitas, 17 were wanted off McDermott's concluding over. An outstanding team effort had brought deserved success for Australia and they delighted the crowd with their lap of honour, the captain, Allan Border, being borne aloft clutching the golden Reliance Cup.

PAKISTAN v SRI LANKA

At Niaz Stadium, Hyderabad, Pakistan, on 8 October 1987.   Toss: Pakistan.
Result: **PAKISTAN** won by 15 runs.   Award: Javed Miandad.
LOI debuts: None.

PAKISTAN		Runs	Balls	4/6
Ramiz Raja	c Ratnayake b Anurasiri	76	115	3
Ijaz Ahmed	c Kuruppu b Ratnayeke	16	34	2
Mansoor Akhtar	c Ratnayake b Ratnayeke	12	23	–
Javed Miandad	b Ratnayeke	103	100	6
Wasim Akram	run out	14	14	–
Salim Malik	not out	18	12	1
*Imran Khan	b Ratnayeke	2	4	–
†Salim Yousuf	not out	1	1	–
Mudassar Nazar				
Abdul Qadir				
Tausif Ahmed				
Extras	(lb 15, w 9, nb 1)	25		
Total	(50 overs; 6 wickets)	**267**		

SRI LANKA		Runs	Balls	4/6
R.S.Mahanama	c Miandad b Mansoor	89	117	7/1
†D.S.B.P.Kuruppu	c Salim Yousuf b Imran	9	24	1
R.L.Dias	b Qadir	5	21	–
A. Ranatunga	b Tausif	24	29	3
*L.R.D.Mendis	run out	1	6	–
A.P.Gurusinha	b Qadir	37	39	2/1
P.A.de Silva	b Imran	42	32	3/1
J.R.Ratnayeke	c Salim Yousuf b Wasim	7	13	–
R.J.Ratnayake	c Mudassar b Wasim	8	9	–
V.B.John	not out	1	4	–
S.D.Anurasiri	run out	0	3	–
Extras	(b 7, lb 14, w 7, nb 1)	29		
Total	(49.2 overs)	**252**		

SRI LANKA	O	M	R	W
John	10	2	37	0
Ratnayake	10	0	64	2
Ratnayeke	9	0	47	2
De Silva	10	0	44	0
Anurasiri	10	0	52	1
Gurusinha	1	0	8	0

PAKISTAN	O	M	R	W
Imran Khan	10	2	42	0
Wasim Akram	9.2	1	41	2
Mudassar Nazar	9	0	63	0
Abdul Qadir	10	1	30	2
Tausif Ahmed	10	0	48	1
Mansoor Akhtar	1	0	7	1

FALL OF WICKETS		
Wkt	P	SL
1st	48	29
2nd	67	57
3rd	180	100
4th	226	103
5th	259	182
6th	266	190
7th	–	209
8th	–	223
9th	–	251
10th	–	252

Umpires: V.K.Ramaswamy (*India*) (4) and S.J.Woodward (*New Zealand*) (8).

ENGLAND v WEST INDIES

At Municipal Stadium, Gujranwala, Pakistan, on 9 October 1987.   Toss: England.
Result: **ENGLAND** won by 2 wickets.   Award: A.J.Lamb.
LOI debuts: None.

WEST INDIES		**Runs**	**Balls**	**4/6**
D.L.Haynes	run out	19	45	1
C.A.Best	b DeFreitas	5	15	–
R.B.Richardson	b Foster	53	80	8
*I.V.A.Richards	b Foster	27	36	3
†P.J.L.Dujon	run out	46	76	3
A.L.Logie	b Foster	49	41	3/1
R.A.Harper	b Small	24	10	3/1
C.L.Hooper	not out	1	2	–
W.K.M.Benjamin	not out	7	2	1
C.A.Walsh				
B.P.Patterson				
Extras	(lb 9, nb 3)	12		
Total	(50 overs; 7 wickets)	**243**		

ENGLAND		**Runs**	**Balls**	**4/6**
G.A.Gooch	c Dujon b Hooper	47	93	3
B.C.Broad	c Dujon b Walsh	3	12	–
R.T.Robinson	run out	12	35	1
*M.W.Gatting	b Hooper	25	23	3
A.J.Lamb	not out	67	68	5/1
D.R.Pringle	c Best b Hooper	12	23	–
†P.R.Downton	run out	3	4	–
J.E.Emburey	b Patterson	22	15	2/1
P.A.J.DeFreitas	b Patterson	23	21	2
N.A.Foster	not out	9	6	1
G.C.Small				
Extras	(lb 14, w 6, nb 3)	23		
Total	(49.3 overs; 8 wickets)	**246**		

ENGLAND	O	M	R	W		**FALL OF WICKETS**		
DeFreitas	10	2	31	1		Wkt	WI	E
Foster	10	0	53	3		1st	8	14
Emburey	10	1	22	0		2nd	53	40
Small	10	0	45	1		3rd	105	98
Pringle	10	0	83	0		4th	122	99
						5th	205	123
WEST INDIES	O	M	R	W		6th	235	131
Patterson	10	0	49	2		7th	235	162
Walsh	9.3	0	65	1		8th	–	209
Harper	10	0	44	0		9th	–	–
Benjamin	10	2	32	0		10th	–	–
Hooper	10	0	42	3				

Umpires: A.R.Crafter (*Australia*) (52) and R.B.Gupta (*India*) (4).

INDIA v AUSTRALIA

At M.A.Chidambaram Stadium, Madras, India, on 9 October 1987.   Toss: India.
Result: **AUSTRALIA** won by 1 run.   Award: G.R.Marsh.
LOI debuts: India – N.S.Sidhu; Australia – T.M.Moody.

AUSTRALIA		Runs	Balls	4/6
D.C.Boon	lbw b Shastri	49	68	5
G.R.Marsh	c Azharuddin b Prabhakar	110	141	7/1
D.M.Jones	c Sidhu b Maninder	39	35	2/2
*A.R.Border	b Binny	16	22	–
T.M.Moody	c Kapil Dev b Prabhakar	8	13	1
S.R.Waugh	not out	19	17	–
S.P.O'Donnell	run out	7	10	–
†G.C.Dyer				
P.L.Taylor				
C.J.McDermott				
B.A.Reid				
Extras	(lb 18, w 2, nb 2)	22		
Total	(50 overs; 6 wickets)	**270**		

INDIA		Runs	Balls	4/6
K.Srikkanth	lbw b Waugh	70	83	7
S.M.Gavaskar	c Reid b Taylor	37	32	6/1
N.S.Sidhu	b McDermott	73	79	4/5
D.B.Vengsarkar	c Jones b McDermott	29	45	2
M.Azharuddin	b McDermott	10	14	1
*Kapil Dev	c Boon b O'Donnell	6	10	–
R.J.Shastri	c and b McDermott	12	11	1
†K.S.More	not out	12	14	2
R.M.H.Binny	run out	0	3	–
M.Prabhakar	run out	5	7	–
Maninder Singh	b Waugh	4	5	–
Extras	(b 2, lb 7, w 2)	11		
Total	(49.5 overs)	**269**		

INDIA	O	M	R	W	FALL OF WICKETS		
					Wkt	A	I
Kapil Dev	10	0	41	0	1st	110	69
Prabhakar	10	0	47	2	2nd	174	131
Binny	7	0	46	1	3rd	228	207
Maninder	10	0	48	1	4th	237	229
Shastri	10	0	50	1	5th	251	232
Azharuddin	3	0	20	0	6th	270	246
					7th	–	256
AUSTRALIA	O	M	R	W	8th	–	256
McDermott	10	0	56	4	9th	–	265
Reid	10	2	35	0	10th	–	269
O'Donnell	9	1	32	1			
Taylor	5	0	46	1			
Waugh	9.5	0	52	2			
Border	6	0	39	0			

Umpires: D.M.Archer (*West Indies*) (11) and H.D.Bird (*England*) (45).

NEW ZEALAND v ZIMBABWE

At Lal Bahadur Stadium, Hyderabad, India, on 10 October 1987.   Toss: Zimbabwe.
Result: **NEW ZEALAND** won by 3 runs.   Award: D.L.Houghton.
LOI debuts: New Zealand – A.H.Jones; Zimbabwe – E.A.Brandes, A.C.Waller.

NEW ZEALAND		Runs	Balls	4/6
M.C.Snedden	c Waller b Rawson	64	96	3
J.G.Wright	c Houghton b Traicos	18	40	1
M.D.Crowe	c and b Rawson	72	88	5/1
A.H.Jones	c Brandes b Shah	0	6	–
*J.J.Crowe	c Brown b Curran	31	35	2
D.N.Patel	lbw b Shah	0	2	–
J.G.Bracewell	not out	13	20	–
†I.D.S.Smith	c Brown b Curran	29	20	2/1
S.L.Boock	not out	0	–	–
W.Watson				
E.J.Chatfield				
Extras	(b 4, lb 4, w 4, nb 3)	15		
Total	(50 overs; 7 wickets)	**242**		

ZIMBABWE		Runs	Balls	4/6
R.D.Brown	c J.J.Crowe b Chatfield	1	10	–
A.H.Shah	lbw b Snedden	5	13	–
†D.L.Houghton	c M.D.Crowe b Snedden	142	137	13/6
A.J.Pycroft	run out	12	22	2
K.M.Curran	c Boock b Watson	4	8	–
A.C.Waller	c Smith b Watson	5	14	–
G.A.Paterson	c Smith b Boock	2	11	–
P.W.E.Rawson	lbw b Boock	1	10	–
I.P.Butchart	run out	54	70	2/1
E.A.Brandes	run out	0		
*A.J.Traicos	not out	4	6	–
Extras	(lb 7, w 1, nb 1)	9		
Total	(49.4 overs)	**239**		

ZIMBABWE	O	M	R	W		FALL OF WICKETS	
Curran	10	0	51	2	Wkt	NZ	Z
Rawson	10	0	62	2	1st	59	8
Brandes	7	2	24	0	2nd	143	10
Traicos	10	2	28	1	3rd	145	61
Butchart	4	0	27	0	4th	166	67
Shah	9	0	42	2	5th	169	86
					6th	205	94
NEW ZEALAND	O	M	R	W	7th	240	104
Chatfield	10	2	26	1	8th	–	221
Snedden	9	0	53	2	9th	–	221
Watson	10	2	36	2	10th	–	239
Bracewell	7	0	48	0			
Patel	5	0	27	0			
Boock	8.4	0	42	2			

Umpires: Mahboob Shah (*Pakistan*) (11) and P.W.Vidanagamage (*Sri Lanka*) (16).

PAKISTAN v ENGLAND

At Pindi Club Ground, Rawalpindi, Pakistan, on 12 (*no play*), 13 October 1987.
Toss: England.
Result: **PAKISTAN** won by 18 runs.   Award: Abdul Qadir.
LOI debuts: None.

PAKISTAN		Runs	Balls	4/6
Mansoor Akhtar	c Downton b Foster	6	24	1
Ramiz Raja	run out	15	40	1
Salim Malik	c Downton b DeFreitas	65	80	8
Javed Miandad	lbw b DeFreitas	23	50	3
Ijaz Ahmed	c Robinson b Small	59	59	4/1
*Imran Khan	b Small	22	32	2
Wasim Akram	b DeFreitas	5	3	1
†Salim Yousuf	not out	16	10	–
Abdul Qadir	not out	12	7	1/1
Tausif Ahmed				
Salim Jaffer				
Extras	(lb 10, w 3, nb 3)	16		
Total	(50 overs; 7 wickets)	**239**		

ENGLAND		Runs	Balls	4/6
G.A.Gooch	b Qadir	21	41	3
B.C.Broad	b Tausif	36	78	2
R.T.Robinson	b Qadir	33	62	1
*M.W.Gatting	b Salim Jaffer	43	47	4
A.J.Lamb	lbw b Qadir	30	38	3
D.R.Pringle	run out	8	14	–
J.E.Emburey	run out	1	1	–
†P.R.Downton	c Salim Yousuf b Qadir	0	2	–
P.A.J.DeFreitas	not out	3	3	–
N.A.Foster	run out	6	5	–
G.C.Small	lbw b Salim Jaffer	0	1	–
Extras	(b 6, lb 26, w 8)	40		
Total	(48.4 overs)	**221**		

ENGLAND	O	M	R	W		FALL OF WICKETS		
DeFreitas	10	1	42	3	Wkt	P	E	
Foster	10	1	35	1	1st	13	52	
Small	10	1	47	2	2nd	51	92	
Pringle	10	0	54	0	3rd	112	141	
Emburey	10	0	51	0	4th	123	186	
					5th	202	206	
PAKISTAN	O	M	R	W	6th	210	207	
Wasim Akram	9	0	32	0	7th	210	207	
Salim Jaffer	9.4	0	42	2	8th	–	213	
Tausif Ahmed	10	0	39	1	9th	–	221	
Abdul Qadir	10	0	31	4	10th	–	221	
Salim Malik	7	0	29	0				
Mansoor Akhtar	3	0	16	0				

Umpires: A.R.Crafter (*Australia*) (53) and R.B.Gupta (*India*) (5).

AUSTRALIA v ZIMBABWE

At M.A.Chidambaram Stadium, Madras, India, on 13 October 1987. Toss: Zimbabwe.
Result: **AUSTRALIA** won by 96 runs.   Award: S.R.Waugh.
LOI debuts: Australia – T.B.A.May; Zimbabwe – M.P.Jarvis.

AUSTRALIA		Runs	Balls	4/6
G.R.Marsh	c Curran b Shah	62	101	8
D.C.Boon	c Houghton b Curran	2	15	–
D.M.Jones	run out	2	12	–
*A.R.Border	c Shah b Butchart	67	88	8
S.R.Waugh	run out	45	41	3/2
S.P.O'Donnell	run out	3	11	–
†G.C.Dyer	c Paterson b Butchart	27	20	1/2
P.L.Taylor	not out	17	13	1
C.J.McDermott	c Brown b Curran	1	3	–
T.B.A.May	run out	1	1	–
B.A.Reid				
Extras	(w 8)	8		
Total	(50 overs; 9 wickets)	**235**		

ZIMBABWE		Runs	Balls	4/6
R.D.Brown	b O'Donnell	3	30	–
G.A.Paterson	run out	16	53	1
†D.L.Houghton	c O'Donnell b May	11	22	1
A.J.Pycroft	run out	9	29	1
K.M.Curran	b O'Donnell	30	38	1/3
A.C.Waller	c and b May	19	22	1/1
A.H.Shah	b McDermott	2	9	–
P.W.E.Rawson	b Reid	15	14	2
I.P.Butchart	c Jones b O'Donnell	18	32	2
*A.J.Traicos	c and b O'Donnell	6	5	1
M.P.Jarvis	not out	1	1	–
Extras	(b 2, lb 3, w 3, nb 1)	9		
Total	(42.4 overs)	**139**		

ZIMBABWE	O	M	R	W
Curran	8	0	29	2
Jarvis	10	0	40	0
Rawson	6	0	39	0
Butchart	10	1	59	2
Traicos	10	0	36	0
Shah	6	0	32	1

AUSTRALIA	O	M	R	W
McDermott	7	1	13	1
Reid	7	1	21	1
O'Donnell	9.4	1	39	4
Waugh	6	3	7	0
May	8	0	29	2
Taylor	5	0	25	0

FALL OF WICKETS		
Wkt	A	Z
1st	10	13
2nd	20	27
3rd	133	41
4th	143	44
5th	155	79
6th	202	97
7th	228	97
8th	230	124
9th	235	137
10th	–	139

Umpires: Khizer Hayat (*Pakistan*) (13) and D.R.Shepherd (*England*) (21).

WEST INDIES v SRI LANKA

At National Stadium, Karachi, Pakistan, on 13 October 1987.　Toss: Sri Lanka.
Result: **WEST INDIES** won by 191 runs.　Award: I.V.A.Richards.
LOI debuts: None.

WEST INDIES		Runs	Balls	4/6
D.L.Haynes	b Gurusinha	105	124	10/1
C.A.Best	b Ratnayeke	18	30	1
R.B.Richardson	c Kuruppu b Ratnayeke	0	1	–
*I.V.A.Richards	c Mahanama b De Mel	181	125	16/7
A.L.Logie	not out	31	25	–
R.A.Harper	not out	5	2	–
C.L.Hooper				
†P.J.L.Dujon				
W.K.M.Benjamin				
C.A.Walsh				
B.P.Patterson				
Extras	(b 4, lb 8, w 4, nb 4)	20		
Total	(50 overs; 4 wickets)	360		

SRI LANKA		Runs	Balls	4/6
R.S.Mahanama	c Dujon b Walsh	12	4	3
†D.S.B.P.Kuruppu	lbw b Patterson	14	14	–
A.P.Gurusinha	b Hooper	36	108	1/1
P.A.de Silva	c Dujon b Hooper	9	27	–
A.Ranatunga	not out	52	93	5
*L.R.D.Mendis	not out	37	45	5
R.S.Madugalle				
J.R.Ratnayeke				
A.L.F.de Mel				
V.B.John				
S.D.Anurasiri				
Extras	(b 1, lb 2, w 6)	9		
Total	(50 overs; 4 wickets)	**169**		

SRI LANKA	O	M	R	W		FALL OF WICKETS		
John	10	1	48	0		Wkt	WI	SL
Ratnayeke	8	0	68	2		1st	45	24
Anurasiri	10	0	39	0		2nd	45	31
De Mel	10	0	97	1		3rd	227	57
De Silva	6	0	35	0		4th	343	112
Ranatunga	2	0	18	0		5th	–	–
Gurusinha	4	0	43	1		6th	–	–
						7th	–	–
WEST INDIES	O	M	R	W		8th	–	–
Patterson	7	0	32	1		9th	–	–
Walsh	7	2	23	1		10th	–	–
Harper	10	2	15	0				
Benjamin	4	0	11	0				
Hooper	10	0	39	2				
Richards	8	0	22	0				
Richardson	4	0	24	0				

Umpires: V.K.Ramaswamy (*India*) (5) and S.J.Woodward (*New Zealand*) (9).

INDIA v NEW ZEALAND

At Chinnaswamy Stadium, Bangalore, India, on 14 October 1987.   Toss: New Zealand.
Result: **INDIA** won by 16 runs.   Award: Kapil Dev.
LOI debuts: None.

INDIA		Runs	Balls	4/6
K.Srikkanth	run out	9	19	1
S.M.Gavaskar	run out	2	14	–
N.S.Sidhu	c Jones b Patel	75	71	4/4
D.B.Vengsarkar	c and b Watson	0	8	–
M.Azharuddin	c Boock b Patel	21	57	1
R.J.Shastri	c and b Patel	22	44	–/1
*Kapil Dev	not out	72	58	4/1
M.Prabhakar	c and b Chatfield	3	5	–
†K.S.More	not out	42	26	5
L.Sivaramakrishnan				
Maninder Singh				
Extras	(lb 4, w 2)	6		
Total	(50 overs; 7 wickets)	**252**		

NEW ZEALAND		Runs	Balls	4/6
M.C.Snedden	c Shastri b Azharuddin	33	63	2
K.R.Rutherford	c Srikkanth b Shastri	75	95	6/2
M.D.Crowe	st More b Maninder	9	12	1
A.H.Jones	run out	64	86	2
*J.J.Crowe	c Vengsarkar b Maninder	7	11	–
D.N.Patel	run out	1	3	–
J.G.Bracewell	c Maninder b Shastri	8	14	–
†I.D.S.Smith	b Prabhakar	10	5	–
S.L.Boock	not out	7	8	–
W. Watson	not out	2	3	–
E.J.Chatfield				
Extras	(b 5, lb 9, w 5, nb 1)	20		
Total	(50 overs; 8 wickets)	**236**		

NEW ZEALAND	O	M	R	W		FALL OF WICKETS		
Chatfield	10	1	39	1		Wkt	I	NZ
Snedden	10	1	56	0		1st	11	67
Watson	9	0	59	1		2nd	16	86
Boock	4	0	26	0		3rd	21	146
Bracewell	7	0	32	0		4th	86	168
Patel	10	0	36	3		5th	114	170
						6th	165	189
INDIA	O	M	R	W		7th	170	206
Kapil Dev	10	1	54	0		8th	–	225
Prabhakar	8	0	38	1		9th	–	–
Azharuddin	4	0	11	1		10th	–	–
Sivaramakrishnan	8	0	34	0				
Maninder	10	0	40	2				
Shastri	10	0	45	2				

Umpires: D.M.Archer (*West Indies*) (12) and H.D.Bird (*England*) (46).

PAKISTAN v WEST INDIES

At Gaddafi Stadium, Lahore, Pakistan, on 16 October 1987.   Toss: West Indies.
Result: **PAKISTAN** won by 1 wicket.   Award: Salim Yousuf.
LOI debuts: West Indies – P.V.Simmons.

WEST INDIES		Runs	Balls	4/6
D.L.Haynes	b Salim Jaffer	37	81	3
P.V.Simmons	c and b Tausif	50	57	8
R.B.Richardson	c Ijaz b Salim Jaffer	11	22	1
*I.V.A.Richards	c Salim Malik b Imran	51	52	4/1
A.L.Logie	c Mansoor b Salim Jaffer	2	4	–
C.L.Hooper	lbw b Wasim	22	37	2
†P.J.L.Dujon	lbw b Wasim	5	12	–
R.A.Harper	c Mansoor b Imran	0	1	–
E.A.E.Baptiste	b Imran	14	20	1
C.A.Walsh	lbw b Imran	7	6	1
B.P.Patterson	not out	0	4	–
Extras	(b 1, lb 14, w 2)	17		
Total	(49.3 overs)	**216**		

PAKISTAN		Runs	Balls	4/6
Ramiz Raja	c Richards b Harper	42	87	1
Mansoor Akhtar	b Patterson	10	24	2
Salim Malik	c Baptiste b Walsh	4	7	1
Javed Miandad	c and b Hooper	33	72	1
Ijaz Ahmed	b Walsh	6	14	–
*Imran Khan	c Logie b Walsh	18	26	–
†Salim Yousuf	c Hooper b Walsh	56	49	7
Wasim Akram	c Richardson b Patterson	7	8	–
Abdul Qadir	not out	16	9	–/1
Tausif Ahmed	run out	0	1	–
Salim Jaffer	not out	1	3	–
Extras	(b 5, lb 12, w 7)	24		
Total	(50 overs; 9 wickets)	**217**		

PAKISTAN	O	M	R	W		FALL OF WICKETS		
Imran Khan	8.3	2	37	4	Wkt	WI	P	
Wasim Akram	10	0	45	2	1st	91	23	
Abdul Qadir	8	0	42	0	2nd	97	28	
Tausif Ahmed	10	2	35	1	3rd	118	92	
Salim Jaffer	10	0	30	3	4th	121	104	
Salim Malik	3	0	12	0	5th	169	110	
					6th	184	183	
WEST INDIES	O	M	R	W	7th	184	200	
Patterson	10	1	51	2	8th	196	202	
Walsh	10	1	40	4	9th	207	203	
Baptiste	8	1	33	0	10th	216	–	
Harper	10	0	28	1				
Hooper	10	0	38	0				
Richards	2	0	10	0				

Umpires: A.R.Crafter (*Australia*) (54) and S.J.Woodward (*New Zealand*) (10).

ENGLAND v SRI LANKA

At Shahi Bagh Stadium, Peshawar, Pakistan, on 17 October 1987.   Toss: England.
Result: **ENGLAND** won by 109 runs (*target revised to 267 from 45 overs*).
Award: A.J.Lamb.   LOI debuts: None.

ENGLAND		Runs	Balls	4/6
G.A.Gooch	c and b Anurasiri	84	100	8
B.C.Broad	c De Silva b Ratnayeke	28	60	1
*M.W.Gatting	b Ratnayeke	58	63	3
A.J.Lamb	c De Silva b Ratnayeke	76	58	3/2
J.E.Emburey	not out	30	19	3/1
C.W.J.Athey	not out	2	2	–
†P.R.Downton				
P.A.J.DeFreitas				
D.R.Pringle				
E.E.Hemmings				
G.C.Small				
Extras	(lb 13, w 5)	18		
Total	(50 overs; 4 wickets)	**296**		

SRI LANKA		Runs	Balls	4/6
R.S.Mahanama	c Gooch b Pringle	11	39	2
†D.S.B.P.Kuruppu	c Hemmings b Emburey	13	26	1
A.P.Gurusinha	run out	1	12	–
R.S.Madugalle	b Hemmings	30	49	3
A.Ranatunga	lbw b DeFreitas	40	67	4
*L.R.D.Mendis	run out	14	33	1
P.A.de Silva	c Emburey b Hemmings	6	14	–
J.R.Ratnayeke	c Broad b Emburey	1	5	–
R.J.Ratnayake	not out	14	22	1
V.B.John	not out	8	7	1
S.D.Anurasiri				
Extras	(b 2, lb 9, w 6, nb 3)	20		
Total	(45 overs; 8 wickets)	**158**		

SRI LANKA	O	M	R	W
Ratnayeke	9	0	62	2
John	10	0	44	0
De Silva	7	0	33	0
Ratnayake	10	0	60	1
Anurasiri	8	0	44	1
Ranatunga	6	0	40	0

ENGLAND	O	M	R	W
DeFreitas	9	2	24	1
Small	7	0	27	0
Pringle	4	0	11	1
Emburey	10	1	26	2
Hemmings	10	1	31	2
Gooch	2	0	9	0
Athey	1	0	10	0
Broad	1	0	6	0
Lamb	1	0	3	0

FALL OF WICKETS		
Wkt	E	SL
1st	89	31
2nd	142	32
3rd	218	37
4th	287	99
5th	–	105
6th	–	113
7th	–	119
8th	–	137
9th	–	–
10th	–	–

Umpires: R.B.Gupta (*India*) (6) and V.K.Ramaswamy (*India*) (6).

INDIA v ZIMBABWE

At Wankhede Stadium, Bombay, India, on 17 October 1987.　Toss: Zimbabwe.
Result: **INDIA** won by 8 wickets.　Award: M.Prabhakar.
LOI debuts: Zimbabwe – K.J.Arnott, M.A.Meman.

ZIMBABWE		**Runs**	**Balls**	**4/6**
G.A.Paterson	b Prabhakar	6	21	–
K.J.Arnott	lbw b Prabhakar	1	6	–
†D.L.Houghton	b Prabhakar	0	12	–
A.J.Pycroft	st More b Shastri	61	102	2
K.M.Curran	c More b Prabhakar	0	1	
A.C.Waller	st More b Maninder	16	42	1
I.P.Butchart	c Sivaramakrishnan b Maninder	10	23	1
A.H.Shah	c More b Maninder	0	1	–
M.A.Meman	run out	19	22	2
*A.J.Traicos	c Gavaskar b Sivaramakrishnan	0	1	–
M.P.Jarvis	not out	8	35	–
Extras	(b 2, lb 6, w 6)	14		
Total	(44.2 overs)	**135**		

INDIA		**Runs**	**Balls**	**4/6**
K.Srikkanth	c Paterson b Traicos	31	38	4
S.M.Gavaskar	st Houghton b Traicos	43	52	9
M.Prabhakar	not out	11	41	1
D.B.Vengsarkar	not out	46	37	4/3
N.S.Sidhu				
M.Azharuddin				
*Kapil Dev				
R.J.Shastri				
†K.S.More				
L.Sivaramakrishnan				
Maninder Singh				
Extras	(lb 1, w 4)	5		
Total	(27.5 overs; 2 wickets)	**136**		

INDIA	O	M	R	W		FALL OF WICKETS		
Kapil Dev	8	1	17	0		Wkt	Z	I
Prabhakar	8	1	19	4		1st	3	76
Maninder	10	0	21	3		2nd	12	80
Azharuddin	1	0	6	0		3rd	13	–
Sivaramakrishnan	9	0	36	1		4th	13	–
Shastri	8.2	0	28	1		5th	47	–
						6th	67	–
ZIMBABWE	O	M	R	W		7th	67	–
Curran	6	0	32	0		8th	98	–
Jarvis	4	0	22	0		9th	99	–
Butchart	3	0	20	0		10th	135	–
Traicos	8	0	27	2				
Meman	6.5	0	34	0				

Umpires: Mahboob Shah (*Pakistan*) (12) and D.R.Shepherd (*England*) (22).

AUSTRALIA v NEW ZEALAND

At Nehru Stadium, Indore, India, on 18 (*no play*), 19 October 1987.   Toss: New Zealand.
Result: **AUSTRALIA** won by 3 runs.   Award: D.C.Boon.
LOI debuts: None.

AUSTRALIA		Runs	Balls	4/6
D.C.Boon	c Wright b Snedden	87	96	5/2
G.R.Marsh	c J.J.Crowe b Snedden	5	9	–
D.M.Jones	c Rutherford b Patel	52	48	1/3
*A.R.Border	c M.D.Crowe b Chatfield	34	28	3
S.R.Waugh	not out	13	8	1/1
T.M.Moody	not out	0	3	–
S.P.O'Donnell				
†G.C.Dyer				
T.B.A.May				
C.J.McDermott				
B.A.Reid				
Extras	(b 1, lb 5, w 2)	8		
Total	(30 overs; 4 wickets)	**199**		

NEW ZEALAND		Runs	Balls	4/6
K.R.Rutherford	b O'Donnell	37	38	2/2
J.G.Wright	c Dyer b O'Donnell	47	44	1/2
M.D.Crowe	c Marsh b Waugh	58	48	5
A.H.Jones	c Marsh b McDermott	15	23	–
*J.J.Crowe	c and b Reid	3	10	–
D.N.Patel	run out	13	9	1
J.G.Bracewell	c and b Reid	6	4	1
†I.D.S.Smith	b Waugh	1	2	–
M.C.Snedden	run out	1	1	–
W.Watson	not out	2	3	–
E.J.Chatfield	not out	0	–	–
Extras	(b 4, lb 5, w 4)	13		
Total	(30 overs; 9 wickets)	**196**		

NEW ZEALAND	O	M	R	W		FALL OF WICKETS		
Snedden	6	0	36	2		Wkt	A	NZ
Chatfield	6	0	27	1		1st	17	83
Watson	6	0	34	0		2nd	134	94
Patel	6	0	45	1		3rd	171	133
Bracewell	6	0	51	0		4th	196	140
						5th	–	165
AUSTRALIA	O	M	R	W		6th	–	183
McDermott	6	0	30	1		7th	–	193
Reid	6	0	38	2		8th	–	193
May	6	0	39	0		9th	–	195
O'Donnell	6	0	44	2		10th	–	–
Waugh	6	0	36	2				

Umpires: D.M.Archer (*West Indies*) (13) and Khizer Hayat (*Pakistan*) (14).

PAKISTAN v ENGLAND

At National Stadium, Karachi, Pakistan, on 20 October 1987.   Toss: Pakistan.
Result: **PAKISTAN** won by 7 wickets.   Award: Imran Khan.
LOI debuts: None.

ENGLAND		Runs	Balls	4/6
G.A.Gooch	c Wasim b Imran	16	27	2
R.T.Robinson	b Qadir	16	26	1
C.W.J.Athey	b Tausif	86	104	6/2
*M.W.Gatting	c Salim Yousuf b Qadir	60	65	3/1
A.J.Lamb	b Imran	9	15	–
J.E.Emburey	lbw b Qadir	3	11	–
†P.R.Downton	c Salim Yousuf b Imran	6	13	–
P.A.J.DeFreitas	c Salim Yousuf b Imran	13	15	1
N.A.Foster	not out	20	20	2
G.C.Small	run out	0	1	–
E.E.Hemmings	not out	4	3	–
Extras	(lb 7, w 4)	11		
Total	(50 overs; 9 wickets)	244		

PAKISTAN		Runs	Balls	4/6
Ramiz Raja	c Gooch b DeFreitas	113	148	5
Mansoor Akhtar	run out	29	49	3
Salim Malik	c Athey b Emburey	88	92	7
Javed Miandad	not out	6	3	1
Ijaz Ahmed	not out	4	2	1
*Imran Khan				
†Salim Yousuf				
Wasim Akram				
Abdul Qadir				
Tausif Ahmed				
Salim Jaffer				
Extras	(lb 6, w 1)	7		
Total	(49 overs; 3 wickets)	247		

PAKISTAN	O	M	R	W		FALL OF WICKETS		
Imran Khan	9	0	37	4		Wkt	E	P
Wasim Akram	8	0	44	0		1st	26	61
Tausif Ahmed	10	0	46	1		2nd	52	228
Abdul Qadir	10	0	31	3		3rd	187	243
Salim Jaffer	8	0	44	0		4th	187	–
Salim Malik	5	0	35	0		5th	192	–
						6th	203	–
ENGLAND	O	M	R	W		7th	206	–
DeFreitas	8	2	41	1		8th	230	–
Foster	10	0	51	0		9th	230	–
Hemmings	10	1	40	0		10th	–	–
Emburey	10	0	34	1				
Small	9	0	63	0				
Gooch	2	0	12	0				

Umpires: A.R.Crafter (*Australia*) (55) and V.K.Ramaswamy (*India*) (7).

WEST INDIES v SRI LANKA

At Green Park, Kanpur, India, on 21 October 1987. Toss: Sri Lanka.
Result: **WEST INDIES** won by 25 runs. Award: P.V.Simmons.
LOI debuts: None.

WEST INDIES		Runs	Balls	4/6
D.L.Haynes	b Anurasiri	24	36	3
P.V.Simmons	c Madugalle b Ratnayeke	89	126	11
R.B.Richardson	c Mahanama b Jeganathan	4	12	–
*I.V.A.Richards	c Ratnayake b De Silva	14	25	–
A.L.Logie	not out	65	66	7
C.L.Hooper	st Kuruppu b De Silva	6	8	1
†P.J.L.Dujon	c Kuruppu b Ratnayeke	6	14	–
R.A.Harper	b Ratnayeke	3	6	–
W.K.M.Benjamin	b Ratnayeke	0	3	–
C.A.Walsh	not out	9	8	1
B.P.Patterson				
Extras	(b 2, lb 7, w 7)	16		
Total	(50 overs; 8 wickets)	**236**		

SRI LANKA		Runs	Balls	4/6
R.S.Mahanama	b Patterson	0	3	–
†D.S.B.P.Kuruppu	c and b Hooper	33	82	1
J.R.Ratnayeke	lbw b Benjamin	15	22	1
R.S.Madugalle	c Haynes b Harper	18	42	–
A.Ranatunga	not out	86	100	7/2
*L.R.D.Mendis	b Walsh	19	34	1
P.A.de Silva	b Patterson	8	9	–
R.J.Ratnayake	c Walsh b Patterson	5	7	–
S.Jeganathan	run out	3	9	–
V.B.John	not out	1	3	–
S.D.Anurasiri				
Extras	(b 2, lb 11, nb 10)	23		
Total	(50 overs; 8 wickets)	**211**		

SRI LANKA	O	M	R	W
Ratnayeke	10	1	41	3
John	5	1	25	0
Ratnayake	5	0	39	1
Jeganathan	10	1	33	1
Anurasiri	10	1	46	1
De Silva	10	0	43	2

WEST INDIES	O	M	R	W
Patterson	10	0	31	3
Walsh	9	2	43	1
Benjamin	10	0	43	1
Harper	10	1	29	1
Hooper	8	0	35	1
Richards	3	0	17	0

FALL OF WICKETS		
Wkt	WI	SL
1st	62	2
2nd	80	28
3rd	115	86
4th	155	86
5th	168	156
6th	199	184
7th	213	200
8th	214	209
9th	–	–
10th	–	–

Umpires: Amanullah Khan (*Pakistan*) (10) and Mahboob Shah (*Pakistan*) (13).

INDIA v AUSTRALIA

At Feroz Shah Kotla, Delhi, India, on 22 October 1987.   Toss: Australia.
Result: **INDIA** won by 56 runs.   Award: M.Azharuddin.
LOI debuts: Australia – A.K.Zesers.

INDIA		**Runs**	**Balls**	**4/6**
K.Srikkanth	c Dyer b McDermott	26	37	3
S.M.Gavaskar	b O'Donnell	61	72	7
N.S.Sidhu	c Moody b McDermott	51	70	2
D.B.Vengsarkar	c O'Donnell b Reid	63	60	3/2
*Kapil Dev	c Dyer b McDermott	3	5	–
M.Azharuddin	not out	54	45	5/1
R.J.Shastri	c and b Waugh	8	7	1
†K.S.More	not out	5	4	–
M.Prabhakar				
C.Sharma				
Maninder Singh				
Extras	(b 1, lb 6, w11)	18		
Total	(50 overs; 6 wickets)	**289**		

AUSTRALIA		**Runs**	**Balls**	**4/6**
G.R.Marsh	st More b Maninder	33	56	2
D.C.Boon	c More b Shastri	62	59	7
D.M.Jones	c Kapil Dev b Maninder	36	55	–
*A.R.Border	c Prabhakar b Maninder	12	24	–
S.R.Waugh	c Sidhu b Kapil Dev	42	52	3
T.M.Moody	run out	2	6	–
S.P.O'Donnell	b Azharuddin	5	10	–
†G.C.Dyer	c Kapil Dev b Prabhakar	15	12	–/1
C.J.McDermott	c and b Azharuddin	4	5	–
A.K.Zesers	not out	2	11	–
B.A.Reid	c Sidhu b Azharuddin	1	6	–
Extras	(lb 11, w 8)	19		
Total	(49 overs)	**233**		

AUSTRALIA	O	M	R	W		**FALL OF WICKETS**		
O'Donnell	9	1	45	1		Wkt	I	A
Reid	10	0	65	1		1st	50	88
Waugh	10	0	59	1		2nd	125	104
McDermott	10	0	61	3		3rd	167	135
Moody	2	0	15	0		4th	178	164
Zesers	9	1	37	0		5th	243	167
						6th	274	182
INDIA	O	M	R	W		7th	–	214
Kapil Dev	8	1	41	1		8th	–	227
Prabhakar	10	0	56	1		9th	–	231
Maninder	10	0	34	3		10th	–	233
Shastri	10	0	35	1				
Sharma	7.1	0	37	0				
Azharuddin	3.5	0	19	3				

Umpires: Khalid Aziz (*Pakistan*) (4) and D.R.Shepherd (*England*) (23).

NEW ZEALAND v ZIMBABWE

At Eden Gardens, Calcutta, India, on 23 October 1987.   Toss: New Zealand.
Result: **NEW ZEALAND** won by 4 wickets.   Award: J.J.Crowe.
LOI debuts: None.

ZIMBABWE		Runs	Balls	4/6
G.A.Paterson	run out	0	8	–
A.H.Shah	c M.D.Crowe b Watson	41	90	2
K.J.Arnott	run out	51	83	5
†D.L.Houghton	c M.D.Crowe b Boock	50	57	5
A.J.Pycroft	not out	52	46	2/1
K.M.Curran	b Boock	12	11	1
A.C.Waller	not out	8	5	1
I.P.Butchart				
E.A.Brandes				
*A.J.Traicos				
M.P.Jarvis				
Extras	(lb 7, w 6)	13		
Total	(50 overs; 5 wickets)	**227**		

NEW ZEALAND		Runs	Balls	4/6
K.R.Rutherford	b Brandes	22	32	2
J.G.Wright	b Shah	12	32	1
M.D.Crowe	c Butchart b Shah	58	58	8
D.N.Patel	c Arnott b Brandes	1	4	–
*J.J.Crowe	not out	88	105	8
A.H.Jones	c Jarvis b Traicos	15	35	1
M.C.Snedden	b Jarvis	4	13	–
†I.D.S.Smith	not out	17	10	2
S.L.Boock				
E.J.Chatfield				
W.Watson				
Extras	(b 1, lb 5, w 4, nb 1)	11		
Total	(47.4 overs; 6 wickets)	**228**		

NEW ZEALAND	O	M	R	W		FALL OF WICKETS		
Chatfield	10	2	47	0	Wkt	Z	NZ	
Snedden	10	2	32	0	1st	1	37	
Watson	10	1	45	1	2nd	82	53	
Boock	10	1	43	2	3rd	121	56	
Patel	10	1	53	0	4th	180	125	
					5th	216	158	
ZIMBABWE	O	M	R	W	6th	–	182	
Curran	2	0	12	0	7th	–	–	
Jarvis	7.4	0	39	1	8th	–	–	
Brandes	10	1	44	2	9th	–	–	
Shah	10	0	34	2	10th	–	–	
Traicos	10	0	43	1				
Butchart	8	0	50	0				

Umpires: Khizer Hayat (*Pakistan*) (15) and P.W.Vidanagamage (*Sri Lanka*) (17).

PAKISTAN v SRI LANKA

At Iqbal Stadium, Faisalabad, Pakistan, on 25 October 1987. Toss: Pakistan.
Result: **PAKISTAN** won by 113 runs.   Award: Salim Malik
LOI debuts: None.

PAKISTAN		Runs	Balls	4/6
Ramiz Raja	c and b Anurasiri	32	49	2
Mansoor Akhtar	b Jeganathan	33	61	2
Salim Malik	b Ratnayeke	100	95	10
Javed Miandad	run out	1	8	–
Wasim Akram	c Ranatunga b De Silva	39	40	2/2
Ijaz Ahmed	c and b John	30	18	5
*Imran Khan	run out	39	20	5/1
Manzoor Elahi	not out	4	6	–
†Salim Yousuf	not out	11	6	–/1
Abdul Qadir				
Tausif Ahmed				
Extras	(lb 6, w 2)	8		
Total	(50 overs; 7 wickets)	**297**		

SRI LANKA		Runs	Balls	4/6
R.S.Mahanama	run out	8	13	1
†D.S.B.P.Kuruppu	c Salim Yousuf b Imran	0	1	–
J.R.Ratnayeke	run out	22	60	2
R.S.Madugalle	c Salim Yousuf b Manzoor	15	38	2
A.Ranatunga	c and b Qadir	50	66	4
*L.R.D.Mendis	b Qadir	58	65	6
P.A.de Silva	not out	13	35	–
A.L.F.de Mel	b Qadir	0	3	–
S.Jeganathan	c Salim Yousuf b Miandad	1	11	–
V.B.John	not out	1	12	–
S.D.Anurasiri				
Extras	(b 4, lb 4, w 6, nb 2)	16		
Total	(50 overs; 8 wickets)	**184**		

SRI LANKA	O	M	R	W		FALL OF WICKETS		
Ratnayeke	10	0	58	1		Wkt	P	SL
John	8	1	53	1		1st	64	4
De Mel	10	0	53	0		2nd	72	11
Jeganathan	9	1	45	1		3rd	77	41
Anurasiri	7	0	45	1		4th	137	70
De Silva	6	0	37	1		5th	197	150
						6th	264	173
PAKISTAN	O	M	R	W		7th	285	173
Imran Khan	3.2	1	13	1		8th	–	179
Wasim Akram	7	0	34	0		9th	–	–
Manzoor Elahi	9.4	0	32	1		10th	–	–
Tausif Ahmed	10	1	23	0				
Abdul Qadir	10	0	40	3				
Salim Malik	7	1	29	0				
Javed Miandad	3	0	5	1				

Umpires: R.B.Gupta (*India*) (7) and S.J.Woodward (*New Zealand*) (11).

ENGLAND v WEST INDIES

At Sawai Mansingh Stadium, Jaipur, India, on 26 October 1987.   Toss: West Indies.
Result: **ENGLAND** won by 34 runs.   Award: G.A.Gooch.
LOI debuts: None.

ENGLAND		Runs	Balls	4/6
G.A.Gooch	c Harper b Patterson	92	137	7
R.T.Robinson	b Patterson	13	19	2
C.W.J.Athey	c Patterson b Harper	21	44	3
*M.W.Gatting	lbw b Richards	25	24	1
A.J.Lamb	c Richardson b Patterson	40	52	3
J.E.Emburey	not out	24	16	4
P.A.J.DeFreitas	not out	16	9	3
†P.R.Downton				
N.A.Foster				
G.C.Small				
E.E.Hemmings				
Extras	(b 5, lb 10, w 22, nb 1)	38		
Total	(50 overs; 5 wickets)	**269**		

WEST INDIES		Runs	Balls	4/6
D.L.Haynes	c Athey b DeFreitas	9	14	2
P.V.Simmons	b Emburey	25	28	5
R.B.Richardson	c Downton b Small	93	130	8/1
*I.V.A.Richards	b Hemmings	51	51	4/3
A.L.Logie	c Hemmings b Emburey	22	21	3
C.L.Hooper	c Downton b DeFreitas	8	11	1
†P.J.L.Dujon	c Downton b Foster	1	4	–
R.A.Harper	run out	3	4	–
W.K.M.Benjamin	c Foster b DeFreitas	8	16	–
C.A.Walsh	b Hemmings	2	3	–
B.P.Patterson	not out	4	8	–
Extras	(lb 7, w 1, nb 1)	9		
Total	(48.1 overs)	**235**		

WEST INDIES	O	M	R	W
Patterson	9	0	56	3
Walsh	10	0	24	0
Benjamin	10	0	63	0
Harper	10	1	52	1
Hooper	3	0	27	0
Richards	8	0	32	1

ENGLAND	O	M	R	W
DeFreitas	9.1	2	28	3
Foster	10	0	52	1
Emburey	9	0	41	2
Small	10	0	61	1
Hemmings	10	0	46	2

FALL OF WICKETS		
Wkt	E	WI
1st	35	18
2nd	90	65
3rd	154	147
4th	209	182
5th	250	208
6th	–	211
7th	–	219
8th	–	221
9th	–	224
10th	–	235

Umpires: Mahboob Shah (*Pakistan*) (14) and P.W.Vidanagamage (*Sri Lanka*) (18).

INDIA v ZIMBABWE

At Gujarat Stadium, Motera, Ahmedabad, India, on 26 October 1987.   Toss: India.
Result: **INDIA** won by 7 wickets.   Award: Kapil Dev.
LOI debuts: None.

ZIMBABWE		Runs	Balls	4/6
R.D.Brown	c More b Sharma	13	52	2
A.H.Shah	run out	0	3	–
K.J.Arnott	b Kapil Dev	60	126	1
A.J.Pycroft	c More b Sharma	2	9	–
†D.L.Houghton	c Kapil Dev b Shastri	22	35	–
A.C.Waller	c Shastri b Maninder	39	44	4/1
I.P.Butchart	b Kapil Dev	13	14	1
P.W.E.Rawson	not out	16	17	–
E.A.Brandes	not out	3	4	–
M.P.Jarvis				
*A.J.Traicos				
Extras	(b 1, lb 12, w 9, nb 1)	23		
Total	(50 overs; 7 wickets)	**191**		

INDIA		Runs	Balls	4/6
K.Srikkanth	lbw b Jarvis	6	9	1
S.M.Gavaskar	c Butchart b Rawson	50	114	3
N.S.Sidhu	c Brandes b Rawson	55	61	5/1
D.B.Vengsarkar	not out	33	43	1
*Kapil Dev	not out	41	25	2/3
M.Azharuddin				
R.J.Shastri				
†K.S.More				
M.Prabhakar				
C.Sharma				
Maninder Singh				
Extras	(lb 6, w3)	9		
Total	(42 overs; 3 wickets)	**194**		

INDIA	O	M	R	W		FALL OF WICKETS		
Kapil Dev	10	2	44	2		Wkt	Z	I
Prabhakar	7	2	12	0		1st	4	11
Sharma	10	0	41	2		2nd	36	105
Maninder	10	1	32	1		3rd	40	132
Shastri	10	0	35	1		4th	83	–
Azharuddin	3	0	14	0		5th	150	–
						6th	155	–
ZIMBABWE	O	M	R	W		7th	184	–
Brandes	6	0	28	0		8th	–	–
Jarvis	8	1	21	1		9th	–	–
Shah	8	0	40	0		10th	–	–
Traicos	10	0	39	0				
Rawson	8	0	46	2				
Butchart	2	0	14	0				

Umpires: D.M.Archer (*West Indies*) (14) and H.D.Bird (*England*) (47).

AUSTRALIA v NEW ZEALAND

At Sector 16 Stadium, Chandigarh, India, on 27 October 1987.   Toss: Australia.
Result: **AUSTRALIA** won by 17 runs.   Award: G.R.Marsh.
LOI debuts: None.

AUSTRALIA		Runs	Balls	4/6
G.R.Marsh	not out	126	149	12/3
D.C.Boon	run out	14	28	1
D.M.Jones	c Smith b Watson	56	80	1/2
*A.R.Border	b Snedden	1	4	–
M.R.J.Veletta	run out	0	1	–
S.R.Waugh	b Watson	1	7	–
†G.C.Dyer	b Chatfield	8	10	–
C.J.McDermott	lbw b Chatfield	5	7	–
T.B.A.May	run out	15	10	1
A.K.Zesers	not out	8	3	1
B.A.Reid				
Extras	(lb 10, w 7)	17		
Total	(50 overs; 8 wickets)	**251**		

NEW ZEALAND		Runs	Balls	4/6
M.C.Snedden	b Waugh	32	56	3
J.G.Wright	c and b Zesers	61	82	4
M.D.Crowe	run out	4	5	–
K.R.Rutherford	c Jones b McDermott	44	57	4
*J.J.Crowe	c and b Border	27	28	3
D.N.Patel	st Dyer b Border	3	10	–
J.G.Bracewell	run out	12	20	–
†I.D.S.Smith	c Boon b Waugh	12	15	–
S.L.Boock	run out	12	8	1
W.Watson	run out	8	8	–/1
E.J.Chatfield	not out	5	6	–
Extras	(b 1, lb 7, w 4, nb 2)	14		
Total	(48.4 overs)	**234**		

NEW ZEALAND	O	M	R	W
Snedden	10	0	48	1
Chatfield	10	2	52	2
Boock	10	1	45	0
Bracewell	4	0	24	0
Watson	8	0	46	2
Patel	8	0	26	0

AUSTRALIA	O	M	R	W
McDermott	10	1	43	1
Reid	6	0	30	0
Waugh	9.4	0	37	2
Zesers	6	0	37	1
May	10	0	52	0
Border	7	0	27	2

FALL OF WICKETS		
Wkt	A	NZ
1st	25	72
2nd	151	82
3rd	158	127
4th	158	173
5th	175	179
6th	193	186
7th	201	206
8th	228	208
9th	–	221
10th	–	234

Umpires: Khizer Hayat (*Pakistan*) (16) and D.R.Shepherd (*England*) (24).

AUSTRALIA v ZIMBABWE

At Barabati Stadium, Cuttack, India, on 30 October 1987.   Toss: Zimbabwe.
Result: **AUSTRALIA** won by 70 runs.   Award: D.C.Boon.
LOI debuts: None.

AUSTRALIA		Runs	Balls	4/6
D.C.Boon	c Houghton b Butchart	93	101	9/1
G.R.Marsh	run out	37	65	1
D.M.Jones	not out	58	72	1/1
C.J.McDermott	c Rawson b Traicos	9	10	–/1
*A.R.Border	st Houghton b Traicos	4	6	–
M.R.J.Veletta	run out	43	39	3
S.R.Waugh	not out	10	14	1
S.P.O'Donnell				
†G.C.Dyer				
T.B.A.May				
B.A.Reid				
Extras	(b 3, lb 3, w 6)	12		
Total	(50 overs; 5 wickets)	**266**		

ZIMBABWE		Runs	Balls	4/6
A.H.Shah	b Waugh	32	90	4
A.C.Waller	c Waugh b McDermott	38	83	2
K.M.Curran	c Waugh b May	29	57	2
A.J.Pycroft	c Dyer b McDermott	38	46	2
†D.L.Houghton	lbw b May	1	11	–
I.P.Butchart	st Dyer b Border	3	5	––
P.W.E.Rawson	not out	24	29	2/1
E.A.Brandes	not out	18	11	1/2
K.J.Arnott				
M.P.Jarvis				
*A.J.Traicos				
Extras	(lb 5, w 6, nb 2)	13		
Total	(50 overs; 6 wickets)	**196**		

ZIMBABWE	O	M	R	W		FALL OF WICKETS		
Rawson	9	0	41	0	Wkt	A	Z	
Jarvis	6	0	33	0	1st	90	55	
Shah	7	0	31	0	2nd	148	89	
Brandes	10	1	58	0	3rd	159	92	
Traicos	10	0	45	2	4th	170	97	
Butchart	8	0	52	1	5th	248	139	
AUSTRALIA	O	M	R	W	6th	–	156	
McDermott	10	0	43	2	7th	–	–	
Reid	9	2	30	0	8th	–	–	
Waugh	4	0	9	1	9th	–	–	
O'Donnell	7	1	21	0	10th	–	–	
May	10	1	30	2				
Border	8	0	36	1				
Jones	1	0	5	0				
Boon	1	0	17	0				

Umpires: Mahboob Shah (*Pakistan*) (15) and P.W.Vidanagamage (*Sri Lanka*) (19).

ENGLAND v SRI LANKA

At Nehru Stadium, Poona, India, on 30 October 1987.   Toss: Sri Lanka.
Result: **ENGLAND** won by 8 wickets.   Award: G.A.Gooch.
LOI debuts: None.

SRI LANKA		Runs	Balls	4/6
R.S.Mahanama	c Emburey b DeFreitas	14	28	1
J.R.Ratnayeke	lbw b Small	7	26	–
†A.P.Gurusinha	run out	34	63	3
R.L.Dias	st Downton b Hemmings	80	105	6/3
*L.R.D.Mendis	b DeFreitas	7	11	1
R.S.Madugalle	c sub (P.W.Jarvis) b Hemmings	22	38	–/1
P.A.de Silva	not out	23	18	2
A.L.F.de Mel	c Lamb b Hemmings	0	2	–
S.Jeganathan	not out	20	15	2/1
V.B.John				
S.D.Anurasiri				
Extras	(lb 3, w 3, nb 5)	11		
Total	(50 overs; 7 wickets)	**218**		

ENGLAND		Runs	Balls	4/6
G.A.Gooch	c and b Jeganathan	61	79	7
R.T.Robinson	b Jeganathan	55	75	7
C.W.J.Athey	not out	40	55	–
*M.W.Gatting	not out	46	40	4
A.J.Lamb				
†P.R.Downton				
J.E.Emburey				
P.A.J.DeFreitas				
N.A.Foster				
G.C.Small				
E.E.Hemmings				
Extras	(b 1, lb 13, w 3)	17		
Total	(41.2 overs; 2 wickets)	**219**		

ENGLAND	O	M	R	W		FALL OF WICKETS		
DeFreitas	10	2	46	2		Wkt	SL	E
Small	10	1	33	1		1st	23	123
Foster	10	0	37	0		2nd	25	132
Emburey	10	1	42	0		3rd	113	–
Hemmings	10	0	57	3		4th	125	–
						5th	170	–
SRI LANKA	O	M	R	W		6th	177	–
Ratnayeke	8	1	37	0		7th	180	–
John	6	2	19	0		8th	–	–
De Mel	4.2	0	34	0		9th	–	–
Jeganathan	10	0	45	2		10th	–	–
Anurasiri	10	0	45	0				
De Silva	3	0	25	0				

Umpires: D.M.Archer (*West Indies*) (15) and Khizer Hayat (*Pakistan*) (17).

PAKISTAN v WEST INDIES

At National Stadium, Karachi, Pakistan, on 30 October 1987.   Toss: West Indies.
Result: **WEST INDIES** won by 28 runs.   Award: R.B.Richardson.
LOI debuts: None.

WEST INDIES		Runs	Balls	4/6
D.L.Haynes	c Imran b Mudassar	25	52	1
P.V.Simmons	b Wasim	6	9	1
R.B.Richardson	c Qadir b Imran	110	135	8/2
*I.V.A.Richards	b Wasim	67	75	2/2
A.L.Logie	c Mudassar b Imran	12	17	–
R.A.Harper	b Wasim	2	7	–
C.L.Hooper	not out	5	7	–
W.K.M.Benjamin	c Mudassar b Imran	0	1	–
†P.J.L.Dujon	not out	1	1	–
C.A.Walsh				
B.P.Patterson				
Extras	(b 3, lb 10, w 16, nb 1)	30		
Total	(50 overs; 7 wickets)	**258**		

PAKISTAN		Runs	Balls	4/6
Mudassar Nazar	b Harper	40	55	3
Ramiz Raja	c Hooper b Patterson	70	111	3
Salim Malik	c Richards b Walsh	23	37	–
Javed Miandad	b Benjamin	38	38	3
Ijaz Ahmed	b Benjamin	6	10	–
*Imran Khan	c Harper b Walsh	8	11	–
†Salim Yousuf	b Patterson	7	11	–
Wasim Akram	lbw b Patterson	0	2	–
Abdul Qadir	not out	8	11	–
Shoaib Mohammed	b Benjamin	0	1	–
Salim Jaffer	not out	8	16	–
Extras	(b 4, lb 6, w 10, nb 2)	22		
Total	(50 overs; 9 wickets)	**230**		

PAKISTAN	O	M	R	W
Imran Khan	9	0	57	3
Wasim Akram	10	0	45	3
Abdul Qadir	10	1	29	0
Mudassar Nazar	10	0	47	1
Salim Jaffer	6	0	37	0
Salim Malik	5	0	30	0

WEST INDIES	O	M	R	W
Patterson	10	0	34	3
Walsh	10	1	34	2
Harper	10	0	38	1
Benjamin	10	0	69	3
Richards	10	0	45	0

FALL OF WICKETS		
Wkt	WI	P
1st	19	78
2nd	84	128
3rd	221	147
4th	242	167
5th	248	186
6th	255	202
7th	255	202
8th	–	208
9th	–	208
10th	–	–

Umpires: R.B.Gupta (*India*) (8) and V.K.Ramaswamy (*India*) (8).

INDIA v NEW ZEALAND

At Vidarbha CA Ground, Nagpur, India, on 31 October 1987.   Toss: New Zealand.
Result: **INDIA** won by 9 wickets.   Awards: S.M.Gavaskar and C.Sharma.
LOI debuts: New Zealand – D.K.Morrison.

NEW ZEALAND		Runs	Balls	4/6
J.G.Wright	run out	35	59	4
P.A.Horne	b Prabhakar	18	35	1
M.D.Crowe	c Pandit b Azharuddin	21	24	2
K.R.Rutherford	b Sharma	26	54	1
*J.J.Crowe	b Maninder	24	24	3
D.N.Patel	c Kapil Dev b Shastri	40	51	3
M.C.Snedden	run out	23	28	2
†I.D.S.Smith	b Sharma	0	1	–
E.J.Chatfield	b Sharma	0	1	–
W.Watson	not out	12	25	1
D.K.Morrison				
Extras	(lb 14, w 7, nb 1)	22		
Total	(50 overs; 9 wickets)	**221**		

INDIA		Runs	Balls	4/6
K.Srikkanth	c Rutherford b Watson	75	58	9/3
S.M.Gavaskar	not out	103	88	10/3
M.Azharuddin	not out	41	51	5
N.S.Sidhu				
D.B.Vengsarkar				
*Kapil Dev				
R.J.Shastri				
†C.S.Pandit				
M.Prabhakar				
C.Sharma				
Maninder Singh				
Extras	(lb 1, w 2, nb 2)	5		
Total	(32.1 overs; 1 wicket)	**224**		

INDIA	O	M	R	W		FALL OF WICKETS		
Kapil Dev	6	0	24	0		Wkt	NZ	I
Prabhakar	7	0	23	1		1st	46	136
Sharma	10	2	51	3		2nd	84	–
Maninder	10	0	51	1		3rd	90	–
Shastri	10	1	32	1		4th	122	–
Azharuddin	7	0	26	1		5th	181	–
						6th	182	–
NEW ZEALAND	O	M	R	W		7th	182	–
Morrison	10	0	69	0		8th	182	–
Chatfield	4.1	1	39	0		9th	221	–
Snedden	4	0	29	0		10th	–	–
Watson	10	0	50	1				
Patel	4	0	36	0				

Umpires: H.D.Bird (*England*) (48) and D.R.Shepherd (*England*) (25).

PAKISTAN v AUSTRALIA (SEMI-FINAL)

At Gaddafi Stadium, Lahore, Pakistan, on 4 November 1987.   Toss: Australia.
Result: **AUSTRALIA** won by 18 runs.   Award: C.J.McDermott.
LOI debuts: None.

AUSTRALIA		Runs	Balls	4/6
G.R.Marsh	run out	31	57	2
D.C.Boon	st Miandad b Salim Malik	65	91	4
D.M.Jones	b Tausif	38	45	3
*A.R.Border	run out	18	22	2
M.R.J.Veletta	b Imran	48	50	2
S.R.Waugh	not out	32	28	4/1
S.P.O'Donnell	run out	0	2	–
†G.C.Dyer	b Imran	0	1	–
C.J.McDermott	b Imran	1	3	–
T.B.A.May	not out	0	2	–
B.A.Reid				
Extras	(b 1, lb 19, w 13, nb 1)	34		
Total	(50 overs; 8 wickets)	**267**		

PAKISTAN		Runs	Balls	4/6
Ramiz Raja	run out	1	1	–
Mansoor Akhtar	b McDermott	9	19	–
Salim Malik	c McDermott b Waugh	25	31	3
Javed Miandad	b Reid	70	103	4
*Imran Khan	c Dyer b Border	58	84	4
Wasim Akram	b McDermott	20	13	–/2
Ijaz Ahmed	c Jones b Reid	8	7	1
†Salim Yousuf	c Dyer b McDermott	21	15	2
Abdul Qadir	not out	20	16	2
Salim Jaffer	c Dyer b McDermott	0	2	–
Tausif Ahmed	c Dyer b McDermott	1	3	–
Extras	(lb 6, w 10)	16		
Total	(49 overs)	**249**		

PAKISTAN	O	M	R	W
Imran Khan	10	1	36	3
Salim Jaffer	6	0	57	0
Wasim Akram	10	0	54	0
Abdul Qadir	10	0	39	0
Tausif Ahmed	10	1	39	1
Salim Malik	4	0	22	1

AUSTRALIA	O	M	R	W
McDermott	10	0	44	5
Reid	10	2	41	2
Waugh	9	1	51	1
O'Donnell	10	1	45	0
May	6	0	36	0
Border	4	0	26	1

FALL OF WICKETS		
Wkt	A	P
1st	73	2
2nd	155	37
3rd	155	38
4th	215	150
5th	236	177
6th	236	192
7th	241	212
8th	249	236
9th	–	247
10th	–	249

Umpires: H.D.Bird (*England*) (49) and D.R.Shepherd (*England*) (26).

INDIA v ENGLAND (SEMI-FINAL)

At Wankhede Stadium, Bombay, India, on 5 November 1987.   Toss: India.
Result: **ENGLAND** won by 35 runs.   Award: G.A.Gooch.
LOI debuts: None.

ENGLAND		Runs	Balls	4/6
G.A.Gooch	c Srikkanth b Maninder	115	136	11
R.T.Robinson	st More b Maninder	13	36	2
C.W.J.Athey	c More b Sharma	4	17	–
*M.W.Gatting	b Maninder	56	62	5
A.J.Lamb	not out	32	29	2
J.E.Emburey	lbw b Kapil Dev	6	10	–
P.A.J.DeFreitas	b Kapil Dev	7	8	1
†P.R.Downton	not out	1	5	–
N.A.Foster				
G.C.Small				
E.E.Hemmings				
Extras	(b 1, lb 18, w 1)	20		
Total	(50 overs; 6 wickets)	**254**		

INDIA		Runs	Balls	4/6
K.Srikkanth	b Foster	31	55	4
S.M.Gavaskar	b DeFreitas	4	7	1
N.S.Sidhu	c Athey b Foster	22	40	–
M.Azharuddin	lbw b Hemmings	64	74	7
C.S.Pandit	lbw b Foster	24	30	3
*Kapil Dev	c Gatting b Hemmings	30	22	3
R.J.Shastri	c Downton b Hemmings	21	32	2
†K.S.More	c and b Emburey	0	5	–
M.Prabhakar	c Downton b Small	4	11	–
C.Sharma	c Lamb b Hemmings	0	1	–
Maninder Singh	not out	0	–	–
Extras	(b 1, lb 9, w 6, nb 3)	19		
Total	(45.3 overs)	**219**		

INDIA	O	M	R	W		FALL OF WICKETS		
Kapil Dev	10	1	38	2		Wkt	E	I
Prabhakar	9	1	40	0		1st	40	7
Maninder	10	0	54	3		2nd	79	58
Sharma	9	0	41	1		3rd	196	73
Shastri	10	0	49	0		4th	203	121
Azharuddin	2	0	13	0		5th	219	168
						6th	231	204
ENGLAND	O	M	R	W		7th	–	205
DeFreitas	7	0	37	1		8th	–	218
Small	6	0	22	1		9th	–	219
Emburey	10	1	35	1		10th	–	219
Foster	10	0	47	3				
Hemmings	9.3	0	52	4				
Gooch	3	0	16	0				

Umpires: A.R.Crafter (*Australia*) (56) and S.J.Woodward (*New Zealand*) (12).

ENGLAND v AUSTRALIA (FINAL)

At Eden Gardens, Calcutta, India, on 8 November 1987.   Toss: Australia.
Result: **AUSTRALIA** won by 7 runs.   Award: D.C.Boon.
LOI debuts: None.

AUSTRALIA		Runs	Balls	4/6
D.C.Boon	c Downton b Hemmings	75	125	7
G.R.Marsh	b Foster	24	49	3
D.M.Jones	c Athey b Hemmings	33	57	1/1
C.J.McDermott	b Gooch	14	8	2
*A.R.Border	run out	31	31	3
M.R.J.Veletta	not out	45	31	6
S.R.Waugh	not out	5	4	–
S.P.O'Donnell				
†G.C.Dyer				
T.B.A.May				
B.A.Reid				
Extras	(b 1, lb 13, w 5, nb 7)	26		
Total	(50 overs; 5 wickets)	**253**		

ENGLAND		Runs	Balls	4/6
G.A.Gooch	lbw b O'Donnell	35	57	4
R.T.Robinson	lbw b McDermott	0	1	–
C.W.J.Athey	run out	58	103	2
*M.W.Gatting	c Dyer b Border	41	45	3/1
A.J.Lamb	b Waugh	45	45	4
†P.R.Downton	c O'Donnell b Border	9	8	1
J.E.Emburey	run out	10	16	–
P.A.J.DeFreitas	c Reid b Waugh	17	10	2/1
N.A.Foster	not out	7	6	–
G.C.Small	not out	3	3	–
E.E.Hemmings				
Extras	(b 1, lb 14, w 2, nb 4)	21		
Total	(50 overs; 8 wickets)	**246**		

ENGLAND	O	M	R	W		FALL OF WICKETS		
DeFreitas	6	1	34	0	Wkt	A	E	
Small	6	0	33	0	1st	75	1	
Foster	10	0	38	1	2nd	151	66	
Hemmings	10	1	48	2	3rd	166	135	
Emburey	10	0	44	0	4th	168	170	
Gooch	8	1	42	1	5th	241	188	
					6th	–	218	
AUSTRALIA	O	M	R	W	7th	–	220	
McDermott	10	1	51	1	8th	–	235	
Reid	10	0	43	0	9th	–	–	
Waugh	9	0	37	2	10th	–	–	
O'Donnell	10	1	35	1				
May	4	0	27	0				
Border	7	0	38	2				

Umpires: R.B.Gupta (9) and Mahboob Shah (*Pakistan*) (16).

THE 1992 WORLD CUP

The fifth World Cup was the largest until 1999, its 39 matches exceeding even the 37 scheduled for the 1996 competition, 14 of them being staged in New Zealand and the remaining 25 in Australia, ten of the latter being day/night games. This was the first World Cup to involve floodlit cricket with its full panoply of coloured clothing, white balls and dark sightscreens. Matches were again 50 overs per innings and, despite there being a dozen more games than in the Reliance Cup, it was completed in 33 days as opposed to six weeks. It was also the fairest in that instead of being divided into groups, each side played the others once before the four leaders played off in the semi-finals.

The competition's only major fault, and it was a vital one, concerned the new rules governing rain-interrupted matches. To accommodate such a compressed schedule of matches and allowing for travelling time involved in an itinerary stretching from Perth to Dunedin, no spare days were allowed. To overcome the imperfection of a straight run-rate calculation when a second innings had to be shortened after rain, the organising committee employed a method whereby the reduction in the target would be proportionate to the lowest-scoring overs of the side batting first. England's encounters with South Africa were the worst affected. At Melbourne, rain deprived England of 9 overs but their target of 237 was reduced by only 11 runs. Thanks to a remarkable innings of 75 not out by Neil Fairbrother, England won by three wickets off the penultimate ball. Their meeting in the Sydney semi-final was again interrupted, a 12-minute downpour arriving when South Africa wanted 22 from 13 balls. At first their target was reduced to 22 from seven but, as the teams took the field, the scoreboard showed that it had been adjusted to 21 from one! England were embarrassed, South Africa distraught and the crowd in uproar. In the case of the final rounds a second day had been put aside and the match could easily have been completed then without reducing the overs, as would have been the case in England. The demands of television proved paramount and the rules quite inflexible. It was an especially unfortunate end for South Africa, newly restored to the fold and slotted into the tournament at the last moments. This was the first tournament to involve nine teams – the eight current full members plus aspiring Zimbabwe, winners of the ICC Trophy.

QUALIFYING TABLES

	P	W	L	NR	Points	Net Run-rate†
NEW ZEALAND	8	7	1	0	14	0.59
ENGLAND	8	5	2	1	11	0.47
SOUTH AFRICA	8	5	3	0	10	0.13
PAKISTAN	8	4	3	1	9	0.16
Australia	8	4	4	0	8	0.20
West Indies	8	4	4	0	8	0.07
India	8	2	5	1	5	0.14
Sri Lanka	8	2	5	1	5	−0.68
Zimbabwe	8	1	7	0	2	−1.14

†*Calculated by subtracting runs conceded per over from runs scored per over, revising figures in shortened matches and discounting those matches not played to a result.*

After three semi-final defeats and a disastrous start in this tournament, Pakistan won the Benson and Hedges World Cup, defeating England by 22 runs at the MCG before a record Australian limited-overs crowd of 87,182 (receipts $A2 million (£880,000)).

NEW ZEALAND v AUSTRALIA

At Eden Park, Auckland, New Zealand, on 22 February 1992.   Toss: New Zealand.
Result: **NEW ZEALAND** won by 37 runs.   Award: M.D.Crowe.
LOI debuts: None.

NEW ZEALAND		Runs	Balls	4/6
J.G.Wright	b McDermott	0	1	–
R.T.Latham	c Healy b Moody	26	44	4
A.H.Jones	lbw b Reid	4	14	1
*M.D.Crowe	not out	100	134	11
K.R.Rutherford	run out	57	71	6
C.Z.Harris	run out	14	15	2
†I.D.S.Smith	c Healy b McDermott	14	14	1
C.L.Cairns	not out	16	11	2
D.N.Patel				
G.R.Larsen				
W.Watson				
Extras	(lb 6, w 7, nb 4)	17		
Total	(50 overs; 6 wickets)	248		

AUSTRALIA		Runs	Balls	4/6
D.C.Boon	run out	100	131	11
G.R.Marsh	c Latham b Larsen	19	56	2
D.M.Jones	run out	21	27	3
*A.R.Border	c Cairns b Patel	3	11	–
T.M.Moody	c and b Latham	7	11	–
M.E.Waugh	lbw b Larsen	2	5	–
S.R.Waugh	c and b Larsen	38	34	3/1
†I.A.Healy	not out	7	9	–
C.J.McDermott	run out	1	1	–
P.L.Taylor	c Rutherford b Watson	1	2	–
B.A.Reid	c Jones b Harris	3	4	–
Extras	(lb 6, w 2, nb 1)	9		
Total	(48.1 overs)	211		

AUSTRALIA	O	M	R	W
McDermott	10	1	43	2
Reid	10	0	39	1
Moody	9	1	37	1
S.R.Waugh	10	0	60	0
Taylor	7	0	36	0
M.E.Waugh	4	0	27	0

NEW ZEALAND	O	M	R	W
Cairns	4	0	30	0
Patel	10	1	36	1
Watson	9	1	39	1
Larsen	10	1	30	3
Harris	7.1	0	35	1
Latham	8	0	35	1

FALL OF WICKETS		
Wkt	NZ	A
1st	2	62
2nd	13	92
3rd	53	104
4th	171	120
5th	191	125
6th	215	199
7th	–	200
8th	–	205
9th	–	206
10th	–	211

Umpires: Khizer Hayat (*Pakistan*) (38) and D.R.Shepherd (*England*) (41).

ENGLAND v INDIA

At WACA Ground, Perth, Australia, on 22 February 1992.   Toss: England.
Result: **ENGLAND** won by 9 runs.   Award: I.T.Botham.
LOI debuts: None.

ENGLAND		Runs	Balls	4/6
*G.A.Gooch	c Tendulkar b Shastri	51	89	1
I.T.Botham	c More b Kapil Dev	9	21	1
R.A.Smith	c Azharuddin b Prabhakar	91	108	8/2
G.A.Hick	c More b Banerjee	5	6	1
N.H.Fairbrother	c Srikkanth b Srinath	24	34	1
†A.J.Stewart	b Prabhakar	13	15	1
C.C.Lewis	c Banerjee b Kapil Dev	10	6	1
D.R.Pringle	c Srikkanth b Srinath	1	3	–
D.A.Reeve	not out	8	8	–
P.A.J.DeFreitas	run out	1	5	–
P.C.R.Tufnell	not out	3	5	–
Extras	(b 1, lb 6, w 13)	20		
Total	(50 overs; 9 wickets)	**236**		

INDIA		Runs	Balls	4/6
R.J.Shastri	run out	57	112	2
K.Srikkanth	c Botham b DeFreitas	39	50	7
*M.Azharuddin	c Stewart b Reeve	0	1	–
S.R.Tendulkar	c Stewart b Botham	35	44	5
V.G.Kambli	c Hick b Botham	3	11	–
P.K.Amre	run out	22	31	–
Kapil Dev	c DeFreitas b Reeve	17	18	2
S.T.Banerjee	not out	25	16	1/1
†K.S.More	run out	1	4	–
M.Prabhakar	b Reeve	0	2	–
J.Srinath	run out	11	8	–
Extras	(lb 9, w 7, nb 1)	17		
Total	(49.2 overs)	**227**		

INDIA	O	M	R	W		FALL OF WICKETS		
Kapil Dev	10	0	38	2		Wkt	E	I
Prabhakar	10	3	34	2		1st	21	63
Srinath	9	1	47	2		2nd	131	63
Banerjee	7	0	45	1		3rd	137	126
Tendulkar	10	0	37	0		4th	197	140
Shastri	4	0	28	1		5th	198	149
						6th	214	187
ENGLAND	O	M	R	W		7th	222	194
Pringle	10	0	53	0		8th	223	200
Lewis	9.2	0	36	0		9th	224	201
DeFreitas	10	0	39	1		10th	–	227
Reeve	6	0	38	3				
Botham	10	0	27	2				
Tufnell	4	0	25	0				

Umpires: J.D.Buultjens (*Sri Lanka*) (13) and P.J.McConnell (63).

FIFTH WORLD CUP (3rd Match)   LOI No. 716/1

SRI LANKA v ZIMBABWE

At Pukekura Park, New Plymouth, New Zealand, on 23 February 1992.   Toss: Sri Lanka.
Result: **SRI LANKA** won by 3 wickets.   Award: A.Flower.
LOI debuts: Zimbabwe – K.G.Duers, A.Flower, W.R.James.

ZIMBABWE		Runs	Balls	4/6
†A.Flower	not out	115	152	8/1
W.R.James	c Tillekeratne b Wickremasinghe	17	21	3
A.J.Pycroft	c Ramanayake b Gurusinha	5	22	–
*D.L.Houghton	c Tillekeratne b Gurusinha	10	19	1
K.J.Arnott	c Tillekeratne b Wickremasinghe	52	56	4/1
A.C.Waller	not out	83	45	9/3
I.P.Butchart				
E.A.Brandes				
K.G.Duers				
M.P.Jarvis				
A.J.Traicos				
Extras	(b 2, lb 6, w 13, nb 9)	30		
Total	(50 overs; 4 wickets)	**312**		

SRI LANKA		Runs	Balls	4/6
R.S.Mahanama	c Arnott b Brandes	59	89	4
M.A.R.Samarasekera	c Duers b Traicos	75	61	11/1
*P.A.de Silva	c Houghton b Brandes	14	28	1
A.P.Gurusinha	run out	5	6	1
A.Ranatunga	not out	88	61	9/1
S.T.Jayasuriya	c Flower b Houghton	32	23	2/2
†H.P.Tillekeratne	b Jarvis	18	12	1/1
R.S.Kalpage	c Houghton b Brandes	11	14	1
C.P.H.Ramanayake	not out	1	1	–
K.I.W.Wijegunawardene				
G.P.Wickremasinghe				
Extras	(lb 5, w 5)	10		
Total	(49.2 overs; 7 wickets)	**313**		

SRI LANKA	O	M	R	W		FALL OF WICKETS		
Ramanayake	10	0	59	0		Wkt	Z	SL
Wijegunawardene	7	0	54	0		1st	30	128
Wickremasinghe	10	1	50	2		2nd	57	144
Gurusinha	10	0	72	2		3rd	82	155
Kalpage	10	0	51	0		4th	167	167
Jayasuriya	3	0	18	0		5th	–	212
						6th	–	273
ZIMBABWE	O	M	R	W		7th	–	308
Jarvis	9.2	0	51	1		8th	–	–
Brandes	10	0	70	3		9th	–	–
Duers	10	0	72	0		10th	–	–
Butchart	8	0	63	0				
Traicos	10	1	33	1				
Houghton	2	0	19	1				

Umpires: P.D.Reporter (*India*) (13) and S.J.Woodward (25).

WEST INDIES v PAKISTAN

At Melbourne Cricket Ground, Australia, on 23 February 1992.   Toss: West Indies.
Result: **WEST INDIES** won by 10 wickets.   Award: B.C.Lara.
LOI debuts: Pakistan – Iqbal Sikander, Wasim Haider.

PAKISTAN		**Runs**	**Balls**	**4/6**
Ramiz Raja	not out	102	158	4
Aamir Sohail	c Logie b Benjamin	23	44	3
Inzamam-ul-Haq	c Hooper b Harper	27	39	–
*Javed Miandad	not out	57	61	5
Salim Malik				
Ijaz Ahmed				
Wasim Akram				
Iqbal Sikander				
Wasim Haider				
†Moin Khan				
Aqib Javed				
Extras	(b 1, lb 3, w 5, nb 2)	11		
Total	(50 overs; 2 wickets)	**220**		

WEST INDIES		**Runs**	**Balls**	**4/6**
D.L.Haynes	not out	93	144	7
B.C.Lara	retired hurt	88	101	11
*R.B.Richardson	not out	20	40	1
C.L.Hooper				
A.L.Logie				
K.L.T.Arthurton				
R.A.Harper				
M.D.Marshall				
W.K.M.Benjamin				
†D.Williams				
C.E.L.Ambrose				
Extras	(b 2, lb 8, w 7, nb 3)	20		
Total	(46.5 overs; 0 wickets)	**221**		

WEST INDIES	O	M	R	W
Marshall	10	1	53	0
Ambrose	10	0	40	0
Benjamin	10	0	49	1
Hooper	10	0	41	0
Harper	10	0	33	1
PAKISTAN	O	M	R	W
Wasim Akram	10	0	37	0
Aqib Javed	8.5	0	42	0
Wasim Haider	8	0	42	0
Ijaz Ahmed	6	1	29	0
Iqbal Sikander	8	1	26	0
Aamir Sohail	6	0	35	0

	FALL OF WICKETS		
	Wkt	P	WI
	1st	45	–
	2nd	97	–
	3rd	–	–
	4th	–	–
	5th	–	–
	6th	–	–
	7th	–	–
	8th	–	–
	9th	–	–
	10th	–	–

Umpires: S.G.Randell (44) and I.D.Robinson (*Zimbabwe*) (1).

NEW ZEALAND v SRI LANKA

At Seddon Park, Hamilton, New Zealand, on 25 February 1992.   Toss: New Zealand.
Result: **NEW ZEALAND** won by 6 wickets.   Award: K.R.Rutherford.
LOI debuts: None.

SRI LANKA		Runs	Balls	4/6
R.S.Mahanama	c and b Harris	80	131	6
M.A.R.Samarasekera	c Wright b Watson	9	20	1
A.P.Gurusinha	c Smith b Harris	9	33	1
*P.A.de Silva	run out	31	45	2
A.Ranatunga	c Rutherford b Harris	20	26	2
S.T.Jayasuriya	run out	5	7	–
†H.P.Tillekeratne	c Crowe b Watson	8	19	–
R.S.Kalpage	c Larsen b Watson	11	17	–
C.P.H.Ramanayake	run out	2	1	–
S.D.Anurasiri	not out	3	2	–
G.P.Wickremasinghe	not out	3	4	–
Extras	(b 1, lb 15, w 4, nb 5)	25		
Total	(50 overs; 9 wickets)	**206**		

NEW ZEALAND		Runs	Balls	4/6
J.G.Wright	c and b Kalpage	57	76	9
R.T.Latham	b Kalpage	20	41	3
A.H.Jones	c Jayasuriya b Gurusinha	49	77	4
*M.D.Crowe	c Ramanayake b Wickremasinghe	5	23	–
K.R.Rutherford	not out	65	71	6/1
C.Z.Harris	not out	5	5	–
†I.D.S.Smith				
D.N.Patel				
D.K.Morrison				
G.R.Larsen				
W.Watson				
Extras	(lb 3, w 3, nb 3)	9		
Total	(48.2 overs; 4 wickets)	**210**		

NEW ZEALAND	O	M	R	W
Morrison	8	0	36	0
Watson	10	0	37	3
Larsen	10	1	29	0
Harris	10	0	43	3
Latham	3	0	13	0
Patel	9	0	32	0

SRI LANKA	O	M	R	W
Ramanayake	9.2	0	46	0
Wickremasinghe	8	1	40	1
Anurasiri	10	1	27	0
Kalpage	10	0	33	2
Gurusinha	4	0	19	1
Ranatunga	4	0	22	0
Jayasuriya	2	0	14	0
De Silva	1	0	6	0

FALL OF WICKETS		
Wkt	SL	NZ
1st	18	77
2nd	50	90
3rd	120	105
4th	172	186
5th	172	–
6th	181	–
7th	195	–
8th	199	–
9th	202	–
10th	–	–

Umpires: P.D.Reporter (*India*) (14) and D.R.Shepherd (*England*) (42).

AUSTRALIA v SOUTH AFRICA

At Sydney Cricket Ground, Australia, on 26 February 1992. Toss: Australia.
Result: **SOUTH AFRICA** won by 9 wickets. Award: K.C.Wessels.
LOI debuts: South Africa – W.J.Cronje, M.W.Pringle, J.N.Rhodes.

AUSTRALIA		**Runs**	**Balls**	**4/6**
G.R.Marsh	c Richardson b Kuiper	25	72	1
D.C.Boon	run out	27	32	4
D.M.Jones	c Richardson b McMillan	24	51	1
*A.R.Border	b Kuiper	0	1	–
T.M.Moody	lbw b Donald	10	33	–
S.R.Waugh	c Cronje b McMillan	27	51	1
†I.A.Healy	c McMillan b Donald	16	24	2
P.L.Taylor	b Donald	4	9	–
C.J.McDermott	run out	6	12	–
M.R.Whitney	not out	9	15	1
B.A.Reid	not out	5	10	–
Extras	(lb 2, w 11, nb 4)	17		
Total	(49 overs; 9 wickets)	**170**		

SOUTH AFRICA		**Runs**	**Balls**	**4/6**
*K.C.Wessels	not out	81	148	9
A.C.Hudson	b Taylor	28	52	3
P.N.Kirsten	not out	49	88	1
A.P.Kuiper				
J.N.Rhodes				
W.J.Cronje				
B.M.McMillan				
†D.J.Richardson				
R.P.Snell				
M.W.Pringle				
A.A.Donald				
Extras	(lb 5, w 6, nb 2)	13		
Total	(46.5 overs; 1 wicket)	**171**		

SOUTH AFRICA	O	M	R	W		FALL OF WICKETS		
Donald	10	0	34	3	Wkt		A	SA
Pringle	10	0	52	0	1st		42	74
Snell	9	1	15	0	2nd		76	–
McMillan	10	0	35	2	3rd		76	–
Kuiper	5	0	15	2	4th		97	–
Cronje	5	1	17	0	5th		108	–
						6th	143	–
AUSTRALIA	O	M	R	W		7th	146	–
McDermott	10	1	23	0	8th		156	–
Reid	8.5	0	41	0	9th		161	–
Whitney	6	0	26	0	10th		–	–
Waugh	4	1	16	0				
Taylor	10	1	32	1				
Border	4	0	13	0				
Moody	4	0	15	0				

Umpires: B.L.Aldridge (*New Zealand*) (19) and S.A.Bucknor (*West Indies*) (4).

PAKISTAN v ZIMBABWE

At Bellerive Oval, Hobart, Australia, on 27 February 1992.　Toss: Zimbabwe.
Result: **PAKISTAN** won by 53 runs.　Award: Aamir Sohail.
LOI debuts: None.

PAKISTAN		Runs	Balls	4/6
Ramiz Raja	c Flower b Jarvis	9	16	1
Aamir Sohail	c Pycroft b Butchart	114	136	12
Inzamam-ul-Haq	c Brandes b Butchart	14	43	–
Javed Miandad	lbw b Butchart	89	94	5
Salim Malik	not out	14	12	–
Wasim Akram	not out	1	1	–
*Imran Khan				
Mushtaq Ahmed				
Iqbal Sikander				
†Moin Khan				
Aqib Javed				
Extras	(lb 9, nb 4)	13		
Total	(50 overs; 4 wickets)	254		

ZIMBABWE		Runs	Balls	4/6
K.J.Arnott	c Wasim b Iqbal	7	61	–
†A.Flower	c Inzamam b Wasim	6	21	–
A.J.Pycroft	b Wasim	0	4	–
*D.L.Houghton	c Ramiz b Aamir	44	82	3
A.H.Shah	b Aamir	33	58	2
A.C.Waller	b Wasim	44	36	3/1
I.P.Butchart	c Miandad b Aqib	33	27	4
E.A.Brandes	not out	2	3	–
A.J.Traicos	not out	8	7	–
W.R.James				
M.P.Jarvis				
Extras	(b 3, lb 15, w 6)	24		
Total	(50 overs; 7 wickets)	201		

ZIMBABWE	O	M	R	W		FALL OF WICKETS		
Brandes	10	1	49	0		Wkt	P	Z
Jarvis	10	1	52	1		1st	29	14
Shah	10	1	24	0		2nd	63	14
Butchart	10	0	57	3		3rd	208	33
Traicos	10	0	63	0		4th	253	103
						5th	–	108
PAKISTAN	O	M	R	W		6th	–	187
Wasim Akram	10	2	21	3		7th	–	190
Aqib Javed	10	1	49	1		8th	–	–
Iqbal Sikander	10	1	35	1		9th	–	–
Mushtaq Ahmed	10	1	34	0		10th	–	–
Aamir Sohail	6	1	26	2				
Salim Malik	4	0	18	0				

Umpires: J.D.Buultjens (*Sri Lanka*) (14) and S.G.Randell (45).

FIFTH WORLD CUP (8th Match – floodlit)LOI No. 721/43

ENGLAND v WEST INDIES

At Melbourne Cricket Ground, Australia, on 27 February 1992.   Toss: England.
Result: **ENGLAND** won by 6 wickets.   Award: C.C.Lewis.
LOI debuts: None.

WEST INDIES		Runs	Balls	4/6
D.L.Haynes	c Fairbrother b DeFreitas	38	68	5
B.C.Lara	c Stewart b Lewis	0	2	–
*R.B.Richardson	c Botham b Lewis	5	17	1
C.L.Hooper	c Reeve b Botham	5	20	–
K.L.T.Arthurton	c Fairbrother b DeFreitas	54	101	2/2
A.L.Logie	run out	20	27	–/1
R.A.Harper	c Hick b Reeve	3	14	–
M.D.Marshall	run out	3	8	–
†D.Williams	c Pringle b DeFreitas	6	19	–
C.E.L.Ambrose	c DeFreitas b Lewis	4	6	–
W.K.M.Benjamin	not out	11	15	1
Extras	(lb 4, w 3, nb 1)	8		
Total	(49.2 overs)	**157**		

ENGLAND		Runs	Balls	4/6
*G.A.Gooch	st Williams b Hooper	65	101	7
I.T.Botham	c Williams b Benjamin	8	28	1
R.A.Smith	c Logie b Benjamin	8	28	–
G.A.Hick	c and b Harper	54	55	3/1
N.H.Fairbrother	not out	13	28	1
†A.J.Stewart	not out	0	1	–
D.A.Reeve				
C.C.Lewis				
D.R.Pringle				
P.A.J.DeFreitas				
P.C.R.Tufnell				
Extras	(lb 7, w 4, nb 1)	12		
Total	(39.5 overs; 4 wickets)	**160**		

ENGLAND	O	M	R	W		FALL OF WICKETS		
Pringle	7	3	16	0		Wkt	WI	E
Lewis	8.2	1	30	3		1st	0	50
DeFreitas	9	2	34	3		2nd	22	71
Botham	10	0	30	1		3rd	36	126
Reeve	10	1	23	1		4th	55	156
Tufnell	5	0	20	0		5th	91	–
						6th	102	–
WEST INDIES	O	M	R	W		7th	116	–
Ambrose	8	1	26	0		8th	131	–
Marshall	8	0	37	0		9th	145	–
Benjamin	9.5	2	22	2		10th	157	–
Hooper	10	1	38	1				
Harper	4	0	30	1				

Umpires: K.E.Liebenberg (*South Africa*) (1) and S.J.Woodward (*New Zealand*) (26).

INDIA v SRI LANKA

At Harrup Park, Mackay, Queensland, Australia, on 28 February 1992.   Toss: Sri Lanka.
NO RESULT.   No award.
LOI debuts: India – A.Jadeja.

INDIA		Runs	Balls	4/6
K.Srikkanth	not out	1	2	–
Kapil Dev	not out	0	–	–
*M.Azharuddin				
S.R.Tendulkar				
V.G.Kambli				
P.K.Amre				
A.Jadeja				
†K.S.More				
M.Prabhakar				
J.Srinath				
S.L.V.Raju				
Extras		–		
Total	(0.2 overs; 0 wickets)	**1**		

SRI LANKA
R.S.Mahanama
U.C.Hathurusinghe
A.P.Gurusinha
*P.A.de Silva
A.Ranatunga
S.T.Jayasuriya
†H.P.Tillekeratne
R.S.Kalpage
C.P.H.Ramanayake
K.I.W.Wijegunawardene
G.P.Wickremasinghe
Extras
Total

SRI LANKA	O	M	R	W
Ramanayake	0.2	0	1	0

Umpires: I.D.Robinson (*Zimbabwe*) (2) and D.R.Shepherd (*England*) (43).

NEW ZEALAND v SOUTH AFRICA

At Eden Park, Auckland, New Zealand, on 29 February 1992.   Toss: South Africa.
Result: **NEW ZEALAND** won by 7 wickets.   Award: M.J.Greatbatch.
LOI debuts: South Africa – T.Bosch.

SOUTH AFRICA		Runs	Balls	4/6
*K.C.Wessels	c Smith b Watson	3	18	–
A.C.Hudson	b Patel	1	16	–
P.N.Kirsten	c Cairns b Watson	90	129	10
W.J.Cronje	c Smith b Harris	7	22	–
†D.J.Richardson	c Larsen b Cairns	28	53	1
A.P.Kuiper	run out	2	2	–
J.N.Rhodes	c Crowe b Cairns	6	13	–
B.M.McMillan	not out	33	40	1
R.P.Snell	not out	11	8	1
A.A.Donald				
T.Bosch				
Extras	(lb 8, nb 1)	9		
Total	(50 overs; 7 wickets)	**190**		

NEW ZEALAND		Runs	Balls	4/6
M.J.Greatbatch	b Kirsten	68	60	9/3
R.T.Latham	c Wessels b Snell	60	69	7
A.H.Jones	not out	34	63	4
†I.D.S.Smith	c Kirsten b Donald	19	8	4
*M.D.Crowe	not out	3	9	–
K.R.Rutherford				
C.Z.Harris				
C.L.Cairns				
D.N.Patel				
G.R.Larsen				
W.Watson				
Extras	(b 1, w 5, nb 1)	7		
Total	(34.3 overs; 3 wickets)	**191**		

NEW ZEALAND	O	M	R	W		FALL OF WICKETS		
Watson	10	2	30	2	Wkt	SA	NZ	
Patel	10	1	28	1	1st	8	114	
Larsen	10	1	29	0	2nd	10	155	
Harris	10	2	33	1	3rd	29	179	
Latham	2	0	19	0	4th	108	–	
Cairns	8	0	43	2	5th	111	–	
					6th	121	–	
SOUTH AFRICA	O	M	R	W	7th	162	–	
Donald	10	0	38	1	8th	–	–	
McMillan	5	1	23	0	9th	–	–	
Snell	7	0	56	1	10th	–	–	
Bosch	2.3	0	19	0				
Cronje	2	0	14	0				
Kuiper	1	0	18	0				
Kirsten	7	1	22	1				

Umpires: Khizer Hayat (*Pakistan*) (39) and P.D.Reporter (*India*) (15).

WEST INDIES v ZIMBABWE

At Woolloongabba, Brisbane, Australia, on 29 February 1992.　Toss: Zimbabwe.
Result: **WEST INDIES** won by 75 runs.　Award: B.C.Lara.
LOI debuts: Zimbabwe – A.D.R.Campbell.

WEST INDIES		Runs	Balls	4/6
P.V.Simmons	b Brandes	21	45	3
B.C.Lara	c Houghton b Shah	72	71	12
*R.B.Richardson	c Brandes b Jarvis	56	76	2/2
C.L.Hooper	c Pycroft b Traicos	63	67	5/1
K.L.T.Arthurton	b Duers	26	18	2/2
A.L.Logie	run out	5	6	–
M.D.Marshall	c Houghton b Brandes	2	10	–
†D.Williams	not out	8	6	1
W.K.M.Benjamin	b Brandes	1	4	–
A.C.Cummins				
B.P.Patterson				
Extras	(b 1, lb 6, w 2, nb 1)	10		
Total	(50 overs; 8 wickets)	**264**		

ZIMBABWE		Runs	Balls	4/6
K.J.Arnott	retired hurt	16	36	1
†A.Flower	b Patterson	6	20	–
A.J.Pycroft	c Williams b Benjamin	10	24	–
*D.L.Houghton	c Patterson b Hooper	55	88	3
A.C.Waller	c Simmons b Benjamin	0	9	–
A.D.R.Campbell	c Richardson b Hooper	1	18	–
A.H.Shah	not out	60	87	4
E.A.Brandes	c and b Benjamin	6	9	–
A.J.Traicos	run out	8	19	–
M.P.Jarvis	not out	5	4	1
K.G.Duers				
Extras	(lb 9, w 5, nb 8)	22		
Total	(50 overs; 7 wickets)	**189**		

ZIMBABWE	O	M	R	W		FALL OF WICKETS		
Brandes	10	1	45	3	Wkt	WI	Z	
Jarvis	10	1	71	1	1st	78	21	
Duers	10	0	52	1	2nd	103	43	
Shah	10	0	39	1	3rd	220	48	
Traicos	10	0	50	1	4th	221	63	
					5th	239	132	
WEST INDIES	O	M	R	W	6th	254	161	
Patterson	10	0	25	1	7th	255	181	
Marshall	6	0	23	0	8th	264	–	
Benjamin	10	2	27	3	9th	–	–	
Cummins	10	0	33	0	10th	–	–	
Hooper	10	0	47	2				
Arthurton	4	0	25	0				

Umpires: K.E.Liebenberg (*South Africa*) (2) and S.J.Woodward (*New Zealand*) (27).

AUSTRALIA v INDIA

At Woolloongabba, Brisbane, Australia, on 1 March 1992.   Toss: Australia.
Result: **AUSTRALIA** won by 1 run (*target revised to 236 from 47 overs*).
Award: D.M.Jones.
LOI debuts: None.

AUSTRALIA		Runs	Balls	4/6
M.A.Taylor	c More b Kapil Dev	13	22	–
G.R.Marsh	b Kapil Dev	8	29	1
†D.C.Boon	c Shastri b Raju	43	61	4
D.M.Jones	c and b Prabhakar	90	109	6/2
S.R.Waugh	b Srinath	29	48	1
T.M.Moody	b Prabhakar	25	23	3
*A.R.Border	c Jadeja b Kapil Dev	10	10	–
C.J.McDermott	c Jadeja b Prabhakar	2	5	–
P.L.Taylor	run out	1	1	–
M.G.Hughes	not out	0	4	–
M.R.Whitney				
Extras	(lb 7, w 5, nb 4)	16		
Total	(50 overs; 9 wickets)	**237**		

INDIA		Runs	Balls	4/6
R.J.Shastri	c Waugh b Moody	25	70	1
K.Srikkanth	b McDermott	0	11	–
*M.Azharuddin	run out	93	103	10
S.R.Tendulkar	c Waugh b Moody	11	19	1
Kapil Dev	lbw b Waugh	21	21	3
S.V.Manjrekar	run out	47	42	3/1
A.Jadeja	b Hughes	1	4	–
†K.S.More	b Moody	14	8	2
J.Srinath	not out	8	8	–
M.Prabhakar	run out	1	1	–
S.L.V.Raju	run out	0	–	–
Extras	(lb 8, w 5)	13		
Total	(47 overs)	**234**		

INDIA	O	M	R	W		FALL OF WICKETS		
Kapil Dev	10	2	41	3		Wkt	A	I
Prabhakar	10	0	41	3		1st	18	6
Srinath	8	0	48	1		2nd	31	53
Tendulkar	5	0	29	0		3rd	102	86
Raju	10	0	37	1		4th	156	128
Jadeja	7	0	34	0		5th	198	194
						6th	230	199
AUSTRALIA	O	M	R	W		7th	235	216
McDermott	9	1	35	1		8th	236	231
Whitney	10	2	36	0		9th	237	232
Hughes	9	1	49	1		10th	–	234
Moody	9	0	56	3				
Waugh	10	0	50	1				

Umpires: B.L.Aldridge (*New Zealand*) (20) and I.D.Robinson (*Zimbabwe*) (3).

ENGLAND v PAKISTAN

At Adelaide Oval, Australia, on 1 March 1992.   Toss: England.
NO RESULT.   No award.
LOI debuts: None.

PAKISTAN		Runs	Balls	4/6
Ramiz Raja	c Reeve b DeFreitas	1	10	–
Aamir Sohail	c and b Pringle	9	39	–
Inzamam-ul-Haq	c Stewart b DeFreitas	0	1	–
*Javed Miandad	b Pringle	3	22	–
Salim Malik	c Reeve b Botham	17	20	3
Ijaz Ahmed	c Stewart b Small	0	15	–
Wasim Akram	b Botham	1	13	–
†Moin Khan	c Hick b Small	2	14	–
Wasim Haider	c Stewart b Reeve	13	46	1
Mushtaq Ahmed	c Reeve b Pringle	17	42	1
Aqib Javed	not out	1	21	–
Extras	(lb 1, w 8, nb 1)	10		
Total	(40.2 overs)	**74**		

ENGLAND		Runs	Balls	4/6
*G.A.Gooch	c Moin b Wasim Akram	3	14	–
I.T.Botham	not out	6	22	–
R.A.Smith	not out	5	13	1
G.A.Hick				
N.H.Fairbrother				
†A.J.Stewart				
C.C.Lewis				
D.A.Reeve				
D.R.Pringle				
P.A.J.DeFreitas				
G.C.Small				
Extras	(b 1, lb 3, w 5, nb 1)	10		
Total	(8 overs; 1 wicket)	**24**		

ENGLAND	O	M	R	W		FALL OF WICKETS		
Pringle	8.2	5	8	3		Wkt	P	E
DeFreitas	7	1	22	2		1st	5	14
Small	10	1	29	2		2nd	5	–
Botham	10	4	12	2		3rd	14	–
Reeve	5	3	2	1		4th	20	–
						5th	32	–
PAKISTAN	O	M	R	W		6th	35	–
Wasim Akram	3	0	7	1		7th	42	–
Aqib Javed	3	1	7	0		8th	47	–
Wasim Haider	1	0	1	0		9th	62	–
Ijaz Ahmed	1	0	5	0		10th	74	–

Umpires: S.A.Bucknor (*West Indies*) (5) and P.J.McConnell (64).

SOUTH AFRICA v SRI LANKA

At Basin Reserve, Wellington, New Zealand, on 2 March 1992. Toss: Sri Lanka.
Result: **SRI LANKA** won by 3 wickets. Award: A.Ranatunga.
LOI debuts: South Africa – O.Henry, M.W.Rushmere.

SOUTH AFRICA		Runs	Balls	4/6
*K.C.Wessels	c and b Ranatunga	40	94	–
A.P.Kuiper	b Anurasiri	18	44	3
P.N.Kirsten	c Hathurusinghe b Kalpage	47	81	5/1
J.N.Rhodes	c Jayasuriya b Wickremasinghe	28	21	2
M.W.Rushmere	c Jayasuriya b Ranatunga	4	9	–
W.J.Cronje	st Tillekeratne b Anurasiri	3	6	–
B.M.McMillan	not out	18	22	–
R.P.Snell	b Anurasiri	9	5	2
†D.J.Richardson	run out	0	–	–
O.Henry	c Kalpage b Ramanayake	11	13	1
A.A.Donald	run out	3	6	–
Extras	(lb 9, w 4, nb 1)	14		
Total	(50 overs)	**195**		

SRI LANKA		Runs	Balls	4/6
R.S.Mahanama	c Richardson b McMillan	68	121	6
U.C.Hathurusinghe	c Wessels b Donald	5	9	1
A.P.Gurusinha	lbw b Donald	0	4	–
*P.A.de Silva	b Donald	7	16	1
†H.P.Tillekeratne	c Rushmere b Henry	17	63	–
A.Ranatunga	not out	64	73	6
S.T.Jayasuriya	st Richardson b Kirsten	3	7	–
R.S.Kalpage	run out	5	11	–
C.P.H.Ramanayake	not out	4	2	1
S.D.Anurasiri				
G.P.Wickremasinghe				
Extras	(b 1, lb 7, w 13, nb 4)	25		
Total	(49.5 overs; 7 wickets)	**198**		

SRI LANKA	O	M	R	W		FALL OF WICKETS		
Ramanayake	9	2	19	1		Wkt	SA	SL
Wickremasinghe	7	0	32	1		1st	27	11
Anurasiri	10	1	41	3		2nd	114	12
Gurusinha	8	0	30	0		3rd	114	35
Kalpage	10	0	38	1		4th	128	87
Ranatunga	6	0	26	2		5th	149	154
						6th	153	168
SOUTH AFRICA	O	M	R	W		7th	165	189
McMillan	10	2	34	1		8th	165	–
Donald	9.5	0	42	3		9th	186	–
Snell	10	1	33	0		10th	195	–
Henry	10	0	31	1				
Kuiper	5	0	25	0				
Kirsten	5	0	25	1				

Umpires: Khizer Hayat (*Pakistan*) (40) and S.J.Woodward (28).

NEW ZEALAND v ZIMBABWE

At McLean Park, Napier, New Zealand, on 3 March 1992.   Toss: Zimbabwe.
Result: **NEW ZEALAND** won by 48 runs (*target revised to 154 from 18 overs*).
Award: M.D.Crowe.
LOI debuts: Zimbabwe – M.G.Burmester.

NEW ZEALAND		Runs	Balls	4/6
M.J.Greatbatch	b Duers	15	16	2
R.T.Latham	b Brandes	2	6	–
A.H.Jones	c Waller b Butchart	57	58	9
*M.D.Crowe	not out	74	44	8/2
C.L.Cairns	not out	1	2	–
K.R.Rutherford				
C.Z.Harris				
†I.D.S.Smith				
D.N.Patel				
D.K.Morrison				
G.R.Larsen				
Extras	(b 6, lb 7)	13		
Total	(20.5 overs; 3 wickets)	**162**		

ZIMBABWE		Runs	Balls	4/6
†A.Flower	b Larsen	30	27	5
A.C.Waller	b Morrison	11	11	1/1
*D.L.Houghton	b Larsen	10	14	2
I.P.Butchart	c Cairns b Larsen	3	7	–
E.A.Brandes	b Harris	6	8	–
A.J.Pycroft	not out	13	20	–
A.D.R.Campbell	c Crowe b Harris	8	9	1
A.H.Shah	b Harris	7	8	1
M.G.Burmester	not out	4	8	–
A.J.Traicos				
K.G.Duers				
Extras	(lb 9, w 3, nb 1)	13		
Total	(18 overs; 7 wickets)	**105**		

ZIMBABWE	O	M	R	W		FALL OF WICKETS		
Brandes	5	1	28	1		Wkt	NZ	Z
Duers	6	0	17	1		1st	9	22
Shah	4	0	34	0		2nd	25	40
Butchart	4	0	53	1		3rd	154	63
Burmester	1.5	0	17	0		4th	–	63
						5th	–	75
NEW ZEALAND	O	M	R	W		6th	–	86
Morrison	4	0	14	1		7th	–	97
Cairns	2	0	27	0		8th	–	–
Larsen	4	0	16	3		9th	–	–
Harris	4	0	15	3		10th	–	–
Latham	3	0	18	0				
Crowe	1	0	6	0				

Umpires: J.D.Buultjens (*Sri Lanka*) (15) and K.E.Liebenberg (*South Africa*) (3).

INDIA v PAKISTAN

At Sydney Cricket Ground, Australia, on 4 March 1992.   Toss: India.
Result: **INDIA** won by 43 runs.   Award: S.R.Tendulkar.
LOI debuts: None.

INDIA		Runs	Balls	4/6
A.Jadeja	c Zahid b Wasim Haider	46	81	2
K.Srikkanth	c Moin b Aqib	5	40	–
*M.Azharuddin	c Moin b Mushtaq	32	51	4
V.G.Kambli	c Inzamam b Mushtaq	24	42	–
S.R.Tendulkar	not out	54	62	3
S.V.Manjrekar	b Mushtaq	0	1	–
Kapil Dev	c Imran b Aqib	35	26	2/1
†K.S.More	run out	4	4	–
M.Prabhakar	not out	2	1	–
J.Srinath				
S.L.V.Raju				
Extras	(lb 3, w 9, nb 2)	14		
Total	(49 overs; 7 wickets)	216		

PAKISTAN		Runs	Balls	4/6
Aamir Sohail	c Srikkanth b Tendulkar	62	103	6
Inzamam-ul-Haq	lbw b Kapil Dev	2	7	–
Zahid Fazal	c More b Prabhakar	2	10	–
Javed Miandad	b Srinath	40	113	2
Salim Malik	c More b Prabhakar	12	9	2
*Imran Khan	run out	0	5	–
Wasim Akram	st More b Raju	4	8	–
Wasim Haider	b Srinath	13	25	–
†Moin Khan	c Manjrekar b Kapil Dev	12	12	1
Mushtaq Ahmed	run out	3	4	–
Aqib Javed	not out	1	12	–
Extras	(lb 6, w 15, nb 1)	22		
Total	(48.1 overs)	173		

PAKISTAN	O	M	R	W		FALL OF WICKETS		
					Wkt	I	P	
Wasim Akram	10	0	45	0	1st	25	8	
Aqib Javed	8	2	28	2	2nd	86	17	
Imran Khan	8	0	25	0	3rd	101	105	
Wasim Haider	10	1	36	1	4th	147	127	
Mushtaq Ahmed	10	0	59	3	5th	148	130	
Aamir Sohail	3	0	20	0	6th	208	141	
INDIA	O	M	R	W	7th	213	141	
Kapil Dev	10	0	30	2	8th	–	161	
Prabhakar	10	1	22	2	9th	–	166	
Srinath	8.1	0	37	2	10th	–	173	
Tendulkar	10	0	37	1				
Raju	10	1	41	1				

Umpires: P.J.McConnell (65) and D.R.Shepherd (*England*) (44).

SOUTH AFRICA v WEST INDIES

At Lancaster Park, Christchurch, New Zealand, on 5 March 1992.   Toss: West Indies.
Result: **SOUTH AFRICA** won by 64 runs.   Award: M.W.Pringle.
LOI debuts: None.

SOUTH AFRICA		Runs	Balls	4/6
*K.C.Wessels	c Haynes b Marshall	1	9	–
A.C.Hudson	c Lara b Cummins	22	60	3
P.N.Kirsten	c Williams b Marshall	56	91	2
M.W.Rushmere	st Williams b Hooper	10	24	–
A.P.Kuiper	b Ambrose	23	29	–/1
J.N.Rhodes	c Williams b Cummins	22	27	–
B.M.McMillan	c Lara b Benjamin	20	29	2
†D.J.Richardson	not out	20	26	1
R.P.Snell	c Haynes b Ambrose	3	6	–
M.W.Pringle	not out	5	6	–
A.A.Donald				
Extras	(lb 8, w 3, nb 7)	18		
Total	(50 overs; 8 wickets)	**200**		

WEST INDIES		Runs	Balls	4/6
D.L.Haynes	c Richardson b Kuiper	30	83	3
B.C.Lara	c Rhodes b Pringle	9	13	2
*R.B.Richardson	lbw b Pringle	1	3	–
C.L.Hooper	c Wessels b Pringle	0	4	–
K.L.T.Arthurton	c Wessels b Pringle	0	4	–
A.L.Logie	c Pringle b Kuiper	61	69	9/1
M.D.Marshall	c Rhodes b Snell	6	10	1
†D.Williams	c Richardson b Snell	0	3	–
C.E.L.Ambrose	run out	12	15	2
A.C.Cummins	c McMillan b Donald	6	24	–
W.K.M.Benjamin	not out	1	4	–
Extras	(lb 9, w 1)	10		
Total	(38.4 overs)	**136**		

WEST INDIES	O	M	R	W
Ambrose	10	1	34	2
Marshall	10	1	26	2
Hooper	10	0	45	1
Cummins	10	0	40	2
Benjamin	10	0	47	1

SOUTH AFRICA	O	M	R	W
Donald	6.4	2	13	1
Pringle	8	4	11	4
Snell	7	2	16	2
McMillan	8	2	36	0
Kuiper	9	0	51	2

FALL OF WICKETS		
Wkt	SA	WI
1st	8	10
2nd	51	19
3rd	73	19
4th	119	19
5th	127	70
6th	159	70
7th	181	116
8th	187	117
9th	–	132
10th	–	136

Umpires: B.L.Aldridge (21) and S.G.Randell (*Australia*) (46).

AUSTRALIA v ENGLAND

At Sydney Cricket Ground, Australia, on 5 March 1992.   Toss: Australia.
Result: **ENGLAND** won by 8 wickets.   Award: I.T.Botham.
LOI debuts: None.

AUSTRALIA		Runs	Balls	4/6
T.M.Moody	b Tufnell	51	91	3
M.A.Taylor	lbw b Pringle	0	11	–
D.C.Boon	run out	18	27	2
D.M.Jones	c Lewis b DeFreitas	22	50	2
S.R.Waugh	run out	27	43	2
*A.R.Border	b Botham	16	22	1
†I.A.Healy	c Fairbrother b Botham	9	7	–/1
P.L.Taylor	lbw b Botham	0	2	–
C.J.McDermott	c DeFreitas b Botham	0	2	–
M.R.Whitney	not out	8	27	1
B.A.Reid	b Reeve	1	22	–
Extras	(b 2, lb 8, w 5, nb 4)	19		
Total	(49 overs)	**171**		

ENGLAND		Runs	Balls	4/6
*G.A.Gooch	b Waugh	58	115	7
I.T.Botham	c Healy b Whitney	53	79	6
R.A.Smith	not out	30	60	5
G.A.Hick	not out	7	5	1
N.H.Fairbrother				
†A.J.Stewart				
C.C.Lewis				
D.A.Reeve				
D.R.Pringle				
P.A.J.DeFreitas				
P.C.R.Tufnell				
Extras	(lb 13, w 8, nb 4)	25		
Total	(40.5 overs; 2 wickets)	**173**		

ENGLAND	O	M	R	W		FALL OF WICKETS		
Pringle	9	1	24	1		Wkt	A	E
Lewis	10	2	28	0		1st	5	107
DeFreitas	10	3	23	1		2nd	35	153
Botham	10	1	31	4		3rd	106	–
Tufnell	9	0	52	1		4th	114	–
Reeve	1	0	3	1		5th	145	–
						6th	155	–
AUSTRALIA	O	M	R	W		7th	155	–
McDermott	10	1	29	0		8th	155	–
Reid	7.5	0	49	0		9th	164	–
Whitney	10	2	28	1		10th	171	–
Waugh	6	0	29	1				
P.L.Taylor	3	0	7	0				
Moody	4	0	18	0				

Umpires: S.A.Bucknor (*West Indies*) (6) and Khizer Hayat (*Pakistan*) (41).

INDIA v ZIMBABWE

At Seddon Park, Hamilton, New Zealand, on 7 March 1992.   Toss: India.
Result: **INDIA** won by 55 runs (*totals revised to 158 and 103 respectively*).
Award: S.R.Tendulkar.
LOI debuts: None.

INDIA		Runs	Balls	4/6
K.Srikkanth	b Burmester	32	32	5
Kapil Dev	lbw b Brandes	10	14	–/1
*M.Azharuddin	c Flower b Burmester	12	15	2
S.R.Tendulkar	c Campbell b Burmester	81	77	8/1
S.V.Manjrekar	c Duers b Traicos	34	34	2
V.G.Kambli	b Traicos	1	2	–
A.Jadeja	c Shah b Traicos	6	6	–
†K.S.More	not out	15	8	–/1
J.Srinath	not out	6	4	1
M.Prabhakar				
S.L.V.Raju				
Extras	(lb 3, w 3)	6		
Total	(32 overs; 7 wickets)	**203**		

ZIMBABWE		Runs	Balls	4/6
A.H.Shah	b Tendulkar	31	51	3
†A.Flower	not out	43	56	3
A.C.Waller	not out	13	7	2
A.J.Pycroft				
*D.L.Houghton				
A.D.R.Campbell				
I.P.Butchart				
E.A.Brandes				
M.G.Burmester				
A.J.Traicos				
K.G.Duers				
Extras	(b 1, lb 11, w 5)	17		
Total	(19.1 overs; 1 wicket)	**104**		

ZIMBABWE	O	M	R	W		FALL OF WICKETS		
Brandes	7	0	43	1		Wkt	I	Z
Duers	7	0	48	0		1st	23	79
Burmester	6	0	36	3		2nd	43	–
Shah	6	1	38	0		3rd	69	–
Traicos	6	0	35	3		4th	168	–
						5th	170	–
INDIA	O	M	R	W		6th	182	–
Kapil Dev	4	0	6	0		7th	184	–
Prabhakar	3	0	14	0		8th	–	–
Srinath	4	0	20	0		9th	–	–
Tendulkar	6	0	35	1		10th	–	–
Raju	2.1	0	17	0				

Umpires: J.D.Buultjens (*Sri Lanka*) (16) and S.G.Randell (*Australia*) (47).

AUSTRALIA v SRI LANKA

At Adelaide Oval, Australia, on 7 March 1992.   Toss: Australia.
Result: **AUSTRALIA** won by 7 wickets.   Award: T.M.Moody.
LOI debuts: None.

SRI LANKA		Runs	Balls	4/6
R.S.Mahanama	run out	7	10	1
M.A.R.Samarasekera	c Healy b Taylor	34	63	3
A.P.Gurusinha	lbw b Whitney	5	23	1
*P.A.de Silva	c Moody b McDermott	62	83	2
A.Ranatunga	c Jones b Taylor	23	52	–
S.T.Jayasuriya	lbw b Border	15	29	1
†H.P.Tillekeratne	run out	5	13	–
R.S.Kalpage	run out	14	15	1
C.P.H.Ramanayake	run out	5	10	–
S.D.Anurasiri	not out	4	4	–
G.P.Wickremasinghe				
Extras	(b 3, lb 6, w 5, nb 1)	15		
Total	(50 overs; 9 wickets)	189		

AUSTRALIA		Runs	Balls	4/6
T.M.Moody	c Mahanama b Wickremasinghe	57	86	4
G.R.Marsh	c Anurasiri b Kalpage	60	113	3/1
M.E.Waugh	c Mahanama b Wickremasinghe	26	26	–/2
D.C.Boon	not out	27	37	1
D.M.Jones	not out	12	8	–/1
S.R.Waugh				
*A.R.Border				
†I.A.Healy				
P.L.Taylor				
C.J.McDermott				
M.R.Whitney				
Extras	(lb 2, w 3, nb 3)	8		
Total	(44 overs; 3 wickets)	190		

AUSTRALIA	O	M	R	W		FALL OF WICKETS	
					Wkt	SL	A
McDermott	10	0	28	1	1st	8	120
S.R.Waugh	7	0	34	0	2nd	28	130
Whitney	10	3	26	1	3rd	72	165
Moody	3	0	18	0	4th	123	–
Taylor	10	0	34	2	5th	151	–
Border	10	0	40	1	6th	163	–
SRI LANKA	O	M	R	W	7th	166	–
Wickremasinghe	10	3	29	2	8th	182	–
Ramanayake	9	1	44	0	9th	189	–
Anurasiri	10	0	43	0	10th	–	–
Gurusinha	6	0	20	0			
Kalpage	8	0	41	1			
Ranatunga	1	0	11	0			

Umpires: P.D.Reporter (*India*) (16) and I.D.Robinson (*Zimbabwe*) (4).

NEW ZEALAND v WEST INDIES

At Eden Park, Auckland, New Zealand, on 8 March 1992.　Toss: New Zealand.
Result: **NEW ZEALAND** won by 5 wickets.　Award: M.D.Crowe.
LOI debuts: None.

WEST INDIES		Runs	Balls	4/6
D.L.Haynes	c and b Harris	22	61	–/1
B.C.Lara	c Rutherford b Larsen	52	81	7
*R.B.Richardson	c Smith b Watson	29	54	1
C.L.Hooper	c Greatbatch b Patel	2	9	–
K.L.T.Arthurton	b Morrison	40	54	3
A.L.Logie	b Harris	3	4	–
M.D.Marshall	b Larsen	5	14	–
†D.Williams	not out	32	24	5
W.K.M.Benjamin	not out	2	1	–
C.E.L.Ambrose				
A.C.Cummins				
Extras	(lb 8, w 7, nb 1)	16		
Total	(50 overs; 7 wickets)	**203**		

NEW ZEALAND		Runs	Balls	4/6
M.J.Greatbatch	c Haynes b Benjamin	63	77	7/3
R.T.Latham	c Williams b Cummins	14	27	1
A.H.Jones	c Williams b Benjamin	10	35	–
*M.D.Crowe	not out	81	81	12
K.R.Rutherford	c Williams b Ambrose	8	32	1
C.Z.Harris	c Williams b Cummins	7	23	–
D.N.Patel	not out	10	18	–
†I.D.S.Smith				
D.K.Morrison				
G.R.Larsen				
W.Watson				
Extras	(lb 7, w 5, nb 1)	13		
Total	(48.3 overs; 5 wickets)	**206**		

NEW ZEALAND	O	M	R	W		FALL OF WICKETS		
Morrison	9	1	33	1	Wkt	WI	NZ
Patel	10	2	19	1	1st	65	67
Watson	10	2	56	1	2nd	95	97
Larsen	10	0	41	2	3rd	100	100
Harris	10	2	32	2	4th	136	135
Latham	1	0	14	0	5th	142	174
					6th	156	–
WEST INDIES	O	M	R	W	7th	201	–
Ambrose	10	1	41	1	8th	–	–
Marshall	9	1	35	0	9th	–	–
Cummins	10	0	53	2	10th	–	–
Hooper	10	0	36	0			
Benjamin	9.3	3	34	2			

Umpires: K.E.Liebenberg (*South Africa*) (4) and P.J.McConnell (*Australia*) (66).

SOUTH AFRICA v PAKISTAN

At Woolloongabba, Brisbane, Australia, on 8 March 1992.   Toss: Pakistan.
Result: **SOUTH AFRICA** won by 20 runs (*target revised to 194 from 36 overs*).
Award: A.C.Hudson.
LOI debuts: None.

SOUTH AFRICA		**Runs**	**Balls**	**4/6**
A.C.Hudson	c Ijaz b Imran	54	81	8
*K.C.Wessels	c Moin b Aqib	7	26	–
M.W.Rushmere	c Aamir b Mushtaq	35	70	2
A.P.Kuiper	c Moin b Imran	5	12	–
J.N.Rhodes	lbw b Iqbal	5	17	–
W.J.Cronje	not out	47	53	4
B.M.McMillan	b Wasim	33	44	1
†D.J.Richardson	b Wasim	5	10	–
R.P.Snell	not out	1	1	–
M.W.Pringle				
A.A.Donald				
Extras	(lb 8, w 9, nb 2)	19		
Total	(50 overs; 7 wickets)	**211**		

PAKISTAN		**Runs**	**Balls**	**4/6**
Aamir Sohail	b Snell	23	53	2
Zahid Fazal	c Richardson b McMillan	11	46	1
Inzamam-ul-Haq	run out	48	45	5
*Imran Khan	c Richardson b McMillan	34	53	5
Salim Malik	c Donald b Kuiper	12	11	–
Wasim Akram	c Snell b Kuiper	9	8	1
Ijaz Ahmed	c Rhodes b Kuiper	6	3	1
†Moin Khan	not out	5	5	–
Mushtaq Ahmed	run out	4	4	–
Iqbal Sikander	not out	1	3	–
Aqib Javed				
Extras	(lb 2, w 17, nb 1)	20		
Total	(36 overs; 8 wickets)	**173**		

PAKISTAN	O	M	R	W
Wasim Akram	10	0	42	2
Aqib Javed	7	1	36	1
Imran Khan	10	0	34	2
Iqbal Sikander	8	0	30	1
Ijaz Ahmed	7	0	26	0
Mushtaq Ahmed	8	1	35	1

SOUTH AFRICA	O	M	R	W
Donald	7	1	31	0
Pringle	7	0	31	0
Snell	8	2	26	1
McMillan	7	0	34	2
Kuiper	6	0	40	3
Cronje	1	0	9	0

FALL OF WICKETS		
Wkt	SA	P
1st	31	50
2nd	98	50
3rd	110	135
4th	111	136
5th	127	156
6th	198	157
7th	207	163
8th	–	171
9th	–	–
10th	–	–

Umpires: B.L.Aldridge (*New Zealand*) (22) and S.A.Bucknor (*West Indies*) (7).

ENGLAND v SRI LANKA

At Eastern Oval, Ballarat, Australia, on 9 March 1992.   Toss: England.
Result: **ENGLAND** won by 106 runs.   Award: C.C.Lewis.
LOI debuts: None.

ENGLAND		Runs	Balls	4/6
*G.A.Gooch	b Labrooy	8	28	1
I.T.Botham	b Anurasiri	47	63	5/2
R.A.Smith	run out	19	39	2
G.A.Hick	b Ramanayake	41	62	3
N.H.Fairbrother	c Ramanayake b Gurusinha	63	70	2/2
†A.J.Stewart	c Jayasuriya b Gurusinha	59	36	7/1
C.C.Lewis	not out	20	6	1/2
D.R.Pringle	not out	0	–	–
D.A.Reeve				
P.A.J.DeFreitas				
R.K.Illingworth				
Extras	(b 1, lb 9, w 9, nb 4)	23		
Total	(50 overs; 6 wickets)	**280**		

SRI LANKA		Runs	Balls	4/6
R.S.Mahanama	c Botham b Lewis	9	19	1
M.A.R.Samarasekera	c Illingworth b Lewis	23	29	4
A.P.Gurusinha	c and b Lewis	7	9	–
*P.A.de Silva	c Fairbrother b Lewis	7	10	1
A.Ranatunga	c Stewart b Botham	36	51	6
†H.P.Tillekeratne	run out	4	30	–
S.T.Jayasuriya	c DeFreitas b Illingworth	19	16	2
G.F.Labrooy	c Smith b Illingworth	19	34	1
C.P.H.Ramanayake	c and b Reeve	12	38	–
S.D.Anurasiri	lbw b Reeve	11	19	–
G.P.Wickremasinghe	not out	6	16	–
Extras	(lb 7, w 8, nb 6)	21		
Total	(44 overs)	**174**		

SRI LANKA	O	M	R	W		FALL OF WICKETS		
Wickremasinghe	9	0	54	0		Wkt	E	SL
Ramanayake	10	1	42	1		1st	44	33
Labrooy	10	1	68	1		2nd	80	46
Anurasiri	10	1	27	1		3rd	105	56
Gurusinha	10	0	67	2		4th	164	60
Jayasuriya	1	0	12	0		5th	244	91
						6th	268	119
ENGLAND	O	M	R	W		7th	–	123
Pringle	7	1	27	0		8th	–	156
Lewis	8	0	30	4		9th	–	158
DeFreitas	5	1	31	0		10th	–	174
Botham	10	0	33	1				
Illingworth	10	0	32	2				
Reeve	4	0	14	2				

Umpires: Khizer Hayat (*Pakistan*) (42) and P.D.Reporter (*India*) (17).

WEST INDIES v INDIA

At Basin Reserve, Wellington, New Zealand, on 10 March 1992.   Toss: India.
Result: **WEST INDIES** won by 5 wickets (*target revised to 195 from 46 overs*).
Award: A.C.Cummins.
LOI debuts: None.

INDIA		Runs	Balls	4/6
A.Jadeja	c Benjamin b Simmons	27	61	2
K.Srikkanth	c Logie b Hooper	40	70	2
*M.Azharuddin	c Ambrose b Cummins	61	84	4
S.R.Tendulkar	c Williams b Ambrose	4	11	–
S.V.Manjrekar	run out	27	40	–
Kapil Dev	c Haynes b Cummins	3	4	–
P.K.Amre	c Hooper b Ambrose	4	8	–
†K.S.More	c Hooper b Cummins	5	5	1
M.Prabhakar	c Richardson b Cummins	8	10	1
J.Srinath	not out	5	5	–
S.L.V.Raju	run out	1	1	–
Extras	(lb 6, w 5, nb 1)	12		
Total	(49.4 overs)	**197**		

WEST INDIES		Runs	Balls	4/6
D.L.Haynes	c Manjrekar b Kapil Dev	16	16	3
B.C.Lara	c Manjrekar b Srinath	41	37	6/1
P.V.Simmons	c Tendulkar b Prabhakar	22	20	2/1
*R.B.Richardson	c Srikkanth b Srinath	3	8	–
K.L.T.Arthurton	not out	58	99	3
A.L.Logie	c More b Raju	7	10	1
C.L.Hooper	not out	34	57	3
†D.Williams				
W.K.M.Benjamin				
C.E.L.Ambrose				
A.C.Cummins				
Extras	(lb 8, w 2, nb 4)	14		
Total	(40.2 overs; 5 wickets)	**195**		

WEST INDIES	O	M	R	W		FALL OF WICKETS		
Ambrose	10	1	24	2		Wkt	I	WI
Benjamin	9.4	0	35	0		1st	56	57
Cummins	10	0	33	4		2nd	102	82
Simmons	9	0	48	1		3rd	115	88
Hooper	10	0	46	1		4th	166	98
Arthurton	1	0	5	0		5th	171	112
						6th	172	–
INDIA	O	M	R	W		7th	180	–
Kapil Dev	8	0	45	1		8th	186	–
Prabhakar	9	0	55	1		9th	193	–
Raju	10	2	32	1		10th	197	–
Srinath	9	2	23	2				
Tendulkar	3	0	20	0				
Srikkanth	1	0	9	0				
Jadeja	0.2	0	5	0				

Umpires: S.G.Randell (*Australia*) (48) and S.J.Woodward (29).

SOUTH AFRICA v ZIMBABWE

At Manuka Oval, Canberra, Australia, on 10 March 1992.   Toss: South Africa.
Result: **SOUTH AFRICA** won by 7 wickets.   Award: P.N.Kirsten.
LOI debuts: None.

ZIMBABWE		Runs	Balls	4/6
W.R.James	lbw b Pringle	5	12	1
†A.Flower	c Richardson b Cronje	19	44	–
A.J.Pycroft	c Wessels b McMillan	19	47	–
*D.L.Houghton	c Cronje b Kirsten	15	53	–
A.C.Waller	c Cronje b Kirsten	15	28	1
A.H.Shah	c Wessels b Kirsten	3	4	–
E.A.Brandes	c Richardson b McMillan	20	28	1/1
M.G.Burmester	c Kuiper b Cronje	1	10	–
A.J.Traicos	not out	16	40	1
M.P.Jarvis	c and b McMillan	17	21	1/1
K.G.Duers	b Donald	5	10	–
Extras	(lb 11, w 13, nb 4)	28		
Total	(48.3 overs)	**163**		

SOUTH AFRICA		Runs	Balls	4/6
*K.C.Wessels	b Shah	70	137	6
A.C.Hudson	b Jarvis	13	22	1
P.N.Kirsten	not out	62	103	3
A.P.Kuiper	c Burmester b Brandes	7	9	–
J.N.Rhodes	not out	3	3	–
W.J.Cronje				
B.M.McMillan				
†D.J.Richardson				
R.P.Snell				
M.W.Pringle				
A.A.Donald				
Extras	(lb 4, w 2, nb 3)	9		
Total	(45.1 overs; 3 wickets)	**164**		

SOUTH AFRICA	O	M	R	W
Donald	9.3	1	25	1
Pringle	9	0	25	1
Snell	10	3	24	0
Cronje	5	0	17	2
Kirsten	5	0	31	3
McMillan	10	1	30	3

ZIMBABWE	O	M	R	W
Brandes	9.1	0	40	1
Jarvis	9	2	23	1
Burmester	5	0	20	0
Shah	8	2	32	1
Duers	8	1	19	0
Traicos	6	0	26	0

FALL OF WICKETS		
Wkt	Z	SA
1st	7	27
2nd	51	139
3rd	72	151
4th	80	–
5th	80	–
6th	115	–
7th	117	–
8th	123	–
9th	151	–
10th	163	–

Umpires: S.A.Bucknor (*West Indies*) (8) and D.R.Shepherd (*England*) (45).

AUSTRALIA v PAKISTAN

At WACA Ground, Perth, Australia, on 11 March 1992.   Toss: Pakistan.
Result: **PAKISTAN** won by 48 runs.   Award: Aamir Sohail.
LOI debuts: None.

PAKISTAN		Runs	Balls	4/6
Aamir Sohail	c Healy b Moody	76	106	8
Ramiz Raja	c Border b Whitney	34	61	4
Salim Malik	b Moody	0	6	–
Javed Miandad	c Healy b S.R.Waugh	46	75	3
*Imran Khan	c Moody b S.R.Waugh	13	22	–/1
Inzamam-ul-Haq	run out	16	16	–
Ijaz Ahmed	run out	0	2	–
Wasim Akram	c M.E.Waugh b S.R.Waugh	0	1	–
†Moin Khan	c Healy b McDermott	5	8	–
Mushtaq Ahmed	not out	3	5	–
Aqib Javed				
Extras	(lb 9, w 16, nb 2)	27		
Total	(50 overs; 9 wickets)	**220**		

AUSTRALIA		Runs	Balls	4/6
T.M.Moody	c Salim b Aqib	4	18	–
G.R.Marsh	c Moin b Imran	39	91	1
D.C.Boon	c Mushtaq b Aqib	5	15	1
D.M.Jones	c Aqib b Mushtaq	47	79	2
M.E.Waugh	c Ijaz b Mushtaq	30	42	2
*A.R.Border	c Ijaz b Mushtaq	1	4	–
S.R.Waugh	c Moin b Imran	5	6	1
†I.A.Healy	c Ijaz b Aqib	8	15	–
C.J.McDermott	lbw b Wasim	0	2	–
M.R.Whitney	b Wasim	5	9	–
B.A.Reid	not out	0	–	–
Extras	(lb 7, w 14, nb 7)	28		
Total	(45.2 overs)	**172**		

AUSTRALIA	O	M	R	W		FALL OF WICKETS		
McDermott	10	0	33	1		Wkt	P	A
Reid	9	0	37	0		1st	78	13
S.R.Waugh	10	0	36	3		2nd	80	31
Whitney	10	1	50	1		3rd	157	116
Moody	10	0	42	2		4th	193	122
M.E.Waugh	1	0	13	0		5th	194	123
						6th	205	130
PAKISTAN	O	M	R	W		7th	205	156
Wasim Akram	7.2	0	28	2		8th	214	162
Aqib Javed	8	1	21	3		9th	220	167
Imran Khan	10	1	32	2		10th	–	172
Ijaz Ahmed	10	0	43	0				
Mushtaq Ahmed	10	0	41	3				

Umpires: K.E.Liebenberg (*South Africa*) (5) and P.D.Reporter (*India*) (18).

NEW ZEALAND v INDIA

At Carisbrook, Dunedin, New Zealand, on 12 March 1992.   Toss: India.
Result: **NEW ZEALAND** won by 4 wickets.   Award: M.J.Greatbatch.
LOI debuts: None.

INDIA		Runs	Balls	4/6
A.Jadeja	retired hurt	13	32	1
K.Srikkanth	c Latham b Patel	0	3	–
*M.Azharuddin	c Greatbatch b Patel	55	98	3/1
S.R.Tendulkar	c Smith b Harris	84	107	6
S.V.Manjrekar	c and b Harris	18	25	–
Kapil Dev	c Larsen b Harris	33	16	5
S.T.Banerjee	c Greatbatch b Watson	11	9	1
†K.S.More	not out	2	8	–
J.Srinath	not out	4	3	–
M.Prabhakar				
S.L.V.Raju				
Extras	(b 1, lb 4, w 4, nb 1)	10		
Total	(50 overs; 6 wickets)	**230**		

NEW ZEALAND		Runs	Balls	4/6
M.J.Greatbatch	c Banerjee b Raju	73	77	5/4
R.T.Latham	b Prabhakar	8	22	1
A.H.Jones	not out	67	107	8
*M.D.Crowe	run out	26	28	3/1
†I.D.S.Smith	c sub b Prabhakar	9	8	1
K.R.Rutherford	lbw b Raju	21	22	3/1
C.Z.Harris	b Prabhakar	4	17	–
C.L.Cairns	not out	4	5	1
D.N.Patel				
G.R.Larsen				
W.Watson				
Extras	(b 4, lb 3, w 4, nb 8)	19		
Total	(47.1 overs; 6 wickets)	**231**		

NEW ZEALAND	O	M	R	W		FALL OF WICKETS		
Cairns	8	1	40	0		Wkt	I	NZ
Patel	10	0	29	2		1st	4	36
Watson	10	1	34	1		2nd	149	118
Larsen	9	0	43	0		3rd	166	162
Harris	9	0	55	3		4th	201	172
Latham	4	0	24	0		5th	222	206
						6th	223	225
INDIA	O	M	R	W		7th	–	–
Kapil Dev	10	0	55	0		8th	–	–
Prabhakar	10	0	46	3		9th	–	–
Banerjee	6	1	40	0		10th	–	–
Srinath	9	0	35	0				
Raju	10	0	38	2				
Tendulkar	1	0	2	0				
Srikkanth	1.1	0	8	0				

Umpires: P.J.McConnell (*Australia*) (67) and I.D.Robinson (*Zimbabwe*) (5).

ENGLAND v SOUTH AFRICA

At Melbourne Cricket Ground, Australia, on 12 March 1992.   Toss: England.
Result: **ENGLAND** won by 3 wickets (*target revised to 226 from 41 overs*).
Award: A.J.Stewart.
LOI debuts: None.

SOUTH AFRICA		Runs	Balls	4/6
*K.C.Wessels	c Smith b Hick	85	126	6
A.C.Hudson	c and b Hick	79	115	7
P.N.Kirsten	c Smith b DeFreitas	11	12	–/1
J.N.Rhodes	run out	18	23	–
A.P.Kuiper	not out	15	12	1
W.J.Cronje	not out	13	15	–
B.M.McMillan				
†D.J.Richardson				
R.P.Snell				
M.W.Pringle				
A.A.Donald				
Extras	(b 4, lb 4, w 4, nb 3)	15		
Total	(50 overs; 4 wickets)	**236**		

ENGLAND		Runs	Balls	4/6
*†A.J.Stewart	run out	77	88	7
I.T.Botham	b McMillan	22	30	1
R.A.Smith	c Richardson b McMillan	0	2	–
G.A.Hick	c Richardson b Snell	1	4	–
N.H.Fairbrother	not out	75	83	6
D.A.Reeve	c McMillan b Snell	10	15	–
C.C.Lewis	run out	33	22	4
D.R.Pringle	c Kuiper b Snell	1	3	–
P.A.J.DeFreitas	not out	1	1	–
R.K.Illingworth				
G.C.Small				
Extras	(lb 3, w 1, nb 2)	6		
Total	(40.5 overs; 7 wickets)	**226**		

ENGLAND	O	M	R	W
Pringle	9	2	34	0
DeFreitas	10	1	41	1
Botham	8	0	37	0
Small	2	0	14	0
Illingworth	10	0	43	0
Reeve	2.4	0	15	0
Hick	8.2	0	44	2

SOUTH AFRICA	O	M	R	W
Donald	9	1	43	0
Pringle	8	0	44	0
Snell	7.5	0	42	3
McMillan	8	1	39	2
Kuiper	4	0	32	0
Cronje	3	0	14	0
Kirsten	1	0	9	0

FALL OF WICKETS		
Wkt	SA	E
1st	151	63
2nd	170	63
3rd	201	64
4th	205	132
5th	–	166
6th	–	216
7th	–	225
8th	–	–
9th	–	–
10th	–	–

Umpires: B.L.Aldridge (*New Zealand*) (23) and J.D.Buultjens (*Sri Lanka*) (17).

WEST INDIES v SRI LANKA

At Berri Oval, South Australia, Australia, on 13 March 1992.   Toss: Sri Lanka.
Result: **WEST INDIES** won by 91 runs.   Award: P.V.Simmons.
LOI debuts: None.

WEST INDIES		Runs	Balls	4/6
D.L.Haynes	c Tillekeratne b Ranatunga	38	47	3/1
B.C.Lara	c and b Ramanayake	1	6	–
P.V.Simmons	c Wickremasinghe b Hathurusinghe	110	125	8/2
*R.B.Richardson	run out	8	23	–
K.L.T.Arthurton	c Tillekeratne b Hathurusinghe	40	54	1
A.L.Logie	b Anurasiri	0	2	–
C.L.Hooper	c Gurusinha b Hathurusinghe	12	12	1
†D.Williams	c Tillekeratne b Hathurusinghe	2	3	–
C.E.L.Ambrose	not out	15	14	–/1
W.K.M.Benjamin	not out	24	20	1
A.C.Cummins				
Extras	(lb 9, w 3, nb 6)	18		
Total	(50 overs; 8 wickets)	**268**		

SRI LANKA		Runs	Balls	4/6
R.S.Mahanama	c Arthurton b Cummins	11	50	–
M.A.R.Samarasekera	lbw b Hooper	40	41	4/1
U.C.Hathurusinghe	run out	16	25	–
*P.A.de Silva	c and b Hooper	11	19	–
A.Ranatunga	c Benjamin b Arthurton	24	40	–/1
A.P.Gurusinha	c Richardson b Ambrose	10	30	–
†H.P.Tillekeratne	b Ambrose	3	9	–
R.S.Kalpage	not out	13	40	–
C.P.H.Ramanayake	b Arthurton	1	13	–
S.D.Anurasiri	b Benjamin	3	11	–
G.P.Wickremasinghe	not out	21	21	1
Extras	(lb 8, w 14, nb 2)	24		
Total	(50 overs; 9 wickets)	**177**		

SRI LANKA	O	M	R	W
Wickremasinghe	7	0	30	0
Ramanayake	7	1	17	1
Anurasiri	10	0	46	1
Gurusinha	1	0	10	0
Ranatunga	7	0	35	1
Kalpage	10	0	64	0
Hathurusinghe	8	0	57	4

WEST INDIES	O	M	R	W
Ambrose	10	2	24	2
Benjamin	10	0	34	1
Cummins	9	0	49	1
Hooper	10	1	19	2
Arthurton	10	0	40	2
Simmons	1	0	3	0

FALL OF WICKETS		
Wkt	WI	SL
1st	6	56
2nd	72	80
3rd	103	86
4th	194	99
5th	195	130
6th	217	135
7th	223	137
8th	228	139
9th	–	149
10th	–	–

Umpires: D.R.Shepherd (*England*) (46) and S.J.Woodward (*New Zealand*) (30).

AUSTRALIA v ZIMBABWE

At Bellerive Oval, Hobart, Australia, on 14 March 1992.   Toss: Zimbabwe.
Result: **AUSTRALIA** won by 128 runs.   Award: S.R.Waugh.
LOI debuts: None.

AUSTRALIA		Runs	Balls	4/6
T.M.Moody	run out	6	8	–
D.C.Boon	b Shah	48	84	4
D.M.Jones	b Burmester	54	71	4
*A.R.Border	st Flower b Traicos	22	29	2
M.E.Waugh	not out	66	39	5/2
S.R.Waugh	b Brandes	55	43	4
†I.A.Healy	lbw b Duers	0	2	–
P.L.Taylor	not out	1	1	–
C.J.McDermott				
M.R.Whitney				
B.A.Reid				
Extras	(b 2, lb 8, w 2, nb 1)	13		
Total	(46 overs; 6 wickets)	**265**		

ZIMBABWE		Runs	Balls	4/6
A.H.Shah	run out	23	47	2
†A.Flower	c Border b S.R.Waugh	20	49	1
A.D.R.Campbell	c M.E.Waugh b Whitney	4	20	1
A.J.Pycroft	c M.E.Waugh b S.R.Waugh	0	1	–
*D.L.Houghton	b McDermott	2	10	–
A.C.Waller	c Taylor b Moody	18	39	2
K.J.Arnott	b Whitney	8	15	–
E.A.Brandes	c McDermott b Taylor	23	28	3
M.G.Burmester	c Border b Reid	12	24	–
A.J.Traicos	c Border b Taylor	3	9	–
K.G.Duers	not out	2	10	–
Extras	(lb 12, w 8, nb 2)	22		
Total	(41.4 overs)	**137**		

ZIMBABWE	O	M	R	W		FALL OF WICKETS		
Brandes	9	0	59	1	Wkt	A	Z	
Duers	9	1	48	1	1st	8	47	
Burmester	9	0	65	1	2nd	102	51	
Shah	9	0	53	1	3rd	134	51	
Traicos	10	0	30	1	4th	144	57	
					5th	257	69	
AUSTRALIA	O	M	R	W	6th	258	88	
McDermott	8	0	26	1	7th	–	97	
Reid	9	2	17	1	8th	–	117	
S.R.Waugh	7	0	28	2	9th	–	132	
Whitney	10	3	15	2	10th	–	137	
Moody	4	0	25	1				
Taylor	3.4	0	14	2				

Umpires: B.L.Aldridge (*New Zealand*) (24) and S.A.Bucknor (*West Indies*) (9).

NEW ZEALAND v ENGLAND

At Basin Reserve, Wellington, New Zealand, on 15 March 1992.   Toss: New Zealand.
Result: **NEW ZEALAND** won by 7 wickets.   Award: A.H.Jones.
LOI debuts: None.

ENGLAND		Runs	Balls	4/6
*†A.J.Stewart	c Harris b Patel	41	59	7
I.T.Botham	b Patel	8	25	1
G.A.Hick	c Greatbatch b Harris	56	70	6/1
R.A.Smith	c Patel b Jones	38	72	3
A.J.Lamb	c Cairns b Watson	12	29	–
C.C.Lewis	c and b Watson	0	1	–
D.A.Reeve	not out	21	27	1
D.R.Pringle	c sub (R.T.Latham) b Jones	10	16	–
P.A.J.DeFreitas	c Cairns b Harris	0	1	–
R.K.Illingworth	not out	2	2	–
G.C.Small				
Extras	(b 1, lb 7, w 4)	12		
Total	(50 overs; 8 wickets)	**200**		

NEW ZEALAND		Runs	Balls	4/6
M.J.Greatbatch	c DeFreitas b Botham	35	37	4/1
J.G.Wright	b DeFreitas	1	5	–
A.H.Jones	run out	78	113	13
*M.D.Crowe	not out	73	81	6
K.R.Rutherford	not out	3	12	–
C.Z.Harris				
C.L.Cairns				
†I.D.S.Smith				
D.N.Patel				
G.R.Larsen				
W.Watson				
Extras	(lb 9, w 1, nb 1)	11		
Total	(40.5 overs; 3 wickets)	**201**		

NEW ZEALAND	O	M	R	W		FALL OF WICKETS		
Patel	10	1	26	2		Wkt	E	NZ
Harris	8	0	39	2		1st	25	5
Watson	10	0	40	2		2nd	95	62
Cairns	3	0	21	0		3rd	135	171
Larsen	10	3	24	0		4th	162	–
Jones	9	0	42	2		5th	162	–
						6th	169	–
ENGLAND	O	M	R	W		7th	189	–
Pringle	6.2	1	34	0		8th	195	–
DeFreitas	8.3	1	45	1		9th	–	–
Botham	4	0	19	1		10th	–	–
Illingworth	9	1	46	0				
Hick	6	0	26	0				
Reeve	3	0	9	0				
Small	4	0	13	0				

Umpires: S.G.Randell (*Australia*) (49) and I.D.Robinson (*Zimbabwe*) (6).

SOUTH AFRICA v INDIA

At Adelaide Oval, Australia, on 15 March 1992.   Toss: South Africa.
Result: **SOUTH AFRICA** won by 6 wickets.   Award: P.N.Kirsten.
LOI debuts: None.

INDIA		Runs	Balls	4/6
K.Srikkanth	c Kirsten b Donald	0	5	–
S.V.Manjrekar	b Kuiper	28	53	–
*M.Azharuddin	c Kuiper b Pringle	79	77	6
S.R.Tendulkar	c Wessels b Kuiper	14	14	1
Kapil Dev	b Donald	42	29	3/1
V.G.Kambli	run out	1	3	–
P.K.Amre	not out	1	1	–
J.Srinath	not out	0	–	–
†K.S.More				
M.Prabhakar				
S.L.V.Raju				
Extras	(lb 7, w 6, nb 2)	15		
Total	(30 overs; 6 wickets)	**180**		

SOUTH AFRICA		Runs	Balls	4/6
A.C.Hudson	b Srinath	53	73	4
P.N.Kirsten	b Kapil Dev	84	86	7
A.P.Kuiper	run out	7	6	–
J.N.Rhodes	c Raju b Prabhakar	7	3	–/1
*K.C.Wessels	not out	9	6	1
W.J.Cronje	not out	8	6	1
B.M.McMillan				
†D.J.Richardson				
R.P.Snell				
M.W.Pringle				
A.A.Donald				
Extras	(lb 10, nb 3)	13		
Total	(29.1 overs; 4 wickets)	**181**		

SOUTH AFRICA	O	M	R	W		FALL OF WICKETS	
Donald	6	0	34	2	Wkt	I	SA
Pringle	6	0	37	1	1st	1	128
Snell	6	1	46	0	2nd	79	149
McMillan	6	0	28	0	3rd	103	157
Kuiper	6	0	28	2	4th	174	163
					5th	177	–
INDIA	O	M	R	W	6th	179	–
Kapil Dev	6	0	36	1	7th	–	–
Prabhakar	5.1	1	33	1	8th	–	–
Tendulkar	6	0	20	0	9th	–	–
Srinath	6	0	39	1	10th	–	–
Raju	6	0	43	0			

Umpires: J.D.Buultjens (*Sri Lanka*) (18) and Khizer Hayat (*Pakistan*) (43).

PAKISTAN v SRI LANKA

At WACA Ground, Perth, Australia, on 15 March 1992.   Toss: Sri Lanka.
Result: **PAKISTAN** won by 4 wickets.   Award: Javed Miandad.
LOI debuts: None.

SRI LANKA		Runs	Balls	4/6
R.S.Mahanama	b Wasim	12	36	1
M.A.R.Samarasekera	st Moin b Mushtaq	38	59	1
U.C.Hathurusinghe	b Mushtaq	5	29	–
*P.A.de Silva	c Aamir b Ijaz	43	56	2
A.P.Gurusinha	c Salim b Imran	37	54	2
A.Ranatunga	c sub (Zahid Fazal) b Aamir	7	19	–
†H.P.Tillekeratne	not out	25	34	3
R.S.Kalpage	not out	13	14	–
C.P.H.Ramanayake				
K.I.W.Wijegunawardene				
G.P.Wickremasinghe				
Extras	(lb 15, w 11, nb 6)	32		
Total	(50 overs; 6 wickets)	**212**		

PAKISTAN		Runs	Balls	4/6
Aamir Sohail	c Mahanama b Ramanayake	1	10	–
Ramiz Raja	c Gurusinha b Wickremasinghe	32	56	3
*Imran Khan	c De Silva b Hathurusinghe	22	69	2
Javed Miandad	c Wickremasinghe b Gurusinha	57	84	3
Salim Malik	c Kalpage b Ramanayake	51	66	2
Inzamam-ul-Haq	run out	11	11	–
Ijaz Ahmed	not out	8	6	1
Wasim Akram	not out	5	5	1
†Moin Khan				
Mushtaq Ahmed				
Aqib Javed				
Extras	(lb 12, w 9, nb 8)	29		
Total	(49.1 overs; 6 wickets)	**216**		

PAKISTAN	O	M	R	W		FALL OF WICKETS		
Wasim Akram	10	0	37	1	Wkt	SL	P	
Aqib Javed	10	0	39	0	1st	29	7	
Imran Khan	8	1	36	1	2nd	48	68	
Mushtaq Ahmed	10	0	43	2	3rd	99	84	
Ijaz Ahmed	8	0	28	1	4th	132	185	
Aamir Sohail	4	0	14	1	5th	158	201	
					6th	187	205	
SRI LANKA	O	M	R	W	7th	–	–	
Wijegunawardene	10	1	34	0	8th	–	–	
Ramanayake	10	1	37	2	9th	–	–	
Wickremasinghe	9.1	0	41	1	10th	–	–	
Gurusinha	9	0	38	1				
Hathurusinghe	9	0	40	1				
Kalpage	2	0	14	0				

Umpires: K.E.Liebenberg (*South Africa*) (6) and P.J.McConnell (68).

NEW ZEALAND v PAKISTAN

At Lancaster Park, Christchurch, New Zealand, on 18 March 1992.   Toss: Pakistan.
Result: **PAKISTAN** won by 7 wickets.   Award: Mushtaq Ahmed.
LOI debuts: None.

NEW ZEALAND		Runs	Balls	4/6
M.J.Greatbatch	c Salim b Mushtaq	42	67	5/1
R.T.Latham	c Inzamam b Aqib	6	9	1
A.H.Jones	lbw b Wasim	2	3	–
*M.D.Crowe	c Aamir b Wasim	3	20	–
K.R.Rutherford	run out	8	35	–
C.Z.Harris	st Moin b Mushtaq	1	6	–
D.N.Patel	c Mushtaq b Aamir	7	13	–
†I.D.S.Smith	b Imran	1	4	–
G.R.Larsen	b Wasim	37	80	3
D.K.Morrison	c Inzamam b Wasim	12	45	1
W.Watson	not out	5	13	–
Extras	(b 3, lb 23, w 12, nb 4)	42		
Total	**(48.2 overs)**	**166**		

PAKISTAN		Runs	Balls	4/6
Aamir Sohail	c Patel b Morrison	0	1	–
Ramiz Raja	not out	119	155	16
Inzamam-ul-Haq	b Morrison	5	8	1
Javed Miandad	lbw b Morrison	30	85	1
Salim Malik	not out	9	23	1
*Imran Khan				
Wasim Akram				
Ijaz Ahmed				
†Moin Khan				
Mushtaq Ahmed				
Aqib Javed				
Extras	(lb 1, w 1, nb 2)	4		
Total	**(44.4 overs; 3 wickets)**	**167**		

PAKISTAN	O	M	R	W		FALL OF WICKETS		
Wasim Akram	9.2	0	32	4		Wkt	NZ	P
Aqib Javed	10	1	34	1		1st	23	0
Mushtaq Ahmed	10	0	18	2		2nd	26	9
Imran Khan	8	0	22	1		3rd	39	124
Aamir Sohail	10	1	29	1		4th	85	–
Ijaz Ahmed	1	0	5	0		5th	88	–
						6th	93	–
NEW ZEALAND	O	M	R	W		7th	96	–
Morrison	10	0	42	3		8th	106	–
Patel	10	2	25	0		9th	150	–
Watson	10	3	26	0		10th	166	–
Harris	4	0	18	0				
Larsen	3	0	16	0				
Jones	3	0	10	0				
Latham	2	0	13	0				
Rutherford	1.4	0	11	0				
Greatbatch	1	0	5	0				

Umpires: S.A.Bucknor (*West Indies*) (10) and S.G.Randell (*Australia*) (50).

ENGLAND v ZIMBABWE

At Lavington Sports Ground, Albury, Australia, on 18 March 1992.   Toss: England.
Result: **ZIMBABWE** won by 9 runs.   Award: E.A.Brandes.
LOI debuts: None.

ZIMBABWE		Runs	Balls	4/6
W.R.James	c and b Illingworth	13	46	1
†A.Flower	b DeFreitas	7	16	1
A.J.Pycroft	c Gooch b Botham	3	13	–
K.J.Arnott	lbw b Botham	11	33	–
*D.L.Houghton	c Fairbrother b Small	29	74	2
A.C.Waller	b Tufnell	8	16	1
A.H.Shah	c Lamb b Tufnell	3	16	–
I.P.Butchart	c Fairbrother b Botham	24	36	2
E.A.Brandes	st Stewart b Illingworth	14	24	1
A.J.Traicos	not out	0	6	–
M.P.Jarvis	lbw b Illingworth	6	6	–
Extras	(lb 8, w 8)	16		
Total	(46.1 overs)	**134**		

ENGLAND		Runs	Balls	4/6
*G.A.Gooch	lbw b Brandes	0	1	–
I.T.Botham	c Flower b Shah	18	34	4
A.J.Lamb	c James b Brandes	17	26	2
R.A.Smith	b Brandes	2	13	–
G.A.Hick	b Brandes	0	6	–
N.H.Fairbrother	c Flower b Butchart	20	77	–
†A.J.Stewart	c Waller b Shah	29	96	3
P.A.J.DeFreitas	c Flower b Butchart	4	17	–
R.K.Illingworth	run out	11	20	–
G.C.Small	c Pycroft b Jarvis	5	18	–
P.C.R.Tufnell	not out	0	–	–
Extras	(b 4, lb 3, w 11, nb1)	19		
Total	(49.1 overs)	**125**		

ENGLAND	O	M	R	W
DeFreitas	8	1	14	1
Small	9	1	20	1
Botham	10	2	23	3
Illingworth	9.1	0	33	3
Tufnell	10	2	36	2
ZIMBABWE	O	M	R	W
Brandes	10	4	21	4
Jarvis	9.1	0	32	1
Shah	10	3	17	2
Traicos	10	4	16	0
Butchart	10	1	32	2

FALL OF WICKETS		
Wkt	Z	E
1st	12	0
2nd	19	32
3rd	30	42
4th	52	42
5th	65	43
6th	77	95
7th	96	101
8th	127	108
9th	127	124
10th	134	125

Umpires: B.L.Aldridge (*New Zealand*) (25) and Khizer Hayat (*Pakistan*) (44).

AUSTRALIA v WEST INDIES

At Melbourne Cricket Ground, Australia, on 18 March 1992.   Toss: Australia.
Result: **AUSTRALIA** won by 57 runs.   Award: D.C.Boon.
LOI debuts: None.

AUSTRALIA		Runs	Balls	4/6
T.M.Moody	c Benjamin b Simmons	42	70	3
D.C.Boon	c Williams b Cummins	100	147	8
D.M.Jones	c Williams b Cummins	6	14	–
*A.R.Border	lbw b Simmons	8	10	1
M.E.Waugh	st Williams b Hooper	21	31	–
S.R.Waugh	b Cummins	6	14	–
†I.A.Healy	not out	11	11	–
P.L.Taylor	not out	10	6	1
C.J.McDermott				
M.R.Whitney				
B.A.Reid				
Extras	(lb 3, w 3, nb 6)	12		
Total	(50 overs; 6 wickets)	**216**		

WEST INDIES		Runs	Balls	4/6
D.L.Haynes	c Jones b McDermott	14	24	2
B.C.Lara	run out	70	97	3
P.V.Simmons	lbw b McDermott	0	1	–
*R.B.Richardson	c Healy b Whitney	10	44	–
K.L.T.Arthurton	c McDermott b Whitney	15	15	2
A.L.Logie	c Healy b Whitney	5	15	–
C.L.Hooper	c M.E.Waugh b Whitney	4	11	–
†D.Williams	c Border b Reid	4	15	–
W.K.M.Benjamin	lbw b S.R.Waugh	15	21	1
C.E.L.Ambrose	run out	2	7	–
A.C.Cummins	not out	5	10	–
Extras	(b 3, lb 5, w 3, nb 4)	15		
Total	(42.4 overs)	**159**		

WEST INDIES	O	M	R	W
Ambrose	10	0	46	0
Benjamin	10	1	49	0
Cummins	10	1	38	3
Hooper	10	0	40	1
Simmons	10	1	40	2
AUSTRALIA	O	M	R	W
McDermott	6	1	29	2
Reid	10	1	26	1
Whitney	10	1	34	4
S.R.Waugh	6.4	0	24	1
Taylor	4	0	24	0
Moody	6	1	14	0

FALL OF WICKETS		
Wkt	A	WI
1st	107	27
2nd	128	27
3rd	141	59
4th	185	83
5th	189	99
6th	200	117
7th	–	128
8th	–	137
9th	–	150
10th	–	159

Umpires: P.D.Reporter (*India*) (19) and D.R.Shepherd (*England*) (47).

NEW ZEALAND v PAKISTAN (SEMI-FINAL)

At Eden Park, Auckland, New Zealand, on 21 March 1992.　Toss: New Zealand.
Result: **PAKISTAN** won by 4 wickets.　Award: Inzamam-ul-Haq.
LOI debuts: None.

NEW ZEALAND		Runs	Balls	4/6
M.J.Greatbatch	b Aqib	17	22	–/2
J.G.Wright	c Ramiz b Mushtaq	13	44	1
A.H.Jones	lbw b Mushtaq	21	53	2
*M.D.Crowe	run out	91	83	7/3
K.R.Rutherford	c Moin b Wasim	50	68	5/1
C.Z.Harris	st Moin b Iqbal	13	12	1
†I.D.S.Smith	not out	18	10	3
D.N.Patel	lbw b Wasim	8	6	1
G.R.Larsen	not out	8	6	1
D.K.Morrison				
W.Watson				
Extras	(lb 11, w 8, nb 4)	23		
Total	(50 overs; 7 wickets)	**262**		

PAKISTAN		Runs	Balls	4/6
Aamir Sohail	c Jones b Patel	14	20	1
Ramiz Raja	c Morrison b Watson	44	55	6
*Imran Khan	c Larsen b Harris	44	93	1/2
Javed Miandad	not out	57	69	4
Salim Malik	c sub (R.T.Latham) b Larsen	1	2	–
Inzamam-ul-Haq	run out	60	37	7/1
Wasim Akram	b Watson	9	8	1
†Moin Khan	not out	20	11	2/1
Mushtaq Ahmed				
Iqbal Sikander				
Aqib Javed				
Extras	(b 4, lb 10, w 1)	15		
Total	(49 overs; 6 wickets)	**264**		

PAKISTAN	O	M	R	W		FALL OF WICKETS		
Wasim Akram	10	1	40	2		Wkt	NZ	P
Aqib Javed	10	2	45	1		1st	35	30
Mushtaq Ahmed	10	0	40	2		2nd	39	84
Imran Khan	10	0	59	0		3rd	87	134
Iqbal Sikander	9	0	56	1		4th	194	140
Aamir Sohail	1	0	11	0		5th	214	227
						6th	221	238
NEW ZEALAND	O	M	R	W		7th	244	–
Patel	10	1	50	1		8th	–	–
Morrison	9	0	55	0		9th	–	–
Watson	10	2	39	2		10th	–	–
Larsen	10	1	34	1				
Harris	10	0	72	1				

Umpires: S.A.Bucknor (*West Indies*) (11) and D.R.Shepherd (*England*) (48).

ENGLAND v SOUTH AFRICA (SEMI-FINAL)

At Sydney Cricket Ground, Australia, on 22 March 1992.   Toss: South Africa.
Result: **ENGLAND** won by 19 runs (*target revised to 252 runs off 43 overs*).
Award: G.A.Hick.
LOI debuts: None.

ENGLAND		Runs	Balls	4/6
*G.A.Gooch	c Richardson b Donald	2	8	–
I.T.Botham	b Pringle	21	27	3
†A.J.Stewart	c Richardson b McMillan	33	58	4
G.A.Hick	c Rhodes b Snell	83	90	9
N.H.Fairbrother	b Pringle	28	50	1
A.J.Lamb	c Richardson b Donald	19	22	1
C.C.Lewis	not out	18	17	2
D.A.Reeve	not out	25	14	4
P.A.J.DeFreitas				
G.C.Small				
R.K.Illingworth				
Extras	(b 1, lb 7, w 9, nb 6)	23		
Total	**(45 overs; 6 wickets)**	**252**		

SOUTH AFRICA		Runs	Balls	4/6
*K.C.Wessels	c Lewis b Botham	17	23	1
A.C.Hudson	lbw b Illingworth	46	53	6
P.N.Kirsten	b DeFreitas	11	26	–
A.P.Kuiper	b Illingworth	36	44	5
W.J.Cronje	c Hick b Small	24	46	1
J.N.Rhodes	c Lewis b Small	43	39	3
B.M.McMillan	not out	21	21	–
†D.J.Richardson	not out	13	10	1
R.P.Snell				
M.W.Pringle				
A.A.Donald				
Extras	(lb 17, w 4)	21		
Total	**(43 overs; 6 wickets)**	**232**		

SOUTH AFRICA	O	M	R	W
Donald	10	0	69	2
Pringle	9	2	36	2
Snell	8	0	52	1
McMillan	9	0	47	1
Kuiper	5	0	26	0
Cronje	4	0	14	0

ENGLAND	O	M	R	W
Botham	10	0	52	1
Lewis	5	0	38	0
DeFreitas	8	1	28	1
Illingworth	10	1	46	2
Small	10	1	51	2

FALL OF WICKETS		
Wkt	E	SA
1st	20	26
2nd	39	61
3rd	110	90
4th	183	131
5th	187	176
6th	221	206
7th	–	–
8th	–	–
9th	–	–
10th	–	–

Umpires: B.L.Aldridge (*New Zealand*) (26) and S.G.Randell (51).

ENGLAND v PAKISTAN (FINAL)

At Melbourne Cricket Ground, Australia, on 25 March 1992.   Toss: Pakistan.
Result: **PAKISTAN** won by 22 runs.   Award: Wasim Akram.
LOI debuts: None.

PAKISTAN		Runs	Balls	4/6
Aamir Sohail	c Stewart b Pringle	4	19	–
Ramiz Raja	lbw b Pringle	8	26	1
*Imran Khan	c Illingworth b Botham	72	110	5/1
Javed Miandad	c Botham b Illingworth	58	98	4
Inzamam-ul-Haq	b Pringle	42	35	4
Wasim Akram	run out	33	19	4
Salim Malik	not out	0	1	–
Ijaz Ahmed				
†Moin Khan				
Mushtaq Ahmed				
Aqib Javed				
Extras	(lb 19, w 6, nb 7)	32		
Total	(50 overs; 6 wickets)	249		

ENGLAND		Runs	Balls	4/6
*G.A.Gooch	c Aqib b Mushtaq	29	66	1
I.T.Botham	c Moin b Wasim	0	6	–
†A.J.Stewart	c Moin b Aqib	7	16	1
G.A.Hick	lbw b Mushtaq	17	36	1
N.H.Fairbrother	c Moin b Aqib	62	70	3
A.J.Lamb	b Wasim	31	41	2
C.C.Lewis	b Wasim	0	1	–
D.A.Reeve	c Ramiz b Mushtaq	15	32	1
D.R.Pringle	not out	18	16	1
P.A.J.DeFreitas	run out	10	8	–
R.K.Illingworth	c Ramiz b Imran	14	11	2
Extras	(lb 5, w 13, nb 6)	24		
Total	(49.2 overs)	227		

ENGLAND	O	M	R	W
Pringle	10	2	22	3
Lewis	10	2	52	0
Botham	7	0	42	1
DeFreitas	10	1	42	0
Illingworth	10	0	50	1
Reeve	3	0	22	0

PAKISTAN	O	M	R	W
Wasim Akram	10	0	49	3
Aqib Javed	10	2	27	2
Mushtaq Ahmed	10	1	41	3
Ijaz Ahmed	3	0	13	0
Imran Khan	6.2	0	43	1
Aamir Sohail	10	0	49	0

FALL OF WICKETS		
Wkt	P	E
1st	20	6
2nd	24	21
3rd	163	59
4th	197	69
5th	249	141
6th	249	141
7th	–	180
8th	–	183
9th	–	208
10th	–	227

Umpires: B.L.Aldridge (*New Zealand*) (27) and S.A.Bucknor (*West Indies*) (12).

THE 1996 WORLD CUP

Sri Lanka, involved in the hosting of World Cup matches for the first time, and having never threatened to reach even the semi-final stage of the previous five World Cup tournaments, became the first host team to win the trophy. Without doubt their batting, the star attraction of the competition, revolutionized limited-overs strategy. Their all-out assaults during the first 15 overs, when the fielding restrictions were in force, was in direct contrast to the established format of a steady start gradually accelerating into a glorious slog in the final ten overs. Sanath Jayasuriya enthralled the vast crowds with his audacious strokeplay and he deservedly won the 'Most Valued Player of the Tournament' prize.

To include three Associate Members, Holland, Kenya and the United Arab Emirates (a motley assortment of very recent immigrants led by a lone denizen of that territory), the ICC laudably expanded the field to 12 teams. However, by introducing a quarter-final stage, the organisers relegated the month-long group stage to practice level. Inevitably it served only to eliminate the newest Test-playing country, Zimbabwe, and the three minnows.

FINAL GROUP TABLES

GROUP A	P	W	L	Pts	NRR	GROUP B	P	W	L	Pts	NRR
SRI LANKA	5	5	0	10	1.60	SOUTH AFRICA	5	5	0	10	2.04
AUSTRALIA	5	3	2	6	0.90	PAKISTAN	5	4	1	8	0.96
INDIA	5	3	2	6	0.45	NEW ZEALAND	5	3	2	6	0.55
WEST INDIES	5	2	3	4	-0.13	ENGLAND	5	2	3	4	0.08
Zimbabwe	5	1	4	2	-0.93	UA Emirates	5	1	4	2	-1.83
Kenya	5	1	4	2	-1.00	Holland	5	0	5	0	-1.92

Political turmoil in Sri Lanka caused Australia and West Indies to refuse to honour their fixtures there, the first cricket internationals to be awarded by default. Crowd disturbances were also a constant threat and it is sad that many will remember this tournament for the Calcutta riot which terminated the home team's semi-final against Sri Lanka.

South Africa dominated the group stage and looked clear favourites to win the Cup when they surprisingly came unstuck against an erratic West Indies side which had been humbled by Kenya. Their 19-run defeat was their first in 12 internationals and it threw the competition wide open. Sri Lanka easily saw off England and India to meet Australia, conquerors of New Zealand and West Indies. Arjuna Ranatunga defied history by putting Australia in to bat at Lahore after the five previous finals had been won by the side batting first. However, this was the first day/night international to be staged in Pakistan and Sri Lanka's captain wanted to avoid fielding under lights in the falling dew. Australia would have been disappointed to total only 241 after being 137-1 and an excellent unbeaten hundred by Aravinda de Silva carried his team to a memorable victory by seven wickets with 22 balls to spare.

This tournament produced more than its fair share of notable records. Sri Lanka savaged Kenya's bowling for a record 398 runs. By responding with a commendable 254-7, the Africans extended the match aggregate record to 652. Gary Kirsten of South Africa recorded the highest World Cup score (188*) and India's Sachin Tendulkar notched the record aggregate for a tournament (523 runs @ 87.16). Australia's Mark Waugh became the first to score hundreds in successive World Cup innings and shared with his twin, Steve, in the highest partnership for any wicket (207). Pakistan's remarkable former captain, Javed Miandad, became the only player to appear in all six World Cups.

ENGLAND v NEW ZEALAND

At Gujarat Stadium, Motera, Ahmedabad, India on 14 February 1996.   Toss: England.
Result: **NEW ZEALAND** won by 11 runs.   Award: N.J.Astle.
LOI debuts: None.

NEW ZEALAND		Runs	Balls	4/6
C.M.Spearman	c and b Cork	5	16	–
N.J.Astle	c Hick b Martin	101	132	8/2
S.P.Fleming	c Thorpe b Hick	28	47	3
R.G.Twose	c Thorpe b Hick	17	26	1
C.L.Cairns	c Cork b Illingworth	36	30	4/1
C.Z.Harris	run out	10	16	1
S.A.Thomson	not out	17	23	1
*†L.K.Germon	not out	13	12	–
G.R.Larsen				
D.J.Nash				
D.K.Morrison				
Extras	(b 4, lb 2, w 4, nb 2)	12		
Total	(50 overs; 6 wickets)	239		

ENGLAND		Runs	Balls	4/6
*M.A.Atherton	b Nash	1	3	–
A.J.Stewart	c and b Harris	34	72	3
G.A.Hick	run out	85	101	9
G.P.Thorpe	b Larsen	9	21	–
N.H.Fairbrother	b Morrison	36	46	1
†R.C.Russell	c Morrison b Larsen	2	9	–
C.White	c Cairns b Thomson	13	12	–/1
D.G.Cork	c Germon b Nash	19	11	2/1
D.Gough	not out	15	17	–
P.J.Martin	c Cairns b Nash	3	7	–
R.K.Illingworth	not out	3	4	–
Extras	(b 1, lb 4, w 1, nb 2)	8		
Total	(50 overs; 9 wickets)	228		

ENGLAND	O	M	R	W		FALL OF WICKETS		
Cork	10	1	36	1	Wkt	NZ	E	
Martin	6	0	37	1	1st	12	1	
Gough	10	0	63	0	2nd	108	100	
Illingworth	10	1	31	1	3rd	141	123	
Hick	9	0	45	2	4th	196	144	
White	5	0	21	0	5th	204	151	
NEW ZEALAND	O	M	R	W	6th	212	180	
Morrison	8	0	38	1	7th	–	185	
Nash	7	1	27	3	8th	–	210	
Cairns	4	0	24	0	9th	–	222	
Larsen	10	1	32	2	10th	–	–	
Thomson	10	0	51	1				
Harris	9	0	45	1				
Astle	2	0	6	0				

Umpires: B.C.Cooray (*Sri Lanka*) (17) and S.G.Randell (*Australia*) (67).
Referee: M.A.K.Pataudi (*India*).

SOUTH AFRICA v UNITED ARAB EMIRATES

At Rawalpindi Cricket Stadium, Pakistan on 15 (*no play*), 16 February 1996.
Toss: United Arab Emirates.
Result: **SOUTH AFRICA** won by 169 runs.　Award: G.Kirsten.
LOI debuts: UAE – S.F.Dukanwala, Mohammad Aslam, G.Mylvaganam, Shahzad Altaf.

SOUTH AFRICA		Runs	Balls	4/6
A.C.Hudson	b Samarasekera	27	33	5
G.Kirsten	not out	188	159	13/4
*W.J.Cronje	st Imtiaz b Zarawani	57	62	1/1
D.J.Cullinan	not out	41	51	2
J.H.Kallis				
J.N.Rhodes				
B.M.McMillan				
S.M.Pollock				
†S.J.Palframan				
C.R.Matthews				
A.A.Donald				
Extras	(b 1, lb 1, w 3, nb 3)	8		
Total	(50 overs; 2 wickets)	**321**		

UNITED ARAB EMIRATES		Runs	Balls	4/6
Azhar Saeed	c McMillan b Pollock	11	24	2
G.Mylvaganam	c Palframan b Donald	23	35	3
Mazhar Hussain	b Donald	14	42	–
V.Mehra	run out	2	11	–
Mohammad Aslam	b McMillan	9	9	1
Arshad Laiq	not out	43	79	4
J.A.Samarasekera	c Hudson b Donald	4	12	–
*Sultan M.Zarawani	c Cronje b McMillan	0	7	–
†Imtiaz Abbasi	c Palframan b McMillan	1	7	–
S.F.Dukanwala	not out	40	77	4
Shahzad Altaf				
Extras	(w 3, nb 2)	5		
Total	(50 overs; 8 wickets)	**152**		

UNITED ARAB EMIRATES	O	M	R	W
Samarasekera	9	2	39	1
Shahzad Altaf	3	0	22	0
Arshad Laiq	6	0	52	0
Dukanwala	10	0	64	0
Azhar Saeed	7	0	41	0
Zarawani	10	0	69	1
Mazhar Hussain	5	0	32	0

SOUTH AFRICA	O	M	R	W
Pollock	9	2	28	1
Matthews	10	0	39	0
Donald	10	0	21	3
Cronje	4	0	17	0
McMillan	8	1	11	3
Kallis	6	0	27	0
Kirsten	3	1	9	0

FALL OF WICKETS		
Wkt	SA	UAE
1st	60	24
2nd	176	42
3rd	–	46
4th	–	60
5th	–	62
6th	–	68
7th	–	70
8th		72
9th	–	–
10th	–	–

Umpires: S.A.Bucknor (*West Indies*) (26) and V.K.Ramaswamy (*India*) (30).
Referee: R.S.Madugalle (*Sri Lanka*).

WEST INDIES v ZIMBABWE

At Lal Bahadur Stadium, Hyderabad, India on 16 February 1996.   Toss: Zimbabwe.
Result: **WEST INDIES** won by 6 wickets.   Award: C.E.L.Ambrose.
LOI debuts: None.

ZIMBABWE		Runs	Balls	4/6
*†A.Flower	c Browne b Ambrose	3	4	–
G.W.Flower	c and b Gibson	31	54	6
G.J.Whittall	run out	14	62	–
A.D.R.Campbell	run out	0	8	–
A.C.Waller	st Browne b Harper	21	44	2
C.N.Evans	c Browne b Ambrose	21	31	2
S.G.Davies	run out	9	35	–
H.H.Streak	lbw b Walsh	7	18	–
P.A.Strang	not out	22	29	2
E.A.Brandes	c Chanderpaul b Ambrose	7	13	1
A.C.I.Lock	not out	1	4	–
Extras	(lb 10, w 4, nb 1)	15		
Total	(50 overs; 9 wickets)	**151**		

WEST INDIES		Runs	Balls	4/6
S.L.Campbell	b Strang	47	88	5
*R.B.Richardson	c Campbell b Strang	32	47	3
B.C.Lara	not out	43	31	5/2
S.Chanderpaul	b Strang	8	4	2
K.L.T.Arthurton	c Campbell b Strang	1	3	–
R.A.Harper	not out	5	6	1
†C.O.Browne				
O.D.Gibson				
I.R.Bishop				
C.E.L.Ambrose				
C.A.Walsh				
Extras	(b 5, lb 3, w 10, nb 1)	19		
Total	(29.3 overs; 4 wickets)	**155**		

WEST INDIES	O	M	R	W		FALL OF WICKETS		
Ambrose	10	2	28	3		Wkt	Z	WI
Walsh	10	3	27	1		1st	11	78
Gibson	9	1	27	1		2nd	53	115
Bishop	10	3	18	0		3rd	56	123
Harper	10	1	30	1		4th	59	136
Arthurton	1	0	11	0		5th	91	–
						6th	103	–
ZIMBABWE	O	M	R	W		7th	115	–
Streak	7	0	34	0		8th	125	–
Lock	6	0	23	0		9th	142	–
Brandes	7	0	42	0		10th	–	–
Whittall	2	0	8	0				
Strang	7.3	1	40	4				

Umpires: R.S.Dunne (*New Zealand*) (32) and S.Venkataraghavan (4).
Referee: R.Subba Row (*England*).

NEW ZEALAND v HOLLAND

At IPCL Sports Complex, Baroda, India on 17 February 1996.   Toss: New Zealand.
Result: **NEW ZEALAND** won by 129 runs.   Award: C.M.Spearman.
LOI debuts: Holland – All.

NEW ZEALAND		Runs	Balls	4/6
C.M.Spearman	c Zuiderent b Lubbers	68	59	8
N.J.Astle	run out	0	5	–
S.P.Fleming	c Zuiderent b Lubbers	66	79	4
R.G.Twose	st Schewe b Lubbers	25	32	1
C.L.Cairns	b Cantrell	52	38	4/2
A.C.Parore	c Clarke b Aponso	55	54	–/3
C.Z.Harris	c Schewe b Bakker	8	12	–
*†L.K.Germon	not out	14	11	1
D.N.Patel	c Schewe b Bakker	11	10	1
D.K.Morrison	not out	0	–	–
R.J.Kennedy				
Extras	(lb 7, w 1)	8		
Total	(50 overs; 8 wickets)	**307**		

HOLLAND		Runs	Balls	4/6
N.E.Clarke	b Kennedy	14	21	2
P.E.Cantrell	c Astle b Harris	45	86	5
G.J.A.F.Aponso	c Astle b Harris	11	31	2
*S.W.Lubbers	run out	5	19	–
R.P.Lefebvre	b Kennedy	45	64	4
T.B.M.de Leede	lbw b Harris	1	4	–
K-J.J.van Noortwijk	c Harris	36	55	3
†M.M.C.Schewe	st Germon b Fleming	12	16	1
B.Zuiderent	not out	1	6	–
P-J.Bakker				
E.L.Gouka				
Extras	(b 4, lb 4, w 8, nb 2)	18		
Total	(50 overs; 7 wickets)	**188**		

HOLLAND	O	M	R	W		FALL OF WICKETS		
Lefebvre	10	0	48	0		Wkt	NZ	H
Bakker	10	0	51	2		1st	1	18
De Leede	7	0	58	0		2nd	117	52
Aponso	10	0	60	1		3rd	155	65
Lubbers	9	0	48	3		4th	165	100
Cantrell	4	0	35	1		5th	253	102
						6th	279	147
NEW ZEALAND	O	M	R	W		7th	292	182
Morrison	4	1	11	0		8th	306	–
Kennedy	10	2	36	2		9th	–	–
Cairns	7	1	24	0		10th	–	–
Harris	10	1	24	3				
Patel	10	0	42	0				
Astle	5	0	19	0				
Fleming	2	0	8	1				
Twose	2	0	16	0				

Umpires: Khizer Hayat (*Pakistan*) (47) and I.D.Robinson (*Zimbabwe*) (26).
Referee: M.A.K.Pataudi (*India*).

SIXTH WORLD CUP (5th Match): SRI LANKA v AUSTRALIA
At R.Premadasa Stadium, Colombo, Sri Lanka on 17 February 1996.
SRI LANKA awarded match by default – Austalia failed to appear.

INDIA v KENYA

At Barabati Stadium, Cuttack, India on 18 February 1996.   Toss: India.
Result: **INDIA** won by 7 wickets.   Award: S.R.Tendulkar.
LOI debuts: Kenya – All.

KENYA		Runs	Balls	4/6
D.Chudasama	c Mongia b Prasad	29	49	5
†K.Otieno	c Mongia b Raju	27	60	3
S.O.Tikolo	c Kumble b Raju	65	80	4/1
*M.O.Odumbe	st Mongia b Kumble	26	52	–
H.S.Modi	c Jadeja b Kumble	2	4	–
T.Odoyo	c Prabhakar b Kumble	8	14	–
E.T.Odumbe	not out	15	22	–
Asif Karim	not out	6	13	–
D.L.Tikolo				
M.Suji				
R.Ali				
Extras	(b 2, lb 11, w 7, nb 1)	21		
Total	(50 overs; 6 wickets)	**199**		

INDIA		Runs	Balls	4/6
A.Jadeja	c Ali b Asif Karim	53	88	4/1
S.R.Tendulkar	not out	127	136	15/1
N.S.Sidhu	c Suji b S.O.Tikolo	1	11	–
V.G.Kambli	c D.L.Tikolo b M.O.Odumbe	2	11	–
†N.R.Mongia	not out	8	6	1
*M.Azharuddin				
M.Prabhakar				
J.Srinath				
A.Kumble				
B.K.V.Prasad				
S.L.V.Raju				
Extras	(lb 5, w 6, nb 1)	12		
Total	(41.5 overs; 3 wickets)	**203**		

INDIA	O	M	R	W		FALL OF WICKETS		
Prabhakar	5	1	19	0		Wkt	K	I
Srinath	10	0	38	0		1st	41	165
Prasad	10	0	41	1		2nd	65	167
Kumble	10	0	28	3		3rd	161	182
Raju	10	2	34	2		4th	161	–
Tendulkar	5	0	26	0		5th	165	–
						6th	184	–
KENYA	O	M	R	W		7th	–	–
Ali	5	0	25	0		8th	–	–
E.T.Odumbe	3	0	18	0		9th	–	–
Suji	5	0	20	0		10th	–	–
Odoyo	3	0	22	0				
Asif Karim	10	1	27	1				
D.L.Tikolo	3	0	21	0				
M.O.Odumbe	9.5	1	39	1				
S.O.Tikolo	3	0	26	1				

Umpires: K.T.Francis (*Sri Lanka*) (23) and D.R.Shepherd (*England*) (58).
Referee: C.H.Lloyd (*West Indies*).

ENGLAND v UNITED ARAB EMIRATES

At Shahi Bagh Stadium, Peshawar, Pakistan on 18 February 1996.
Toss: United Arab Emirates.
Result: **ENGLAND** won by 8 wickets.　Award: N.M.K.Smith.
LOI debuts: None.

UNITED ARAB EMIRATES		Runs	Balls	4/6
Azhar Saeed	lbw b DeFreitas	9	36	1
G.Mylvaganam	c Fairbrother b DeFreitas	0	6	–
Mazhar Hussain	b Smith	33	59	6
V.Mehra	c Russell b Smith	1	34	–
Mohammad Aslam	b Gough	23	47	1
Arshad Laiq	b Smith	0	6	–
Salim Raza	b Cork	10	31	–
J.A.Samarasekera	run out	29	39	3
*Sultan M.Zarawani	b Cork	2	8	–
S.F.Dukanwala	lbw b Illingworth	15	21	1
†Imtiaz Abbasi	not out	1	5	–
Extras	(b 4, lb 4, w 4, nb 1)	13		
Total	(48.3 overs)	**136**		

ENGLAND		Runs	Balls	4/6
A.J.Stewart	c Mylvaganam b Arshad	23	52	3
N.M.K.Smith	retired ill	27	31	4
G.P.Thorpe	not out	44	66	5
*M.A.Atherton	b Azhar	20	40	1
N.H.Fairbrother	not out	12	29	1
†R.C.Russell				
C.White				
D.G.Cork				
P.A.J.DeFreitas				
D.Gough				
R.K.Illingworth				
Extras	(b 4, lb 2, w 2, nb 6)	14		
Total	(35 overs; 2 wickets)	**140**		

ENGLAND	O	M	R	W		FALL OF WICKETS		
						Wkt	UAE	E
Cork	10	1	33	2		1st	3	52
DeFreitas	9.3	3	16	2		2nd	32	109
Gough	8	3	23	1		3rd	48	–
White	1.3	1	2	0		4th	49	–
Smith	9.3	2	29	3		5th	49	–
Illingworth	10	2	25	1		6th	80	–
						7th	88	–
UNITED ARAB	O	M	R	W		8th	100	–
EMIRATES						9th	135	–
Samarasekera	7	1	35	0		10th	136	–
Arshad Laiq	7	0	25	1				
Salim Raza	5	1	20	0				
Azhar Saeed	10	1	26	1				
Zarawani	6	0	28	0				

Umpires: B.C.Cooray (*Sri Lanka*) (18) and V.K.Ramaswamy (*India*) (31).
Referee: J.R.Reid (*New Zealand*).

SOUTH AFRICA v NEW ZEALAND

At Iqbal Stadium, Faisalabad, Pakistan on 20 February 1996.   Toss: New Zealand.
Result: **SOUTH AFRICA** won by 5 wickets.   Award: W.J.Cronje.
LOI debuts: None.

NEW ZEALAND		Runs	Balls	4/6
C.M.Spearman	c Palframan b Matthews	14	14	3
N.J.Astle	run out	1	4	–
S.P.Fleming	b McMillan	33	79	2
R.G.Twose	c McMillan b Pollock	13	17	2
C.L.Cairns	b Donald	9	20	2
A.C.Parore	run out	27	48	–
C.Z.Harris	run out	8	21	–
S.A.Thomson	c Cronje b Donald	29	55	4
*†L.K.Germon	not out	31	32	2
G.R.Larsen	c Cullinan b Donald	1	7	–
D.K.Morrison	not out	5	6	–
Extras	(lb 4, nb 2)	6		
Total	(50 overs; 9 wickets)	**177**		

SOUTH AFRICA		Runs	Balls	4/6
G.Kirsten	lbw b Harris	35	46	5
†S.J.Palframan	b Morrison	16	26	3
*W.J.Cronje	c Fleming b Astle	78	64	11/3
D.J.Cullinan	c Thomson b Astle	27	42	2
J.H.Kallis	not out	11	26	1
J.N.Rhodes	c and b Larsen	9	12	1
B.M.McMillan	not out	2	10	
S.M.Pollock				
P.L.Symcox				
C.R.Matthews				
A.A.Donald				
Extras		0		
Total	(37.3 overs; 5 wickets)	**178**		

SOUTH AFRICA	O	M	R	W		FALL OF WICKETS		
Pollock	10	1	45	1	Wkt	NZ	SA	
Matthews	10	2	30	1	1st	7	41	
Donald	10	0	34	3	2nd	17	87	
Cronje	3	0	13	0	3rd	36	146	
Symcox	10	1	25	0	4th	54	159	
McMillan	7	1	26	1	5th	85	170	
					6th	103	–	
NEW ZEALAND	O	M	R	W	7th	116	–	
Morrison	8	0	44	1	8th	158	–	
Cairns	6	0	24	0	9th	165	–	
Larsen	8	1	41	1	10th	–	–	
Harris	4	0	25	1				
Thomson	8.3	0	34	0				
Astle	3	1	10	2				

Umpires: S.G.Randell (*Australia*) (68) and S.Venkataraghavan (*India*) (5).
Referee: R.S.Madugalle (*Sri Lanka*).

SRI LANKA v ZIMBABWE

At Sinhalese Sports Club, Colombo, Sri Lanka on 21 February 1996.   Toss: Zimbabwe.
Result: **SRI LANKA** won by 6 wickets.   Award: P.A.de Silva.
LOI debuts: None.

ZIMBABWE		Runs	Balls	4/6
*†A.Flower	run out	8	17	1
G.W.Flower	run out	15	32	–
G.J.Whittall	c Jayasuriya b Muralitharan	35	64	5
A.D.R.Campbell	c Muralitharan b Vaas	75	102	7
A.C.Waller	b Jayasuriya	19	37	–/1
C.N.Evans	not out	39	35	5
H.H.Streak	c De Silva b Vaas	15	13	–
P.A.Strang	not out	0	1	–
A.C.I.Lock				
E.A.Brandes				
S.G.Peall				
Extras	(b 1, lb 16, w 4, nb 1)	22		
Total	(50 overs; 6 wickets)	**228**		

SRI LANKA		Runs	Balls	4/6
S.T.Jayasuriya	b Streak	6	11	1
†R.S.Kaluwitharana	c Peall b Streak	0	1	–
A.P.Gurusinha	run out	87	100	5/6
P.A.de Silva	lbw b Streak	91	86	10/2
*A.Ranatunga	not out	13	11	1
H.P.Tillekeratne	not out	7	16	1
R.S.Mahanama				
W.P.U.C.J.Vaas				
H.D.P.K.Dharmasena				
G.P.Wickremasinghe				
M.Muralitharan				
Extras	(lb 5, w 17, nb 3)	25		
Total	(37 overs; 4 wickets)	**229**		

SRI LANKA	O	M	R	W		FALL OF WICKETS		
Vaas	10	0	30	2		Wkt	Z	SL
Wickremasinghe	8	0	36	0		1st	19	5
Ranatunga	2	0	14	0		2nd	51	23
Muralitharan	10	0	37	1		3rd	92	195
Dharmasena	10	1	50	0		4th	160	209
Jayasuriya	10	0	44	1		5th	194	–
						6th	227	–
ZIMBABWE	O	M	R	W		7th	–	–
Streak	10	0	60	3		8th	–	–
Lock	4	0	17	0		9th	–	–
Brandes	8	0	35	0		10th	–	–
Peall	3	0	23	0				
Strang	5	0	43	0				
Whittall	2	0	20	0				
G.W.Flower	5	1	26	0				

Umpires: R.S.Dunne (*New Zealand*) (33) and Mahboob Shah (*Pakistan*) (27).
Referee: Nasim-ul-Ghani (*Pakistan*).

INDIA v WEST INDIES

At Roop Singh Stadium, Gwalior, India on 21 February 1996.   Toss: West Indies.
Result: **INDIA** won by 5 wickets.   Award: S.R.Tendulkar.
LOI debuts: None.

WEST INDIES		Runs	Balls	4/6
S.L.Campbell	b Srinath	5	14	1
*R.B.Richardson	c Kambli b Prabhakar	47	70	4
B.C.Lara	c Mongia b Srinath	2	5	–
S.Chanderpaul	c Azharuddin b Kapoor	38	66	6
R.I.C.Holder	b Kumble	0	3	–
R.A.Harper	b Kumble	23	42	1/1
†C.O.Browne	b Prabhakar	18	43	–
O.D.Gibson	b Kumble	6	5	–/1
I.R.Bishop	run out	9	26	–
C.E.L.Ambrose	c Kumble b Prabhakar	8	17	1
C.A.Walsh	not out	9	11	2
Extras	(lb 2, w 5, nb 1)	8		
Total	(41 overs)	**173**		

INDIA		Runs	Balls	4/6
A.Jadeja	b Ambrose	1	3	–
S.R.Tendulkar	run out	70	91	8
N.S.Sidhu	b Ambrose	1	5	–
*M.Azharuddin	c Walsh b Harper	32	59	4
V.G.Kambli	not out	33	48	4/1
M.Prabhakar	c and b Harper	1	12	–
†N.R.Mongia	not out	24	33	3
A.R.Kapoor				
A.Kumble				
J.Srinath				
B.K.V.Prasad				
Extras	(lb 3, w 1, nb 8)	12		
Total	(39.4 overs; 5 wickets)	**174**		

INDIA	O	M	R	W
Prabhakar	10	0	39	3
Srinath	10	0	22	2
Kumble	10	0	35	3
Prasad	10	0	34	0
Kapoor	10	2	41	1

WEST INDIES	O	M	R	W
Ambrose	8	1	41	2
Walsh	9	3	18	0
Bishop	5	0	28	0
Gibson	8.4	0	50	0
Harper	9	1	34	2

FALL OF WICKETS		
Wkt	WI	I
1st	16	2
2nd	24	15
3rd	91	94
4th	99	125
5th	99	127
6th	141	–
7th	141	–
8th	149	–
9th	162	–
10th	173	–

Umpires: Khizer Hayat (*Pakistan*) (48) and I.D.Robinson (*Zimbabwe*) (27).
Referee: R.Subba Row (*England*).

ENGLAND v HOLLAND

At Shahi Bagh Stadium, Peshawar, Pakistan on 22 February 1996.   Toss: England.
Result: **ENGLAND** won by 49 runs.   Award: G.A.Hick.
LOI debuts: Holland – F.Jansen.

ENGLAND		Runs	Balls	4/6
A.J.Stewart	b Bakker	5	13	–
N.M.K.Smith	c Clarke b Jansen	31	33	5
G.A.Hick	not out	104	133	6/2
G.P.Thorpe	lbw b Lefebvre	89	82	7/1
*M.A.Atherton	b Lubbers	10	10	–
N.H.Fairbrother	not out	24	29	1
†R.C.Russell				
D.G.Cork				
P.A.J.DeFreitas				
D.Gough				
P.J.Martin				
Extras	(lb 12, w 4)	16		
Total	(50 overs; 4 wickets)	**279**		

HOLLAND		Runs	Balls	4/6
N.E.Clarke	lbw b Cork	0	8	–
P.E.Cantrell	lbw b DeFreitas	28	44	4
T.B.M.de Leede	lbw b DeFreitas	41	42	7
*S.W.Lubbers	c Russell b DeFreitas	9	8	1
K-J.J.van Noortwijk	c Gough b Martin	64	82	3/2
B.Zuiderent	c Thorpe b Martin	54	93	2
R.P.Lefebvre	not out	11	14	–
†M.M.C.Schewe	not out	11	13	1
G.J.A.F.Aponso				
F.Jansen				
P-J.Bakker				
Extras	(lb 4, w 6, nb 2)	12		
Total	(50 overs; 6 wickets)	**230**		

HOLLAND	O	M	R	W
Lefebvre	10	1	40	1
Bakker	8	0	46	1
Jansen	7	0	40	1
Aponso	8	0	55	0
Lubbers	10	0	51	1
De Leede	2	0	9	0
Cantrell	5	0	26	0

ENGLAND	O	M	R	W
Cork	8	0	52	1
DeFreitas	10	3	31	3
Smith	8	0	27	0
Gough	3	0	23	0
Martin	10	1	42	2
Hick	5	0	23	0
Thorpe	6	0	28	0

FALL OF WICKETS		
Wkt	E	H
1st	11	1
2nd	42	46
3rd	185	70
4th	212	84
5th	–	195
6th	–	210
7th	–	–
8th	–	–
9th	–	–
10th	–	–

Umpires: S.A.Bucknor (*West Indies*) (27) and K.T.Francis (*Sri Lanka*) (24).
Referee: J.R.Reid (*New Zealand*).

AUSTRALIA v KENYA

At Indira Priyadarshani Stadium, Vishakhapatnam, India on 23 February 1996.
Toss: Kenya.
Result: **AUSTRALIA** won by 97 runs.   Award: M.E.Waugh.
LOI debuts: None.

AUSTRALIA		Runs	Balls	4/6
*M.A.Taylor	c Modi b Suji	6	20	–
M.E.Waugh	c Suji b Ali	130	130	14/1
R.T.Ponting	c Otieno b Ali	6	14	1
S.R.Waugh	c and b Suji	82	92	5/1
S.G.Law	run out	35	32	3
M.G.Bevan	b Ali	12	13	–
†I.A.Healy	c E.T.Odumbe b Asif Karim	17	11	2
P.R.Reiffel	not out	3	2	–
S.K.Warne	not out	0	2	–
C.J.McDermott				
G.D.McGrath				
Extras	(b 1, w 10, nb 2)	13		
Total	(50 overs; 7 wickets)	**304**		

KENYA		Runs	Balls	4/6
†K.Otieno	b McGrath	85	141	8/1
D.Chudasama	c Healy b McDermott	5	8	1
S.O.Tikolo	c Ponting b Reiffel	6	8	1
*M.O.Odumbe	c Reiffel b Bevan	50	53	7
H.S.Modi	b Bevan	10	21	1
E.T.Odumbe	c Bevan b Reiffel	14	34	–
D.L.Tikolo	not out	11	34	–
T.Odoyo	st Healy b Warne	10	6	2
M.Suji	not out	1	4	–
Asif Karim				
R.Ali				
Extras	(lb 7, w 6, nb 2)	15		
Total	(50 overs; 7 wickets)	**207**		

KENYA	O	M	R	W		FALL OF WICKETS		
Suji	10	1	55	2		Wkt	A	K
Ali	10	0	45	3		1st	10	12
Odoyo	8	0	58	0		2nd	26	30
E.T.Odumbe	4	0	21	0		3rd	233	132
Asif Karim	10	1	54	1		4th	237	167
M.O.Odumbe	4	0	35	0		5th	261	188
D.L.Tikolo	3	0	21	0		6th	301	195
S.O.Tikolo	1	0	14	0		7th	301	206
						8th	–	–
AUSTRALIA	O	M	R	W		9th	–	–
McDermott	3	0	12	1		10th	–	–
Reiffel	7	1	18	2				
McGrath	10	0	44	1				
S.R.Waugh	7	0	43	0				
Warne	10	0	25	1				
Bevan	8	0	35	2				
M.E.Waugh	5	0	23	0				

Umpires: C.J.Mitchley (*South Africa*) (24) and D.R.Shepherd (*England*) (59).
Referee: C.H.Lloyd (*West Indies*).

PAKISTAN v UNITED ARAB EMIRATES

At Municipal Stadium, Gujranwala, Pakistan on 24 February 1996.   Toss: Pakistan.
Result: **PAKISTAN** won by 9 wickets.   Award: Mushtaq Ahmed.
LOI debuts: None.

UNITED ARAB EMIRATES		Runs	Balls	4/6
G.Mylvaganam	b Mushtaq	13	50	1
Salim Raza	c Miandad b Aqib	22	20	2/1
Azhar Saeed	run out	1	13	–
Mazhar Hussain	c Waqar b Mushtaq	7	22	–
Mohammad Aslam	b Mushtaq	5	9	1
Mohammad Ishaq	b Wasim	12	20	1
Arshad Laiq	c Ijaz b Aqib	9	19	2
J.A.Samarasekera	b Waqar	10	21	–
S.F.Dukanwala	not out	21	19	1/1
*Sultan M.Zarawani	b Wasim	1	3	–
†Imtiaz Abbasi	not out	0	4	–
Extras	(lb 1, w 5, nb 2)	8		
Total	(33 overs; 9 wickets)	**109**		

PAKISTAN		Runs	Balls	4/6
Aamir Sohail	b Samarasekera	5	5	1
Saeed Anwar	not out	40	49	4
Ijaz Ahmed	not out	50	58	4/1
Inzamam-ul-Haq				
Javed Miandad				
Salim Malik				
*Wasim Akram				
†Rashid Latif				
Mushtaq Ahmed				
Aqib Javed				
Waqar Younis				
Extras	(lb 1, w 12, nb 4)	17		
Total	(18 overs; 1 wicket)	**112**		

PAKISTAN	O	M	R	W
Wasim Akram	7	1	25	2
Waqar Younis	7	1	33	1
Aqib Javed	6	0	18	2
Mushtaq Ahmed	7	0	16	3
Aamir Sohail	6	1	16	0
UNITED ARAB EMIRATES	O	M	R	W
Samarasekera	3	0	17	1
Arshad Laiq	4	0	24	0
Dukanwala	3	1	14	0
Salim Raza	3	0	17	0
Zarawani	3	0	23	0
Azhar Saeed	2	0	16	0

FALL OF WICKETS			
Wkt	UAE	P	
1st	27	7	
2nd	40	–	
3rd	47	–	
4th	53	–	
5th	54	–	
6th	70	–	
7th	80	–	
8th	108	–	
9th	109	–	
10th	–	–	

Umpires: B.C.Cooray (*Sri Lanka*) (19) and S.Venkataraghavan (*India*) (6).
Referee: R.S.Madugalle (*Sri Lanka*).

ENGLAND v SOUTH AFRICA

At Rawalpindi Cricket Stadium, Pakistan on 25 February 1996.   Toss: South Africa.
Result: **SOUTH AFRICA** won by 78 runs.   Award: J.N.Rhodes.
LOI debuts: None.

SOUTH AFRICA		Runs	Balls	4/6
G.Kirsten	run out	38	60	4
†S.J.Palframan	c Russell b Martin	28	36	3
*W.J.Cronje	c Russell b Gough	15	31	1
D.J.Cullinan	b DeFreitas	34	42	2
J.H.Kallis	c Russell b Cork	26	42	2
J.N.Rhodes	b Martin	37	32	3
B.M.McMillan	b Smith	11	17	–
S.M.Pollock	c Fairbrother b Cork	12	13	–
P.L.Symcox	c Thorpe b Martin	1	4	–
C.R.Matthews	not out	9	13	–
P.S.de Villiers	c Smith b Gough	12	11	1
Extras	(lb 1, w 5, nb 1)	7		
Total	(50 overs)	**230**		

ENGLAND		Runs	Balls	4/6
*M.A.Atherton	c Palframan b Pollock	0	4	–
N.M.K.Smith	b De Villiers	11	24	1
G.A.Hick	c McMillan b De Villiers	14	27	1
G.P.Thorpe	c Palframan b Symcox	46	69	3
A.J.Stewart	run out	7	29	–
N.H.Fairbrother	c Palframan b Symcox	3	10	–
†R.C.Russell	c Rhodes b Pollock	12	32	–
D.G.Cork	b Matthews	17	32	1
P.A.J.DeFreitas	run out	22	24	1/1
D.Gough	b Matthews	11	13	2
P.J.Martin	not out	1	3	–
Extras	(lb 7, w 1)	8		
Total	(44.3 overs)	**152**		

ENGLAND	O	M	R	W
Cork	10	0	36	2
DeFreitas	10	0	55	1
Gough	10	0	48	2
Martin	10	0	33	3
Smith	8	0	40	1
Thorpe	2	0	17	0

SOUTH AFRICA	O	M	R	W
Pollock	8	1	16	2
De Villiers	7	1	27	2
Matthews	9.3	0	30	2
McMillan	6	0	17	0
Symcox	10	0	38	2
Cronje	4	0	17	0

FALL OF WICKETS		
Wkt	SA	E
1st	56	0
2nd	85	22
3rd	88	33
4th	137	52
5th	163	62
6th	195	97
7th	199	97
8th	202	139
9th	213	141
10th	230	152

Umpires: S.G.Randell (*Australia*) (69) and I.D.Robinson (*Zimbabwe*) (28).
Referee: J.R.Reid (*New Zealand*).

SIXTH WORLD CUP (15th Match): SRI LANKA v WEST INDIES
At. R.Premadasa Stadium, Colombo, Sri Lanka on 26 February 1996.
SRI LANKA awarded match by default – West Indies failed to appear.

PAKISTAN v HOLLAND

At Gaddafi Stadium, Lahore, Pakistan on 26 February 1996.   Toss: Holland.
Result: **PAKISTAN** won by 8 wickets.   Award: Waqar Younis.
LOI debuts: None.

HOLLAND		Runs	Balls	4/6
N.E.Clarke	c Rashid b Aqib	4	27	–
P.E.Cantrell	c Ijaz b Waqar	17	33	1
T.B.M.de Leede	c Rashid b Waqar	0	18	–
K-J.J.van Noortwijk	c Mushtaq b Aqib	33	89	2/1
G.J.A.F.Aponso	b Waqar	58	106	3/1
*R.P.Lefebvre	b Waqar	10	26	–
B.Zuiderent	run out	6	6	1
E.L.Gouka	not out	0	1	–
†M.M.C.Schewe				
F.Jansen				
P-J.Bakker				
Extras	(lb 7, w 4, nb 6)	17		
Total	(50 overs; 7 wickets)	**145**		

PAKISTAN		Runs	Balls	4/6
Aamir Sohail	c Jansen b Lefebvre	9	24	1
Saeed Anwar	not out	83	93	9/3
Ijaz Ahmed	c Lefebvre b Cantrell	39	54	2/1
Inzamam-ul-Haq	not out	18	14	–/1
Javed Miandad				
Salim Malik				
*Wasim Akram				
†Rashid Latif				
Mushtaq Ahmed				
Aqib Javed				
Waqar Younis				
Extras	(lb 1, w 1)	2		
Total	(30.4 overs; 2 wickets)	**151**		

PAKISTAN	O	M	R	W
Wasim Akram	10	1	30	0
Waqar Younis	10	0	26	4
Aqib Javed	9	2	25	2
Mushtaq Ahmed	10	2	27	0
Aamir Sohail	9	0	21	0
Salim Malik	2	0	9	0

HOLLAND	O	M	R	W
Lefebvre	7	1	20	1
Bakker	7	1	13	0
Jansen	2	0	22	0
De Leede	4	0	20	0
Aponso	5	0	38	0
Cantrell	4	0	18	1
Gouka	1.4	0	19	0

FALL OF WICKETS		
Wkt	H	P
1st	16	10
2nd	28	104
3rd	29	–
4th	102	–
5th	130	–
6th	142	–
7th	145	–
8th	–	–
9th	–	–
10th	–	–

Umpires: S.A.Bucknor (*West Indies*) (28) and K.T.Francis (*Sri Lanka*) (25).
Referee: R.Subba Row (*England*).

ZIMBABWE v KENYA 1995-96

At Moin-ul-Haq Stadium, Patna, India on 26 February 1996.   Toss: Zimbabwe.
NO RESULT – match declared void‡ and replayed.
LOI debuts: Kenya – Tariq Ali.

ZIMBABWE		Runs	Balls	4/6
G.W.Flower	not out	25		
A.C.Waller	c E.T.Odumbe b Ali	3		
G.J.Whittall	c M.O.Odumbe b E.T.Odumbe	12		
A.D.R.Campbell	lbw b E.T.Odumbe	0		
*†A.Flower	not out	0		
C.N.Evans				
H.H.Streak				
P.A.Strang				
S.G.Peall				
B.C.Strang				
A.C.I.Lock				
Extras	(lb 2, w 3)	5		
Total	**(15.5 overs; 3 wickets)**	**45**		

KENYA
D.Chudasama
†Tariq Iqbal
K.Otieno
S.O.Tikolo
*M.O.Odumbe
H.S.Modi
E.T.Odumbe
T.Odoyo
Asif Karim
M.Suji
R.Ali

KENYA	O	M	R	W	FALL OF WICKETS	
Suji	5	1	11	0	Wkt	Z
Ali	5	0	14	1	1st	8
E.T.Odumbe	2.5	0	8	2	2nd	44
Odoyo	3	0	10	0	3rd	45
					4th	–
					5th	–
					6th	–
					7th	–
					8th	–
					9th	–
					10th	–

Umpires: Khizer Hayat (*Pakistan*) (49) and C.J.Mitchley (*South Africa*) (25).
Referee: M.A.K.Pataudi (*India*).

‡ An ICC committee subsequently ruled that such matches should count for records purposes.

ZIMBABWE v KENYA

At Moin-ul-Haq Stadium, Patna, India on 27 February 1996.   Toss: Zimbabwe.
Result: **ZIMBABWE** won by 5 wickets.   Award: P.A.Strang.
LOI debuts: None.

KENYA		Runs	Balls	4/6
D.Chudasama	run out	34	66	5
†Tariq Iqbal	b Lock	1	20	–
K.Otieno	b Peall	19	51	1
S.O.Tikolo	st A.Flower b B.C.Strang	0	6	–
*M.O.Odumbe	c B.C.Strang b P.A.Strang	30	64	1
H.S.Modi	b B.C.Strang	3	10	–
E.T.Odumbe	c Campbell b P.A.Strang	20	55	–
T.Odoyo	c G.W.Flower b P.A.Strang	0	2	–
Asif Karim	lbw b P.A.Strang	0	1	–
M.Suji	c G.W.Flower b P.A.Strang	15	24	1
R.Ali	not out	0	–	–
Extras	(lb 3, w 8, nb 1)	12		
Total	(49.4 overs)	**134**		

ZIMBABWE		Runs	Balls	4/6
A.C.Waller	c Tikolo b M.O.Odumbe	30	32	3
G.W.Flower	b Ali	45	112	4
A.D.R.Campbell	c Tikolo b M.O.Odumbe	6	26	1
G.J.Whittall	c E.T.Odumbe b Ali	6	36	1
*†A.Flower	lbw b Ali	5	8	1
C.N.Evans	not out	8	18	1
H.H.Streak	not out	15	27	1
P.A.Strang				
S.G.Peall				
B.C.Strang				
A.C.I.Lock				
Extras	(b 3, lb 4, w 12, nb 3)	22		
Total	(42.2 overs; 5 wickets)	**137**		

ZIMBABWE	O	M	R	W		FALL OF WICKETS		
Streak	7	2	23	0	Wkt	K	Z	
Lock	8	2	19	1	1st	7	59	
Whittall	5	0	21	0	2nd	60	79	
Peall	10	1	23	1	3rd	61	104	
B.C.Strang	10	0	24	2	4th	63	108	
P.A.Strang	9.4	1	21	5	5th	67	113	
					6th	109	–	
KENYA	O	M	R	W	7th	109	–	
Suji	9.2	0	37	0	8th	109	–	
Ali	8	1	22	3	9th	134	–	
E.T.Odumbe	2	0	14	0	10th	134	–	
Odoyo	2	0	7	0				
Asif Karim	10	1	21	0				
M.O.Odumbe	10	2	24	2				
Tikolo	1	0	5	0				

Umpires: Khizer Hayat (*Pakistan*) (50) and C.J.Mitchley (*South Africa*) (26).
Referee: M.A.K.Pataudi (*India*).

NEW ZEALAND v UNITED ARAB EMIRATES

At Iqbal Stadium, Faisalabad, Pakistan on 27 February 1996.
Toss: United Arab Emirates.
Result: **NEW ZEALAND** won by 109 runs. Award: R.G.Twose.
LOI debuts: None.

NEW ZEALAND

		Runs	Balls	4/6
C.M.Spearman	b Salim Raza	78	77	10
N.J.Astle	b Samarasekera	2	2	–
S.P.Fleming	c and b Dukanwala	16	11	4
R.G.Twose	c Mazhar b Azhar Saeed	92	112	8
C.L.Cairns	c Abbasi b Zarawani	6	11	–
A.C.Parore	c Azhar Saeed b Zarawani	15	18	–
S.A.Thomson	not out	31	36	2
*†L.K.Germon	b Azhar Saeed	3	6	–
D.J.Nash	lbw b Azhar Saeed	8	12	–
D.K.Morrison	not out	10	2	1/1
R.J.Kennedy				
Extras	(b 2, lb 12, nb 1)	15		
Total	(47 overs; 8 wickets)	**276**		

UNITED ARAB EMIRATES

		Runs	Balls	4/6
Azhar Saeed	c Fleming b Nash	5	22	–
Salim Raza	c Kennedy b Morrison	21	17	3/1
Mazhar Hussain	c Cairns b Thomson	29	54	5
V.Mehra	c Cairns b Thomson	12	31	1
Mohammad Ishaq	c Fleming b Kennedy	8	11	1
Mohammad Aslam	c Twose b Thomson	1	13	–
S.F.Dukanwala	c and b Cairns	8	18	–
Arshad Laiq	run out	14	37	2
J.A.Samarasekera	not out	47	59	7
*Sultan M.Zarawani	c Thomson b Nash	13	18	1
†Imtiaz Abbasi	not out	2	6	–
Extras	(lb 2, w 3, nb 2)	7		
Total	(47 overs; 9 wickets)	**167**		

UNITED ARAB EMIRATES	O	M	R	W
Samarasekera	6	0	30	1
Arshad Laiq	2	0	16	0
Dukanwala	10	0	46	1
Mazhar Hussain	3	0	28	0
Azhar Saeed	7	0	45	3
Salim Raza	9	0	48	1
Zarawani	10	0	49	2

NEW ZEALAND	O	M	R	W
Morrison	7	0	37	1
Nash	9	1	34	2
Cairns	10	2	31	1
Kennedy	6	0	20	1
Thomson	10	2	20	3
Astle	5	0	23	0

FALL OF WICKETS

Wkt	NZ	UAE
1st	11	23
2nd	42	29
3rd	162	65
4th	173	70
5th	210	81
6th	228	88
7th	239	92
8th	266	124
9th	–	162
10th	–	–

Umpires: B.C.Cooray (*Sri Lanka*) (20) and S.Venkataraghavan (*India*) (7).
Referee: R.S.Madugalle (*Sri Lanka*).

INDIA v AUSTRALIA

At Wankhede Stadium, Bombay, India on 27 February 1996.   Toss: Australia.
Result: **AUSTRALIA** won by 16 runs.   Award: M.E.Waugh.
LOI debuts: None.

AUSTRALIA		Runs	Balls	4/6
M.E.Waugh	run out	126	135	8/3
*M.A.Taylor	c Srinath b Raju	59	75	8/1
R.T.Ponting	c Manjrekar b Raju	12	21	–
S.R.Waugh	run out	7	15	–
S.G.Law	c and b Kumble	21	31	1
M.G.Bevan	run out	6	5	–
S.Lee	run out	9	10	–
†I.A.Healy	c Kumble b Prasad	6	9	–
S.K.Warne	c Azharuddin b Prasad	0	1	–
D.W.Fleming	run out	0	1	–
G.D.McGrath	not out	0	–	–
Extras	(lb 8, w 2, nb 2)	12		
Total	(50 overs)	**258**		

INDIA		Runs	Balls	4/6
A.Jadeja	lbw b Fleming	1	17	–
S.R.Tendulkar	st Healy b M.E.Waugh	90	88	14/1
V.G.Kambli	b Fleming	0	2	–
*M.Azharuddin	b Fleming	10	17	1
S.V.Manjrekar	c Healy b S.R.Waugh	62	93	7
M.Prabhakar	run out	3	6	–
†N.R.Mongia	c Taylor b Warne	27	32	3
A.Kumble	b Fleming	17	23	3
J.Srinath	c Lee b Fleming	7	12	1
B.K.V.Prasad	c Bevan b S.R.Waugh	0	3	–
S.L.V.Raju	not out	3	4	–
Extras	(b 5, lb 8, w 8, nb 1)	22		
Total	(48 overs)	**242**		

INDIA	O	M	R	W
Prabhakar	10	0	55	0
Srinath	10	1	51	0
Prasad	10	0	49	2
Kumble	10	1	47	1
Raju	10	0	48	2

AUSTRALIA	O	M	R	W
McGrath	8	3	48	0
Fleming	9	0	36	5
Warne	10	1	28	1
Lee	3	0	23	0
M.E.Waugh	10	0	44	1
Bevan	5	0	28	0
S.R.Waugh	3	0	22	2

FALL OF WICKETS		
Wkt	A	I
1st	103	7
2nd	140	7
3rd	157	70
4th	232	143
5th	237	147
6th	244	201
7th	258	205
8th	258	224
9th	258	231
10th	258	242

Umpires: R.S.Dunne (*New Zealand*) (34) and D.R.Shepherd (*England*) (60).
Referee: C.H.Lloyd (*West Indies*).

WEST INDIES v KENYA

At Nehru Stadium, Poona, India on 29 February 1996.   Toss: West Indies.
Result: **KENYA** won by 73 runs.   Award: M.O.Odumbe.
LOI debuts: None.

KENYA		Runs	Balls	4/6
D.Chudasama	c Lara b Walsh	8	7	2
†Tariq Iqbal	c Cuffy b Walsh	16	32	2
K.Otieno	c Adams b Walsh	2	5	–
S.O.Tikolo	c Adams b Harper	29	51	3/1
*M.O.Odumbe	hit wicket b Bishop	6	30	–
H.S.Modi	c Adams b Ambrose	28	74	1
M.Suji	c Lara b Harper	0	4	–
T.Odoyo	st Adams b Harper	24	59	3
E.T.Odumbe	b Cuffy	1	4	–
Asif Karim	c Adams b Ambrose	11	26	1
R.Ali	not out	6	19	–
Extras	(lb 8, w 14, nb 13)	35		
Total	(49.3 overs)	**166**		

WEST INDIES		Runs	Balls	4/6
S.L.Campbell	b Suji	4	21	1
*R.B.Richardson	b Ali	5	11	1
B.C.Lara	c Tariq Iqbal b Ali	8	11	1
S.Chanderpaul	c Tikolo b M.O.Odumbe	19	47	3
K.L.T.Arthurton	run out	0	6	–
†J.C.Adams	c Modi b M.O.Odumbe	9	37	–
R.A.Harper	c Tariq Iqbal b M.O.Odumbe	17	18	2
I.R.Bishop	not out	6	42	–
C.E.L.Ambrose	run out	3	13	–
C.A.Walsh	c Chudasama b Asif Karim	4	8	1
C.E.Cuffy	b Ali	1	8	–
Extras	(b 5, lb 6, w 4, nb 2)	17		
Total	(35.2 overs)	**93**		

WEST INDIES	O	M	R	W
Ambrose	8.3	3	21	2
Walsh	9	0	46	3
Bishop	10	2	30	1
Cuffy	8	0	31	1
Harper	10	4	15	3
Arthurton	4	0	15	0

KENYA	O	M	R	W
Suji	7	2	16	1
Ali	7.2	2	17	3
Asif Karim	8	1	19	1
M.O.Odumbe	10	3	15	3
Odoyo	3	0	15	0

FALL OF WICKETS		
Wkt	K	WI
1st	15	18
2nd	19	22
3rd	45	33
4th	72	35
5th	77	55
6th	81	65
7th	125	78
8th	126	83
9th	155	89
10th	166	93

Umpires: Khizer Hayat (*Pakistan*) (51) and V.K.Ramaswamy (32).
Referee: M.A.K.Pataudi (*India*).

PAKISTAN v SOUTH AFRICA

At National Stadium, Karachi, Pakistan on 29 February 1996.   Toss: Pakistan.
Result: **SOUTH AFRICA** won by 5 wickets.   Award: W.J.Cronje.
LOI debuts: None.

PAKISTAN		Runs	Balls	4/6
Aamir Sohail	c Cronje b Pollock	111	139	8
Saeed Anwar	c McMillan b Cronje	25	30	3
Ijaz Ahmed	lbw b Cronje	0	2	–
Inzamam-ul-Haq	run out	23	39	3
Salim Malik	c Palframan b Adams	40	66	3
*Wasim Akram	not out	32	25	3
†Rashid Latif	lbw b Matthews	0	1	–
Ramiz Raja	not out	2	2	–
Mushtaq Ahmed				
Saqlain Mushtaq				
Waqar Younis				
Extras	(b 1, lb 2, w 4, nb 2)	9		
Total	(50 overs; 6 wickets)	**242**		

SOUTH AFRICA		Runs	Balls	4/6
A.C.Hudson	b Waqar	33	26	6
G.Kirsten	b Saqlain	44	57	5
B.M.McMillan	lbw b Waqar	1	4	–
D.J.Cullinan	b Waqar	65	76	6
J.H.Kallis	c and b Saqlain	9	14	–
*W.J.Cronje	not out	45	72	2
S.M.Pollock	not out	20	27	1
†S.J.Palframan				
C.R.Matthews				
A.A.Donald				
P.R.Adams				
Extras	(b 8, lb 4, w 6, nb 8)	26		
Total	(44.2 overs; 5 wickets)	**243**		

SOUTH AFRICA	O	M	R	W
Pollock	9	0	49	1
Matthews	10	0	47	1
Cronje	5	0	20	2
Donald	8	0	50	0
Adams	10	0	42	1
McMillan	8	0	31	0

PAKISTAN	O	M	R	W
Wasim Akram	9.2	0	49	0
Waqar Younis	8	0	50	3
Mushtaq Ahmed	10	0	54	0
Aamir Sohail	6	0	35	0
Saqlain Mushtaq	10	1	38	2
Salim Malik	1	0	5	0

FALL OF WICKETS		
Wkt	P	SA
1st	52	51
2nd	52	53
3rd	112	111
4th	189	125
5th	233	203
6th	235	–
7th	–	–
8th	–	–
9th	–	–
10th	–	–

Umpires: S.A.Bucknor (*West Indies*) (29) and K.T.Francis (*Sri Lanka*) (26).
Referee: R.Subba Row (*England*).

AUSTRALIA v ZIMBABWE

At Vidarbha CA Ground, Nagpur, India on 1 March 1996.　Toss: Zimbabwe.
Result: **AUSTRALIA** won by 8 wickets.　Award: S.K.Warne.
LOI debuts: None.

ZIMBABWE		Runs	Balls	4/6
A.C.Waller	run out	67	102	10
G.W.Flower	b McGrath	4	16	–
G.J.Whittall	c and b S.R.Waugh	6	22	1
A.D.R.Campbell	c M.E.Waugh b S.R.Waugh	5	10	1
*†A.Flower	st Healy b Warne	7	15	1
C.N.Evans	c Healy b Warne	18	25	2/1
H.H.Streak	c S.R.Waugh b Fleming	13	42	–
P.A.Strang	not out	16	29	1
B.C.Strang	b Fleming	0	2	–
S.G.Peall	c Healy b Warne	0	4	–
A.C.I.Lock	b Warne	5	11	1
Extras	(lb 8, w 3, nb 2)	13		
Total	(45.3 overs)	**154**		

AUSTRALIA		Runs	Balls	4/6
*M.A.Taylor	c B.C.Strang b P.A.Strang	34	51	5
M.E.Waugh	not out	76	109	10
R.T.Ponting	c and b P.A.Strang	33	51	4
S.R.Waugh	not out	5	7	1
S.G.Law				
M.G.Bevan				
S.Lee				
†I.A.Healy				
S.K.Warne				
D.W.Fleming				
G.D.McGrath				
Extras	(b 6, lb 2, w 1, nb 1)	10		
Total	(36 overs; 2 wickets)	**158**		

AUSTRALIA	O	M	R	W		FALL OF WICKETS		
McGrath	8	2	12	1		Wkt	Z	A
Fleming	9	1	30	2		1st	21	92
Lee	4	2	8	0		2nd	41	150
S.R.Waugh	7	2	22	2		3rd	55	–
Warne	9.3	1	34	4		4th	68	–
M.E.Waugh	5	0	30	0		5th	106	–
Law	3	0	10	0		6th	126	–
						7th	140	–
ZIMBABWE	O	M	R	W		8th	140	–
Streak	10	3	29	0		9th	145	–
Lock	4	0	25	0		10th	154	–
B.C.Strang	3	0	20	0				
Whittall	2	0	11	0				
P.A.Strang	10	2	33	2				
Peall	4	0	20	0				
G.W.Flower	3	0	12	0				

Umpires: R.S.Dunne (*New Zealand*) (35) and D.R.Shepherd (*England*) (61).
Referee: C.H.Lloyd (*West Indies*).

HOLLAND v UNITED ARAB EMIRATES

At Gaddafi Stadium, Lahore, Pakistan on 1 March 1996.   Toss: United Arab Emirates.
Result: **UNITED ARAB EMIRATES** won by 7 wickets.
Awards: S.F.Dukanwala and Salim Raza.
LOI debuts: Holland – R.F.van Oosterom; UAE – Saeed-al-Saffar.

HOLLAND		Runs	Balls	4/6
N.E.Clarke	c Mehra b Shahzad	0	11	–
P.E.Cantrell	c Abbasi b Azhar Saeed	47	106	1
G.J.A.F.Aponso	c and b Dukanwala	45	80	7
T.B.M.de Leede	c and b Azhar Saeed	36	47	3
K-J.J.van Noortwijk	c Zarawani b Dukanwala	26	19	3
*S.W.Lubbers	c Saeed-al-Saffar b Zarawani	8	8	1
R.P.Lefebvre	c Ishaq b Dukanwala	12	9	–/1
B.Zuiderent	st Abbasi b Dukanwala	3	5	–
†M.M.C.Schewe	b Dukanwala	6	6	–
R.F.van Oosterom	not out	2	5	–
P-J.Bakker	not out	0	4	–
Extras	(b 5, lb 15, w 11)	31		
Total	(50 overs; 9 wickets)	**216**		

UNITED ARAB EMIRATES		Runs	Balls	4/6
Azhar Saeed	run out	32	82	3
Salim Raza	c Zuiderent b Lubbers	84	68	7/6
Mazhar Hussain	c Clarke b Lefebvre	16	15	3
V.Mehra	not out	29	48	2
Mohammad Ishaq	not out	51	53	8
J.A.Samarasekera				
S.F.Dukanwala				
*Sultan M.Zarawani				
Saeed-al-Saffar				
Imtiaz Abbasi				
†Shahzad Altaf				
Extras	(lb 7, w 1)	8		
Total	(44.2 overs; 3 wickets)	**220**		

UNITED ARAB EMIRATES	O	M	R	W		FALL OF WICKETS		
					Wkt	1st	H	UAE
Shahzad Altaf	10	3	15	1	1st	3	117
Samarasekera	9	1	35	0	2nd	77	135
Saeed-al-Saffar	3	0	25	0	3rd	148	138
Dukanwala	10	0	29	5	4th	153	–
Zarawani	8	0	40	1	5th	168	–
Salim Raza	5	0	23	0	6th	200	–
Azhar Saeed	5	0	29	2	7th	200	–
					8th	209	–
HOLLAND	O	M	R	W	9th	210	–
Bakker	8	0	41	0	10th	–	–
Lefebvre	8	0	24	1			
Lubbers	9	0	38	1			
Cantrell	8	0	30	0			
Aponso	7.2	0	47	0			
De Leede	4	0	33	0			

Umpires: Mahboob Shah (28) and S.G.Randell (*Australia*) (70).
Referee: Nasim-ul-Ghani (*Pakistan*).

INDIA v SRI LANKA

At Feroz Shah Kotla, Delhi, India on 2 March 1996.   Toss: Sri Lanka.
Result: **SRI LANKA** won by 6 wickets.   Award: S.T.Jayasuriya.
LOI debuts: None.

INDIA		Runs	Balls	4/6
M.Prabhakar	c Gurusinha b Pushpakumara	7	36	1
S.R.Tendulkar	run out	137	137	8/5
S.V.Manjrekar	c Kaluwitharana b Dharmasena	32	46	2/1
*M.Azharuddin	not out	72	80	4
V.G.Kambli	not out	1	1	–
A.Jadeja				
†N.R.Mongia				
J.Srinath				
A.Kumble				
S.A.Ankola				
B.K.V.Prasad				
Extras	(b 4, lb 7, w 11)	22		
Total	(50 overs; 3 wickets)	**271**		

SRI LANKA		Runs	Balls	4/6
S.T.Jayasuriya	c Prabhakar b Kumble	79	76	9/2
†R.S.Kaluwitharana	c Kumble b Prasad	26	16	6
A.P.Gurusinha	run out	25	27	2/1
P.A.de Silva	st Mongia b Kumble	8	14	1
*A.Ranatunga	not out	46	63	2
H.P.Tillekeratne	not out	70	98	6
R.S.Mahanama				
H.D.P.K.Dharmasena				
W.P.U.C.J.Vaas				
K.R.Pushpakumara				
M.Muralitharan				
Extras	(b 4, lb 9, w 2, nb 3)	18		
Total	(48.4 overs; 4 wickets)	**272**		

SRI LANKA	O	M	R	W		FALL OF WICKETS		
Vaas	9	3	37	0		Wkt	I	SL
Pushpakumara	8	0	53	1		1st	27	53
Muralitharan	10	1	42	0		2nd	93	129
Dharmasena	9	0	53	1		3rd	268	137
Jayasuriya	10	0	52	0		4th	–	141
Ranatunga	4	0	23	0		5th	–	–
						6th	–	–
INDIA	O	M	R	W		7th	–	–
Prabhakar	4	0	47	0		8th	–	–
Srinath	9.4	0	51	0		9th	–	–
Prasad	10	1	53	1		10th	–	–
Ankola	5	0	28	0				
Kumble	10	1	39	2				
Tendulkar	10	0	41	0				

Umpires: C.J.Mitchley (*South Africa*) (27) and I.D.Robinson (*Zimbabwe*) (29).
Referee: J.R.Reid (*New Zealand*).

PAKISTAN v ENGLAND

At National Stadium, Karachi, Pakistan on 3 March 1996.   Toss: England.
Result: **PAKISTAN** won by 7 wickets.   Award: Aamir Sohail.
LOI debuts: None.

ENGLAND		Runs	Balls	4/6
R.A.Smith	c Waqar b Salim	75	92	8/1
*M.A.Atherton	b Aamir	66	91	6
G.A.Hick	st Rashid b Aamir	1	2	–
G.P.Thorpe	not out	52	64	3
N.H.Fairbrother	c Wasim b Mushtaq	13	21	1
†R.C.Russell	c and b Mushtaq	4	7	–
D.A.Reeve	b Mushtaq	3	5	–
D.G.Cork	lbw b Waqar	0	2	–
D.Gough	b Wasim	14	15	1
P.J.Martin	run out	2	4	–
R.K.Illingworth	not out	1	1	–
Extras	(lb 11, w 4, nb 3)	18		
Total	(50 overs; 9 wickets)	249		

PAKISTAN		Runs	Balls	4/6
Aamir Sohail	c Thorpe b Illingworth	42	56	6
Saeed Anwar	c Russell b Cork	71	72	8
Ijaz Ahmed	c Russell b Cork	70	83	6
Inzamam-ul-Haq	not out	53	54	6
Javed Miandad	not out	11	21	1
Salim Malik				
*Wasim Akram				
†Rashid Latif				
Mushtaq Ahmed				
Waqar Younis				
Aqib Javed				
Extras	(lb 1, w 2)	3		
Total	(47.4 overs; 3 wickets)	250		

PAKISTAN	O	M	R	W	FALL OF WICKETS		
					Wkt	E	P
Wasim Akram	7	1	31	1	1st	147	81
Waqar Younis	10	1	45	1	2nd	151	139
Aqib Javed	7	0	34	0	3rd	156	214
Mushtaq Ahmed	10	0	53	3	4th	194	–
Aamir Sohail	10	0	48	2	5th	204	–
Salim Malik	6	1	27	1	6th	212	–
ENGLAND	O	M	R	W	7th	217	–
Cork	10	0	59	2	8th	241	–
Martin	9	0	45	0	9th	247	–
Gough	10	0	45	0	10th	–	–
Illingworth	10	0	46	1			
Reeve	6.4	0	37	0			
Hick	2	0	17	0			

Umpires: B.C.Cooray (*Sri Lanka*) (21) and S.Venkataraghavan (*India*) (8).
Referee: R.S.Madugalle (*Sri Lanka*).

AUSTRALIA v WEST INDIES

At Sawai Mansingh Stadium, Jaipur, India on 4 March 1996.　Toss: Australia.
Result: **WEST INDIES** won by 4 wickets.　Award: R.B.Richardson.
LOI debuts: None.

AUSTRALIA		Runs	Balls	4/6
M.E.Waugh	st Browne b Harper	30	62	1
*M.A.Taylor	c Browne b Walsh	9	38	–
R.T.Ponting	run out	102	112	5/1
S.R.Waugh	b Walsh	57	64	3/1
M.G.Bevan	run out	2	3	–
S.G.Law	not out	12	12	–
†I.A.Healy	run out	3	5	–
P.R.Reiffel	not out	4	6	–
S.K.Warne				
D.W.Fleming				
G.D.McGrath				
Extras	(lb 3, w 6, nb 1)	10		
Total	(50 overs; 6 wickets)	229		

WEST INDIES		Runs	Balls	4/6
S.L.Campbell	c Healy b Fleming	1	5	–
†C.O.Browne	run out	10	18	2
B.C.Lara	c McGrath b M.E.Waugh	60	70	7
*R.B.Richardson	not out	93	132	10/1
S.Chanderpaul	b M.E.Waugh	10	17	–
R.A.Harper	lbw b Reiffel	22	28	2
K.L.T.Arthurton	lbw b M.E.Waugh	0	3	–
J.C.Adams	not out	17	22	3
I.R.Bishop				
C.E.L.Ambrose				
C.A.Walsh				
Extras	(lb 12, w 5, nb 2)	19		
Total	(48.5 overs; 6 wickets)	232		

WEST INDIES	O	M	R	W		FALL OF WICKETS		
Ambrose	10	4	25	0		Wkt	A	WI
Walsh	9	2	35	2		1st	22	1
Bishop	9	0	52	0		2nd	84	26
Harper	10	0	46	1		3rd	194	113
Arthurton	9	0	53	0		4th	200	146
Adams	3	0	15	0		5th	216	194
						6th	224	196
AUSTRALIA	O	M	R	W		7th	–	–
Reiffel	10	3	45	1		8th	–	–
Fleming	7.5	1	44	1		9th	–	–
McGrath	9	0	46	0		10th	–	–
Warne	10	1	30	0				
M.E.Waugh	10	1	38	3				
Bevan	2	0	17	0				

Umpires: Mahboob Shah (*Pakistan*) (29) and D.R.Shepherd (*England*) (62).
Referee: R.Subba Row (*England*).

SOUTH AFRICA v HOLLAND

At Rawalpindi Cricket Stadium, Pakistan on 5 March 1996.   Toss: South Africa.
Result: **SOUTH AFRICA** won by 160 runs.   Award: A.C.Hudson.
LOI debuts: None.

SOUTH AFRICA		Runs	Balls	4/6
G.Kirsten	c Zuiderent b Aponso	83	98	6
A.C.Hudson	c Van Oosterom b Gouka	161	133	13/4
*W.J.Cronje	c Lubbers b Cantrell	41	38	3
D.J.Cullinan	not out	19	17	1
J.H.Kallis	not out	17	16	–
B.M.McMillan				
S.M.Pollock				
†S.J.Palframan				
P.L.Symcox				
C.R.Matthews				
A.A.Donald				
Extras	(lb 5, w 2)	7		
Total	(50 overs; 3 wickets)	**328**		

HOLLAND		Runs	Balls	4/6
N.E.Clarke	c Pollock b Donald	32	46	4/2
P.E.Cantrell	c and b Matthews	23	39	4
T.B.M.de Leede	b Donald	12	26	2
K-J.J.van Noortwijk	c Palframan b Symcox	9	24	1
G.J.A.F.Aponso	c Kirsten b Symcox	6	31	–
B.Zuiderent	run out	27	50	2
†M.M.C.Schewe	b Matthews	20	34	1
E.L.Gouka	c Kallis b Pollock	19	35	2
R.F.van Oosterom	not out	5	15	–
*S.W.Lubbers	not out	2	2	–
P-J.Bakker				
Extras	(lb 7, w 5, nb 1)	13		
Total	(50 overs; 8 wickets)	**168**		

HOLLAND	O	M	R	W
Bakker	10	1	64	0
Lubbers	8	0	50	0
De Leede	10	0	59	0
Aponso	10	0	57	1
Cantrell	10	0	61	1
Gouka	2	0	32	1

SOUTH AFRICA	O	M	R	W
Pollock	8	0	35	1
Matthews	10	0	38	2
Donald	6	0	21	2
Cronje	3	1	3	0
Symcox	10	2	22	2
McMillan	4	2	5	0
Kallis	7	1	30	0
Cullinan	2	0	7	0

FALL OF WICKETS		
Wkt	SA	H
1st	186	56
2nd	274	70
3rd	301	81
4th	–	86
5th	–	97
6th	–	126
7th	–	158
8th	–	163
9th	–	–
10th	–	–

Umpires: Khizer Hayat (52) and S.G.Randell (*Australia*) (71).
Referee: Nasim-ul-Ghani (*Pakistan*).

INDIA v ZIMBABWE

At Green Park, Kanpur, India on 6 March 1996.   Toss: Zimbabwe.
Result: **INDIA** won by 40 runs.   Award: A.Jadeja.
LOI debuts: None.

INDIA		Runs	Balls	4/6
S.R.Tendulkar	b Streak	3	12	–
N.S.Sidhu	c Streak b P.A.Strang	80	116	5
S.V.Manjrekar	c Campbell b Lock	2	18	–
*M.Azharuddin	c Campbell b B.C.Strang	2	10	–
V.G.Kambli	c G.W.Flower b Lock	106	110	11
A.Jadeja	not out	44	27	3/2
†N.R.Mongia	not out	6	9	–
A.Kumble				
J.Srinath				
B.K.V.Prasad				
S.L.V.Raju				
Extras	(lb 1, w 3)	4		
Total	(50 overs; 5 wickets)	**247**		

ZIMBABWE		Runs	Balls	4/6
A.C.Waller	c Tendulkar b Kumble	22	36	1
G.W.Flower	c Azharuddin b Raju	30	42	1
G.J.Whittall	run out	10	28	–
A.D.R.Campbell	c and b Jadeja	28	56	4
*†A.Flower	b Raju	28	40	1
C.N.Evans	c Srinath b Jadeja	6	6	1
H.H.Streak	lbw b Raju	30	38	3
P.A.Strang	b Srinath	14	22	1
B.C.Strang	lbw b Srinath	3	13	–
S.G.Peall	c Raju b Kumble	9	14	2
A.C.I.Lock	not out	2	4	–
Extras	(b 4, lb 9, w 11, nb 1)	25		
Total	(49.4 overs)	**207**		

ZIMBABWE	O	M	R	W
Streak	10	4	29	1
Lock	10	1	57	2
B.C.Strang	5	1	22	1
P.A.Strang	10	0	55	1
Peall	6	0	35	0
Whittall	3	0	19	0
G.W.Flower	3	1	16	0
Campbell	3	0	13	0

INDIA	O	M	R	W
Srinath	10	1	36	2
Prasad	7	0	40	0
Kumble	9.4	1	33	2
Raju	10	2	30	3
Tendulkar	6	0	23	0
Jadeja	7	0	32	2

FALL OF WICKETS		
Wkt	I	Z
1st	5	59
2nd	25	59
3rd	32	96
4th	174	99
5th	219	106
6th	–	165
7th	–	173
8th	–	193
9th	–	195
10th	–	207

Umpires: S.A.Bucknor (*West Indies*) (30) and C.J.Mitchley (*South Africa*) (28).
Referee: J.R.Reid (*New Zealand*).

SRI LANKA v KENYA

At Asgiriya Stadium, Kandy, Sri Lanka on 6 March 1996.   Toss: Kenya.
Result: **SRI LANKA** won by 144 runs.   Award: P.A.de Silva.
LOI debuts: Kenya – L.Onyango.

SRI LANKA		Runs	Balls	4/6
S.T.Jayasuriya	c D.L.Tikolo b E.T.Odumbe	44	27	5/3
†R.S.Kaluwitharana	b E.T.Odumbe	33	18	4/2
A.P.Gurusinha	c Onyango b Asif Karim	84	103	7/3
P.A.de Silva	c Modi b Suji	145	115	14/5
*A.Ranatunga	not out	75	40	13/1
H.P.Tillekeratne	run out	0	1	–
R.S.Mahanama	not out	0	–	–
W.P.U.C.J.Vaas				
H.D.P.K.Dharmasena				
K.R.Pushpakumara				
M.Muralitharan				
Extras	(lb 6, w 11)	17		
Total	(50 overs; 5 wickets)	**398**		

KENYA		Runs	Balls	4/6
D.Chudasama	b Muralitharan	27	23	5
†K.Otieno	b Vaas	14	28	1/1
S.O.Tikolo	b Dharmasena	96	95	8/4
*M.O.Odumbe	st Kaluwitharana b Muralitharan	0	2	–
H.S.Modi	run out	41	82	2
D.L.Tikolo	not out	25	40	2/1
E.T.Odumbe	c Muralitharan b Ranatunga	4	13	–
L.Onyango	c sub b Ranatunga	23	18	2/1
M.Suji	not out	2	4	–
Asif Karim				
R.Ali				
Extras	(b 1, lb 9, w 7, nb 5)	22		
Total	(50 overs; 7 wickets)	**254**		

KENYA	O	M	R	W		FALL OF WICKETS		
Suji	9	0	85	1	Wkt	SL	K	
Ali	6	0	67	0	1st	83	47	
Onyango	4	0	31	0	2nd	88	51	
E.T.Odumbe	5	0	34	2	3rd	272	51	
Asif Karim	10	0	50	1	4th	378	188	
D.L.Tikolo	2	0	13	0	5th	384	196	
M.O.Odumbe	9	0	74	0	6th	–	215	
S.O.Tikolo	5	0	38	0	7th	–	246	
					8th	–	–	
SRI LANKA	O	M	R	W	9th	–	–	
Vaas	10	0	44	1	10th	–	–	
Pushpakumara	7	0	46	0				
Muralitharan	10	1	40	2				
Dharmasena	10	0	45	1				
Jayasuriya	7	0	34	0				
Ranatunga	5	0	31	2				
Tillekeratne	1	0	4	0				

Umpires: R.S.Dunne (*New Zealand*) (36) and V.K.Ramaswamy (*India*) (33).
Referee: M.A.K.Pataudi (*India*).

PAKISTAN v NEW ZEALAND

At Gaddafi Stadium, Lahore, Pakistan on 6 March 1996.   Toss: New Zealand.
Result: **PAKISTAN** won by 46 runs.   Award: Salim Malik.
LOI debuts: None.

PAKISTAN		Runs	Balls	4/6
Aamir Sohail	c Thomson b Kennedy	50	62	10
Saeed Anwar	run out	62	67	6/1
Ijaz Ahmed	c Spearman b Cairns	26	46	–
Inzamam-ul-Haq	run out	39	41	4/1
Javed Miandad	run out	5	19	–
Salim Malik	not out	55	47	6
*Wasim Akram	not out	28	26	3
†Rashid Latif				
Waqar Younis				
Mushtaq Ahmed				
Aqib Javed				
Extras	(lb 5, w 5, nb 6)	16		
Total	(50 overs; 5 wickets)	281		

NEW ZEALAND		Runs	Balls	4/6
C.M.Spearman	c Rashid b Aqib	14	13	2
N.J.Astle	c Rashid b Waqar	6	17	1
*†L.K.Germon	c sub (Ata-ur-Rehman) b Mushtaq	41	67	1
S.P.Fleming	st Rashid b Salim	42	43	7
R.G.Twose	c Salim b Mushtaq	24	38	–
C.L.Cairns	c Rashid b Aamir	32	34	1/2
A.C.Parore	c Mushtaq b Salim	36	34	3
S.A.Thomson	c Rashid b Waqar	13	25	–
D.J.Nash	not out	5	13	–
R.J.Kennedy	b Aqib	2	3	–
D.K.Morrison	absent hurt			
Extras	(b 4, lb 9, w 6, nb 1)	20		
Total	(47.3 overs)	235		

NEW ZEALAND	O	M	R	W
Morrison	2	0	17	0
Nash	10	1	49	0
Cairns	10	1	53	1
Kennedy	5	0	32	1
Astle	9	0	50	0
Thomson	6	0	35	0
Twose	8	0	40	0

PAKISTAN	O	M	R	W
Waqar Younis	9	2	32	2
Aqib Javed	7.3	0	45	2
Mushtaq Ahmed	10	0	32	2
Salim Malik	7	0	41	2
Ijaz Ahmed	4	0	21	0
Aamir Sohail	10	0	51	1

FALL OF WICKETS		
Wkt	P	NZ
1st	70	23
2nd	139	23
3rd	155	83
4th	173	132
5th	200	132
6th	–	182
7th	–	221
8th	–	228
9th	–	235
10th	–	–

Umpires: K.T.Francis (*Sri Lanka*) (27) and I.D.Robinson (*Zimbabwe*) (30).
Referee: C.H.Lloyd (*West Indies*).

ENGLAND v SRI LANKA (QUARTER-FINAL)

At Iqbal Stadium, Faisalabad, Pakistan on 9 March 1996.   Toss: England.
Result: **SRI LANKA** won by 5 wickets.   Award: S.T.Jayasuriya.
LOI debuts: None.

ENGLAND		Runs	Balls	4/6
R.A.Smith	run out	25	41	3
*M.A.Atherton	c Kaluwitharana b Vaas	22	27	2
G.A.Hick	c Ranatunga b Muralitharan	8	21	–
G.P.Thorpe	b Dharmasena	14	31	1
P.A.J.DeFreitas	lbw b Jayasuriya	67	64	5/2
A.J.Stewart	b Muralitharan	17	38	–
†R.C.Russell	b Dharmasena	9	17	–
D.A.Reeve	b Jayasuriya	35	34	5
D.Gough	not out	26	26	2
P.J.Martin	not out	0	1	–
R.K.Illingworth				
Extras	(lb 8, w 4)	12		
Total	(50 overs; 8 wickets)	**235**		

SRI LANKA		Runs	Balls	4/6
S.T.Jayasuriya	st Russell b Reeve	82	44	13/3
†R.S.Kaluwitharana	b Illingworth	8	3	2
A.P.Gurusinha	run out	45	63	5
P.A.de Silva	c Smith b Hick	31	30	5
*A.Ranatunga	lbw b Gough	25	17	5
H.P.Tillekeratne	not out	19	50	1
R.S.Mahanama	not out	22	38	2
H.D.P.K.Dharmasena				
W.P.U.C.J.Vaas				
M.Muralitharan				
G.P.Wickremasinghe				
Extras	(lb 1, w 2, nb 1)	4		
Total	(40.4 overs; 5 wickets)	**236**		

SRI LANKA	O	M	R	W		FALL OF WICKETS	
Wickremasinghe	7	0	43	0	Wkt	E	SL
Vaas	8	1	29	1	1st	31	12
Muralitharan	10	1	37	2	2nd	58	113
Dharmasena	10	0	30	2	3rd	66	165
Jayasuriya	9	0	46	2	4th	94	194
De Silva	6	0	42	0	5th	145	198
					6th	171	–
ENGLAND	O	M	R	W	7th	173	–
Martin	9	0	41	0	8th	235	–
Illingworth	10	1	72	1	9th	–	–
Gough	10	1	36	1	10th	–	–
DeFreitas	3.4	0	38	0			
Reeve	4	1	14	1			
Hick	4	0	34	1			

Umpires: Mahboob Shah (30) and I.D.Robinson (*Zimbabwe*) (31).
Referee: Nasim-ul-Ghani (*Pakistan*).

INDIA v PAKISTAN (QUARTER-FINAL)

At Chinnaswamy Stadium, Bangalore, India on 9 March 1996.   Toss: India.
Result: **INDIA** won by 39 runs.   Award: N.S.Sidhu.
LOI debuts: None.

INDIA		Runs	Balls	4/6
N.S.Sidhu	b Mushtaq	93	115	11
S.R.Tendulkar	b Rehman	31	59	3
S.V.Manjrekar	c Miandad b Aamir Sohail	20	43	–
*M.Azharuddin	c Rashid b Waqar	27	23	1/1
V.G.Kambli	b Mushtaq	24	26	1
A.Jadeja	c Aamir b Waqar	45	26	4/2
†N.R.Mongia	run out	3	3	–
A.Kumble	c Miandad b Aqib	10	6	2
J.Srinath	not out	12	4	2
B.K.V.Prasad	not out	0	–	–
S.L.V.Raju				
Extras	(lb 3, w 15, nb 4)	22		
Total	(50 overs; 8 wickets)	**287**		

PAKISTAN		Runs	Balls	4/6
*Aamir Sohail	b Prasad	55	46	9/1
Saeed Anwar	c Kumble b Srinath	48	32	5/2
Ijaz Ahmed	c Srinath b Prasad	12	16	1
Inzamam-ul-Haq	c Mongia b Prasad	12	22	1
Salim Malik	lbw b Kumble	38	50	4
Javed Miandad	run out	38	68	2
†Rashid Latif	st Mongia b Raju	26	25	1/2
Mushtaq Ahmed	c and b Kumble	0	2	–
Waqar Younis	not out	4	19	–
Ata-ur-Rehman	lbw b Kumble	0	1	–
Aqib Javed	not out	6	10	–
Extras	(b 1, lb 3, w 5)	9		
Total	(49 overs; 9 wickets)	**248**		

PAKISTAN	O	M	R	W
Waqar Younis	10	1	67	2
Aqib Javed	10	0	67	1
Ata-ur-Rehman	10	0	40	1
Mushtaq Ahmed	10	0	56	2
Aamir Sohail	5	0	29	1
Salim Malik	5	0	25	0

INDIA	O	M	R	W
Srinath	9	0	61	1
Prasad	10	0	45	3
Kumble	10	0	48	3
Raju	10	0	46	1
Tendulkar	5	0	25	0
Jadeja	5	0	19	0

FALL OF WICKETS		
Wkt	I	P
1st	90	84
2nd	138	113
3rd	168	122
4th	200	132
5th	226	184
6th	236	231
7th	260	232
8th	279	239
9th	–	239
10th	–	–

Umpires: S.A.Bucknor (*West Indies*) (31) and D.R.Shepherd (*England*) (63).
Referee: R.Subba Row (*England*).

SOUTH AFRICA v WEST INDIES (QUARTER-FINAL)

At National Stadium, Karachi, Pakistan on 11 March 1996.   Toss: West Indies.
Result: **WEST INDIES** won by 19 runs.   Award: B.C.Lara.
LOI debuts: None.

WEST INDIES		Runs	Balls	4/6
S.Chanderpaul	c Cullinan b McMillan	56	93	4
†C.O.Browne	c Cullinan b Matthews	26	18	3
B.C.Lara	c Pollock b Symcox	111	94	16
*R.B.Richardson	c Hudson b Symcox	10	27	–
R.A.Harper	lbw b McMillan	9	15	1
R.I.C.Holder	run out	5	9	–
K.L.T.Arthurton	c Kirsten b Adams	1	5	–
J.C.Adams	not out	13	17	1
I.R.Bishop	b Adams	17	22	1/1
C.E.L.Ambrose	not out	0	1	–
C.A.Walsh				
Extras	(b 2, lb 11, w 2, nb 1)	16		
Total	(50 overs; 8 wickets)	**264**		

SOUTH AFRICA		Runs	Balls	4/6
A.C.Hudson	c Walsh b Adams	54	79	8
G.Kirsten	hit wicket b Ambrose	3	14	–
D.J.Cullinan	c Bishop b Adams	69	78	3/3
*W.J.Cronje	c Arthurton b Adams	40	47	2/2
J.N.Rhodes	c Adams b Harper	13	24	–
B.M.McMillan	lbw b Harper	6	7	–
†S.J.Palframan	c and b Harper	1	7	–
S.M.Pollock	c Adams b Harper	6	2	–
P.L.Symcox	c Harper b Arthurton	24	20	1/2
C.R.Matthews	not out	8	12	–
P.R.Adams	b Walsh	10	14	–
Extras	(b 1, lb 4, w 2, nb 4)	11		
Total	(49.3 overs)	**245**		

SOUTH AFRICA	O	M	R	W
Pollock	9	0	46	0
Matthews	10	0	42	1
Cronje	3	0	17	0
McMillan	10	1	37	2
Symcox	10	0	64	2
Adams	8	0	45	2

WEST INDIES	O	M	R	W
Ambrose	10	0	29	1
Walsh	8.3	1	51	1
Bishop	5	1	31	0
Harper	10	0	47	4
Adams	10	0	53	3
Arthurton	6	0	29	1

FALL OF WICKETS		
Wkt	WI	SA
1st	42	21
2nd	180	119
3rd	210	140
4th	214	186
5th	227	196
6th	230	196
7th	230	198
8th	254	227
9th	–	228
10th	–	245

Umpires: K.T.Francis (*Sri Lanka*) (28) and S.G.Randell (*Australia*) (72).
Referee: R.S.Madugalle (*Sri Lanka*).

AUSTRALIA v NEW ZEALAND (QUARTER-FINAL)

At M.A.Chidambaram Stadium, Madras, India on 11 March 1996.   Toss: New Zealand.
Result: **AUSTRALIA** won by 6 wickets.   Award: M.E.Waugh.
LOI debuts: None.

NEW ZEALAND		Runs	Balls	4/6
C.M.Spearman	c Healy b Reiffel	12	12	3
N.J.Astle	c Healy b Fleming	1	6	–
*†L.K.Germon	c Fleming b McGrath	89	96	9/1
S.P.Fleming	c S.R.Waugh b McGrath	8	18	1
C.Z.Harris	c Reiffel b Warne	130	124	13/4
R.G.Twose	b Bevan	4	12	–
C.L.Cairns	c Reiffel b M.E.Waugh	4	9	–
A.C.Parore	lbw b Warne	11	13	–
S.A.Thomson	run out	11	10	1
D.N.Patel	not out	3	4	–
D.J.Nash				
Extras	(lb 6, w 3, nb 4)	13		
Total	(50 overs; 9 wickets)	**286**		

AUSTRALIA		Runs	Balls	4/6
*M.A.Taylor	c Germon b Patel	10	24	1
M.E.Waugh	c Parore b Nash	110	112	6/2
R.T.Ponting	c sub (R.J.Kennedy) b Thomson	31	43	4
S.K.Warne	lbw b Astle	24	14	1/2
S.R.Waugh	not out	59	71	4
S.G.Law	not out	42	28	4/1
M.G.Bevan				
†I.A.Healy				
P.R.Reiffel				
D.W.Fleming				
G.D.McGrath				
Extras	(b 1, lb 6, w 3, nb 3)	13		
Total	(47.5 overs; 4 wickets)	**289**		

AUSTRALIA	O	M	R	W		FALL OF WICKETS		
Reiffel	4	0	38	1		Wkt	NZ	A
Fleming	5	1	20	1		1st	15	19
McGrath	9	2	50	2		2nd	16	84
M.E.Waugh	8	0	43	1		3rd	44	126
Warne	10	0	52	2		4th	212	213
Bevan	10	0	52	1		5th	227	–
S.R.Waugh	4	0	25	0		6th	240	–
						7th	259	–
NEW ZEALAND	O	M	R	W		8th	282	–
Nash	9	1	44	1		9th	286	–
Patel	8	0	45	1		10th	–	–
Cairns	6.5	0	51	0				
Harris	10	0	41	0				
Thomson	8	0	57	1				
Astle	3	0	21	1				
Twose	3	0	23	0				

Umpires: C.J.Mitchley (*South Africa*) (29) and S.Venkataraghavan (9).
Referee: M.A.K.Pataudi (*India*).

INDIA v SRI LANKA (SEMI-FINAL)

At Eden Gardens, Calcutta, India on 13 March 1996.   Toss: India.
Result: **SRI LANKA** won by default.   Award: P.A.de Silva.
LOI debuts: None.

SRI LANKA		Runs	Balls	4/6
S.T.Jayasuriya	c Prasad b Srinath	1	3	–
†R.S.Kaluwitharana	c Manjrekar b Srinath	0	1	–
A.P.Gurusinha	c Kumble b Srinath	1	16	–
P.A.de Silva	b Kumble	66	47	14
R.S.Mahanama	retired ill	58	101	6
*A.Ranatunga	lbw b Tendulkar	35	42	4
H.P.Tillekeratne	c Tendulkar b Prasad	32	43	2
H.D.P.K.Dharmasena	b Tendulkar	9	20	–
W.P.U.C.J.Vaas	run out	23	16	3
G.P.Wickremasinghe	not out	4	9	–
M.Muralitharan	not out	5	4	–
Extras	(b 1, lb 10, w 4, nb 2)	17		
Total	(50 overs; 8 wickets)	**251**		

INDIA		Runs	Balls	4/6
S.R.Tendulkar	st Kaluwitharana b Jayasuriya	65	88	9
N.S.Sidhu	c Jayasuriya b Vaas	3	8	–
S.V.Manjrekar	b Jayasuriya	25	48	1
*M.Azharuddin	c and b Dharmasena	0	6	–
V.G.Kambli	not out	10	29	–
J.Srinath	run out	6	6	1
A.Jadeja	b Jayasuriya	0	11	–
†N.R.Mongia	c Jayasuriya b De Silva	1	8	–
A.R.Kapoor	c De Silva b Muralitharan	0	1	–
A.Kumble	not out	0	–	–
B.K.V.Prasad				
Extras	(b 1, lb 4, w 5)	10		
Total	(34.1 overs; 8 wickets)	**120**		

INDIA	O	M	R	W
Srinath	7	1	34	3
Kumble	10	0	51	1
Prasad	8	0	50	1
Kapoor	10	0	40	0
Jadeja	5	0	31	0
Tendulkar	10	1	34	2

SRI LANKA	O	M	R	W
Wickremasinghe	5	0	24	0
Vaas	6	1	23	1
Muralitharan	7.1	0	29	1
Dharmasena	7	0	24	1
Jayasuriya	7	1	11	3
De Silva	2	1	4	1

FALL OF WICKETS		
Wkt	SL	I
1st	1	8
2nd	1	98
3rd	35	99
4th	85	101
5th	168	110
6th	206	115
7th	236	120
8th	244	120
9th	–	–
10th	–	–

Umpires: R.S.Dunne (*NZ*) (37) and C.J.Mitchley (*South Africa*) (30).
Referee: C.H.Lloyd (*West Indies*).

AUSTRALIA v WEST INDIES (SEMI-FINAL)

At Punjab CA Stadium, Mohali, Chandigarh, India on 14 March 1996.   Toss: Australia.
Result: **AUSTRALIA** won by 5 runs.   Award: S.K.Warne.
LOI debuts: None.

AUSTRALIA		Runs	Balls	4/6
M.E.Waugh	lbw b Ambrose	0	2	–
*M.A.Taylor	b Bishop	1	11	–
R.T.Ponting	lbw b Ambrose	0	15	–
S.R.Waugh	b Bishop	3	18	–
S.G.Law	run out	72	105	5
M.G.Bevan	c Richardson b Harper	69	110	4/1
†I.A.Healy	run out	31	28	2
P.R.Reiffel	run out	7	11	–
S.K.Warne	not out	6	6	–
D.W.Fleming				
G.D.McGrath				
Extras	(lb 11, w 5, nb 2)	18		
Total	(50 overs; 8 wickets)	**207**		

WEST INDIES		Runs	Balls	4/6
S.Chanderpaul	c Fleming b McGrath	80	126	7
†C.O.Browne	c and b Warne	10	18	–
B.C.Lara	b S.R.Waugh	45	45	5
*R.B.Richardson	not out	49	83	4
R.A.Harper	lbw b McGrath	2	5	–
O.D.Gibson	c Healy b Warne	1	2	–
J.C.Adams	lbw b Warne	2	11	–
K.L.T.Arthurton	c Healy b Fleming	0	4	–
I.R.Bishop	lbw b Warne	3	3	–
C.E.L.Ambrose	run out	2	2	–
C.A.Walsh	b Fleming	0	1	–
Extras	(lb 4, w 2, nb 2)	8		
Total	(49.3 overs)	**202**		

WEST INDIES	O	M	R	W
Ambrose	10	1	26	2
Bishop	10	1	35	2
Walsh	10	1	33	0
Gibson	2	0	13	0
Harper	9	0	47	1
Adams	9	0	42	0

AUSTRALIA	O	M	R	W
McGrath	10	2	30	2
Fleming	8.3	0	48	2
Warne	9	0	36	4
M.E.Waugh	4	0	16	0
S.R.Waugh	7	0	30	1
Reiffel	5	0	13	0
Bevan	4	1	12	0
Law	2	0	13	0

FALL OF WICKETS		
Wkt	A	WI
1st	0	25
2nd	7	93
3rd	8	165
4th	15	173
5th	153	178
6th	171	183
7th	186	187
8th	207	194
9th	–	202
10th	–	202

Umpires: B.C.Cooray (*Sri Lanka*) (22) and S.Venkataraghavan (10).
Referee: J.R.Reid (*New Zealand*).

AUSTRALIA v SRI LANKA (FINAL)

At Gaddafi Stadium, Lahore, Pakistan on 17 March 1996. Toss: Sri Lanka.
Result: **SRI LANKA** won by 7 wickets. Award: P.A.de Silva.
Tournament Award: S.T.Jayasuriya. LOI debuts: None.

AUSTRALIA		Runs	Balls	4/6
*M.A.Taylor	c Jayasuriya b De Silva	74	83	8/1
M.E.Waugh	c Jayasuriya b Vaas	12	15	1
R.T.Ponting	b De Silva	45	73	2
S.R.Waugh	c De Silva b Dharmasena	13	25	–
S.K.Warne	st Kaluwitharana b Muralitharan	2	5	–
S.G.Law	c De Silva b Jayasuriya	22	30	–/1
M.G.Bevan	not out	36	49	2
†I.A.Healy	b De Silva	2	3	–
P.R.Reiffel	not out	13	18	–
D.W.Fleming				
G.D.McGrath				
Extras	(lb 10, w 11, nb 1)	22		
Total	(50 overs; 7 wickets)	**241**		

SRI LANKA		Runs	Balls	4/6
S.T.Jayasuriya	run out	9	7	1
†R.S.Kaluwitharana	c Bevan b Fleming	6	13	–
A.P.Gurusinha	b Reiffel	65	99	6/1
P.A.de Silva	not out	107	124	13
*A.Ranatunga	not out	47	37	4/1
H.P.Tillekeratne				
R.S.Mahanama				
H.D.P.K.Dharmasena				
W.P.U.C.J.Vaas				
G.P.Wickremasinghe				
M.Muralitharan				
Extras	(b 1, lb 4, w 5, nb 1)	11		
Total	(46.2 overs; 3 wickets)	**245**		

SRI LANKA	O	M	R	W
Wickremasinghe	7	0	38	0
Vaas	6	1	30	1
Muralitharan	10	0	31	1
Dharmasena	10	0	47	1
Jayasuriya	8	0	43	1
De Silva	9	0	42	3

AUSTRALIA	O	M	R	W
McGrath	8.2	1	28	0
Fleming	6	0	43	1
Warne	10	0	58	0
Reiffel	10	0	49	1
M.E.Waugh	6	0	35	0
S.R.Waugh	3	0	15	0
Bevan	3	0	12	0

FALL OF WICKETS		
Wkt	A	SL
1st	36	12
2nd	137	23
3rd	152	148
4th	156	–
5th	170	–
6th	202	–
7th	205	–
8th	–	–
9th	–	–
10th	–	–

Umpires: S.A.Bucknor (*West Indies*) (32) and D.R.Shepherd (*England*) (64).
Referee: C.H.Lloyd (*West Indies*).

WORLD CUP RECORDS 1975 to 1995-96

RESULTS SUMMARY

	Played	Won	Lost	No Result	Semi-Finalist	Runner-Up	Winner
West Indies	38	25	12	1	1	1	2
England	40	25	14	1	2	3	–
Australia	37	22	15	–	–	2	1
Pakistan	37	21	15	1	3	–	1
New Zealand	35	19	16	–	3	–	–
India	36	18	17	1	2	–	1
South Africa	15	10	5	–	1	–	–
Sri Lanka	32	10	20	2	–	–	1
Zimbabwe	25	3	22	–	–	–	–
Kenya	5	1	4	–	–	–	–
UAE	5	1	4	–	–	–	–
Canada	3	–	3	–	–	–	–
East Africa	3	–	3	–	–	–	–
Holland	5	–	5	–	–	–	–

WORLD CUP FINALS

1975	WEST INDIES (291-8) beat Australia (274) by 17 runs	Lord's
1979	WEST INDIES (286-9) beat England (194) by 92 runs	Lord's
1983	INDIA (183) beat West Indies (140) by 43 runs	Lord's
1987-88	AUSTRALIA (253-5) beat England (246-8) by 7 runs	Calcutta
1991-92	PAKISTAN (249-6) beat England (227) by 22 runs	Melbourne
1995-96	SRI LANKA (245-3) beat Australia (241-7) by 7 wickets	Lahore

TEAM RECORDS

HIGHEST TOTAL

398-5	Sri Lanka v Kenya	Kandy	1995-96

HIGHEST TOTAL – BATTING SECOND

313-7	Sri Lanka v Zimbabwe	New Plymouth	1991-92

LOWEST TOTAL

45	Canada v England	Manchester	1979

HIGHEST MATCH AGGREGATE

652-12	Sri Lanka v Kenya	Kandy	1995-96

LARGEST MARGINS OF VICTORY

10wkts	India beat East Africa	Leeds	1975
10wkts	West Indies beat Zimbabwe	Birmingham	1983
10wkts	West Indies beat Pakistan	Melbourne	1991-92
202 runs	England beat India	Lord's	1975

NARROWEST MARGINS OF VICTORY

1wkt	West Indies beat Pakistan	Birmingham	1975
1wkt	Pakistan beat West Indies	Lahore	1987-88
1 run	Australia beat India	Madras	1987-88
1 run	Australia beat India	Brisbane	1991-92

INDIVIDUAL RECORDS – BATTING

MOST RUNS

		M	I	NO	HS	Runs	Avge	100
Javed Miandad	P	33	30	5	103	1083	43.32	1
I.V.A.Richards	WI	23	21	5	181	1013	63.31	3
G.A.Gooch	E	21	21	1	115	897	44.85	1
M.D.Crowe	NZ	21	21	5	100*	880	55.00	1
D.L.Haynes	WI	25	25	2	105	854	37.13	1
A.Ranatunga	SL	25	24	8	88*	835	52.18	–
D.C.Boon	A	16	16	1	100	815	54.33	2
S.R.Tendulkar	I	15	14	2	137	806	67.16	2

HIGHEST INDIVIDUAL SCORE

188*	G.Kirsten	South Africa v UAE	Rawalpindi	1995-96

HUNDRED BEFORE LUNCH

101	A.Turner	Australia v Sri Lanka	The Oval	1975

MOST HUNDREDS

3	I.V.A.Richards (West Indies), Ramiz Raja (Pakistan), M.E.Waugh (Australia)

HIGHEST PARTNERSHIP FOR EACH WICKET

1st	186	G.Kirsten/A.C.Hudson	SA v H	Rawalpindi	1995-96
2nd	176	D.L.Amiss/K.W.R.Fletcher	E v I	Lord's	1975
3rd	207	M.E.Waugh/S.R.Waugh	A v K	Vishakhapatnam	1995-96
4th	168	L.K.Germon/C.Z.Harris	NZ v A	Madras	1995-96
5th	145*	A.Flower/A.C.Waller	Z v SL	New Plymouth	1991-92
6th	144	Imran Khan/Shahid Mahboob	P v SL	Leeds	1983
7th	75*	D.A.G.Fletcher/I.P.Butchart	Z v A	Nottingham	1983
8th	117	D.L.Houghton/I.P.Butchart	Z v NZ	Hyderabad	1987-88
9th	126*	Kapil Dev/S.M.H.Kirmani	I v Z	Tunbridge Wells	1983
10th	71	A.M.E.Roberts/J.Garner	WI v I	Manchester	1983

INDIVIDUAL RECORDS – BOWLING

MOST WICKETS

		Balls	Runs	Wkts	Avge	Best	4w
Imran Khan	P	1017	655	34	19.26	4-37	2
I.T.Botham	E	1332	762	30	25.40	4-31	1
Kapil Dev	I	1422	892	28	31.85	5-43	1
Wasim Akram	P	1118	768	28	27.42	4-32	1
C.J.McDermott	A	894	599	27	22.18	5-44	2
Mushtaq Ahmed	P	810	549	26	21.11	3-16	–
A.M.E.Roberts	WI	1021	552	26	21.23	3-32	–

BEST ANALYSIS

7-51	W.W.Davis	West Indies v Australia	Leeds	1983

HAT-TRICK

(All bowled)	C.Sharma	India v New Zealand	Nagpur	1987-88

MOST ECONOMICAL BOWLING

12-8-6-1   B.S.Bedi   India v East Africa   Leeds   1975

MOST EXPENSIVE BOWLING

12-1-105-2   M.C.Snedden   New Zealand v England   The Oval   1983

INDIVIDUAL RECORDS – WICKET-KEEPING
MOST DISMISSALS

22	(18ct, 4st)	Wasim Bari	Pakistan
20	(19ct, 1st)	P.J.L.Dujon	West Indies
20	(17ct, 3st)	I.A.Healy	Australia
18	(17ct, 1st)	R.W.Marsh	Australia
18	(12ct, 6st)	K.S.More	India
16	(16ct)	D.L.Murray	West Indies
15	(14ct, 1st)	D.J.Richardson	South Africa

MOST DISMISSALS IN AN INNINGS

5(5ct)	S.M.H.Kirmani	India v Zimbabwe	Leicester	1983
5(4ct,1st)	J.C.Adams	West Indies v Kenya	Poona	1995-96
5(4ct,1st)	Rashid Latif	Pakistan v New Zealand	Lahore	1995-96

INDIVIDUAL RECORDS – FIELDING
MOST CATCHES

12	C.H.Lloyd	West Indies
12	Kapil Dev	India
12	D.L.Haynes	West Indies
11	C.L.Cairns	New Zealand
10	I.T.Botham	England
10	A.R.Border	Australia

MOST CATCHES IN AN INNINGS

3	C.H.Lloyd	West Indies v Sri Lanka	Manchester	1975
3	D.A.Reeve	England v Pakistan	Adelaide	1991-92
3	Ijaz Ahmed	Pakistan v Australia	Perth	1991-92
3	A.R.Border	Australia v Zimbabwe	Hobart	1991-92
3	C.L.Cairns	New Zealand v UAE	Faisalabad	1995-96

INDIVIDUAL RECORDS – GENERAL
MOST APPEARANCES

33 Javed Miandad (Pakistan)	25 A.R.Border (Australia)
28 Imran Khan (Pakistan)	D.L.Haynes (West Indies)
26 Kapil Dev (India)	A.Ranatunga (Sri Lanka)

ENGLAND

			Opponents	Venue	Tournament
HIGHEST TOTAL	334-4	(60 overs)	India	Lord's	1975
LOWEST TOTAL	93	(36.2 overs)	Australia	Leeds	1975

HUNDREDS (6)

137	D.L.Amiss	India	Lord's	1975
131	K.W.R.Fletcher	New Zealand	Nottingham	1975
130	D.I.Gower	Sri Lanka	Taunton	1983
115	G.A.Gooch	India	Bombay	1987-88
104*	G.A.Hick	Holland	Peshawar	1995-96
102	A.J.Lamb	New Zealand	The Oval	1983

RECORD WICKET PARTNERSHIPS

1st	158	B.Wood/D.L.Amiss	East Africa	Birmingham	1975
2nd	176	D.L.Amiss/K.W.R.Fletcher	India	Lord's	1975
3rd	143	G.A.Hick/G.P.Thorpe	Holland	Peshawar	1995-96
4th	115	A.J.Lamb/M.W.Gatting	New Zealand	The Oval	1983
5th	89*	M.H.Denness/C.M.Old	India	Lord's	1975
6th	98	D.I.Gower/I.J.Gould	Sri Lanka	Taunton	1983
7th	44*	I.J.Gould/G.R.Dilley	New Zealand	The Oval	1983
8th	62	D.A.Reeve/D.Gough	Sri Lanka	Faisalabad	1995-96
9th	43	R.W.Taylor/R.G.D.Willis	Pakistan	Leeds	1979
10th	20	G.G.Arnold/P.Lever	Australia	Leeds	1975

FOUR OR MORE WICKETS (11)

5-39	V.J.Marks	Sri Lanka	Taunton	1983
4-8	C.M.Old	Canada	Manchester	1979
4-11	J.A.Snow	East Africa	Birmingham	1975
4-11	R.G.D.Willis	Canada	Manchester	1979
4-15	M.Hendrick	Pakistan	Leeds	1979
4-30	C.C.Lewis	Sri Lanka	Ballarat	1991-92
4-31	I.T.Botham	Australia	Sydney	1991-92
4-42	R.G.D.Willis	New Zealand	Birmingham	1983
4-45	A.W.Greig	New Zealand	Nottingham	1975
4-45	G.R.Dilley	Sri Lanka	Taunton	1983
4-52	E.E.Hemmings	India	Bombay	1987-88

AUSTRALIA

			Opponents	Venue	Tournament
HIGHEST TOTAL	328-5	(60 overs)	Sri Lanka	The Oval	1975
LOWEST TOTAL	129	(38.2 overs)	India	Chelmsford	1983

HUNDREDS (10)

		Opponents	Venue	Tournament
130	M.E.Waugh	Kenya	Vishakhapatnam	1995-96
126*	G.R.Marsh	New Zealand	Chandigarh	1987-88
126	M.E.Waugh	India	Bombay	1995-96
110	T.M.Chappell	India	Nottingham	1983
110	G.R.Marsh	India	Madras	1987-88
110	M.E.Waugh	New Zealand	Madras	1995-96
102	R.T.Ponting	West Indies	Jaipur	1995-96
101	A.Turner	Sri Lanka	The Oval	1975
100	D.C.Boon	New Zealand	Auckland	1991-92
100	D.C.Boon	West Indies	Melbourne	1991-92

RECORD WICKET PARTNERSHIPS

			Opponents	Venue	Tournament
1st	182	R.B.McCosker/A.Turner	Sri Lanka	The Oval	1975
2nd	144	T.M.Chappell/K.J.Hughes	India	Nottingham	1983
3rd	207	M.E.Waugh/S.R.Waugh	Kenya	Vishakhapatnam	1995-96
4th	117	G.S.Chappell/K.D.Walters	Sri Lanka	The Oval	1975
5th	113	M.E.Waugh/S.R.Waugh	Zimbabwe	Hobart	1991-92
6th	99	R.Edwards/R.W.Marsh	West Indies	The Oval	1975
7th	55*	K.D.Walters/G.J.Gilmour	England	Leeds	1975
8th	50*	R.W.Marsh/R.M.Hogg	Zimbabwe	Nottingham	1983
9th	23*	G.R.Marsh/A.K.Zesers	New Zealand	Chandigarh	1987-88
10th	41	J.R.Thomson/D.K.Lillee	West Indies	Lord's	1975

FOUR OR MORE WICKETS (12)

		Opponents	Venue	Tournament
6-14	G.J.Gilmour	England	Leeds	1975
6-39	K.H.Macleay	India	Nottingham	1983
5-21	A.G.Hurst	Canada	Birmingham	1979
5-34	D.K.Lillee	Pakistan	Leeds	1975
5-36	D.W.Fleming	India	Bombay	1995-96
5-44	C.J.McDermott	Pakistan	Lahore	1987
5-48	G.J.Gilmour	West Indies	Lord's	1975
4-34	M.R.Whitney	West Indies	Melbourne	1991-92
4-34	S.K.Warne	Zimbabwe	Nagpur	1995-96
4-36	S.K.Warne	West Indies	Chandigarh	1995-96
4-39	S.P.O'Donnell	Zimbabwe	Madras	1987-88
4-56	C.J.McDermott	India	Madras	1987-88

SOUTH AFRICA

			Opponents	Venue	Tournament
HIGHEST TOTAL	328-3	(50 overs)	Holland	Rawalpindi	1995-96
LOWEST TOTAL	195	(50 overs)	Sri Lanka	Wellington	1991-92

HUNDREDS (2)

188*	G.Kirsten	UAE	Rawalpindi	1995-9
161	A.C.Hudson	Holland	Rawalpindi	1995-96

RECORD WICKET PARTNERSHIPS

1st	186	G.Kirsten/A.C.Hudson	Holland	Rawalpindi	1995-96
2nd	116	G.Kirsten/W.J.Cronje	UAE	Rawalpindi	1995-96
3rd	145*	G.Kirsten/D.J.Cullinan	UAE	Rawalpindi	1995-96
4th	79	P.N.Kirsten/D.J.Richardson	New Zealand	Auckland	1991-92
5th	78	D.J.Cullinan/W.J.Cronje	Pakistan	Karachi	1995-96
6th	71	W.J.Cronje/B.M.McMillan	Pakistan	Brisbane	1991-92
7th	41	P.N.Kirsten/B.M.McMillan	New Zealand	Auckland	1991-92
8th	29	S.M.Pollock/P.L.Symcox	West Indies	Karachi	1995-96
9th	21	B.M.McMillan/O.Henry	Sri Lanka	Wellington	1991-92
10th	17	C.R.Matthews/P.S.de Villiers	England	Rawalpindi	1995-96
	17	C.R.Matthews/P.R.Adams	West Indies	Karachi	1995-96

FOUR OR MORE WICKETS (1)

4-11	M.W.Pringle	West Indies	Christchurch	1991-92

WEST INDIES

			Opponents	Venue	Tournament
HIGHEST TOTAL	360-4	(50 overs)	Sri Lanka	Karachi	1987-88
LOWEST TOTAL	93	(35.2 overs)	Kenya	Poona	1995-96

HUNDREDS (10)

181	I.V.A.Richards	Sri Lanka	Karachi	1987-88
138*	I.V.A.Richards	England	Lord's	1979
119	I.V.A.Richards	India	The Oval	1983
111	B.C.Lara	South Africa	Karachi	1995-96
110	R.B.Richardson	Pakistan	Karachi	1987-88
110	P.V.Simmons	Sri Lanka	Berri	1991-92
106*	C.G.Greenidge	India	Birmingham	1979
105*	C.G.Greenidge	Zimbabwe	Worcester	1983
105	D.L.Haynes	Sri Lanka	Karachi	1987-88
102	C.H.Lloyd	Australia	Lord's	1975

RECORD WICKET PARTNERSHIPS

1st	175*	D.L.Haynes/B.C.Lara	Pakistan	Melbourne	1991-92
2nd	125	C.G.Greenidge/A.I.Kallicharran	New Zealand	The Oval	1975
3rd	195*	C.G.Greenidge/H.A.Gomes	Zimbabwe	Worcester	1983
4th	149	R.B.Kanhai/C.H.Lloyd	Australia	Lord's	1975
5th	139	I.V.A.Richards/C.L.King	England	Lord's	1979
6th	83*	K.L.T.Arthurton/C.L.Hooper	India	Wellington	1991-92
7th	52	K.D.Boyce/B.D.Julien	Australia	Lord's	1975
8th	40*	C.H.Lloyd/J.Garner	New Zealand	Nottingham	1979
9th	41	M.A.Holding/W.W.Daniel	Australia	Leeds	1983
10th	71	A.M.E.Roberts/J.Garner	India	Manchester	1983

Although the first wicket added 221* v Pakistan at Melbourne in 1991-92, this consisted of two partnerships: D.L.Haynes added 175* with B.C.Lara (retired hurt), and a further 46 with R.B.Richardson.

FOUR OR MORE WICKETS (9)

7-51	W.W.Davis	Australia	Leeds	1983
5-38	J.Garner	England	Lord's	1979
4-20	B.D.Julien	Sri Lanka	Manchester	1975
4-27	B.D.Julien	New Zealand	The Oval	1975
4-33	M.A.Holding	India	Birmingham	1979
4-33	A.C.Cummins	India	Wellington	1991-92
4-40	C.A.Walsh	Pakistan	Lahore	1987-88
4-47	R.A.Harper	South Africa	Karachi	1995-96
4-50	K.D.Boyce	Australia	Lord's	1975

NEW ZEALAND

			Opponents	Venue	Tournament
HIGHEST TOTAL	309-5	(60 overs)	East Africa	Birmingham	1975
LOWEST TOTAL	158	(52.2 overs)	West Indies	The Oval	1975

HUNDREDS (5)

171*	G.M.Turner	East Africa	Birmingham	1975
130	C.Z.Harris	Australia	Madras	1995-96
114*	G.M.Turner	India	Manchester	1975
101	N.J.Astle	England	Ahmedabad	1995-96
100*	M.D.Crowe	Australia	Auckland	1991-92

RECORD WICKET PARTNERSHIPS

1st	114	M.J.Greatbatch/R.T.Latham	South Africa	Auckland	1991-92
2nd	126*	G.M.Turner/G.P.Howarth	Sri Lanka	Nottingham	1979
3rd	149	G.M.Turner/J.M.Parker	East Africa	Birmingham	1975
4th	168	L.K.Germon/C.Z.Harris	Australia	Madras	1995-96
5th	71	G.P.Howarth/J.V.Coney	England	Birmingham	1983
6th	46	J.V.Coney/M.D.Crowe	Pakistan	Birmingham	1983
7th	70	J.V.Coney/R.J.Hadlee	England	Birmingham	1983
8th	48	B.J.McKechnie/D.R.Hadlee	England	Nottingham	1975
9th	59	W.K.Lees/J.G.Bracewell	Pakistan	Nottingham	1983
10th	65	M.C.Snedden/E.J.Chatfield	Sri Lanka	Derby	1983

FOUR OR MORE WICKETS (1)

5-25	R.J.Hadlee	Sri Lanka	Bristol	1983

INDIA

			Opponents	Venue	Tournament
HIGHEST TOTAL	289-6	(50 overs)	Australia	Delhi	1987-88
LOWEST TOTAL	158	(37.5 overs)	Australia	Nottingham	1983

HUNDREDS (5)

175*	Kapil Dev	Zimbabwe	Tunbridge Wells	1983
137	S.R.Tendulkar	Sri Lanka	Delhi	1995-96
127*	S.R.Tendulkar	Kenya	Cuttack	1995-96
106	V.G.Kambli	Zimbabwe	Kanpur	1995-96
103*	S.M.Gavaskar	New Zealand	Nagpur	1987-88

RECORD WICKET PARTNERSHIPS

1st	165	A.Jadeja/S.R.Tendulkar	Kenya	Cuttack	1995-96
2nd	127	M.Azharuddin/S.R.Tendulkar	New Zealand	Dunedin	1991-92
3rd	175	S.R.Tendulkar/M.Azharuddin	Sri Lanka	Delhi	1995-96
4th	142	N.S.Sidhu/V.G.Kambli	Zimbabwe	Kanpur	1995-96
5th	66	M.Azharuddin/S.V.Manjrekar	Australia	Brisbane	1991-92
6th	73	Yashpal Sharma/R.M.H.Binny	West Indies	Manchester	1983
7th	58	Kapil Dev/Madan Lal	Australia	Nottingham	1983
8th	82*	Kapil Dev/K.S.More	New Zealand	Bangalore	1987-88
9th	126*	Kapil Dev/S.M.H.Kirmani	Zimbabwe	Tunbridge Wells	1983
10th	27	S.Venkataraghavan/B.S.Bedi	West Indies	Birmingham	1979

Although the second wicket added 145 v New Zealand at Dunedin in 1991-92, this consisted of two partnerships: M.Azharuddin added 18 with A.Jadeja (retired hurt), and a further 127 with S.R.Tendulkar.

FOUR OR MORE WICKETS (4)

5-43	Kapil Dev	Australia	Nottingham	1983
4-19	M.Prabhakar	Zimbabwe	Bombay	1987-88
4-20	Madan Lal	Australia	Chelmsford	1983
4-29	R.M.H.Binny	Australia	Chelmsford	1983

PAKISTAN

		Opponents	Venue	Tournament
HIGHEST TOTAL 338-5	(60 overs)	Sri Lanka	Swansea	1983
LOWEST TOTAL 74	(40.2 overs)	England	Adelaide	1991-92

HUNDREDS (9)

119*	Ramiz Raja	New Zealand	Christchurch	1991-92
114	Aamir Sohail	Zimbabwe	Hobart	1991-92
113	Ramiz Raja	England	Karachi	1987-88
111	Aamir Sohail	South Africa	Karachi	1995-96
103*	Zaheer Abbas	New Zealand	Nottingham	1983
103	Javed Miandad	Sri Lanka	Hyderabad	1987-88
102*	Imran Khan	Sri Lanka	Leeds	1983
102*	Ramiz Raja	West Indies	Melbourne	1991-92
100	Salim Malik	Sri Lanka	Faisalabad	1987-88

RECORD WICKET PARTNERSHIPS

1st	159	Sadiq Mohammed/Majid Khan	Sri Lanka	Nottingham	1975
2nd	167	Ramiz Raja/Salim Malik	England	Karachi	1987-88
3rd	145	Aamir Sohail/Javed Miandad	Zimbabwe	Hobart	1991-92
4th	147*	Zaheer Abbas/Imran Khan	New Zealand	Nottingham	1983
5th	87	Javed Miandad/Asif Iqbal	Australia	Nottingham	1979
	87	Javed Miandad/Inzamam-ul-Haq	New Zealand	Auckland	1991-92
6th	144	Imran Khan/Shahid Mahboob	Sri Lanka	Leeds	1983
7th	52	Asif Iqbal/Wasim Raja	England	Leeds	1979
8th	36	Zaheer Abbas/Sarfraz Nawaz	England	Lord's	1983
9th	39*	Zaheer Abbas/Wasim Bari	England	Lord's	1983
10th	28	Abdul Qadir/Rashid Khan	New Zealand	Birmingham	1983

FOUR OR MORE WICKETS (9)

5-44	Abdul Qadir	Sri Lanka	Leeds	1983
4-21	Abdul Qadir	New Zealand	Birmingham	1983
4-26	Waqar Younis	Holland	Lahore	1995-96
4-31	Abdul Qadir	England	Rawalpindi	1987-88
4-32	Wasim Akram	New Zealand	Christchurch	1991-92
4-37	Imran Khan	West Indies	Lahore	1987-88
4-37	Imran Khan	England	Karachi	1987-88
4-44	Sarfraz Nawaz	West Indies	Birmingham	1975
4-56	Asif Iqbal	West Indies	The Oval	1979

SRI LANKA

			Opponents	Venue	Tournament
HIGHEST TOTAL	398-5	(50 overs)	Kenya	Kandy	1995-96
LOWEST TOTAL	86	(37.2 overs)	West Indies	Manchester	1975

HUNDREDS (2)

		Opponents	Venue	Tournament
145	P.A.de Silva	Kenya	Kandy	1995-96
107*	P.A.de Silva	Australia	Lahore	1995-96

RECORD WICKET PARTNERSHIPS

			Opponents	Venue	Tournament
1st	128	R.S.Mahanama/ M.A.R.Samarasekera	Zimbabwe	New Plymouth	1991-92
2nd	101	S.T.Jayasuriya/A.P.Gurusinha	England	Faisalabad	1995-96
3rd	184	A.P.Gurusinha/P.A.de Silva	Kenya	Kandy	1995-96
4th	106	P.A.de Silva/A.Ranatunga	Kenya	Kandy	1995-96
5th	131*	A.Ranatunga/H.P.Tillekeratne	India	Delhi	1995-96
6th	61	A.Ranatunga/H.P.Tillekeratne	Zimbabwe	New Plymouth	1991-92
7th	35	A.Ranatunga/R.S.Kalpage	Zimbabwe	New Plymouth	1991-92
8th	54	D.S.de Silva/R.G.de Alwis	Pakistan	Swansea	1983
	54	R.G.de Alwis/A.L.F.de Mel	England	Taunton	1983
9th	35	R.G.de Alwis/R.J.Ratnayake	England	Taunton	1983
10th	33	R.J.Ratnayake/V.B.John	England	Leeds	1983

FOUR OR MORE WICKETS (3)

		Opponents	Venue	Tournament
5-32	A.L.F.de Mel	New Zealand	Derby	1983
5-39	A.L.F.de Mel	Pakistan	Leeds	1983
4-57	U.C.Hathurusinghe	West Indies	Berri	1991-92

ZIMBABWE

			Opponents	Venue	Tournament
HIGHEST TOTAL	312-4	(50 overs)	Sri Lanka	New Plymouth	1991-92
LOWEST TOTAL	134	(46.1 overs)	England	Albury	1991-92

HUNDREDS (2)

142	D.L.Houghton	New Zealand	Hyderabad, India	1987-88
115*	A.Flower	Sri Lanka	New Plymouth	1991-92

RECORD WICKET PARTNERSHIPS

1st	79	A.H.Shah/A.Flower	India	Hamilton	1991-92
2nd	81	A.H.Shah/K.J.Arnott	New Zealand	Calcutta	1987-88
3rd	51	D.L.Houghton/A.J.Pycroft	New Zealand	Hyderabad, India	1987-88
4th	85	A.Flower/K.J.Arnott	Sri Lanka	New Plymouth	1991-92
5th	145*	A.Flower/A.C.Waller	Sri Lanka	New Plymouth	1991-92
6th	103	D.L.Houghton/K.M.Curran	Australia	Southampton	1983
7th	75*	D.A.G.Fletcher/I.P.Butchart	Australia	Nottingham	1983
8th	117	D.L.Houghton/I.P.Butchart	New Zealand	Hyderabad, India	1987-88
9th	55	K.M.Curran/P.W.E.Rawson	West Indies	Birmingham	1983
10th	36	A.J.Pycroft/M.P.Jarvis	India	Bombay	1987-88

FOUR OR MORE WICKETS (4)

5-21	P.A.Strang	Kenya	Patna	1995-96
4-21	E.A.Brandes	England	Albury	1991-92
4-40	P.A.Strang	West Indies	Hyderabad, India	1995-96
4-42	D.A.G.Fletcher	Australia	Nottingham	1983

KENYA

			Opponents	Venue	Tournament
HIGHEST TOTAL	254-7	(50 overs)	Sri Lanka	Kandy	1995-96
LOWEST TOTAL	134	(49.4 overs)	Zimbabwe	Patna	1995-96

HUNDREDS (0)

Highest Score

96		S.O.Tikolo	Sri Lanka	Kandy	1995-96

RECORD WICKET PARTNERSHIPS

1st	47	D.Chudasama/K.Otieno	Sri Lanka	Kandy	1995-96
2nd	53	D.Chudasama/K.Otieno	Zimbabwe	Patna	1995-96
3rd	102	K.Otieno/M.O.Odumbe	Australia	Vishakhapatnam	1995-96
4th	137	S.O.Tikolo/H.Modi	Sri Lanka	Kandy	1995-96
5th	21	M.O.Odumbe/E.T.Odumbe	Australia	Vishakhapatnam	1995-96
6th	42	M.O.Odumbe/E.T.Odumbe	Zimbabwe	Patna	1995-96
7th	44	H.Modi/T.Odoyo	West Indies	Poona	1995-96
8th	8*	D.L.Tikolo/M.Suji	Sri Lanka	Kandy	1995-96
9th	29	T.Odoyo/Asif Karim	West Indies	Poona	1995-96
10th	11	Asif Karim/R.Ali	West Indies	Poona	1995-96

FOUR OR MORE WICKETS (0)

Best Analysis

3-15	M.O.Odumbe	West Indies	Poona	1995-96

LIMITED-OVERS INTERNATIONALS
CAREER RECORDS

These records, complete until 14 February 1999, encompass players who have appeared in limited-overs internationals since 1 September 1997, England players currently registered for county cricket and any others included in provisional lists for the 1999 World Cup. Players chosen for those lists are shown in bold.

ENGLAND – BATTING AND FIELDING

	M	I	NO	HS	Runs	Avge	100	50	Ct/St
C.J.Adams	2	2	–	25	28	14.00	–	–	2
M.W.Alleyne	4	4	1	38*	76	25.33	–	–	–
M.A.Atherton	54	54	3	127	1791	35.11	2	12	15
I.D.Austin	4	3	1	11*	29	14.50	–	–	–
R.J.Bailey	4	4	2	43*	137	68.50	–	–	1
K.J.Barnett	1	1	–	84	84	84.00	–	1	–
J.E.Benjamin	2	1	–	0	0	0.00	–	–	–
M.P.Bicknell	7	6	2	31*	96	24.00	–	–	2
R.J.Blakey	3	2	–	25	25	12.50	–	–	2/1
A.D.Brown	13	13	–	118	333	25.61	1	1	6
D.R.Brown	9	8	4	21	99	24.75	–	–	1
A.R.Caddick	9	5	4	20*	35	35.00	–	–	2
D.G.Cork	25	15	2	31*	132	10.15	–	–	6
J.P.Crawley	13	12	1	73	235	21.36	–	2	1/1
R.D.B.Croft	40	28	11	32	274	16.11	–	–	9
P.A.J.DeFreitas	103	66	23	67	690	16.04	–	1	26
M.A.Ealham	30	22	1	45	380	18.09	–	–	3
N.H.Fairbrother	66	64	17	113	1918	40.80	1	15	32
M.V.Fleming	11	10	1	34	140	15.55	–	–	1
A.Flintoff	–								
A.R.C.Fraser	37	16	7	38*	122	13.55	–	–	2
A.F.Giles	5	3	2	10*	17	17.00	–	–	1
D.Gough	56	37	13	45	269	11.20	–	–	7
D.W.Headley	13	6	4	10*	22	11.00	–	–	3
G.A.Hick	87	86	9	126*	2990	38.83	5	19	40
A.J.Hollioake	31	28	6	83*	582	26.45	–	3	12
B.C.Hollioake	7	6	–	63	122	20.33	–	1	1
N.Hussain	28	28	5	93	549	23.86	–	2	14
R.K.Illingworth	25	11	5	14	68	11.33	–	–	8
R.C.Irani	10	10	2	45*	78	9.75	–	–	2
P.W.Jarvis	16	8	2	16*	31	5.16	–	–	1
N.V.Knight	40	40	3	125*	1498	40.48	3	8	14
C.C.Lewis	53	40	14	33	374	14.38	–	–	20
G.D.Lloyd	6	5	1	22	39	9.75	–	–	2
D.L.Maddy	2	1	–	1	1	1.00	–	–	–
D.E.Malcolm	10	5	2	4	9	3.00	–	–	1
P.J.Martin	20	13	7	6	38	6.33	–	–	1
M.P.Maynard	10	10	1	41	153	17.00	–	–	3
J.E.Morris	8	8	1	63*	167	23.85	–	1	2
A.D.Mullally	22	9	2	20	42	6.00	–	–	5
M.R.Ramprakash	13	13	3	51	265	26.50	–	1	6
S.J.Rhodes	9	8	2	56	107	17.83	–	1	9/2
R.T.Robinson	26	26	–	83	597	22.96	–	3	6
R.C.Russell	40	31	7	50	423	17.62	–	1	41/6
I.D.K.Salisbury	4	2	1	5	7	7.00	–	–	1
C.E.W.Silverwood	6	4	–	12	17	4.25	–	–	–

	M	I	NO	HS	Runs	Avge	100	50	Ct/St
G.C.Small	53	24	9	18*	98	6.53	–	–	7
N.M.K.Smith	7	6	1	31	100	20.00	–	–	1
R.A.Smith	71	70	8	167*	2419	39.01	4	15	26
A.J.Stewart	116	111	8	116	3211	31.17	2	18	101/11
J.P.Taylor	1	1	–	1	1	1.00	–	–	–
G.P.Thorpe	44	44	7	89	1482	40.05	–	14	23
P.C.R.Tufnell	20	10	9	5*	15	15.00	–	–	4
S.D.Udal	10	6	4	11*	35	17.50	–	–	1
S.L.Watkin	4	2	–	4	4	2.00	–	–	–
M.Watkinson	1	–	–	–	–	–	–	–	–
A.P.Wells	1	1	–	15	15	15.00	–	–	–
V.J.Wells	7	5	–	39	131	26.20	–	–	3
J.J.Whitaker	2	2	1	44*	48	48.00	–	–	1
C.White	15	13	–	38	187	14.38	–	–	2

ENGLAND – BOWLING

	O	R	W	Avge	Best	4wI
M.W.Alleyne	15	58	3	19.33	3-27	–
I.D.Austin	37.3	179	3	59.66	2-37	–
R.J.Bailey	6	25	0			
J.E.Benjamin	12	47	1	47.00	1-22	–
M.P.Bicknell	68.5	347	13	26.69	3-55	–
A.D.Brown	1	5	0			
D.R.Brown	54	305	7	43.57	2-28	–
A.R.Caddick	87	398	15	26.53	3-35	–
D.G.Cork	240	1071	35	30.60	3-27	–
R.D.B.Croft	351	1464	40	36.60	3-51	–
P.A.J.DeFreitas	952	3775	115	32.82	4-35	1
M.A.Ealham	245.2	1047	30	34.90	5-32	1
N.H.Fairbrother	1	9	0			
M.V.Fleming	87.1	434	17	25.52	4-45	1
A.R.C.Fraser	348.4	1245	42	29.64	4-22	1
A.F.Giles	38	197	5	39.40	2-37	–
D.Gough	519.2	2203	89	24.75	5-44	6
D.W.Headley	99	520	11	47.27	2-38	–
G.A.Hick	149.1	741	19	39.00	3-41	–
A.J.Hollioake	178.2	899	31	29.00	4-23	2
B.C.Hol[l]ioake	25	122	2	61.00	2-43	–
R.K.Illingworth	250.1	1059	30	35.30	3-33	–
R.C.Irani	54.5	246	4	61.50	1-23	–
P.W.Jarvis	146.3	672	24	28.00	5-35	2
C.C.Lewis	437.3	1942	66	29.42	4-30	4
D.E.Malcolm	87.4	404	16	25.25	3-40	–
P.J.Martin	174.4	806	27	29.85	4-44	1
A.D.Mullally	194.3	772	28	27.57	4-18	1
M.R.Ramprakash	2	14	0			
I.D.K.Salisbury	31	177	5	35.40	3-41	–
G.C.Small	465.3	1942	58	33.48	4-31	1
C.E.W.Silverwood	42	201	3	67.00	2-27	–
N.M.K.Smith	43.3	190	6	31.66	3-29	–
J.P.Taylor	3	20	0			
G.P.Thorpe	20	97	2	48.50	2-15	–
P.C.R.Tufnell	170	699	19	36.78	4-22	1
S.D.Udal	95	371	8	46.37	2-37	–
S.L.Watkin	36.5	193	7	27.57	4-49	1

ENGLAND – BOWLING (continued)

	O	R	W		Avge	Best	4wI
M.Watkinson	9	43	0				
V.J.Wells	**32.4**	**153**	**8**		**19.12**	**3-30**	**–**
C.White	101.2	445	15		29.66	4-37	1

AUSTRALIA – BATTING AND FIELDING

	M	I	NO	HS	Runs	Avge	100	50	Ct/St
M.G.Bevan	**97**	**86**	**33**	**108***	**3244**	**61.20**	**3**	**22**	**37**
A.J.Bichel	17	11	4	27*	99	14.14	–	–	2
G.S.Blewett	32	30	3	57*	550	20.37	–	2	7
A.C.Dale	**24**	**9**	**6**	**15***	**56**	**18.66**	**–**	**–**	**9**
M.J.Di Venuto	9	9	–	89	241	26.77	–	2	1
D.W.Fleming	**44**	**14**	**9**	**5***	**32**	**6.40**	**–**	**–**	**6**
A.C.Gilchrist	**51**	**49**	**4**	**154**	**1660**	**36.88**	**5**	**5**	**63/10**
J.N.Gillespie	**14**	**8**	**2**	**26**	**65**	**10.83**	**–**	**–**	**–**
I.J.Harvey	**11**	**9**	**2**	**43**	**101**	**14.42**	**–**	**–**	**6**
B.P.Julian	**18**	**12**	**–**	**25**	**129**	**10.75**	**–**	**–**	**7**
M.S.Kasprowicz	16	8	6	28*	60	30.00	–	–	3
S.G.Law	**54**	**51**	**5**	**110**	**1237**	**26.89**	**1**	**7**	**12**
S.Lee	**16**	**14**	**3**	**41**	**207**	**18.81**	**–**	**–**	**9**
D.S.Lehmann	**38**	**36**	**5**	**103**	**1102**	**35.54**	**1**	**7**	**7**
S.C.G.MacGill	–								
G.D.McGrath	**85**	**27**	**15**	**10**	**49**	**4.08**	**–**	**–**	**11**
J.P.Maher	2	2	–	13	21	10.50	–	–	–
D.R.Martyn	**31**	**28**	**6**	**59***	**572**	**26.00**	**–**	**3**	**7**
T.M.Moody	**58**	**52**	**5**	**89**	**1013**	**21.55**	**–**	**8**	**16**
R.T.Ponting	**68**	**68**	**8**	**145**	**2492**	**41.53**	**5**	**14**	**16**
P.R.Reiffel	**83**	**54**	**20**	**58**	**496**	**14.58**	**–**	**1**	**23**
G.R.Robertson	13	7	4	15	45	15.00	–	–	3
A.Symonds	1	–	–	–	–	–	–	–	–
S.K.Warne	**108**	**64**	**19**	**55**	**512**	**11.37**	**–**	**1**	**40**
M.E.Waugh	**174**	**169**	**13**	**130**	**6044**	**38.74**	**11**	**39**	**68**
S.R.Waugh	**251**	**228**	**44**	**102***	**5707**	**31.01**	**1**	**34**	**87**
P.Wilson	11	5	2	2	4	1.33	–	–	1
B.E.Young	**6**	**3**	**1**	**18**	**31**	**15.50**	**–**	**–**	**2**

AUSTRALIA – BOWLING

	O	R	W		Avge	Best	4wI
M.G.Bevan	**255.2**	**1266**	**30**		**42.20**	**3-36**	**–**
A.J.Bichel	148.2	701	21		33.38	3-17	–
G.S.Blewett	124.5	646	14		46.14	2- 6	–
A.C.Dale	**212**	**821**	**27**		**30.40**	**3-18**	**–**
D.W.Fleming	**387.4**	**1704**	**70**		**24.34**	**5-36**	**4**
J.N.Gillespie	**126.1**	**607**	**13**		**46.69**	**2-39**	**–**
I.J.Harvey	**69.3**	**325**	**7**		**46.42**	**3-17**	**–**
B.P.Julian	**144**	**733**	**21**		**34.90**	**3-40**	**–**
M.S.Kasprowicz	136.1	709	22		32.22	3-50	–
S.G.Law	**134.3**	**635**	**12**		**52.91**	**2-22**	**–**
S.Lee	**94.1**	**405**	**12**		**33.75**	**5-33**	**1**
D.S.Lehmann	**60**	**323**	**7**		**46.14**	**2-11**	**–**
G.D.McGrath	**768.1**	**3084**	**122**		**25.27**	**5-40**	**7**
D.R.Martyn	**19.4**	**107**	**1**		**107.00**	**1-30**	**–**
T.M.Moody	**336.1**	**1469**	**37**		**39.70**	**3-39**	**–**
R.T.Ponting	**14**	**62**	**1**		**62.00**	**1-41**	**–**
P.R.Reiffel	**711.4**	**2757**	**97**		**28.42**	**4-13**	**5**
G.R.Robertson	99.3	430	8		53.75	3-29	–

AUSTRALIA – BOWLING (continued)

	O	R	W	Avge	Best	4wI
A.Symonds	2	14	0			
S.K.Warne	1012.2	4235	169	25.05	5-33	10
M.E.Waugh	520.3	2499	80	31.23	5-24	2
S.R.Waugh	1404.5	6374	185	34.45	4-33	3
P.Wilson	93.4	450	13	34.61	3-39	–
B.E.Young	39	251	1	251.00	1-26	–

SOUTH AFRICA – BATTING AND FIELDING

	M	I	NO	HS	Runs	Avge	100	50	Ct/St
P.R.Adams	11	6	3	15*	25	8.33	–	–	1
A.M.Bacher	8	8	–	45	168	21.00	–	–	3
D.M.Benkenstein	7	7	3	69	188	47.00	–	1	1
N.Boje	13	7	2	28	62	12.40	–	–	5
M.V.Boucher	23	17	4	51	179	13.76	–	1	30/2
W.J.Cronje	152	142	24	112	4695	39.78	2	33	60
D.N.Crookes	24	17	4	54	243	18.69	–	1	16
D.J.Cullinan	107	104	12	124	3198	34.76	3	20	45
A.C.Dawson	1	–	–	–	–	–	–	–	–
P.S.de Villiers	83	36	15	20*	170	8.09	–	–	15
A.A.Donald	108	26	11	12	73	4.86	–	–	14
S.Elworthy	11	2	1	14*	14	14.00	–	–	4
H.H.Gibbs	22	22	–	125	485	22.04	1	–	11
A.J.Hall	1	1	1	9*	9	–	–	–	1
M.Haywood	1	–	–	–	–	–	–	–	–
A.C.Hudson	89	88	1	161	2559	29.41	2	18	17
J.H.Kallis	58	57	10	113*	1804	38.38	3	10	23
G.Kirsten	96	96	9	188*	3600	41.37	8	20	32/1
L.Klusener	46	38	7	99	1093	35.25	–	8	10
G.F.J.Liebenberg	4	4	–	39	94	23.50	–	–	–
B.M.McMillan	78	52	16	127	840	23.33	1	–	42
V.P.Mpitsang	1	1	1	1*	1	–	–	–	–
M.Ntini	1	–	–	–	–	–	–	–	1
S.M.Pollock	63	48	17	75	960	30.96	–	4	14
N.Pothas	–								
J.N.Rhodes	146	135	28	121	3532	33.00	1	16	70
D.J.Richardson	122	77	33	53	868	19.72	–	1	149/16
M.J.R.Rindel	22	22	1	106	575	27.38	1	2	8
P.L.Symcox	77	53	13	61	694	17.35	–	3	22
R.Telemachus	5	1	1	1*	1	–	–	–	–
H.S.Williams	1	1	1	1*	1	–	–	–	–

SOUTH AFRICA – BOWLING

	O	R	W	Avge	Best	4wI
P.R.Adams	83	377	14	26.92	3-26	–
N.Boje	106.4	461	16	28.81	3-33	–
W.J.Cronje	774.2	3347	98	34.15	5-32	2
D.N.Crookes	143.5	688	15	45.86	3-30	–
D.J.Cullinan	28	120	5	24.00	2-30	–
A.C.Dawson	9	51	1	51.00	1-51	–
P.S.de Villiers	737	2635	95	27.73	4-27	2
A.A.Donald	959	3896	182	21.40	6-23	9
S.Elworthy	76.4	397	16	24.81	3-21	–
A.J.Hall	7	38	0			
M.Haywood	4	35	0			
A.C.Hudson	1	3	0			

SOUTH AFRICA – BOWLING (continued)

	O	R	W	Avge	Best	4wl
J.H.Kallis	234.1	1125	37	30.40	5-30	1
G.Kirsten	5	23	0			
L.Klusener	369.4	1835	65	28.23	6-49	4
B.M.McMillan	603.5	2590	70	37.00	4-32	1
V.P.Mpitsang	7	49	2	24.50	2-49	–
M.Ntini	10	31	2	15.50	2-31	–
S.M.Pollock	561.4	2184	92	23.73	6-35	4
M.J.R.Rindel	45	242	6	40.33	2-15	–
P.L.Symcox	640	2622	72	36.41	4-28	1
R.Telemachus	43.4	174	12	14.50	4-43	1
H.S.Williams	8	55	0			

WEST INDIES – BATTING AND FIELDING

	M	I	NO	HS	Runs	Avge	100	50	Ct/St
J.C.Adams	74	57	20	81*	1038	28.05	–	7	48/5
C.E.L.Ambrose	157	86	34	31*	588	11.30	–	–	41
K.L.T.Arthurton	98	88	19	84	1871	27.11	–	9	27
I.R.Bishop	84	44	19	33*	405	16.20	–	–	12
H.R.Bryan	–								
S.L.Campbell	38	38	–	86	841	22.13	–	3	10
S.Chanderpaul	61	57	3	150	1909	35.35	2	12	19
M.Dillon	11	2	2	5*	5	–	–	–	1
D.Ganga	2	2	–	1	1	0.50	–	–	1
R.I.C.Holder	37	31	6	65	599	23.96	–	2	8
C.L.Hooper	177	161	36	113*	4500	36.00	6	25	85
R.D.Jacobs	18	14	3	28*	103	9.36	–	–	18/6
D.R.E.Joseph	–								
R.D.King	9	7	6	7*	26	26.00	–	–	2
C.B.Lambert	11	11	–	119	368	33.45	1	2	–
B.C.Lara	137	135	13	169	5579	45.72	12	37	63
R.N.Lewis	16	12	3	49	157	17.44	–	–	5
N.C.McGarrell	5	3	1	19	25	12.50	–	–	4
N.A.M.McLean	16	11	–	23	69	6.27	–	–	4
J.R.Murray	55	36	6	86	678	22.60	–	5	46/7
S.Ragoonath	–								
F.L.Reifer	2	2	–	22	31	15.50	–	–	1
F.A.Rose	13	11	2	24	83	9.22	–	–	2
K.F.Semple	7	6	–	23	64	10.66	–	–	3
P.V.Simmons	133	130	10	122	3532	29.43	5	18	53
C.M.Tuckett	1	–	–						
P.A.Wallace	26	26	–	103	554	21.30	1	2	8
C.A.Walsh	185	68	29	30	292	7.48	–	–	27
D.Williams	36	23	7	32*	147	9.18	–	–	35/10
L.R.Williams	6	4	–	14	21	5.25	–	–	5
S.C.Williams	46	46	4	105*	1501	35.73	1	12	11

WEST INDIES – BOWLING

	O	R	W	Avge	Best	4wl
J.C.Adams	139	669	22	30.40	5-37	1
C.E.L.Ambrose	1391.5	4939	210	23.51	5-17	10
K.L.T.Arthurton	197.4	990	40	24.75	4-31	3
I.R.Bishop	722	3127	118	26.50	5-25	9
S.Chanderpaul	89.4	469	12	39.08	3-18	–
M.Dillon	90.5	464	12	38.66	3-32	–
C.L.Hooper	1223.1	5321	160	33.25	4-34	3

WEST INDIES – BOWLING (continued)

	O	R	W	Avge	Best	4wI
R.D.King	82	320	9	35.55	3-40	–
C.B.Lambert	2	8	0			
B.C.Lara	5	34	2	17.00	2- 5	–
R.N.Lewis	119.1	614	12	51.16	2-40	–
N.C.McGarrell	34	211	3	70.33	2-43	–
N.A.M.McLean	117.5	590	16	36.87	3-41	–
F.A.Rose	101	517	10	51.70	3-25	–
K.F.Semple	22	121	3	40.33	2-35	–
P.V.Simmons	584.1	2606	74	35.21	4- 3	2
C.M.Tuckett	8	41	2	20.50	2-41	–
C.A.Walsh	1628.4	6312	204	30.94	5- 1	6
L.R.Williams	33.5	173	8	21.62	3-16	–
S.C.Williams	4	30	1	30.00	1-30	–

NEW ZEALAND – BATTING AND FIELDING

	M	I	NO	HS	Runs	Avge	100	50	Ct/St
G.I.Allott	6	4	2	7*	14	7.00	–	–	3
N.J.Astle	75	75	2	120	2512	34.41	5	16	27
M.D.Bailey	1	–	–	–	–	–	–	–	–
M.D.Bell	2	2	–	16	18	9.00	–	–	–
C.E.Bulfin	–								
C.L.Cairns	100	92	6	115	2335	27.15	2	12	31
S.B.Doull	38	25	12	22	166	12.76	–	–	9
C.J.Drum	1	–	–	–	–	–	–	–	1
S.P.Fleming	96	94	9	116*	2799	32.92	3	16	43
C.Z.Harris	120	106	34	130	2198	30.52	1	9	45
M.N.Hart	11	6	–	16	49	8.16	–	–	7
M.J.Horne	29	28	–	61	542	19.35	–	3	8
L.G.Howell	12	12	–	68	287	23.91	–	4	2
G.R.Larsen	106	63	24	37	572	14.66	–	–	21
C.D.McMillan	36	34	1	86	884	26.78	–	5	11
D.J.Nash	51	34	9	40*	382	15.28	–	–	17
S.B.O'Connor	23	8	4	8	21	5.25	–	–	7
A.C.Parore	107	101	17	108	2500	29.76	1	13	61/15
M.W.Priest	18	14	4	24	103	10.30	–	–	2
C.M.Spearman	31	31	–	78	531	17.12	–	2	8
A.R.Tait	2	2	1	10*	17	17.00	–	–	–
R.G.Twose	30	29	1	92	745	26.60	–	5	7
D.L.Vettori	31	19	8	25*	159	14.45	–	–	10
P.J.Wiseman	6	2	1	16	23	23.00	–	–	1
B.A.Young	73	72	5	74	1644	24.53	–	9	28

NEW ZEALAND – BOWLING

	O	R	W	Avge	Best	4wI
G.I.Allott	41.2	222	9	24.66	3-54	–
N.J.Astle	375.4	1666	50	33.32	4-43	1
C.L.Cairns	661.3	3031	93	32.59	5-42	3
S.B.Doull	266.5	1336	34	39.29	4-25	1
C.J.Drum	6	46	0			
S.P.Fleming	4.5	28	1	28.00	1- 8	–
C.Z.Harris	944.1	4005	117	34.23	5-42	2
M.N.Hart	91.2	347	13	26.69	5-22	1
G.R.Larsen	934.2	3525	103	34.22	4-24	1
C.D.McMillan	94.5	462	16	28.87	2-17	–
D.J.Nash	369.5	1734	44	39.40	4-38	1

LOI **NEW ZEALAND – BOWLING (continued)**

	O	R	W	Avge	Best	4wI
S.B.O'Connor	150.1	794	29	27.37	5-39	2
M.W.Priest	125.2	590	8	73.75	2-27	–
C.M.Spearman	0.3	6	0			
A.R.Tait	9	46	2	23.00	2-37	–
R.G.Twose	45.2	237	4	59.25	2-31	–
D.L.Vettori	204.3	993	25	39.72	4-49	1
P.J.Wiseman	19	95	2	47.50	1-21	–

INDIA – BATTING AND FIELDING

	M	I	NO	HS	Runs	Avge	100	50	Ct/St
A.B.Agarkar	30	13	2	30	177	16.09	–	–	13
M.Azharuddin	310	285	51	153*	8868	37.89	7	55	147
S.V.Bahutule	7	3	1	11	12	6.00	–	–	3
R.K.Chauhan	35	18	5	32	132	10.15	–	–	10
N.Chopra	11	6	1	39	77	15.40	–	–	2
R.Dravid	70	63	5	123*	2017	34.77	2	14	33
S.C.Ganguly	90	85	7	124	3146	40.33	5	22	26
Harbhajan Singh	13	5	2	4	9	3.00	–	–	4
Harvinder Singh	13	4	1	3*	5	1.66	–	–	4
A.Jadeja	154	139	27	119	4020	35.89	4	23	45
S.B.Joshi	34	20	4	48	181	11.31	–	–	12
V.G.Kambli	86	79	19	106	2225	37.08	2	13	12
H.H.Kanitkar	27	21	8	57	290	22.30	–	1	11
S.S.Karim	26	20	2	55	295	16.38	–	1	23/2
G.K.Khoda	2	2	–	89	115	57.50	–	1	–
A.R.Khurasiya	–								
N.M.Kulkarni	10	5	3	4*	10	5.00	–	–	2
A.Kumble	158	77	26	24	518	10.15	–	–	58
A.Kuruvilla	25	11	4	7	27	3.85	–	–	4
V.V.S.Laxman	7	6	1	23*	62	12.40	–	–	4
P.L.Mhambrey	1	–		–	–	–	–	–	–
D.S.Mohanty	20	5	4	4*	9	9.00	–	–	5
N.R.Mongia	123	82	25	69	1125	19.73	–	2	97/38
G.K.Pandey	–								
J.V.Paranjpe	4	4	1	27	54	18.00	–	–	2
B.K.V.Prasad	104	42	20	19	121	5.50	–	–	28
M.K.S.Prasad	2	1	1	11*	11	–	–	–	1
S.Ramesh	–								
R.Sanghvi	10	2	–	8	8	4.00	–	–	4
V.Shewag	–								
L.R.Shukla	–								
N.S.Sidhu	136	127	8	134*	4414	37.09	6	33	20
R.R.Singh	72	56	14	100	1215	28.92	1	5	15
J.Srinath	153	79	24	53	643	11.69	–	1	24
S.R.Tendulkar	211	204	20	142	7800	42.39	21	43	71

INDIA – BOWLING

	O	R	W	Avge	Best	4wI
A.B.Agarkar	267.5	1378	58	23.75	4-35	3
M.Azharuddin	92	479	12	39.91	3-19	–
S.V.Bahutule	46	259	2	129.50	1-31	–
R.K.Chauhan	272.2	1215	29	41.89	3-29	–
N.Chopra	84	322	7	46.00	2-21	–
R.Dravid	14	71	0			
S.C.Ganguly	216.1	1013	26	38.96	5-16	1
Harbhajan Singh	115	491	18	27.27	3-36	–

	O	R	W		Avge	Best	4wI
Harvinder Singh	85.2	477	20		23.85	3-44	–
A.Jadeja	**198.4**	**1044**	**14**		**74.57**	**2-16**	**–**
S.B.Joshi	279.4	1223	36		33.97	3-17	–
V.G.Kambli	**0.4**	**7**	**1**		**7.00**	**1- 7**	**–**
H.H.Kanitkar	**157.4**	**750**	**17**		**44.11**	**2-22**	**–**
N.M.Kulkarni	67	357	11		32.45	3-27	–
A.Kumble	**1420.2**	**5842**	**212**		**27.55**	**6-12**	**7**
A.Kuruvilla	188.3	890	25		35.60	4-43	1
V.V.S.Laxman	6	32	0				
P.L.Mhambrey	6	22	1		22.00	1-22	–
D.S.Mohanty	138	739	20		36.95	3-15	–
B.K.V.Prasad	**862.5**	**4104**	**119**		**34.48**	**4-17**	**3**
R.Sanghvi	83	398	10		39.80	3-29	–
N.S.Sidhu	0.4	3	0				
R.R.Singh	**369.1**	**1778**	**44**		**40.40**	**5-22**	**1**
J.Srinath	**1328.1**	**5754**	**212**		**27.14**	**5-23**	**5**
S.R.Tendulkar	**744**	**3646**	**78**		**46.74**	**5-32**	**3**

PAKISTAN – BATTING AND FIELDING

	M	I	NO	HS	Runs	Avge	100	50	Ct/St
Aamir Sohail	149	148	5	134	4655	32.55	5	31	49
Abdul Razzak	**13**	**10**	**2**	**46***	**101**	**12.62**	**–**	**–**	**1**
Akhtar Sarfraz	4	4	–	25	66	16.50	–	–	
Aqib Javed	163	51	26	45*	267	10.68	–	–	24
Arshad Khan	**12**	**8**	**6**	**13***	**42**	**21.00**	**–**	**–**	**3**
Asif Mahmood	2	2	–	14	14	7.00	–	–	
Azam Khan	6	5	–	72	116	23.20	–	1	2
Azhar Mahmood	**49**	**36**	**9**	**65***	**452**	**16.74**	**–**	**2**	**16**
Fazal-e-Akber	1	1	–	7	7	7.00	–	–	
Hasan Raja	11	9	–	46	122	13.55	–	–	1
Ijaz Ahmed	**215**	**198**	**26**	**139***	**5577**	**32.42**	**9**	**30**	**79**
Imran Nazir	**–**								
Inzamam-ul-Haq	**171**	**161**	**21**	**137***	**5369**	**38.35**	**5**	**37**	**46**
Kabir Khan	7	3	2	5	7	7.00	–	–	1
Manzoor Akhtar	7	4	–	44	97	24.25	–	–	1
Mohammad Akram	13	8	6	7*	13	6.50	–	–	5
Mohammad Hussain	14	13	7	31*	174	29.00	–	–	5
Mohammad Wasim	**20**	**20**	**2**	**76**	**479**	**26.61**	**–**	**3**	**6**
Mohammad Zahid	9	4	2	7*	15	7.50	–	–	
Moin Khan	**118**	**98**	**27**	**69***	**1684**	**23.71**	**–**	**5**	**104/41**
Mushtaq Ahmed	**130**	**69**	**31**	**26**	**343**	**9.02**	**–**	**–**	**28**
Ramiz Raja	198	197	15	119*	5841	32.09	9	31	33
Rashid Latif	101	66	18	50	748	15.58	–	1	94/28
Saeed Anwar	**161**	**159**	**14**	**194**	**5848**	**40.33**	**15**	**27**	**30**
Sajid Shah	**–**								
Salim Elahi	18	18	1	102*	509	29.94	1	3	4
Salim Malik	276	250	37	102	7055	33.12	5	46	81
Saqlain Mushtaq	**88**	**50**	**15**	**30***	**415**	**11.85**	**–**	**–**	**27**
Shahid Afridi	**71**	**68**	**2**	**109**	**1604**	**24.30**	**2**	**8**	**24**
Shahid Nazir	**14**	**6**	**5**	**8**	**25**	**25.00**	**–**	**–**	**2**
Shoaib Akhtar	**5**	**2**	**1**	**36**	**44**	**44.00**	**–**	**–**	**1**
Wajahatullah Wasti	**–**								
Waqar Younis	**172**	**85**	**31**	**37**	**537**	**9.94**	**–**	**–**	**19**
Wasim Akram	**254**	**200**	**36**	**86**	**2508**	**15.29**	**–**	**5**	**62**
Yousuf Youhana	**13**	**11**	**2**	**100**	**479**	**53.22**	**1**	**4**	**3**

PAKISTAN – BOWLING

	O	R	W	Avge	Best	4wI
Aamir Sohail	778.2	3547	82	43.25	4-22	1
Abdul Razzak	**82.4**	**435**	**12**	**36.25**	**3-48**	**–**
Aqib Javed	1335.3	5721	182	31.43	7-37	6
Arshad Khan	**94**	**437**	**10**	**43.70**	**3-70**	**–**
Azhar Mahmood	**352.3**	**1682**	**34**	**49.47**	**3-34**	**–**
Fazal-e-Akber	2	19	0			
Ijaz Ahmed	**103.3**	**464**	**4**	**116.00**	**2-31**	**–**
Inzamam-ul-Haq	**6.4**	**52**	**2**	**26.00**	**1- 4**	**–**
Kabir Khan	39.5	197	7	28.14	2-23	–
Manzoor Akhtar	33.1	184	5	36.80	4-50	1
Mohammad Akram	87	434	12	36.16	2-28	–
Mohammad Hussain	112	547	13	42.07	4-33	1
Mohammad Zahid	65.2	288	7	41.14	2-20	–
Mushtaq Ahmed	**1121.1**	**4842**	**144**	**33.62**	**5-36**	**3**
Ramiz Raja	1	10	0			
Saeed Anwar	**31.2**	**167**	**3**	**55.66**	**1- 9**	**–**
Salim Malik	582.1	2942	89	33.05	5-35	2
Saqlain Mushtaq	**768.1**	**3295**	**176**	**18.72**	**5-29**	**13**
Shahid Afridi	**515.1**	**2441**	**45**	**54.24**	**3-33**	**–**
Shahid Nazir	**105**	**498**	**15**	**33.20**	**3-14**	**–**
Shoaib Akhtar	**39**	**207**	**5**	**41.40**	**3-44**	**–**
Waqar Younis	**1426.5**	**6545**	**283**	**23.12**	**6-26**	**20**
Wasim Akram	**2185.2**	**8387**	**363**	**23.10**	**5-15**	**20**

SRI LANKA – BATTING AND FIELDING

	M	I	NO	HS	Runs	Avge	100	50	Ct/St
R.P.Arnold	3	2	–	11	14	7.00	–	–	2
M.S.Atapattu	**66**	**65**	**8**	**132***	**1972**	**34.59**	**2**	**14**	**26**
M.R.C.N.Bandaratilake	3	1	–	–	–	–	–	–	–
H.Boteju	–								
U.D.U.Chandana	47	36	7	50	466	16.06	–	1	23
P.A.de Silva	**250**	**243**	**25**	**145**	**7863**	**36.06**	**11**	**53**	**77**
K.S.C.de Silva	33	15	9	13*	35	5.83	–	–	11
S.K.L.de Silva	11	6	3	57	161	53.66	–	2	9/6
H.D.P.K.Dharmasena	**94**	**57**	**25**	**69***	**849**	**26.53**	**–**	**4**	**26**
D.A.Gunawardena	**7**	**7**	**–**	**75**	**164**	**23.42**	**–**	**2**	**1**
U.C.Hathurusinghe	**34**	**32**	**1**	**66**	**669**	**21.58**	**–**	**4**	**6**
S.T.Jayasuriya	**178**	**170**	**7**	**151***	**4672**	**28.66**	**7**	**29**	**59**
D.P.M.D.Jayawardena	**16**	**16**	**2**	**120**	**319**	**22.78**	**1**	**1**	**7**
R.S.Kalpage	**82**	**65**	**27**	**51**	**810**	**21.31**	**–**	**1**	**31**
R.S.Kaluwitharana	**112**	**108**	**6**	**100***	**1930**	**18.92**	**1**	**12**	**74/49**
D.K.Liyanage	15	10	2	43	142	17.75	–	–	6
R.S.Mahanama	208	193	23	119*	5026	29.56	4	35	108
M.Muralitharan	**110**	**49**	**23**	**18**	**151**	**5.80**	**–**	**–**	**53**
M.N.Nawaz	1	1	–	5	5	5.00	–	–	–
A.S.A.Perera	**6**	**2**	**1**	**17**	**17**	**17.00**	**–**	**–**	**–**
R.L.Perera	2	2	–	3	3	1.50	–	–	–
K.R.Pushpakumara	29	8	5	14*	36	12.00	–	–	8
A.Ranatunga	**260**	**246**	**47**	**131***	**7248**	**36.42**	**4**	**48**	**61**
T.T.Samaraweera	6	4	–	20	39	9.75	–	–	–
H.P.Tillekeratne	**176**	**149**	**36**	**104**	**3303**	**29.23**	**2**	**12**	**76/5**
K.E.A.Upashanta	**3**	**2**	**1**	**8***	**11**	**11.00**	**–**	**–**	**1**
W.P.U.C.J.Vaas	**105**	**61**	**22**	**33**	**506**	**12.97**	**–**	**–**	**16**
G.P.Wickremasinghe	**107**	**46**	**16**	**21***	**235**	**7.83**	**–**	**–**	**16**
D.N.T.Zoysa	9	4	2	4	9	4.50	–	–	–

LOI   SRI LANKA – BOWLING

	O	R	W	Avge	Best	4wI
R.P.Arnold	4	24	0			
M.S.Atapattu	9.3	45	0			
M.R.C.N.Bandaratilake	24	111	2	55.50	2-34	–
U.D.U.Chandana	289.1	1405	44	31.93	4-31	2
P.A.de Silva	655.2	3232	81	39.90	4-45	1
K.S.C.de Silva	238.2	1155	48	24.06	3-18	–
H.D.P.K.Dharmasena	783	3498	92	38.02	4-37	1
U.C.Hathurusinghe	149	670	14	47.85	4-57	1
S.T.Jayasuriya	1097.5	5348	152	35.18	6-29	6
D.P.M.D.Jayawardena	34	187	1	187.00	1-24	–
R.S.Kalpage	626	2780	71	39.15	4-36	1
D.K.Liyanage	101	487	9	54.11	3-49	–
R.S.Mahanama	0.2	7	0			
M.Muralitharan	995.3	4224	151	27.97	5-23	5
A.S.A.Perera	45.3	231	8	28.87	2-25	–
R.L.Perera	20	126	3	42.00	3-55	–
K.R.Pushpakumara	221.2	1110	24	46.25	3-25	–
A.Ranatunga	785	3757	79	47.55	4-14	1
T.T.Samaraweera	56	265	6	44.16	3-34	–
H.P.Tillekeratne	30	141	6	23.50	1- 3	–
K.E.A.Upashanta	19	91	3	30.33	2-24	–
W.P.U.C.J.Vaas	841.4	3512	132	26.60	4-20	3
G.P.Wickremasinghe	756.1	3393	79	42.94	3-20	–
D.N.T.Zoysa	69	311	12	25.91	2-22	–

                     ZIMBABWE – BATTING AND FIELDING

	M	I	NO	HS	Runs	Avge	100	50	Ct/St
E.A.Brandes	54	38	9	55	330	11.37	–	1	10
G.B.Brent	3	3	–	24	25	8.33	–	–	–
A.D.R.Campbell	92	89	9	131*	2293	28.66	3	13	35
S.V.Carlisle	8	8	1	28	79	11.28	–	–	4
C.N.Evans	47	41	5	96*	665	18.47	–	1	11
A.Flower	100	98	6	115*	2942	31.97	1	24	72/20
G.W.Flower	87	85	4	112	2867	35.39	2	22	35
M.W.Goodwin	26	26	–	111	722	27.76	1	4	7
D.L.Houghton	63	60	2	142	1530	26.37	1	12	29/2
A.G.Huckle	13	6	4	5*	9	4.50	–	–	3
N.C.Johnson	9	9	–	103	351	39.00	1	2	5
T.N.Madondo	2	2	–	10	10	5.00	–	–	–
E.Z.Matambanadzo	7	5	3	5*	8	4.00	–	–	1
M.Mbangwa	13	7	2	11	24	4.80	–	–	2
M.Nkala	1	–	–	–	–	–	–	–	–
H.K.Olonga	6	2	1	6	8	8.00	–	–	1
G.J.Rennie	16	16	3	76	332	25.53	–	2	9
J.A.Rennie	33	19	10	27	139	15.44	–	–	11
B.C.Strang	18	11	4	15	38	5.42	–	–	9
P.A.Strang	69	58	20	47	955	25.13	–	–	20
H.H.Streak	69	58	20	59	755	19.86	–	1	15
D.P.Viljoen	9	8	–	36	125	15.62	–	–	1
A.R.Whittall	40	23	10	31	135	10.38	–	–	12
G.J.Whittall	68	68	8	83	1360	22.66	–	8	18
C.B.Wishart	39	34	2	102	644	20.12	1	1	13

LOI   ZIMBABWE – BOWLING

	O	R	W	Avge	Best	4wI
E.A.Brandes	436.2	2090	67	31.19	5-28	3
G.B.Brent	19.2	108	1	108.00	1-53	–
A.D.R.Campbell	37.3	179	4	44.75	2-22	–
C.N.Evans	143.4	717	18	39.83	3-11	–
A.Flower	5	23	0			
G.W.Flower	243.2	1221	34	35.91	3-15	–
M.W.Goodwin	34.2	173	3	57.66	1-12	–
D.L.Houghton	2	19	1	19.00	1-19	–
A.G.Huckle	99	476	3	158.66	2-27	–
N.C.Johnson	69.3	372	5	74.40	2-51	–
E.Z.Matambanadzo	49.3	217	11	19.72	4-32	1
M.Mbangwa	109.1	546	7	78.00	2-24	–
M.Nkala	5	32	1	32.00	1-32	–
H.K.Olonga	42	287	7	41.00	4-46	1
J.A.Rennie	237.3	1211	25	48.44	3-27	–
B.C.Strang	134.2	576	23	25.04	6-20	2
P.A.Strang	533	2244	72	31.16	5-21	3
H.H.Streak	596.4	2666	85	31.36	5-32	4
D.P.Viljoen	32	134	4	33.50	2-31	–
A.R.Whittall	337.2	1430	32	44.68	3-23	–
G.J.Whittall	359.3	1859	49	37.93	3-43	–
C.B.Wishart	2	12	0			

BANGLADESH – BATTING AND FIELDING

	M	I	NO	HS	Runs	Avge	100	50	Ct/St
Akram Khan	21	21	1	59	453	22.65	–	2	6
Al Shariar Rokon	–								
Aminul Islam	21	21	5	70	497	31.06	–	2	7
Aminul Islam Bhola	–								
Anisur Rahman	2	2	–	2	2	1.00	–	–	–
Athar Ali Khan	19	19	1	82	532	29.55	–	3	2
Enamul Huq	12	11	2	18	71	7.88	–	–	3
Faruque Ahmed	5	5	–	57	89	17.80	–	1	1
Habibul Bashar	8	8	–	70	113	14.12	–	1	3
Hasibul Hussain	15	13	2	21*	96	8.72	–	–	3
Jahangir Alam	2	2	–	3	4	2.00	–	–	–
Jahangir Shah	2	2	–	3	4	2.00	–	–	–
Javed Omer	4	4	–	18	48	12.00	–	–	–
Khaled Mahmud	6	5	–	47	132	26.40	–	–	–
Khaled Masud	16	15	4	27*	117	10.63	–	–	13/2
Mafizur Rahman	4	4	1	16	53	17.66	–	–	1
Mahbubur Rahman	–								
Mehrab Hossain	1	1	–	6	6	6.00	–	–	–
Minhazul Abedin	23	22	–	45	313	14.22	–	–	2
Mohammed Rafique	12	12	–	77	194	16.16	–	1	1
Monjurul Islam	–								
Morshed Ali Khan	3	1	1	2*	2	–	–	–	2
Naimur Rahman	8	8	1	47	135	19.28	–	–	4
Neeyamur Rashid	–								
Saiful Islam	7	4	2	22*	37	18.50	–	–	–
Sanwar Hossain	3	3	–	13	22	7.33	–	–	1
Shafiuddin Ahmed	5	5	3	11	27	13.50	–	–	–
Shahriar Hossain	5	5	–	16	41	8.20	–	–	2
Shariful Haq	1	1	–	–	–	–	–	–	–
Sheikh Salahuddin	6	5	3	12	24	12.00	–	–	–
Zakir Hassan	2	1	–	–	–	–	–	–	–

LOI BANGLADESH – BOWLING

	O	R	W	Avge	Best	4wI
Akram Khan	**19.3**	**138**	**0**			
Aminul Islam	**36.4**	**219**	**3**	73.00	3-57	–
Anisur Rahman	8	68	0			
Athar Ali Khan	70	365	6	60.83	2-33	–
Enamul Huq	**67**	**365**	**5**	73.00	2-46	–
Habibul Bashar	6	26	0			
Hasibul Hussain	**107.2**	**636**	**13**	48.92	2-44	–
Jahangir Alam	**7**	**36**	**0**			
Khaled Mahmud	**38.4**	**162**	**7**	23.14	2-12	–
Mafizur Rahman	11	73	0			
Minhazul Abedin	71	404	9	44.88	2-39	–
Mohammed Rafique	**99.4**	**480**	**15**	32.00	3-55	–
Morshed Ali Khan	23	85	2	42.50	1-26	–
Naimur Rahman	**41.4**	**209**	**2**	104.50	1-29	–
Saiful Islam	50.3	256	6	42.66	4-36	1
Shafiuddin Ahmed	**39**	**192**	**6**	32.00	3-42	–
Shariful Haq	3	21	0			
Sheikh Salahuddin	41	249	4	62.25	2-48	–
Zakir Hassan	6	35	0			

KENYA – BATTING AND FIELDING

	M	I	NO	HS	Runs	Avge	100	50	Ct/St
R.Ali	9	3	3	6*	7	–	–	–	1
J.O.Angara	3	2	1	3*	6	6.00	–	–	–
Asif Karim	20	13	1	53	135	11.25	–	1	2
D.Chudasama	18	17	–	122	432	25.41	1	1	2
S.K.Gupta	3	3	–	41	43	14.33	–	–	–
J.Kamande	–								
H.S.Modi	20	17	1	78*	453	28.31	–	4	5
T.Odoyo	19	17	2	41	217	14.46	–	–	5
M.O.Odumbe	20	18	1	83	446	26.23	–	3	2
P.J.Ongondo	–								
L.Onyango	3	3	–	23	29	9.66	–	–	1
F.Otieno	–								
K.Otieno	20	19	1	144	592	32.88	1	2	7/4
B.Patel	–								
R.Shah	5	5	–	70	213	42.60	–	3	3
M.Sheikh	11	6	3	6*	19	6.33	–	–	5
A.Suji	8	7	1	67	115	19.16	–	1	1
M.Suji	19	14	10	15	46	11.50	–	–	5
S.O.Tikolo	20	19	–	96	501	26.36	–	4	11
A.Vadher	8	7	4	42*	93	31.00	–	–	4

KENYA – BOWLING

	O	R	W	Avge	Best	4wI
R.Ali	56.2	255	11	23.18	3-17	–
J.Angara	18	90	2	45.00	1-19	–
Asif Karim	161.5	655	17	38.52	5-33	1
H.S.Modi	2	14	0			
T.Odoyo	112	584	11	53.09	3-25	–
M.O.Odumbe	124.5	589	17	34.64	3-14	–
L.Onyango	9	96	1	96.00	1-45	–
R.Shah	1	5	0			
M.Sheikh	74.4	337	10	33.70	2-41	–
A.Suji	33.2	154	3	51.33	1-16	–
M.Suji	138	643	14	45.92	4-24	1
S.O.Tikolo	89.4	444	13	34.15	3-29	–

LIMITED-OVERS INTERNATIONALS
RESULTS SUMMARY

1970-71 to 13 February 1999

Opponents	Matches	Won by E	A	SA	WI	NZ	I	P	SL	Z	B	C	EA	H	K	UAE	Tied	NR
England Australia	67	31	34	–	–	–	–	–	–	–	–	–	–	–	–	–	1	1
South Africa	17	6	–	11	–	–	–	–	–	–	–	–	–	–	–	–	–	–
West Indies	58	25	–	–	31	–	–	–	–	–	–	–	–	–	–	–	–	2
New Zealand	47	23	–	–	–	20	–	–	–	–	–	–	–	–	–	–	1	3
India	33	19	–	–	–	–	13	–	–	–	–	–	–	–	–	–	–	1
Pakistan	41	26	–	–	–	–	–	14	–	–	–	–	–	–	–	–	–	1
Sri Lanka	19	12	–	–	–	–	–	–	7	–	–	–	–	–	–	–	–	–
Zimbabwe	6	1	–	–	–	–	–	–	–	5	–	–	–	–	–	–	–	–
Canada	1	1	–	–	–	–	–	–	–	–	–	0	–	–	–	–	–	–
East Africa	1	1	–	–	–	–	–	–	–	–	–	–	0	–	–	–	–	–
Holland	1	1	–	–	–	–	–	–	–	–	–	–	–	0	–	–	–	–
U A Emirates	1	1	–	–	–	–	–	–	–	–	–	–	–	–	–	0	–	–
Australia South Africa	37	–	18	19	–	–	–	–	–	–	–	–	–	–	–	–	–	–
West Indies	84	–	33	–	49	–	–	–	–	–	–	–	–	–	–	–	1	1
New Zealand	73	–	51	–	–	20	–	–	–	–	–	–	–	–	–	–	–	2
India	54	–	29	–	–	–	22	–	–	–	–	–	–	–	–	–	–	3
Pakistan	49	–	25	–	–	–	–	21	–	–	–	–	–	–	–	–	1	2
Sri Lanka	40	–	26	–	–	–	–	–	12	–	–	–	–	–	–	–	–	2
Zimbabwe	11	–	10	–	–	–	–	–	–	1	–	–	–	–	–	–	–	–
Bangladesh	1	–	1	–	–	–	–	–	–	–	0	–	–	–	–	–	–	–
Canada	1	–	1	–	–	–	–	–	–	–	–	0	–	–	–	–	–	–
Kenya	1	–	1	–	–	–	–	–	–	–	–	–	–	–	0	–	–	–
S Africa West Indies	18	–	–	12	6	–	–	–	–	–	–	–	–	–	–	–	–	–
N Zealand	12	–	–	7	–	5	–	–	–	–	–	–	–	–	–	–	–	–
India	27	–	–	18	–	–	8	–	–	–	–	–	–	–	–	–	–	1
Pakistan	21	–	–	14	–	–	–	7	–	–	–	–	–	–	–	–	–	–
Sri Lanka	15	–	–	8	–	–	–	–	6	–	–	–	–	–	–	–	–	1
Zimbabwe	7	–	–	6	–	–	–	–	–	0	–	–	–	–	–	–	–	1
Holland	1	–	–	1	–	–	–	–	–	–	–	–	–	0	–	–	–	–
Kenya	1	–	–	1	–	–	–	–	–	–	–	–	–	–	0	–	–	–
U A Emirates	1	–	–	1	–	–	–	–	–	–	–	–	–	–	–	0	–	–
W Indies New Zealand	24	–	–	–	18	4	–	–	–	–	–	–	–	–	–	–	–	2
India	57	–	–	–	37	–	19	–	–	–	–	–	–	–	–	–	1	–
Pakistan	84	–	–	–	56	–	–	26	–	–	–	–	–	–	–	–	2	–
Sri Lanka	29	–	–	–	20	–	–	–	8	–	–	–	–	–	–	–	–	1
Zimbabwe	5	–	–	–	5	–	–	–	–	0	–	–	–	–	–	–	–	–
Kenya	1	–	–	–	0	–	–	–	–	–	–	–	–	–	1	–	–	–
N Zealand India	51	–	–	–	–	21	27	–	–	–	–	–	–	–	–	–	–	3
Pakistan	48	–	–	–	–	18	–	28	–	–	–	–	–	–	–	–	1	1
Sri Lanka	40	–	–	–	–	24	–	–	13	–	–	–	–	–	–	–	1	2
Zimbabwe	17	–	–	–	–	13	–	–	–	3	–	–	–	–	–	–	1	–
Bangladesh	1	–	–	–	–	1	–	–	–	–	0	–	–	–	–	–	–	–
East Africa	1	–	–	–	–	1	–	–	–	–	–	–	0	–	–	–	–	–
Holland	1	–	–	–	–	1	–	–	–	–	–	–	–	0	–	–	–	–
U A Emirates	1	–	–	–	–	1	–	–	–	–	–	–	–	–	–	0	–	–
India Pakistan	71	–	–	–	–	–	25	42	–	–	–	–	–	–	–	–	–	4
Sri Lanka	57	–	–	–	–	–	30	–	22	–	–	–	–	–	–	–	–	5
Zimbabwe	24	–	–	–	–	–	18	–	–	4	–	–	–	–	–	–	2	–
Bangladesh	7	–	–	–	–	–	7	–	–	–	0	–	–	–	–	–	–	–
East Africa	1	–	–	–	–	–	1	–	–	–	–	–	0	–	–	–	–	–
Kenya	4	–	–	–	–	–	3	–	–	–	–	–	–	–	1	–	–	–
U A Emirates	1	–	–	–	–	–	1	–	–	–	–	–	–	–	–	0	–	–
Pakistan Sri Lanka	71	–	–	–	–	–	–	46	23	–	–	–	–	–	–	–	–	2
Zimbabwe	19	–	–	–	–	–	–	16	–	2	–	–	–	–	–	–	1	–
Bangladesh	5	–	–	–	–	–	–	5	–	–	0	–	–	–	–	–	–	–
Canada	1	–	–	–	–	–	–	1	–	–	–	0	–	–	–	–	–	–
Holland	1	–	–	–	–	–	–	1	–	–	–	–	–	0	–	–	–	–
Kenya	1	–	–	–	–	–	–	1	–	–	–	–	–	–	0	–	–	–
U A Emirates	2	–	–	–	–	–	–	2	–	–	–	–	–	–	–	0	–	–

	Opponents	Matches	E	A	SA	WI	NZ	I	P	SL	Z	B	C	EA	H	K	UAE	Tied	NR
Sri Lanka	Zimbabwe	15	–	–	–	–	–	–	–	11	4	–	–	–	–	–	–	–	–
	Bangladesh	5	–	–	–	–	–	–	–	5	–	0	–	–	–	–	–	–	–
	Kenya	2	–	–	–	–	–	–	–	2	–	–	–	–	–	0	–	–	–
Zimbabwe	Kenya	6	–	–	–	–	–	–	–	–	5	–	–	–	–	0	–	–	1
	Bangladesh	2	–	–	–	–	–	–	–	–	2	0	–	–	–	–	–	–	–
Kenya	Bangladesh	4	–	–	–	–	–	–	–	–	–	1	–	–	–	3	–	–	–
Holland	U A Emirates	1	–	–	–	–	–	–	–	–	–	–	–	–	0	–	1	–	–
		1406	147	229	98	222	129	174	210	109	26	1	0	0	0	5	1	13	42

MERIT TABLE OF ALL L-O INTERNATIONALS

1970-71 to 13 February 1999

	Matches	Won	Lost	Tied	No Result	% Won (exc NR)
South Africa	157	98	56	–	3	63.63
West Indies	360	222	128	4	6	62.71
Australia	418	229	175	3	11	56.26
Pakistan	414	210	189	5	10	51.98
England	292	147	135	2	8	51.76
India	387	174	193	3	17	47.02
New Zealand	316	129	170	4	13	42.57
Sri Lanka	293	109	170	1	13	38.92
Kenya	20	5	14	–	1	26.31
Zimbabwe	112	26	80	4	2	23.63
United Arab Emirates	7	1	6	–	–	14.28
Bangladesh	25	1	24	–	–	4.00
Canada	3	–	3	–	–	–
East Africa	3	–	3	–	–	–
Holland	5	–	5	–	–	–

LOI RECORDS

To 13 February 1999

TEAM RECORDS
HIGHEST TOTALS

398-5	(50 overs)	Sri Lanka v Kenya	Kandy	1995-96
371-9	(50 overs)	Pakistan v Sri Lanka	Nairobi	1996-97
363-7	(55 overs)	England v Pakistan	Nottingham	1992
360-4	(50 overs)	West Indies v Sri Lanka	Karachi	1987-88
349-9	(50 overs)	Sri Lanka v Pakistan	Singapore	1995-96
348-8	(50 overs)	New Zealand v India	Nagpur	1995-96
347-3	(50 overs)	Kenya v Bangladesh	Nairobi	1997-98
339-4	(50 overs)	Sri Lanka v Pakistan	Chandigarh	1996-97
338-4	(50 overs)	New Zealand v Bangladesh	Sharjah	1989-90

338-5	(60 overs)	Pakistan v Sri Lanka	Swansea	1983
334-4	(60 overs)	England v India	Lord's	1975
333-7	(50 overs)	West Indies v Sri Lanka	Sharjah	1995-96
333-8	(45 overs)	West Indies v India	Jamshedpur	1983-84
333-9	(60 overs)	England v Sri Lanka	Taunton	1983
332-3	(50 overs)	Australia v Sri Lanka	Sharjah	1989-90
330-6	(60 overs)	Pakistan v Sri Lanka	Nottingham	1975

The highest for South Africa is 328-3 (v Holland, Rawalpindi, 1995-96); for India 316-7 (v Pakistan, Dhaka, 1997-98); for Zimbabwe 312-4 (v Sri Lanka, New Plymouth, 1991-92); and for Bangladesh 257 (v Zimbabwe, Nairobi, 1997-98).

HIGHEST TOTALS BATTING SECOND

WINNING:	316-4	(48.5 overs)	Australia v Pakistan	Lahore	1998-99
	316-7	(47.5 overs)	India v Pakistan	Dhaka	1997-98
LOSING:	329	(49.3 overs)	Sri Lanka v West Indies	Sharjah	1995-96

HIGHEST MATCH AGGREGATES

664-19	(99.4 overs)	Pakistan v Sri Lanka	Singapore	1995-96
662-17	(99.3 overs)	West Indies v Sri Lanka	Sharjah	1995-96
652-12	(100 overs)	Sri Lanka v Kenya	Kandy	1995-96

LARGEST RUNS MARGINS OF VICTORY

232 runs	Australia beat Sri Lanka	Adelaide	1984-85
206 runs	New Zealand beat Australia	Adelaide	1985-86
202 runs	England beat India	Lord's	1975

LOWEST TOTALS (Excluding reduced innings)

43	(19.5 overs)	Pakistan v West Indies	Cape Town	1992-93
45	(40.3 overs)	Canada v England	Manchester	1979
55	(28.3 overs)	Sri Lanka v West Indies	Sharjah	1986-87
63	(25.5 overs)	India v Australia	Sydney	1980-81
64	(35.5 overs)	New Zealand v Pakistan	Sharjah	1985-86
69	(28 overs)	South Africa v Australia	Sydney	1993-94
70	(25.2 overs)	Australia v England	Birmingham	1977
70	(26.3 overs)	Australia v New Zealand	Adelaide	1985-86

The lowest for England is 93 (v Australia, Leeds, 1975); for West Indies 87 (v Australia, Sydney, 1992-93); for Zimbabwe 94 (v Pakistan, Sharjah, 1996-97); for Bangladesh 92 (v Zimbabwe, Nairobi, 1997-98); and for Kenya 103 (v South Africa, Nairobi, 1996-97).

LOWEST MATCH AGGREGATE

88-13	(32.2 overs)	West Indies v Pakistan	Cape Town	1992-93

BATTING RECORDS

HIGHEST INDIVIDUAL INNINGS

194	Saeed Anwar	Pakistan v India	Madras	1996-97
189*	I.V.A.Richards	West Indies v England	Manchester	1984
188*	G.Kirsten	South Africa v UAE	Rawalpindi	1995-96
181	I.V.A.Richards	West Indies v Sri Lanka	Karachi	1987-88
175*	Kapil Dev	India v Zimbabwe	Tunbridge Wells	1983
171*	G.M.Turner	New Zealand v East Africa	Birmingham	1975
169*	D.J.Callaghan	South Africa v New Zealand	Pretoria	1994-95
169	B.C.Lara	West Indies v Sri Lanka	Sharjah	1995-96
167*	R.A.Smith	England v Australia	Birmingham	1993
161	A.C.Hudson	South Africa v Holland	Rawalpindi	1995-96

158	D.I.Gower	England v New Zealand	Brisbane	1982-83
154	A.C.Gilchrist	Australia v Sri Lanka	Melbourne	1998-99
153*	I.V.A.Richards	West Indies v Australia	Melbourne	1979-80
153*	M.Azharuddin	India v Zimbabwe	Cuttack	1997-98
153	B.C.Lara	West Indies v Pakistan	Sharjah	1993-94
152*	D.L.Haynes	West Indies v India	Georgetown	1988-89
151*	S.T.Jayasuriya	Sri Lanka v India	Bombay	1996-97
150	S.Chanderpaul	West Indies v South Africa	East London	1998-99

The highest for Zimbabwe is 142 by D.L.Houghton (v New Zealand, Hyderabad, India, 1987-88); for Bangladesh 82 by Athar Ali Khan (v Pakistan, Colombo, 1997-98); and for Kenya 144 by K.Otieno (v Bangladesh, Nairobi, 1997-98).

HUNDRED ON DEBUT

D.L.Amiss	103	England v Australia	Manchester	1972
D.L.Haynes	148	West Indies v Australia	St John's	1977-78
A.Flower	115*	Zimbabwe v Sri Lanka	New Plymouth	1991-92
Salim Elahi	102*	Pakistan v Sri Lanka	Gujranwala	1995-96
N.V.Knight	113	England v Pakistan	Birmingham	1996

Fastest 100 37 balls Shahid Afridi (102) P v SL Nairobi 1996-97
Fastest 50 17 balls S.T.Jayasuriya (76) SL v P Singapore 1995-96

CARRYING BAT THROUGH COMPLETED INNINGS

G.W.Flower	84*	Zimbabwe (205) v England	Sydney	1994-95
Saeed Anwar	103*	Pakistan (219) v Zimbabwe	Harare	1994-95
N.V.Knight	125*	England (246) v Pakistan	Nottingham	1996

HIGHEST PARTNERSHIP FOR EACH WICKET

1st	252	S.C.Ganguly/S.R.Tendulkar	India v Sri Lanka	Colombo (RPS)	1997-98
2nd	263	Aamir Sohail/Inzamam-ul-Haq	Pakistan v New Zealand	Sharjah	1993-94
3rd	230	Saeed Anwar/Ijaz Ahmed	Pakistan v India	Dhaka	1997-98
4th	275*	M.Azharuddin/A.Jadeja	India v Zimbabwe	Cuttack	1997-98
5th	223	M.Azharuddin/A.Jadeja	India v Sri Lanka	Colombo (RPS)	1997-98
6th	154	R.B.Richardson/P.J.L.Dujon	West Indies v Pakistan	Sharjah	1991-92
7th	119	T.Odoyo/A.Suji	Kenya v Zimbabwe	Nairobi	1997-98
8th	119	P.R.Reiffel/S.K.Warne	Australia v South Africa	Port Elizabeth	1993-94
9th	126*	Kapil Dev/S.M.H.Kirmani	India v Zimbabwe	Tunbridge Wells	1983
10th	106*	I.V.A.Richards/M.A.Holding	West Indies v England	Manchester	1984

4000 RUNS IN A CAREER

		LOI	I	NO	HS	Runs	Avge	100	50
M.Azharuddin	I	310	285	51	153*	**8868**	37.89	7	55
D.L.Haynes	WI	238	237	28	152*	**8648**	41.37	17	57
P.A.de Silva	SL	250	243	25	145	**7863**	36.06	11	53
S.R.Tendulkar	I	211	204	20	142	**7800**	42.39	21	43
Javed Miandad	P	233	218	41	119*	**7381**	41.70	8	50
A.Ranatunga	SL	260	246	47	131*	**7248**	36.42	4	48
Salim Malik	P	276	250	37	102	**7055**	33.12	5	46
I.V.A.Richards	WI	187	167	24	189*	**6721**	47.00	11	45
A.R.Border	A	273	252	39	127*	**6524**	30.62	3	39
R.B.Richardson	WI	224	217	30	122	**6248**	33.41	5	44
D.M.Jones	A	164	161	25	145	**6068**	44.61	7	46
M.E.Waugh	A	174	169	13	130	**6044**	38.74	11	39
D.C.Boon	A	181	177	16	122	**5964**	37.04	5	37
Saeed Anwar	P	161	159	14	194	**5848**	40.33	15	27
Ramiz Raja	P	198	197	15	119*	**5841**	32.09	9	31
S.R.Waugh	A	251	228	44	102*	**5707**	31.01	1	34

		LOI	I	NO	HS	Runs	Avge	100	50
B.C.Lara	WI	137	135	13	169	**5579**	45.72	12	37
Ijaz Ahmed	P	215	198	26	139*	**5577**	32.42	9	30
Inzamam-ul-Haq	P	171	161	21	137*	**5369**	38.35	5	37
C.G.Greenidge	WI	128	127	13	133*	**5134**	45.03	11	31
R.S.Mahanama	SL	208	193	23	119*	**5026**	29.56	4	35
M.D.Crowe	NZ	143	141	19	107*	**4704**	38.55	4	34
W.J.Cronje	SA	152	142	24	112	**4695**	39.78	2	33
S.T.Jayasuriya	SL	178	170	7	151*	**4672**	28.66	7	29
Aamir Sohail	P	149	148	5	134	**4655**	32.55	5	31
C.L.Hooper	WI	177	161	36	113*	**4500**	36.00	6	25
N.S.Sidhu	I	136	127	8	134*	**4414**	37.09	6	33
G.R.Marsh	A	117	115	6	126*	**4357**	39.97	9	22
G.A.Gooch	E	125	122	6	142	**4290**	36.98	8	23
K.Srikkanth	I	146	145	4	123	**4092**	29.02	4	27
A.Jadeja	I	154	139	27	119	**4020**	35.89	4	23
A.J.Lamb	E	122	118	16	118	**4010**	39.31	4	26

The highest for Zimbabwe is 2942 in 98 innings by A.Flower; for Bangladesh 532 in 19 innings by Athar Ali Khan; and for Kenya 592 in 19 innings by K.Otieno.

TEN HUNDREDS IN A CAREER

		LOI	100	E	A	SA	WI	NZ	I	P	SL	Z	K
S.R.Tendulkar	I	211	**21**	–	5	1	1	2	–	2	4	4	2
D.L.Haynes	WI	238	**17**	2	6	–	–	2	2	4	1	–	–
Saeed Anwar	P	161	**15**	–	1	–	2	2	3	–	6	1	–
B.C.Lara	WI	137	**12**	1	2	2	–	2	–	4	1	–	–
C.G.Greenidge	WI	128	**11**	–	1	–	–	3	3	2	1	1	–
M.E.Waugh	A	174	**11**	1	–	2	1	3	1	1	1	–	1
I.V.A.Richards	WI	187	**11**	3	3	–	–	1	3	–	1	–	–
P.A.de Silva	SL	250	**11**	–	2	–	–	3	1	–	4	1	

The most for England is 8 by G.A.Gooch; for South Africa 8 by G.Kirsten; for New Zealand 5 by N.J.Astle; for Zimbabwe 3 by A.D.R.Campbell; and for Kenya 1 by D.Chudasama and by K.Otieno.

BOWLING RECORDS
BEST ANALYSES

7-37	Aqib Javed	Pakistan v India	Sharjah	1991-92
7-51	W.W.Davis	West Indies v Australia	Leeds	1983
6-12	A.Kumble	India v West Indies	Calcutta	1993-94
6-14	G.J.Gilmour	Australia v England	Leeds	1975
6-14	Imran Khan	Pakistan v India	Sharjah	1984-85
6-15	C.E.H.Croft	West Indies v England	Kingstown	1980-81
6-20	B.C.Strang	Zimbabwe v Bangladesh	Nairobi	1997-98
6-23	A.A.Donald	South Africa v Kenya	Nairobi	1996-97
6-26	Waqar Younis	Pakistan v Sri Lanka	Sharjah	1989-90
6-29	B.P.Patterson	West Indies v India	Nagpur	1987-88
6-29	S.T.Jayasuriya	Sri Lanka v England	Moratuwa	1992-93
6-30	Waqar Younis	Pakistan v New Zealand	Auckland	1993-94
6-35	S.M.Pollock	South Africa v West Indies	East London	1998-99
6-39	K.H.Macleay	Australia v India	Nottingham	1983
6-41	I.V.A.Richards	West Indies v India	Delhi	1989-90
6-44	Waqar Younis	Pakistan v New Zealand	Sharjah	1996-97
6-49	L.Klusener	South Africa v Sri Lanka	Lahore	1997-98
6-50	A.H.Gray	West Indies v Australia	Port-of-Spain	1990-91

The best for England is 5-20 by V.J.Marks (v New Zealand, Wellington, 1983-84); for New Zealand 5-22 by M.N.Hart (v West Indies, Margao, 1994-95); for Bangladesh 4-36 by Saiful Islam (v Sri Lanka, Sharjah, 1994-95); and for Kenya 5-33 by Asif Karim (v Bangladesh, Nairobi, 1997-98).

HAT-TRICKS

Jalaluddin	Pakistan v Australia	Hyderabad	1982-83
B.A.Reid	Australia v New Zealand	Sydney	1985-86
C.Sharma	India v New Zealand	Nagpur	1987-88
Wasim Akram	Pakistan v West Indies	Sharjah	1989-90
Wasim Akram	Pakistan v Australia	Sharjah	1989-90
Kapil Dev	India v Sri Lanka	Calcutta	1990-91
Aqib Javed	Pakistan v India	Sharjah	1991-92
D.K.Morrison	New Zealand v India	Napier	1993-94
Waqar Younis	Pakistan v New Zealand	East London	1994-95
Saqlain Mushtaq	Pakistan v Zimbabwe	Peshawar	1996-97
E.A.Brandes	Zimbabwe v England	Harare	1996-97
A.M.Stuart	Australia v Pakistan	Melbourne	1996-97

100 WICKETS IN A CAREER

		LOI	O	R	W	Avge	Best	4w	R/Over
Wasim Akram	P	254	2185.2	8387	**363**	23.10	5-15	20	3.83
Waqar Younis	P	172	1426.5	6545	**283**	23.12	6-26	20	4.58
Kapil Dev	I	224	1867	6945	253	27.45	5-43	4	3.71
J.Srinath	I	153	1328.1	5754	212	27.14	5-23	5	4.33
A.Kumble	I	158	1420.2	5842	212	27.55	6-12	7	4.11
C.E.L.Ambrose	WI	157	1391.5	4939	210	23.51	5-17	10	3.54
C.A.Walsh	WI	185	1628.4	6312	204	30.94	5- 1	6	3.87
C.J.McDermott	A	138	1243.3	5018	203	24.71	5-44	5	4.03
S.R.Waugh	A	251	1404.5	6374	185	34.45	4-33	3	4.53
A.A.Donald	SA	108	959	3896	182	21.40	6-23	9	4.06
Aqib Javed	P	163	1335.3	5721	182	31.43	7-37	6	4.28
Imran Khan	P	175	1243.3	4845	182	26.62	6-14	4	3.89
Saqlain Mushtaq	P	88	768.1	3295	176	18.72	5-29	13	4.28
S.K.Warne	A	108	1012.2	4235	169	25.05	5-33	10	4.18
C.L.Hooper	WI	177	1223.1	5321	160	33.25	4-34	3	4.35
R.J.Hadlee	NZ	115	1030.2	3407	158	21.56	5-25	5	3.30
M.Prabhakar	I	129	1060	4534	157	28.87	5-33	6	4.27
M.D.Marshall	WI	136	1195.5	4233	157	26.96	4-18	6	3.53
S.T.Jayasuriya	SL	178	1097.5	5348	152	35.18	6-29	6	4.87
M.Muralitharan	SL	110	995.3	4224	151	27.97	5-23	5	4.24
J.Garner	WI	98	888.2	2752	146	18.84	5-31	5	3.09
I.T.Botham	E	116	1045.1	4139	145	28.54	4-31	3	3.96
Mushtaq Ahmed	P	130	1121.1	4842	144	33.62	5-36	3	4.31
M.A.Holding	WI	102	912.1	3034	142	21.36	5-26	6	3.32
E.J.Chatfield	NZ	114	1010.5	3618	140	25.84	5-34	4	3.57
Abdul Qadir	P	104	850	3453	132	26.15	5-44	6	4.06
W.P.U.C.J.Vaas	SL	105	841.4	3512	132	26.60	4-20	3	4.17
R.J.Shastri	I	150	1102.1	4650	129	36.04	5-15	3	4.21
D.K.Morrison	NZ	96	764.2	3470	126	27.53	5-34	3	4.53
G.D.McGrath	A	85	768.1	3084	122	25.27	5-40	7	4.01
B.K.V.Prasad	I	104	862.5	4104	119	34.48	4-17	3	4.75
I.R.Bishop	WI	84	722	3127	118	26.50	5-25	9	4.33
I.V.A.Richards	WI	187	940.4	4228	118	35.83	6-41	3	4.49
C.Z.Harris	NZ	120	944.1	4005	117	34.23	5-42	2	4.24
P.A.J.DeFreitas	E	103	952	3775	115	32.82	4-35	1	3.96
M.C.Snedden	NZ	93	754.1	3237	114	28.39	4-34	1	4.29
Mudassar Nazar	P	122	809.1	3432	111	30.91	5-28	2	4.24
S.P.O'Donnell	A	87	725	3102	108	28.72	5-13	6	4.27
D.K.Lillee	A	63	598.5	2145	103	20.82	5-34	6	3.58
C.Pringle	NZ	64	552.2	2455	103	23.83	5-45	3	4.44
G.R.Larsen	NZ	106	934.2	3525	103	34.22	4-24	1	3.77
W.K.M.Benjamin	WI	85	740.2	3079	100	30.79	5-22	1	4.15
R.A.Harper	WI	105	862.3	3431	100	34.31	4-40	3	3.97

The most for Zimbabwe is 85 in 69 matches by H.H.Streak; for Bangladesh 15 in 12 matches by Mohammad Rafiq; and for Kenya 17 in 20 matches by M.O.Odumbe.

WICKET-KEEPING RECORDS

FIVE DISMISSALS IN AN INNINGS

5 – R.W.Marsh (Australia); D.J.Richardson (2) (South Africa); C.O.Browne, J.C.Adams, R.D.Jacobs (West Indies); A.C.Parore (New Zealand); S.M.H.Kirmani, S.Viswanath, K.S.More, N.R.Mongia (2) (India); Moin Khan, Rashid Latif (Pakistan); R.G.de Alwis, H.P.Tillekeratne, R.S.Kaluwitharana (Sri Lanka); A.Flower (2) (Zimbabwe).

100 DISMISSALS IN A CAREER
(Including catches taken in the field)

		LOI	Ct	St	Dis
I.A.Healy	Australia	168	195	39	**234**
P.J.L.Dujon	West Indies	169	183	21	**204**
D.J.Richardson	South Africa	122	149	16	**165**
Moin Khan	Pakistan	118	104	41	**145**
N.R.Mongia	India	123	97	38	**135**
R.W.Marsh	Australia	92	120	4	**124**
R.S.Kaluwitharana	Sri Lanka	112	74	49	**123**
Rashid Latif	Pakistan	101	94	28	**122**
A.J.Stewart	England	116	101	11	**112**
Salim Yousuf	Pakistan	86	80	22	**102**

The most for Zimbabwe is 92 (72 ct, 20 st) in 100 matches by A.Flower.

FIELDING RECORDS

FIVE CATCHES IN AN INNINGS

5   J.N.Rhodes   South Africa v West Indies   Bombay   1993-94

The following held four catches in an innings: M.A.Taylor (Australia), K.C.Wessels (South Africa), C.L.Hooper, R.B.Richardson and P.V.Simmons (West Indies), K.R.Rutherford (New Zealand), S.M.Gavaskar (India) and Salim Malik (Pakistan). J.G.Bracewell (New Zealand) held four catches as a substitute.

100 CATCHES IN A CAREER
(Excluding catches taken while keeping wicket)

		LOI	Ct
M.Azharuddin	India	310	**147**
A.R.Border	Australia	273	**127**
R.S.Mahanama	Sri Lanka	208	**108**
I.V.A.Richards	West Indies	187	**101**

The most for England is 45 in 125 matches by G.A.Gooch; for South Africa 70 in 146 matches by J.N.Rhodes; for New Zealand 66 in 143 matches by M.D.Crowe; for Pakistan 81 in 276 matches by Salim Malik; and for Zimbabwe 35 in 87 matches by G.W.Flower and in 92 matches by A.D.R.Campbell.

ALL-ROUND RECORDS

50 RUNS AND 5 WICKETS IN A MATCH

I.V.A.Richards	119	5-41	West Indies v New Zealand	Dunedin	1986-87
K.Srikkanth	70	5-27	India v New Zealand	Vishakhapatnam	1988-89
M.E.Waugh	57	5-24	Australia v West Indies	Melbourne	1992-93

1000 RUNS AND 100 WICKETS

		LOI	Runs	Wkts
I.T.Botham	England	116	2113	145
R.J.Hadlee	New Zealand	115	1751	158
C.Z.Harris	New Zealand	120	2198	117
C.L.Hooper	West Indies	177	4500	160
Imran Khan	Pakistan	175	3709	182
S.T.Jayasuriya	Sri Lanka	178	4672	152
Kapil Dev	India	225	3783	253
Mudassar Nazar	Pakistan	122	2653	111
S.P.O'Donnell	Australia	87	1242	108
M.Prabhakar	India	130	1858	157
I.V.A.Richards	West Indies	187	6721	118
R.J.Shastri	India	150	3108	129
Wasim Akram	Pakistan	254	2508	363
S.R.Waugh	Australia	251	5707	185

1000 RUNS AND 100 DISMISSALS

		LOI	Runs	Dis
P.J.L.Dujon	West Indies	169	1945	204
I.A.Healy	Australia	168	1764	234
R.S.Kaluwitharana	Sri Lanka	112	1930	123
R.W.Marsh	Australia	92	1225	124
N.R.Mongia	India	123	1125	135
Moin Khan	Pakistan	118	1684	145
A.J.Stewart	England	116	3211	112

INDIVIDUAL RECORDS – GENERAL

200 APPEARANCES

310	M.Azharuddin	India	238	D.L.Haynes	West Indies
276	Salim Malik	Pakistan	233	Javed Miandad	Pakistan
273	A.R.Border	Australia	224	Kapil Dev	India
260	A.Ranatunga	Sri Lanka	224	R.B.Richardson	West Indies
254	Wasim Akram	Pakistan	215	Ijaz Ahmed	Pakistan
251	S.R.Waugh	Australia	211	S.R.Tendulkar	India
250	P.A.de Silva	Sri Lanka	208	R.S.Mahanama	Sri Lanka

The most for England is 125 by G.A.Gooch; for South Africa 152 by W.J.Cronje; for New Zealand 149 by J.G.Wright; and for Zimbabwe 100 by A.Flower.

50 MATCHES AS CAPTAIN

184	A.Ranatunga	Sri Lanka	72	Wasim Akram	Pakistan
178	A.R.Border	Australia	67	M.A.Taylor	Australia
160	M.Azharuddin	India	62	Javed Miandad	Pakistan
139	Imran Khan	Pakistan	61	L.R.D.Mendis	Sri Lanka
108	I.V.A.Richards	West Indies	60	G.P.Howarth	New Zealand
102	W.J.Cronje	South Africa	55	A.D.R.Campbell	Zimbabwe
87	R.B.Richardson	West Indies	54	S.R.Tendulkar	India
81	C.H.Lloyd	West Indies	52	K.C.Wessels	South Africa
74	Kapil Dev	India	50	G.A.Gooch	England

ENGLAND

BEST PERFORMANCES IN LIMITED-OVERS INTERNATIONALS
(Number of matches shown in brackets)

v AUSTRALIA (67)

Highest Total	320-8	(55 overs)	Birmingham	1980
Lowest Total	93	(36.2 overs)	Leeds	1975
Highest Score	167*	R.A.Smith	Birmingham	1993
Best Bowling	5-31	M.Hendrick	The Oval	1980

v SOUTH AFRICA (17)

Highest Total	281-7	(50 overs)	Dhaka	1998-99
Lowest Total	115	(43.4 overs)	East London	1995-96
Highest Score	85	M.A.Atherton	Bloemfontein	1995-96
Best Bowling	4-33	D.Gough	Port Elizabeth	1995-96

v WEST INDIES (58)

Highest Total	306-5	(55 overs)	The Oval	1995
Lowest Total	114	(39 overs)	Bridgetown	1985-86
Highest Score	129*	G.A.Gooch	Port-of-Spain	1985-86
Best Bowling	4-23	G.R.Dilley	Brisbane	1986-87

v NEW ZEALAND (47)

Highest Total	322-6	(60 overs)	The Oval	1983
Lowest Total	127	(40.1 overs)	Christchurch	1982-83
Highest Score	158	D.I.Gower	Brisbane	1982-83
Best Bowling	5-20	V.J.Marks	Wellington	1983-84

v INDIA (33)

Highest Total	334-4	(60 overs)	Lord's	1975
Lowest Total	149	(41.4 overs)	Sydney	1984-85
Highest Score	137	D.L.Amiss	Lord's	1975
Best Bowling	5-35	P.W.Jarvis	Bangalore	1992-93

v PAKISTAN (41)

Highest Total	363-7	(55 overs)	Nottingham	1992
Lowest Total	122	(31.6 *8-ball* overs)	Lahore	1977-78
Highest Score	142	G.A.Gooch	Karachi	1987-88
Best Bowling	4-15	R.G.D.Willis	Manchester	1978

v SRI LANKA (19)

Highest Total	333-9	(60 overs)	Taunton	1983
Lowest Total	170	(36.1 overs)	Colombo	1992-93
Highest Score	130	D.I.Gower	Taunton	1983
Best Bowling	5-32	M.A.Ealham	Perth	1998-99

v ZIMBABWE (6)

Highest Total	200-8	(50 overs)	Brisbane	1994-95
Lowest Total	118	(30 overs)	Harare	1996-97
Highest Score	89	G.P.Thorpe	Brisbane	1994-95
Best Bowling	5-44	D.Gough	Sydney	1994-95

v BANGLADESH (0)

Highest Total	–
Lowest Total	–
Highest Score	–
Best Bowling	–

v KENYA (0)

Highest Total	–
Lowest Total	–
Highest Score	–
Best Bowling	–

AUSTRALIA

BEST PERFORMANCES IN LIMITED-OVERS INTERNATIONALS

(Number of matches shown in brackets)

v ENGLAND (67)
Highest Total	283-5	(50 overs)	Brisbane	1990-91
Lowest Total	70	(25.2 overs)	Birmingham	1977
Highest Score	145	D.M.Jones	Brisbane	1990-91
Best Bowling	6-14	G.J.Gilmour	Leeds	1975

v SOUTH AFRICA (37)
Highest Total	287-5	(49 overs)	Pretoria	1996-97
Lowest Total	125	(39.1 overs)	Melbourne	1997-98
Highest Score	115*	M.E.Waugh	Port Elizabeth	1996-97
Best Bowling	4-13	P.R.Reiffel	Sydney	1993-94

v WEST INDIES (84)
Highest Total	286-9	(50 overs)	Georgetown	1994-95
Lowest Total	91	(35.4 overs)	Perth	1986-87
Highest Score	127*	A.R.Border	Sydney	1984-85
Best Bowling	5-24	M.E.Waugh	Melbourne	1992-93

v NEW ZEALAND (73)
Highest Total	302-8	(50 overs)	Melbourne	1982-83
Lowest Total	70	(26.3 overs)	Adelaide	1985-86
Highest Score	138*	G.S.Chappell	Sydney	1980-81
Best Bowling	5-13	S.P.O'Donnell	Christchurch	1989-90

v INDIA (54)
Highest Total	320-9	(60 overs)	Nottingham	1983
Lowest Total	101	(37.5 overs)	Perth	1991-92
Highest Score	126	M.E.Waugh	Bombay	1995-96
Best Bowling	6-39	K.H.Macleay	Nottingham	1983

v PAKISTAN (49)
Highest Total	324-8	(50 overs)	Karachi	1998-99
Lowest Total	120	(41.3 overs)	Hobart	1996-97
Highest Score	125*	G.R.Marsh	Melbourne	1988-89
Best Bowling	5-16	C.G.Rackemann	Adelaide	1983-84

v SRI LANKA (40)
Highest Total	332-3	(50 overs)	Sharjah	1989-90
Lowest Total	168-9	(45 overs)	Colombo	1982-83
Highest Score	154	A.C.Gilchrist	Melbourne	1998-99
Best Bowling	5-21	A.I.C.Dodemaide	Perth	1987-88

v ZIMBABWE (11)
Highest Total	294-3	(50 overs)	Delhi	1997-98
Lowest Total	226-7	(60 overs)	Nottingham	1983
Highest Score	145	R.T.Ponting	Delhi	1997-98
Best Bowling	4-34	S.K.Warne	Nagpur	1995-96

v BANGLADESH (1)
Highest Total	140-3	(25.4 overs)	Sharjah	1989-90
Lowest Total	–			
Highest Score	54*	P.L.Taylor	Sharjah	1989-90
Best Bowling	2-22	P.L.Taylor	Sharjah	1989-90
	2-22	S.R.Waugh	Sharjah	1989-90

v KENYA (1)
Highest Total	304-7	(50 overs)	Vishakhapatnam	1995-96
Lowest Total	304-7	(50 overs)	Vishakhapatnam	1995-96
Highest Score	130	M.E.Waugh	Vishakhapatnam	1995-96
Best Bowling	2-18	P.R.Reiffel	Vishakhapatnam	1995-96

SOUTH AFRICA

BEST PERFORMANCES IN LIMITED-OVERS INTERNATIONALS

(Number of matches shown in brackets)

v ENGLAND (17)

Highest Total	283-4	(46.4 overs)	Dhaka	1998-99
Lowest Total	129	(41.4 overs)	East London	1995-96
Highest Score	116	G.Kirsten	Pretoria	1995-96
Best Bowling	5-40	R.P.Snell	Melbourne	1993-94

v AUSTRALIA (37)

Highest Total	310-6	(50 overs)	Bloemfontein	1996-97
Lowest Total	69	(28 overs)	Sydney	1993-94
Highest Score	112*	G.Kirsten	Melbourne	1993-94
Best Bowling	5-24	L.Klusener	Melbourne	1997-98

v WEST INDIES (18)

Highest Total	297-5	(48.1 overs)	Lahore	1997-98
Lowest Total	140-9	(50 overs)	Cape Town	1992-93
Highest Score	125	H.H.Gibbs	Port Elizabeth	1998-99
Best Bowling	6-35	S.M.Pollock	East London	1998-99

v NEW ZEALAND (12)

Highest Total	314-7	(50 overs)	Pretoria	1994-95
Lowest Totals	147-7	(50 overs)	Hobart	1993-94
Highest Score	169*	D.J.Callaghan	Pretoria	1994-95
Best Bowling	4-38	C.R.Matthews	Hobart	1993-94

v INDIA (27)

Highest Total	288-2	(46.4 overs)	Delhi	1991-92
	288-6	(50 overs)	Sharjah	1995-96
Lowest Total	178-9	(50 overs)	Chandigarh	1993-94
Highest Score	115*	G.Kirsten	Sharjah	1995-96
Best Bowling	5-29	A.A.Donald	Calcutta	1991-92

v PAKISTAN (21)

Highest Total	321-8	(50 overs)	Nairobi	1996-97
Lowest Total	162	(30.1 overs)	East London	1992-93
Highest Score	124	D.J.Cullinan	Nairobi	1996-97
Best Bowling	5-25	L.Klusener	Cape Town	1997-98

v SRI LANKA (15)

Highest Total	311-9	(50 overs)	Lahore	1997-98
Lowest Total	154	(46.1 overs)	Colombo	1993-94
Highest Score	113*	J.H.Kallis	Dhaka	1998-99
Best Bowling	6-49	L.Klusener	Lahore	1997-98

v ZIMBABWE (7)

Highest Total	303-5	(50 overs)	Harare	1995-96
Lowest Total	239	(49.2 overs)	Harare	1995-96
Highest Score	127	B.M.McMillan	Harare	1995-96
Best Bowling	4-33	W.J.Cronje	Harare	1995-96

v BANGLADESH (0)

Highest Total	–			
Lowest Total	–			
Highest Score	–			
Best Bowling	–			

v KENYA (1)

Highest Total	305-8	(50 overs)	Nairobi	1996-97
Lowest Total	305-8	(50 overs)	Nairobi	1996-97
Highest Score	66	G.Kirsten	Nairobi	1996-97
Best Bowling	6-23	A.A.Donald	Nairobi	1996-97

WEST INDIES

BEST PERFORMANCES IN LIMITED-OVERS INTERNATIONALS

(Number of matches shown in brackets)

v ENGLAND (58)

Highest Total	313-6	(50 overs)	Kingstown	1993-94
Lowest Total	127	(47.2 overs)	Kingstown	1980-81
Highest Score	189*	I.V.A.Richards	Manchester	1984
Best Bowling	6-15	C.E.H.Croft	Kingstown	1980-81

v AUSTRALIA (84)

Highest Total	313-9	(50 overs)	St John's	1977-78
Lowest Total	87	(29.3 overs)	Sydney	1992-93
Highest Score	153*	I.V.A.Richards	Melbourne	1979-80
Best Bowling	7-51	W.W.Davis	Leeds	1983

v SOUTH AFRICA (18)

Highest Total	293-8	(50 overs)	Lahore	1997-98
Lowest Total	132	(42.4 overs)	Cape Town	1998-99
Highest Score	150	S.Chanderpaul	East London	1998-99
Best Bowling	4-44	K.L.T.Arthurton	Bloemfontein	1998-99

v NEW ZEALAND (24)

Highest Total	306-6	(50 overs)	Gauhati	1994-95
Lowest Total	123	(39.1 overs)	Margao	1994-95
Highest Score	146*	B.C.Lara	Port-of-Spain	1995-96
Best Bowling	5-41	I.V.A.Richards	Dunedin	1986-87

v INDIA (57)

Highest Total	333-8	(45 overs)	Jamshedpur	1983-84
Lowest Total	121	(43.5 overs)	Port-of-Spain	1996-97
Highest Score	152*	D.L.Haynes	Georgetown	1988-89
Best Bowling	6-29	B.P.Patterson	Nagpur	1987-88

v PAKISTAN (84)

Highest Total	315-4	(47 overs)	Port-of-Spain	1987-88
Lowest Total	103	(40.3 overs)	Melbourne	1996-97
Highest Score	153	B.C.Lara	Sharjah	1993-94
Best Bowling	5-25	I.R.Bishop	Brisbane	1992-93

v SRI LANKA (29)

Highest Total	360-4	(50 overs)	Karachi	1987-88
Lowest Total	160-8	(50 overs)	Adelaide	1995-96
Highest Score	181	I.V.A.Richards	Karachi	1987-88
Best Bowling	5-1	C.A.Walsh	Sharjah	1986-87

v ZIMBABWE (5)

Highest Total	264-8	(50 overs)	Brisbane	1991-92
Lowest Total	233-9	(50 overs)	Hyderabad, India	1993-94
Highest Score	105*	C.G.Greenidge	Worcester	1983
Best Bowling	3-23	P.V.Simmons	Hyderabad, India	1993-94

v BANGLADESH (0)

Highest Total	–
Lowest Total	–
Highest Score	–
Best Bowling	–

v KENYA (1)

Highest Total	93	(35.2 overs)	Poona	1995-96
Lowest Total	93	(35.2 overs)	Poona	1995-96
Highest Score	19	S.Chanderpaul	Poona	1995-96
Best Bowling	3-15	R.A.Harper	Poona	1995-96

NEW ZEALAND

BEST PERFORMANCES IN LIMITED-OVERS INTERNATIONALS

(Number of matches shown in brackets)

v ENGLAND (47)

Highest Total	298-6	(54.5 overs)	Leeds	1990
Lowest Total	134	(42.1 overs)	Christchurch	1983-84
Highest Score	111	M.J.Greatbatch	The Oval	1990
Best Bowling	5-28	B.L.Cairns	Scarborough	1978

v AUSTRALIA (73)

Highest Total	286-9	(50 overs)	Madras	1995-96
Lowest Total	74	(29 overs)	Wellington	1981-82
Highest Score	130	C.Z.Harris	Madras	1995-96
Best Bowling	5-26	R.J.Hadlee	Sydney	1980-81

v SOUTH AFRICA (12)

Highest Total	298-9	(50 overs)	Brisbane	1997-98
Lowest Total	134	(39.5 overs)	Cape Town	1994-95
Highest Score	108	A.C.Parore	Pretoria	1994-95
Best Bowling	4-59	M.L.Su'a	Pretoria	1994-95

v WEST INDIES (24)

Highest Total	243	(49.1 overs)	Kingston	1995-96
Lowest Total	116	(42.2 overs)	Port-of-Spain	1984-85
Highest Score	106*	S.P.Fleming	Port-of-Spain	1995-96
Best Bowling	5-22	M.N.Hart	Margao	1994-95

v INDIA (51)

Highest Total	348-8	(50 overs)	Nagpur	1995-96
Lowest Total	126	(35 overs)	Bombay	1995-96
Highest Score	115	C.L.Cairns	Christchurch	1998-99
Best Bowling	5-23	R.O.Collinge	Christchurch	1975-76

v PAKISTAN (48)

Highest Total	285-7	(50 overs)	Chandigarh	1996-97
Lowest Total	64	(35.5 overs)	Sharjah	1985-86
Highest Score	117	N.J.Astle	Chandigarh	1996-97
Best Bowling	5-38	R.J.Hadlee	Dunedin	1988-89

v SRI LANKA (40)

Highest Total	304-5	(50 overs)	Auckland	1982-83
Lowest Total	116	(34 overs)	Moratuwa	1983-84
Highest Score	140	G.M.Turner	Auckland	1982-83
Best Bowling	5-25	R.J.Hadlee	Bristol	1983

v ZIMBABWE (17)

Highest Total	294-7	(50 overs)	Harare	1997-98
Lowest Total	185-9	(50 overs)	Harare	1997-98
Highest Score	120	N.J.Astle	Auckland	1995-96
Best Bowling	5-39	S.B.O'Connor	Wellington	1997-98

v BANGLADESH (1)

Highest Total	338-4	(50 overs)	Sharjah	1989-90
Lowest Total	338-4	(50 overs)	Sharjah	1989-90
Highest Score	93	J.G.Wright	Sharjah	1989-90
	93	A.H.Jones	Sharjah	1989-90
Best Bowling	2-41	J.P.Millmow	Sharjah	1989-90

v KENYA (0)

Highest Total	–	
Lowest Total	–	
Highest Score	–	
Best Bowling	–	

INDIA

BEST PERFORMANCES IN LIMITED-OVERS INTERNATIONALS

(Number of matches shown in brackets)

v ENGLAND (33)
Highest Total	282-5	(53 overs)	Nottingham	1990
Lowest Total	158	(40.2 overs)	Leeds	1996
Highest Score	134*	N.S.Sidhu	Gwalior	1992-93
Best Bowling	5-41	J.Srinath	Bangalore	1992-93

v AUSTRALIA (54)
Highest Total	309-5	(50 overs)	Cochin	1997-98
Lowest Total	63	(25.5 overs)	Sydney	1980-81
Highest Score	143	S.R.Tendulkar	Sharjah	1997-98
Best Bowling	5-15	R.J.Shastri	Perth	1991-92

v SOUTH AFRICA (27)
Highest Total	287-4	(50 overs)	Delhi	1991-92
Lowest Total	147	(49.4 overs)	Port Elizabeth	1992-93
Highest Score	114	W.V.Raman	Pretoria	1992-93
	114	S.R.Tendulkar	Bombay	1996-97
Best Bowling	4-25	A.Kumble	Bombay	1996-97

v WEST INDIES (57)
Highest Total	282-5	(47 overs)	Berbice	1982-83
Lowest Total	100	(28.3 overs)	Ahmedabad	1993-94
Highest Score	114*	N.S.Sidhu	Vishakhapatnam	1994-95
Best Bowling	6-12	A.Kumble	Calcutta	1993-94

v NEW ZEALAND (51)
Highest Total	289-3	(50 overs)	Delhi	1994-95
Lowest Total	113	(44.2 overs)	Perth	1985-86
Highest Score	123	R.Dravid	Taupo	1998-99
Best Bowling	5-27	K.Srikkanth	Indore	1988-89

v PAKISTAN (71)
Highest Total	316-7	(47.5 overs)	Dhaka	1997-98
Lowest Total	79	(34.2 overs)	Sialkot	1978-79
Highest Score	124	S.C.Ganguly	Dhaka	1997-98
Best Bowling	5-16	S.C.Ganguly	Toronto	1997

v SRI LANKA (57)
Highest Total	307-6	(50 overs)	Colombo	1997-98
Lowest Total	78	(24.1 overs)	Kanpur	1986-87
Highest Score	137	S.R.Tendulkar	Delhi	1995-96
Best Bowling	5-22	R.R.Singh	Gauhati	1997-98

v ZIMBABWE (24)
Highest Total	301-3	(50 overs)	Cuttack	1997-98
Lowest Total	168	(43.5 overs)	Bulawayo	1996-97
Highest Score	175*	Kapil Dev	Tunbridge Wells	1983
Best Bowling	4-19	M.Prabhakar	Bombay	1987-88

v BANGLADESH (7)
Highest Total	191-6	(46.2 overs)	Dhaka	1997-98
Lowest Total	–			
Highest Score	104*	N.S.Sidhu	Chandigarh	1990-91
Best Bowling	5-23	J.Srinath	Dhaka	1997-98

v KENYA (4)
Highest Total	224-6	(47 overs)	Bangalore	1997-98
Lowest Total	196	(47.1 overs)	Gwalior	1997-98
Highest Score	127*	S.R.Tendulkar	Cuttack	1995-96
Best Bowling	4-23	B.K.V.Prasad	Calcutta	1997-98

PAKISTAN

BEST PERFORMANCES IN LIMITED-OVERS INTERNATIONALS

(Number of matches shown in brackets)

v ENGLAND (41)

Highest Total	263	(50.5 overs)	The Oval	1992
Lowest Total	74	(40.2 overs)	Adelaide	1991-92
Highest Score	113	Javed Miandad	The Oval	1987
Best Bowling	4-26	Saqlain Mushtaq	Sharjah	1997-98

v AUSTRALIA (49)

Highest Total	315-8	(50 overs)	Lahore	1998-99
Lowest Total	140	(49 overs)	Adelaide	1983-84
Highest Score	109	Zaheer Abbas	Lahore	1982-83
Best Bowling	5-21	Wasim Akram	Melbourne	1984-85

v SOUTH AFRICA (21)

Highest Total	262-9	(50 overs)	Lahore	1997-98
Lowest Total	109	(32.3 overs)	Johannesburg	1994-95
Highest Score	114*	Ijaz Ahmed	Durban	1994-95
Best Bowling	5-16	Wasim Akram	East London	1992-93

v WEST INDIES (84)

Highest Total	294-6	(50 overs)	Sharjah	1988-89
Lowest Total	43	(19.5 overs)	Cape Town	1992-93
Highest Score	131	Saeed Anwar	Sharjah	1993-94
Best Bowling	5-28	Mudassar Nazar	Melbourne	1984-85

v NEW ZEALAND (48)

Highest Total	328-2	(50 overs)	Sharjah	1993-94
Lowest Total	139	(47.4 overs)	Auckland	1992-93
Highest Score	137*	Inzamam-ul-Haq	Sharjah	1993-94
Best Bowling	6-30	Waqar Younis	Auckland	1993-94

v INDIA (71)

Highest Total	327-5	(50 overs)	Madras	1996-97
Lowest Total	87	(32.5 overs)	Sharjah	1984-85
Highest Score	194	Saeed Anwar	Madras	1996-97
Best Bowling	7-37	Aqib Javed	Sharjah	1991-92

v SRI LANKA (71)

Highest Total	338-5	(60 overs)	Swansea	1983
Lowest Total	131	(36 overs)	Sharjah	1996-97
Highest Score	126	Saeed Anwar	Adelaide	1989-90
Best Bowling	6-26	Waqar Younis	Sharjah	1989-90

v ZIMBABWE (19)

Highest Total	302-6	(50 overs)	Rawalpindi	1998-99
Lowest Total	148	(43.3 overs)	Harare	1994-95
Highest Score	132	Ijaz Ahmed	Rawalpindi	1998-99
Best Bowling	5-15	Wasim Akram	Karachi	1993-94

v BANGLADESH (5)

Highest Total	319-5	(50 overs)	Colombo	1997-98
Lowest Total	284-3	(45 overs)	Chittagong	1988-89
Highest Score	124*	Ijaz Ahmed	Chittagong	1988-89
Best Bowling	5-38	Saqlain Mushtaq	Colombo	1997-98

v KENYA (1)

Highest Total	149-6	(40.2 overs)	Nairobi	1996-97
Lowest Total	–			
Highest Score	50*	Moin Khan	Nairobi	1996-97
Best Bowling	3-27	Saqlain Mushtaq	Nairobi	1996-97

SRI LANKA

BEST PERFORMANCES IN LIMITED-OVERS INTERNATIONALS

(Number of matches shown in brackets)

v ENGLAND (19)

Highest Total	303-9	(49.3 overs)	Adelaide	1998-99
Lowest Total	99	(33.3 overs)	Perth	1998-99
Highest Score	132*	M.S.Atapattu	Lord's	1998
Best Bowling	6-29	S.T.Jayasuriya	Moratuwa	1992-93

v AUSTRALIA (40)

Highest Total	276-4	(60 overs)	The Oval	1975
Lowest Total	91	(35.5 overs)	Adelaide	1984-85
Highest Score	107*	P.A.de Silva	Lahore	1995-96
Best Bowling	4-35	U.D.U.Chandana	Colombo	1996-97

v SOUTH AFRICA (15)

Highest Total	258	(47.5 overs)	Nottingham	1998
Lowest Total	98	(34 overs)	Colombo	1993-94
Highest Score	93*	A.Ranatunga	Port Elizabeth	1997-98
Best Bowling	4-17	C.P.H.Ramanayake	Colombo	1993-94

v WEST INDIES (29)

Highest Total	329	(49.3 overs)	Sharjah	1995-96
Lowest Total	55	(28.3 overs)	Sharjah	1986-87
Highest Score	104	H.P.Tillekeratne	Bombay	1993-94
Best Bowling	5-58	S.T.Jayasuriya	Port-of-Spain	1996-97

v NEW ZEALAND (40)

Highest Total	293-4	(50 overs)	Colombo	1997-98
Lowest Total	115	(38.1 overs)	Colombo	1983-84
Highest Score	140	S.T.Jayasuriya	Bloemfontein	1994-95
Best Bowling	5-26	S.H.U.Karnain	Moratuwa	1983-84

v INDIA (57)

Highest Total	301-4	(50 overs)	Colombo	1997-98
Lowest Total	96	(41 overs)	Sharjah	1983-84
Highest Score	151*	S.T.Jayasuriya	Bombay	1996-97
Best Bowling	5-57	G.F.Labrooy	Baroda	1986-87

v PAKISTAN (71)

Highest Total	349-9	(50 overs)	Singapore	1995-96
Lowest Total	116	(33.5 overs)	Colombo	1985-86
Highest Score	134*	S.T.Jayasuriya	Lahore	1997-98
Best Bowling	5-23	M.Muralitharan	Benoni	1997-98

v ZIMBABWE (15)

Highest Total	313-7	(49.2 overs)	New Plymouth	1991-92
Lowest Total	153	(46.2 overs)	Sharjah	1996-97
Highest Score	127*	P.A.de Silva	Colombo	1996-97
Best Bowling	4-19	S.T.Jayasuriya	Patna	1993-94

v BANGLADESH (5)

Highest Total	296-4	(46 overs)	Colombo	1997-98
Lowest Total	233	(49.4 overs)	Sharjah	1994-95
Highest Score	108	S.T.Jayasuriya	Colombo	1997-98
Best Bowling	4-23	J.R.Ratnayeke	Dhaka	1988-89
	4-23	M.Muralitharan	Sharjah	1994-95

v KENYA (2)

Highest Total	398-5	(50 overs)	Kandy	1995-96
Lowest Total	398-5	(50 overs)	Kandy	1995-96
Highest Score	145	P.A.de Silva	Kandy	1995-96
Best Bowling	4-18	M.Muralitharan	Nairobi	1996-97

ZIMBABWE

BEST PERFORMANCES IN LIMITED-OVERS INTERNATIONALS

(Number of matches shown in brackets)

v ENGLAND (6)

Highest Total	249-7	(50 overs)	Harare	1996-97
Lowest Total	134	(46.1 overs)	Albury	1991-92
Highest Score	84*	G.W.Flower	Sydney	1994-95
Best Bowling	5-28	E.A.Brandes	Harare	1996-97

v AUSTRALIA (11)

Highest Total	278-9	(50 overs)	Delhi	1997-98
Lowest Total	137	(41.4 overs)	Hobart	1991-92
Highest Score	102	A.D.R.Campbell	Ahmedabad	1997-98
Best Bowling	4-42	D.A.G.Fletcher	Nottingham	1983

v SOUTH AFRICA (7)

Highest Total	256-8	(50 overs)	Johannesburg	1996-97
Lowest Total	127	(42.5 overs)	Harare	1995-96
Highest Score	90	G.W.Flower	Pretoria	1996-97
Best Bowling	4-25	H.H.Streak	Harare	1995-96

v WEST INDIES (5)

Highest Total	217-7	(60 overs)	Worcester	1983
Lowest Total	99	(36.3 overs)	Hyderabad, India	1993-94
Highest Score	71*	D.A.G.Fletcher	Worcester	1983
Best Bowling	4-40	P.A.Strang	Hyderabad, India	1995-96

v NEW ZEALAND (17)

Highest Total	271-6	(50 overs)	Harare	1992-93
Lowest Total	138	(49 overs)	Wellington	1997-98
Highest Score	142	D.L.Houghton	Hyderabad, India	1987-88
Best Bowling	5-44	A.C.I.Lock	Napier	1995-96

v INDIA (24)

Highest Total	269	(48.4 overs)	Cuttack	1997-98
Lowest Total	135	(44.2 overs)	Bombay	1987-88
Highest Score	102	G.W.Flower	Cuttack	1997-98
	102	C.B.Wishart	Harare	1998-99
Best Bowling	5-32	H.H.Streak	Bulawayo	1996-97

v PAKISTAN (19)

Highest Total	272-4	(50 overs)	Harare	1997-98
Lowest Total	94	(31.4 overs)	Sharjah	1996-97
Highest Score	103	N.C.Johnson	Sheikhupura	1998-99
Best Bowling	4-18	H.H.Streak	Sharjah	1996-97

v SRI LANKA (15)

Highest Total	312-4	(50 overs)	New Plymouth	1991-92
Lowest Total	105	(48.1 overs)	Harare	1994-95
Highest Score	131*	A.D.R.Campbell	Harare	1994-95
Best Bowling	4-32	P.A.Strang	Sharjah	1998-99

v BANGLADESH (2)

Highest Total	305-4	(50 overs)	Nairobi	1997-98
Lowest Total	284	(50 overs)	Nairobi	1997-98
Highest Score	81	A.Flower	Nairobi	1997-98
Best Bowling	6-20	B.C.Strang	Nairobi	1997-98

v KENYA (6)

Highest Total	281-8	(50 overs)	Nairobi	1997-98
Lowest Total	272-6	(49 overs)	Nairobi	1997-98
Highest Score	83	G.J.Whittall	Nairobi	1997-98
Best Bowling	5-21	P.A.Strang	Patna	1995-96

BANGLADESH

BEST PERFORMANCES IN LIMITED-OVERS INTERNATIONALS

(Number of matches shown in brackets)

v ENGLAND (0)

Highest Total	–			
Lowest Total	–			
Highest Score	–			
Best Bowling	–			

v AUSTRALIA (1)

Highest Total	134-8	(50 overs)	Sharjah	1989-90
Lowest Total	134-8	(50 overs)	Sharjah	1989-90
Highest Score	41*	Aminul Islam	Sharjah	1989-90
Best Bowling	2-43	Minhazul Abedin	Sharjah	1989-90

v SOUTH AFRICA (0)

Highest Total	–			
Lowest Total	–			
Highest Score	–			
Best Bowling	–			

v WEST INDIES (0)

Highest Total	–			
Lowest Total	–			
Highest Score	–			
Best Bowling	–			

v NEW ZEALAND (1)

Highest Total	177-5	(50 overs)	Sharjah	1989-90
Lowest Total	177-5	(50 overs)	Sharjah	1989-90
Highest Score	54	Azhar Hussain	Sharjah	1989-90
Best Bowling	2-39	Minhazul Abedin	Sharjah	1989-90

v INDIA (7)

Highest Total	190	(48 overs)	Dhaka	1997-98
Lowest Total	115	(36.3 overs)	Bombay	1997-98
Highest Score	70	Aminul Islam	Chandigarh	1997-98
Best Bowling	2-12	Khaled Mahmud	Bombay	1997-98

v PAKISTAN (5)

Highest Total	210	(49.3 overs)	Colombo	1997-98
Lowest Total	94	(35.3 overs)	Moratuwa	1985-86
Highest Score	82	Athar Ali Khan	Colombo	1997-98
Best Bowling	2-23	Jahangir Shah	Moratuwa	1985-86

v SRI LANKA (5)

Highest Total	193-8	(46 overs)	Colombo	1997-98
Lowest Total	126	(44.2 overs)	Sharjah	1994-95
Highest Score	78*	Athar Ali Khan	Calcutta	1990-91
Best Bowling	4-36	Saiful Islam	Sharjah	1994-95

v ZIMBABWE (2)

Highest Total	257	(47.1 overs)	Nairobi	1997-98
Lowest Total	92	(32.3 overs)	Nairobi	1997-98
Highest Score	70	Habibul Bashar	Nairobi	1997-98
Best Bowling	3-42	Shafiuddin Ahmed	Nairobi	1997-98

v KENYA (4)

Highest Total	236-4	(47.5 overs)	Hyderabad, India	1997-98
Lowest Total	100	(41.2 overs)	Nairobi	1997-98
Highest Score	77	Mohammed Rafique	Hyderabad, India	1997-98
Best Bowling	3-55	Mohammed Rafique	Hyderabad, India	1997-98

KENYA

BEST PERFORMANCES IN LIMITED-OVERS INTERNATIONALS

(Number of matches shown in brackets)

v ENGLAND (0)

Highest Total	–			
Lowest Total	–			
Highest Score	–			
Best Bowling	–			

v AUSTRALIA (1)

Highest Total	207-7	(50 overs)	Vishakhapatnam	1995-96
Lowest Total	207-7	(50 overs)	Vishakhapatnam	1995-96
Highest Score	85	K.Otieno	Vishakhapatnam	1995-96
Best Bowling	3-45	R.Ali	Vishakhapatnam	1995-96

v SOUTH AFRICA (1)

Highest Total	103	(25.1 overs)	Nairobi	1996-97
Lowest Total	103	(25.1 overs)	Nairobi	1996-97
Highest Score	29	D.Chudasama	Nairobi	1996-97
Best Bowling	2-44	Asif Karim	Nairobi	1996-97

v WEST INDIES (1)

Highest Total	166	(49.3 overs)	Poona	1995-96
Lowest Total	166	(49.3 overs)	Poona	1995-96
Highest Score	29	S.O.Tikolo	Poona	1995-96
Best Bowling	3-15	M.O.Odumbe	Poona	1995-96

v NEW ZEALAND (0)

Highest Total	–			
Lowest Total	–			
Highest Score	–			
Best Bowling	–			

v INDIA (4)

Highest Total	265-5	(50 overs)	Gwalior	1997-98
Lowest Total	196	(46.3 overs)	Calcutta	1997-98
Highest Score	83	M.O.Odumbe	Gwalior	1997-98
Best Bowling	3-14	M.O.Odumbe	Gwalior	1997-98

v PAKISTAN (1)

Highest Total	148	(47 overs)	Nairobi	1996-97
Lowest Total	148	(47 overs)	Nairobi	1996-97
Highest Score	51	D.Chudasama	Nairobi	1996-97
Best Bowling	3-25	T.Odoyo	Nairobi	1996-97

v SRI LANKA (2)

Highest Total	254-7	(50 overs)	Kandy	1995-96
Lowest Total	188-9	(50 overs)	Nairobi	1996-97
Highest Score	96	S.O.Tikolo	Kandy	1995-96
Best Bowling	2-29	E.T.Odumbe	Nairobi	1996-97

v ZIMBABWE (6)

Highest Total	249-8	(50 overs)	Nairobi	1997-98
Lowest Total	134	(49.4 overs)	Patna	1995-96
Highest Score	87	K.Otieno	Nairobi	1997-98
Best Bowling	3-22	R.Ali	Patna	1995-96

v BANGLADESH (4)

Highest Total	347-3	(50 overs)	Nairobi	1997-98
Lowest Total	226-8	(50 overs)	Madras	1997-98
Highest Score	144	K.Otieno	Nairobi	1997-98
Best Bowling	5-33	Asif Karim	Nairobi	1997-98

1999 WORLD CUP

HOSTING ARRANGEMENTS

May 4 to 13

Host		*Host*	
Derbyshire	PAKISTAN	Kent	ENGLAND
Durham	SCOTLAND	Leicestershire	INDIA
Essex	BANGLADESH	Northamptonshire	SRI LANKA
Glamorgan	AUSTRALIA	Somerset	KENYA
Gloucestershire	WEST INDIES	Sussex	SOUTH AFRICA
Hampshire	NEW ZEALAND	Worcestershire	ZIMBABWE

WARM-UP MATCH SCHEDULE

Fri	May 7	Canterbury	Kent v ENGLAND
		Leicester	Leicestershire v INDIA
		Taunton	Somerset v KENYA
		Hove	Sussex v SOUTH AFRICA
		Northampton	Northamptonshire v SRI LANKA
		Worcester	Worcestershire v ZIMBABWE
Sat	May 8	Cardiff	Glamorgan v AUSTRALIA
		Chelmsford	Essex v BANGLADESH
		Southampton	Hampshire v NEW ZEALAND
		Derby	Derbyshire v PAKISTAN
		Chester-le-Street	Durham v SCOTLAND
		Bristol	Gloucestershire v WEST INDIES
Sun	May 9	Chelmsford	Essex v ENGLAND
		Harrogate	Yorkshire v INDIA
		Bristol	Gloucestershire v KENYA
		Canterbury	Kent v SOUTH AFRICA
		Nottingham	Nottinghamshire v SRI LANKA
		Derby	Derbyshire v ZIMBABWE
Mon	May 10	Worcester	Worcestershire v AUSTRALIA
		Southgate	Middlesex v BANGLADESH
		The Oval	Surrey v NEW ZEALAND
		Chester-le-Street	Durham v PAKISTAN
		Manchester	Lancashire v SCOTLAND
		Birmingham	Warwickshire v WEST INDIES
Tue	May 11	Southampton	Hampshire v ENGLAND
		Nottingham	Nottinghamshire v INDIA
		Cardiff	Glamorgan v KENYA
		Southgate	Middlesex v SOUTH AFRICA
		Leicester	Leicestershire v SRI LANKA
		Birmingham	Warwickshire v ZIMBABWE
Wed	May 12	Taunton	Somerset v AUSTRALIA
		Northampton	Northamptonshire v BANGLADESH
		Arundel	Sussex v NEW ZEALAND
		Manchester	Lancashire v PAKISTAN
		Scarborough	Yorkshire v SCOTLAND
		The Oval	Surrey v WEST INDIES

1999 WORLD CUP FIXTURES

One reserve day per match (two for the Final)

Match	Group		May	Venue	Team 1 v Team 2	TV
1	A	Fri	14	Lord's	England v Sri Lanka	SKY
2	A	Sat	15	Hove	India v South Africa	SKY
3	A	Sat	15	Taunton	Zimbabwe v Kenya	SKY
4	B	Sun	16	Worcester	Australia v Scotland	BBC
5	B	Sun	16	Bristol	West Indies v Pakistan	BBC
6	B	Mon	17	Chelmsford	New Zealand v Bangladesh	SKY
7	A	Tue	18	Canterbury	England v Kenya	BBC
8	A	Wed	19	Northampton	Sri Lanka v South Africa	SKY
9	A	Wed	19	Leicester	India v Zimbabwe	SKY
10	B	Thu	20	Cardiff	Australia v New Zealand	BBC
11	B	Thu	20	Chester-le-Street	Pakistan v Scotland	BBC
12	B	Fri	21	Dublin	West Indies v Bangladesh	SKY
13	A	Sat	22	The Oval	England v South Africa	BBC
14	A	Sat	22	Worcester	Zimbabwe v Sri Lanka	BBC
15	A	Sun	23	Bristol	Kenya v India	SKY
16	B	Sun	23	Leeds	Australia v Pakistan	SKY
17	B	Mon	24	Southampton	West Indies v New Zealand	BBC
18	B	Mon	24	Edinburgh	Scotland v Bangladesh	BBC
19	A	Tue	25	Nottingham	England v Zimbabwe	SKY
20	A	Wed	26	Taunton	Sri Lanka v India	BBC
21	A	Wed	26	Amstelveen	South Africa v Kenya	BBC
22	B	Thu	27	Leicester	West Indies v Scotland	SKY
23	B	Thu	27	Chester-le-Street	Australia v Bangladesh	SKY
24	B	Fri	28	Derby	New Zealand v Pakistan	SKY
25	A	Sat	29	Birmingham	England v India	SKY
26	A	Sat	29	Chelmsford	Zimbabwe v South Africa	SKY
27	A	Sun	30	Southampton	Sri Lanka v Kenya	BBC
28	B	Sun	30	Manchester	West Indies v Australia	BBC
29	B	Mon	31	Edinburgh	Scotland v New Zealand	SKY
30	B	Mon	31	Northampton	Pakistan v Bangladesh	SKY
SUPER SIX						
31		Fri	Jun 4	The Oval	Group A – 2nd v Group B – 2nd	SKY
32		Sat	Jun 5	Nottingham	Group A – 1st v Group B – 1st	BBC
33		Sun	Jun 6	Leeds	Group A – 3rd v Group B – 3rd	SKY
34		Tue	Jun 8	Manchester	Group A – 2nd v Group B – 1st	BBC
35		Wed	Jun 9	Lord's	Group A – 3rd v Group B – 2nd	BBC
36		Thu	Jun 10	Birmingham	Group A – 1st v Group B – 3rd	SKY
37		Fri	Jun 11	The Oval	Group A – 3rd v Group B – 1st	BBC
38		Sat	Jun 12	Nottingham	Group A – 2nd v Group B – 3rd	BBC
39		Sun	Jun 13	Leeds	Group A – 1st v Group B – 2nd	SKY
SEMI-FINALS†						
40		Wed	Jun 16	Manchester	Semi-Final I	BBC
41		Thu	Jun 17	Birmingham	Semi-Final II	SKY
FINAL						
42		Sun	Jun 20	Lord's		BOTH

† Super Six 1st v 4th and 2nd v 3rd – venues to be decided after that phase is completed.

TV: Group stage – one match will be covered live each day with the second match covered as back-up in the event of rain interruptions, and for highlights and overseas telecasts.

RADIO: Ball-by-ball Radio 4 (LW) coverage, starting at 9.45am, of all England's matches, all Super Six matches, both Semi-Finals and the Final. Reports of other matches can be heard on Radio 5.